UNDERSTANDING THE UN SECURITY COUNCIL

Dedicated to the memory of Captain Mbaye Diagne and his courage.

Understanding the UN Security Council

Coercion or Consent?

NEIL FENTON

LONDON AND NEW YORK

First published 2004 by Ashgate Publishing

Reissued 2018 by Routledge
2 Park Square, Milton Park, Abingdon, Oxon OX14 4RN
605 Third Avenue, New York, NY 10017

First issued in paperback 2021

Routledge is an imprint of the Taylor & Francis Group, an informa business

© Neil Fenton 2004

Neil Fenton has asserted his right under the Copyright, Designs and Patents Act, 1988, to be identified as the author of this work.

All rights reserved. No part of this book may be reprinted or reproduced or utilised in any form or by any electronic, mechanical, or other means, now known or hereafter invented, including photocopying and recording, or in any information storage or retrieval system, without permission in writing from the publishers.

A Library of Congress record exists under LC control number: 2003064719

Notice:
Product or corporate names may be trademarks or registered trademarks, and are used only for identification and explanation without intent to infringe.

Publisher's Note
The publisher has gone to great lengths to ensure the quality of this reprint but points out that some imperfections in the original copies may be apparent.

Disclaimer
The publisher has made every effort to trace copyright holders and welcomes correspondence from those they have been unable to contact.

ISBN 13: 978-0-815-39873-8 (hbk)
ISBN 13: 978-1-351-14376-9 (ebk)
ISBN 13: 978-1-138-35786-0 (pbk)

DOI: 10.4324/9781351143769

Contents

Preface	*vi*
Acknowledgements	*vii*
List of Acronyms	*viii*
1 Understanding the Centrality of Consent	1
2 Northern Iraq 1991	37
3 Somalia	64
4 Haiti	98
5 Rwanda	125
6 Bosnia	148
7 Back to Iraq	181
8 Beyond Consent and Sovereignty?	205
List of Interviews	*223*
Selected Bibliography	*225*
Index	*242*

Preface

This book examines UN Security Council decision making with regard to the use of force and state sovereignty. It seeks to better understand how the post-Cold War optimism that invigorated the Security Council in the early 1990s has seemingly evaporated and left it fighting for relevance and credibility in the wake of the second Gulf War. Focusing on UN peacekeeping initiatives between 1991 and 1995, it examines the degree to which consent-based peacekeeping doctrine has been modified in practice in preference for Chapter VII enforcement methods. It also asks whether these decisions indicated an increasing humanitarian imperative at the expense of state sovereignty. It begins by analysing the debates on sovereignty, humanitarian intervention, and peacekeeping doctrine. Focus then shifts to UNSC actions in northern Iraq, Somalia, Haiti, Rwanda, and Bosnia. The aim of each case study is to understand the challenges of consent-based peacekeeping, how the UNSC members responded to them and why, and what implications their actions had for the sovereignty of the host state involved. These operations offer crucial lessons on the developing attitudes of the UNSC members towards force, sovereignty and intervention as they were forced to quickly respond to a number of international crises. These results are then compared with an analysis of Security Council decision making prior to the outbreak of the second Gulf War in order to determine the degree to which the attitudes towards force and intervention that were formulated in the early 1990s were reflected in the attitudes of the Security Council members towards the Iraqi crisis.

Acknowledgements

The development of this book was greatly assisted by the thoughtful feedback of S. Neil MacFarlane, to whom I am most grateful. I would also like to thank the Rhodes Trust and New College, Oxford for providing valuable research funding. Finally, I would like to thank my parents who lead by example and never cease to convey the excitement and benefits of learning.

List of Acronyms

ABC	American Broadcasting Corporation
ANC	Armeeé Nationale Congolaise
BBC	British Broadcasting Corporation
CIA	Central Intelligence Agency
CNG	Conseil National de Gouvernment
CSCE	Conference on Security and Cooperation in Europe
DHA	Department of Humanitarian Affairs
DPA	Department of Political Affairs
DPKO	Department of Peacekeeping Operations
EC	European Community
EU	European Union
FAR	Forces Armées Rwandaises
FRAPH	Front Révolutionnaire pour l'Avancement et le Progrès Haitien
GAOR	General Assembly Official Records
GIA	Governors Island Agreement
GNU	Government of National Unity
GRULAC	Group of Latin American and Caribbean Countries at the United Nations
IAEA	International Atomic Energy Agency
IDP	Internally Displaced Persons
JNA	Yugoslav National Army
LAS	League of Arab States
MFN	Most Favoured Nation
MICIVIH	International Civilian Mission in Haiti
MNF	Multi-National Force
MOU	Memorandum of Understanding
NAC	North Atlantic Council
NATO	North Atlantic Treaty Organisation
NMOG	Neutral Military Observer Group
OAS	Organisation of American States
OAU	Organisation of African Unity
OIC	Organisation of the Islamic Conference
ONUC	United Nations Operation in the Congo
OSCE	Organisation for Security and Cooperation in Europe
P-5	Permanent Five Members of the Security Council
PDD	Presidential Decision Directive

List of Acronyms ix

PKK	Kurdish Workers' Party
PSO	Peace Support Operation
QRF	Quick Reaction Force
ROE	Rules of Engagement
RPF	Rwandan Patriotic Front
RRF	Rapid Reaction Force
SCOR	Security Council Official Records
SNA	Somali National Alliance
SOFA	Status of Forces Agreement
SRSG	Special Representative of the Secretary General
UAR	United Arab Republic
UK	United Kingdom
UN	United Nations
UNAMIR	United Nations Assistance Mission in Rwanda
UNEF	United Nations Emergency Force
UNGA	United Nations General Assembly
UNGCI	United Nations Guards Contingent in Iraq
UNHCR	United Nations High Commissioner for Refugees
UNITAF	Unified Task Force
UNMET	United Nations Mission in East Timor
UNMIH	United Nations Mission in Haiti
UNMO	United Nations Military Observer
UNMOVIC	United Nations Monitoring, Verification and Inspection Commission
UNOMUR	United Nations Observer Mission Uganda-Rwanda
UNOSOM	United Nations Operation in Somalia
UNPA	United Nations Protected Area
UNPF	United Nations Peace Forces
UNPROFOR	United Nations Protection Force
UNSC	United Nations Security Council
UNSCOM	United Nations Special Commission
UNTAC	United Nations Transitional Authority in Cambodia
USAID	United States Agency for International Development
USC	United Somali Congress
USSR	Union of Soviet Socialist Republics
VOPP	Vance-Owen Peace Plan
WFP	World Food Program
WMD	Weapons of Mass Destruction

Chapter 1

Understanding the Centrality of Consent

The whirlwind of international crises, conflicts and tensions that have arisen in the wake of the Cold War have resulted in a dramatically fluid landscape of international politics that stands in stark contrast to the quondam predictability of the bi-polar rivalry. The lone super power is engaged in a war on terror and embroiled in an increasingly chaotic civil insurgency in Iraq. The United Nations Security Council (UNSC) appears marginalized, seemingly unable to fulfill its main role to "save succeeding generations from the scourge of war" as intended by its founding Charter. Yet a few short years ago, the UN Security Council was hailed as the focal point of international peace and security, emboldened to address the myriad conflicts that arose following the end of the Cold War and the collapse of the bi-polar order that had structured international politics since 1945.

The end of the Cold War reinvigorated the United Nations (UN) organization with purpose and potential. The new collegiality of the Security Council allowed its members to act with increased flexibility in seeking to fulfill their primary responsibility of preserving international peace and security. To be sure, once extricated from the shadow of the super power rivalry, the UN had plenty of demand for its services. Conflicts and humanitarian crises in northern Iraq, Somalia, and the former Yugoslavia were only a few of the trouble spots that saw the capabilities of the United Nations tested as never before.

Just as demand for the security provisions of the United Nations increased after the collapse of the bi-polar order, so did the willingness of the Security Council members and the UN Secretariat to engage the organisation in demanding situations across the globe. Building on the success of the Gulf War, US President George Bush highlighted the prospect of a "new world order," and the centrality of the United Nations to that order.[1] UN Secretary-General Boutros Boutros-Ghali also suggested "a conviction has grown, among nations large and small, that an opportunity has been regained to achieve the great objectives of the Charter..."[2]

Yet a decade later, the grand plans for the reinvigoration of the UNSC seemed to be in tatters. Boutros-Gali's successor as UN Secretary General, Kofi Annan, was warning:

---

[1] "Bush, Clinton Say US Support for UN Will Continue," Statements of President Bush and Presidential Candidate Bill Clinton to the UN Association of the USA, *United States Information Agency*, 9 October, 1992.
[2] Boutros Boutros-Ghali, "An Agenda for Peace: Preventive Diplomacy, Peacemaking and Peace-keeping," *UN Document*, S/24111, 17 June, 1992.

2 *Understanding the UN Security Council*

...a renewal of the effectiveness and relevance of the Security Council must become a cornerstone of our efforts to promote peace and security in the next century...there has been a regrettable tendency for the Security Council not to be involved in the efforts to maintain international peace and security.[3]

Similarly, George W. Bush, issued a challenge to the UN organisation:

All the world now faces a test, and the United Nations a difficult and defining moment. Are Security Council resolutions to be honoured and enforced, or case aside without consequence? Will the United Nations serve the purpose of its founding, or will it be irrelevant?[4]

In spite of the enthusiasm for reaffirming the key role of the UN Security Council in preserving international peace and security, the council was instead fighting for its very relevance and credibility.

This dramatic contrast between an international community looking towards the Security Council for leadership, resolve and resolution in the 1990s and a Security Council in 2003 that is searching for relevance in the wake of American and British intervention in Iraq is puzzling. What has happened to the post-Cold War "intoxication" of purpose and possibility that once flowed through the Security Council?

The answer lies in understanding the politics of the Security Council itself. The manner in which the UN Security Council members dealt with the recent Iraqi crisis, the attitudes, opinions and positions they supported were in many ways determined by their experiences of the many crises in international peace and security that occurred during the early 1990s. During this time the UNSC members were abruptly forced to develop new means and methods of conflict resolution in a short period of time. Indeed, these experiences are increasingly being viewed as critical factors that have shaped many recent decisions taken by the council in regard to intervention and the use of force.[5] In order to understand the Security Council's stalemate on Iraq, the attitudes of its members towards the use of force and intervention, it is therefore vital that we understand the manner in which they approached these same issues in the immediate post-Cold War period.

Understanding the Past

In the early 1990s the familiar signposts that once defined the limits of international peacekeeping action had vanished in the wake of changed priorities.

---

[3] "Text of Kofi Annan's Speech in The Hague," *UN Press Release SG/SM/6997*, 18 May, 1999.

[4] "President's Remarks at the United Nations General Assembly," *Office of the Press Secretary*, 12 September, 2002.

[5] See Mats Berdal, "Lessons Not Learned: The Use of Force in 'Peace Operations" in the 1990s," *International Peacekeeping*, vol. 7, no. 4, 2000.

Understanding the Centrality of Consent

As the United Nations tried to rapidly expand its capabilities in order to fulfil the new role that was demanded of it in the immediate post-Cold War period, the challenges posed by new conflicts exposed the limitations of UN peacekeeping methods. In response, some UN operations gradually began to stray from the tried and tested operational norms that formed the backbone of this traditional approach. One such norm was the principle of consent. Rather than relying on a purely co-operative basis with the host state for UN deployments, the members of the UNSC seemed willing to authorize more coercive measures under Chapter VII of the UN Charter in order to meet the myriad challenges of the post-Cold War period.

Some analysts noted that the Security Council was increasingly circumventing the restrictions of Article 2(7) in the pursuit of humanitarian goals, and as a result was becoming increasingly interventionist.[6] The United Nations Charter had always encompassed the dual objectives of preserving international peace and security while also furthering individual human rights. In early 1992, the five permanent members of the Security Council (P-5) agreed that the time had come to place a greater emphasis on the latter objective - though not necessarily at the expense of the former.[7] The UN's involvement in Somalia, northern Iraq and Bosnia-Herzegovina led a number of commentators to suggest that the actions of the UN Security Council demonstrated that the international community had begun a shift away from the centrality of state sovereignty towards the development of a doctrine of humanitarian intervention.[8] Some even concluded that actions such as the UNSC's adoption of resolution 688 after the Gulf War indicate that "both sovereignty and statehood as legal terms are undergoing an identity crisis, a crisis so fundamental that the special role of states as the principal global actors is likely

---

[6] See, for example, Sean D. Murphy, *Humanitarian Intervention: The United Nations in an Evolving World Order*, University of Pennsylvania Press, Philadelphia, 1996, p. 284.

[7] Security Council debate on International Peace and Security, *UN Document* S/PV .3046, 31 January, 1992. China was careful to qualify its support for human rights, stating that the issue fell within the sovereignty of each state.

[8] Christopher Ryan argues that "there has been a shift in the willingness of international society to consider humanitarian intervention in what would previously have been regarded as 'internal' matters of states;" Christopher M. Ryan, "Sovereignty, Intervention, and the Law: A Tenuous Relationship of Competing Principles," *Millennium*, vol. 26, no. 1, 1997, p. 77. Similarly Thomas Weiss suggests that "the significant precedent set in northern Iraq, along with actions in Somalia and Bosnia-Herzegovina, moved the international community to begin developing tenets in stark contrast to the conventional wisdom of the past, which held that sovereignty overrides all other principles of international behaviour;" Thomas G. Weiss, "Triage: Humanitarian Interventions in a New Era," *World Policy Journal*, vol. 11, no. 1, 1994, p. 59. Dorinda Dallmeyer also argues that "the Security Council has begun to chip away at the principle of non-intervention", highlighting the concern of many developing countries that a UNSC "hegemonic directorate" could mean the end of the long standing UN principle of consent; Dorinda G. Dallmeyer, "National Perspectives on International Interventions: From the Outside Looking In," in Donald C.F. Daniel and Bradd C. Hayes, eds., *Beyond Traditional Peacekeeping*, Macmillan Press Ltd., London, 1995. pp. 20, 31.

to be displaced."[9] Other commentators were more cautious in reaching conclusions based on the actions of the Security Council. Adam Roberts, for example, argued that there was no new doctrine "but only an emerging, limited and fragile body of state and UN practice in the matter."[10] James Mayall also argued in 1991 that based on the coalition incursion into northern Iraq "it would be imprudent in practice, and wrong in theory, to generalise from the international obligations towards the Kurds in favour of an international enforcement mechanism for human rights wherever they are abused."[11]

One means of analysing the relative significance of the UNSC decisions in regard to the deployment of peacekeeping and peace enforcement operations during this time is to examine the degree to which such operations were deployed according to the principle of consent and the extent to which the UNSC members relied on coercion to address many of the conflicts of the post-Cold War period.[12] It will then be possible to see the extent to which such decisions similarly influenced UNSC attitudes in regard to Iraq in 2002. To this end, this book attempts to answer the following questions:

- To what extent did the members of the UN Security Council downgrade the principle of consent as the basis for peacekeeping operations in the early 1990s in preference for more coercive measures under Article 42 of the UN Charter?

- Do the UNSC's decisions with regard to consent and coercion in these peacekeeping operation indicate an increased willingness among its members to narrow the scope of Article 2(7) in order to permit the UN to deploy a Chapter VII peace enforcement operations for humanitarian reasons and what, if any, are the implications for state sovereignty?

- To what extent can the decisions of the Security Council taken in regard to Iraq in 2002 and 2003 be viewed as consistent with their attitudes towards force and sovereignty as developed during the early 1990s?

---

[9] Jarat Chopra, "The Obsolescence of Intervention under International Law," in Marianne Heiberg, ed., *Subduing Sovereignty: Sovereignty and the Right to Intervene*, Pinter Press Ltd., London, 1994, p. 34.
[10] Adam Roberts, "Humanitarian War: Military Intervention and Human Rights," *International Affairs*, vol. 69, no. 3, 1993, p. 448.
[11] James Mayall, "Non-intervention, Self-determination and the 'New World Order'," *International Affairs*, vol. 67, no. 3, 1991, p. 428.
[12] "Consent" refers to the voluntary agreement of a host government or belligerent party to a UN peacekeeping or peace enforcement operation.

The Concept of Sovereignty

The contention that the sovereign authority of states is being eroded by the actions of the Security Council can only be considered if one understands the centrality of sovereignty to the modern state system. Conceptually, its development occurred alongside the construction of the modern nation-state. As this development slowly solidified during the sixteenth and seventeenth centuries it was accompanied by a parallel evolution in the way men thought about authority and power. The original notion of sovereignty emerged as a particular formulation of ideas intended to answer the questions "where in the body politic does ultimate authority reside?" and "to what extent is this authority accountable?"[13] It represented a new way of thinking about the problems of the location of political power and the exercising of that power, emerging at a particular point in the evolution of political man in order to "explain and legitimize the rise of the centralized and absolutist state."[14] Jean Bodin, to whom credit for first formulating the modern idea of sovereignty is attributed, defined it as the "...absolute and perpetual power of a commonwealth..."[15] From this initial formulation the term came to refer to a variety of rights and obligations on the state because of its location within a larger community of states.

A collection of sovereign states that share common interests and perceive themselves to be bound by a common set of rules is termed an international society.[16] Each state relies on its sovereign identity in order to belong to this society. When a state is placed in a community of other states, the idea of sovereignty takes on two elements; internal sovereignty, which means that states assert supremacy over all other authorities within a particular territory and over a particular population in that territory, and external sovereignty, which means that the state is independent of outside authorities. This feature of external sovereignty is manifest in the principle of *sovereign equality*, which asserts that a sovereign state, in a system of similar states, is an equal member regardless of size, power, or population. This status requires the state to accept a set of constitutive rules that assist in ordering the state system by governing the interactions of its members.[17] These rules include the acceptance of the legal equality of states, mutual recognition, non-intervention, making and honouring of treaties, diplomacy based on accepted practices, and a basic framework of international law.[18] Since no higher authority exists above that of the sovereign state, international laws are only

---

[13] F.H. Hinsley, *Sovereignty*, C.A. Watts & Co. Ltd., London, 1966. p.1.

[14] Joseph A. Camilleri and Jim Falk, *The End of Sovereignty?*, Edward Elgar Publishing Ltd., Aldershot, 1992, p. 239.

[15] Jean Bodin, *On Sovereignty*, J.H. Franklin, ed., Cambridge University Press, Cambridge, 1992. p. 1.

[16] Hedley Bull, *The Anarchical Society*, Macmillan Press Ltd., London, 1977, p. 8.

[17] R.J. Vincent, *Nonintervention and International Order*, Princeton University Press, Princeton, 1974, p. 29.

[18] Robert H. Jackson, *Quasi-States: Sovereignty, International Relations, and the Third World*, Cambridge University Press, Cambridge, 1990, p. 35.

Understanding the UN Security Council

created with the consent of the states themselves.[19] However, failure to abide by these laws and norms of behaviour not only threatens a state's acceptance into the community of sovereigns, but also jeopardises the basic order of the international society. This order is directed towards securing certain basic goals of coexistence: the assurance that life will be to some extent secured against violence, the expectation that promises and agreements reached between members will be honoured, and the expectation that the possession of things will remain somewhat stable and not be subject to constant challenges.[20]

If states wish to fulfil these individual long-term goals - goals which can only be achieved in the context of the society of states and the order it provides - they agree not to intervene in the internal affairs of any other state.[21] This *norm of non-intervention* is one of the key prescriptions of state behaviour within international society that facilitates the preservation of order and stems from the principle of sovereign equality.

Intervention and the Practice of States

For the purpose of this study the term "intervention" will be taken to mean the coercive threat or use of force by a state, group of states or international organisation in the sphere of jurisdiction of a sovereign state.[22] "Humanitarian intervention" will be taken to mean the coercive threat or use of force by a state, group of states or international organisation in the sphere of jurisdiction of a sovereign state for the purpose of protecting the nationals of that sovereign state from widespread deprivations of internationally recognised human rights.[23]

---

[19] Anthony C. Arend and Robert J. Beck, *International Law and the Use of Force*, Routledge, New York, 1993, p. 16.

[20] Hedley Bull, *The Anarchical Society*, p. 4.

[21] Ibid., p. 14.

[22] This definition is based on that used by Hedley Bull in *Intervention in World Politics*, p. 1 and Neil MacFarlane, *Intervention and Regional Security*, Adelphi Paper No. 196, International Institute for Strategic Studies, London, 1985, p. 1. For an excellent discussion of the numerous component elements of the term "intervention" see R.J. Vincennt *Nonintervention and International Order*, Princeton University Press, Princeton, 1974, pp. 3-13. The meaning of "intervention" is a highly debated issue in international relations. See for example Hedley Bull, *Intervention in World Politics*, Clarendon Press, Oxford, 1984, pp. 1-3; Ellery C. Stowell, *Intervention in International Law*, John Byrne & Co., Washington D.C., 1921. pp. 51-53; Gene M. Lyons and Michael Mastanduno, eds., *Beyond Westphalia? State Sovereignty and International Intervention*, The Johns Hopkins University Press, Baltimore, 1995, p. 10; Oliver Ramsbotham and Tom Woodhouse, *Humanitarian Intervention in Contemporary Conflict*, Polity Press, Cambridge, 1996, pp. 1-2.

[23] This definition is derived from combining Bull's definition of intervention with Sean D. Murphy's definition of "humanitarian intervention." See Murphy, *Humanitarian Intervention: the United Nations in an Evolving World Order*, University of Pennsylvania Press, Philadelphia, 1996, p. 12.

Understanding the Centrality of Consent

Intervention by one state into the affairs of another has been discouraged in international relations since the emergence of the society of states in the seventeenth century. Christian Wolff, for example, built on the idea that states were equal entities in international law to arrive at the absolute principle of non-intervention. Vattel suggested that the concept of sovereignty meant that states were entitled to absolute independence and equality, though he arrived at a slightly less restrictive prescription.[24] The idea of non-intervention fitted well into a society of states "which exalted peace as the highest and most 'natural' condition of mankind."[25]

In practice, respect for the norm of non-intervention remained paramount among the Great Powers during the Concert of Europe and, as Ian Brownlie argues, the very concept of the Concert "raised a strong presumption against unilateral changes in the *status quo*."[26] Ellery Stowell similarly suggested that although states were justified under international law to intervene in the affairs of other states in response to instances of repression, oppression, or uncivilised warfare, preservation of the international order remained the order of the day.[27] E.M. Brochard stressed the this same point with regard to humanitarian intervention:

> the right of the sovereign state to act without interference within its own territory...is of such importance to the well being of international society, that the states in their wisdom, as evidenced in their practice, have been jealous of lightly admitting the plea of humanity as a justification for action against a sister state; and we find that intervention on this ground has been rather rigidly limited to specific cases...[28]

When intervention did occur, it was primarily to reinforce the balance of power and preserve the international order. This is demonstrated by the experience of the Concert of Europe. Its formation established the centrality of the Great Powers, around which were clustered a series of secondary states that had a lesser role in the balance of power and thus were only formally considered sovereign equals. When the compromise of a secondary state's sovereign status was viewed as essential for the maintenance of peace and order within Europe, the Great Powers readily violated any norm of sovereign equality that had been extended to these lesser states. Similarly, when it suited the objectives of the Concert, the Great Powers had no qualms about creating a new "sovereign state" in order to readjust the balance of Europe.[29]

---

[24] Vincent, *Nonintervention and International Order*, pp. 29-30.

[25] Geoffrey Best, *Humanity in Warfare*, Weidenfield and Nicolson, London, 1980, p. 129.

[26] Ian Brownlie, *International Law and the Use of Force by States*, Clarendon Press, Oxford, 1963, pp. 19-20.

[27] Ellery C. Stowell, *International Law: A Restatement of Principles in Conformity with Actual Practice*, Sir Issac Pitman & Sons Ltd., London, 1931.

[28] E.M. Brochard as quoted in Ibid., p. 315.

[29] Thus Belgium was admitted to the community of sovereigns in 1830 in order to meet its claims for independence, remove it as a destabilising influence on the administration of the Netherlands, and also pre-empt any potential intervention by France or Prussia. A neutral

8 *Understanding the UN Security Council*

Yet despite the strong emphasis on the preservation of the international order guiding the actions of states on questions of intervention, the moral basis of the sovereign state, even in the nineteenth century, was a source of debate. One early attempt at ensuring that the actions of states were directed according to normative guidelines occurred with the formation of the short-lived Holy Alliance in 1815. The Tsar of Russia, Alexander I, sought to establish a pact among the main European powers based on Christian principles.[30] The protection of such principles was regarded as conducive to the furthering of peace within Europe. While the Alliance did not have much practical effect in reordering the relations among sovereign states, the manner in which the signatories to the Treaties arrogated to themselves the right of intervention in the affairs of other states was to have implications for the rest of the century.[31]

The scope for the inclusion of normative concerns in the conduct of foreign policy spread along with the growth of liberal and national ideals. The rise of popular power during the French and American revolutions saw a shift towards the idea of popular sovereignty, in which the ultimate sovereign authority in a state was its people.[32] A government became viewed simply as a representation of the ultimate sovereign authority vested in the people. The Liberal revolutions that swept continental Europe in 1848 also helped to redefine the locus of sovereign authority. Though short lived, these revolutions provided a brief glimpse of the issues which were to become increasingly important during the following hundred years. Demands for civic freedom and participation in government made conservative European rulers realise that the liberal agitators commanded a dynamic force that had to be channelled into controlled and safe forms of constitutional government - in effect shifting sovereign authority away from the monarch and towards the populace.[33] This was subsequently demonstrated in Prussia when Frederick William extended suffrage, created a bicameral parliament, established a constitution and began a general process of liberal reform.[34]

Despite this increasing scope for individual rights in domestic politics, in international politics there remained no established doctrine of humanitarian

---

and sovereign Belgium was the only arrangement which was acceptable to all of the Great Powers and accordingly it was 'given' a sovereign identity. See Rene Albrecht-Carrie, *The Concert of Europe*, Macmillan Press, London, 1968, pp. 60-65.

[30] H.G. Schenk, *The Aftermath of the Napoleonic Wars*, Kegan, Paul, Trench, Trubner & Co. Ltd., London, 1947, pp. 24-36.

[31] The text of the treaty which established the Holy Alliance in 1815 reads "...the sole principle of force, whether between the said Governments or between their subjects, shall be that of doing each other reciprocal service, and of testifying by unalterable good will the mutual affection with which they ought to be animated, to consider themselves all as members of one and the same Christian nation." The treaty as whole expressed the common responsibility of the rulers of Europe (excluding Great Britain) for the order and functioning of the whole. Albrecht-Carrie, *The Concert of Europe*, p. 35.

[32] Ramsbotham and Woodhouse, *Humanitarian Intervention in Contemporary Conflict*, p. 37.

[33] J.A.S. Grenville, *Europe Reshaped 1848-1878*, The Harvester Press, Sussex, 1976, p. 12.

[34] Ibid., p. 134.

intervention and the principle of non-intervention remained a central feature of nineteenth century international politics.[35] As R.J. Vincent argued:

> statesmen developed doctrines of non-intervention and used them to defend their own policies and to criticize the policies of others, to advance their own objectives and to hamper the achievement of the objectives of others.[36]

The League of Nations

The qualifications necessary for sovereign identity gradually changed and became more formalised as the influence and functioning of the Concert of Europe faded. The first article of the Montevideo Convention of 1933 identified a state as having a permanent population, a defined territory, and the capacity to enter into relations with other states.[37] These criteria assumed the presence of a stable, effective government but the formalised and codified requirement of sovereignty as identified by the Convention still failed to encompass the variety of actors within the international system. Sovereign status still remained an exclusive club to which states were admitted depending upon their level of "civilization."[38] In 1919, the Great Powers decided that there were four different groups of "states". The first group included the European powers, the United States, and a limited number of other countries. The three other classifications divided the peoples of the world according to the likelihood of their attaining sovereign status. "Group A" states of the Middle East were considered well on their way to sovereignty, whereas "Group B" states of tropical Africa were expected to require a number of years of further economic and political development. "Group C" states, including the "primitive" people of the Pacific territories and Southwest Africa were considered to be centuries away from comparable levels of development.[39] This categorization simply served to formalize existing attitudes of the Great Powers towards other,

---

[35] Some commonly cited examples of nineteenth century "humanitarian intervention" include the British French and Russian incursion into Greece in 1827, French intervention into Syria in 1860, and Russia into Bulgaria in 1877. However, in each of these cases the intervening powers, while claiming "humanitarian" motives, were also motivated by strategic considerations. See Murphy, *Humanitarian Intervention*, pp. 52-56. The case of the 1860 French intervention into Turkey in order to protect Turkish Christians is also subject to similar concerns about the "humanitarian" nature of the intervention. See Thomas M. Frank and Nigel S. Rodley, "After Bangladesh: The Law of Humanitarian Intervention By Military Force," *The American Journal of International Law*, vol. 67, 1973, pp. 281-282.

[36] Vincent, *Nonintervention and the International Order*, p. 64.

[37] Oyvind Osterud, "The Narrow Gate: Entry to the Club of Sovereign States," *Review of International Studies*, no. 23, 1997, p. 175.

[38] Gerrit W. Gong, *The Standard of 'Civilization' in International Society*, Clarendon Press, Oxford, 1984, pp. 52-58.

[39] W. Roger Lowis, "The Era of the Mandates System and the Non-European World," in Hedley Bull and Adam Watson, eds., *The Expansion of International Society*, Clarendon Press, Oxford, 1984, pp. 201-203.

non-sovereign states. Lacking sovereignty, these lesser states were not expected to act in accordance with international law and, conversely, international law, with its prohibition on intervention, was not extended to them unless they were under the formal jurisdiction of a recognized sovereign power. Similarly, the relations between the European or sovereign power and its territory or "aspiring sovereign state" were not governed by international law.[40]

The problems of minorities and their demands for self-determination in particular remained a destabilizing force that threatened the European and international orders. The fulfilment of claims for self-determination could have led to the break-up of the individual sovereign states in which the malcontent minorities existed. The redrawing of sovereign borders might then have threatened the European or international balance of power.[41] By the end of the Great War in 1918, the fulfilment of these minority claims was viewed as an effective way to contribute to the stability of the international system. The creation of the League of Nations and the implementation of Wilsonian ideals were intended to resolve the destabilizing issue of minority rights and self-determination. By meeting the demands of minorities through negotiation, just as had been done with Belgium and Greece in the previous century, the League's Minorities Treaties sought to remove the potential for insurrection as well as any pretence for external intervention by the Great Powers. The principle of non-intervention was intended by the signatories of the League to continue as a behavioural norm of states and the resolution of minority claims was considered to be synonymous with the stability of the international order.[42]

Formally, no part of the League Covenant prohibited humanitarian intervention, though the first paragraph of the League Covenant read:

> The High Contracting Parties,
> In order to promote international co-operation and to achieve international peace and security by the acceptance of obligations not to resort to war...

This prohibition on recourse to war limited the potential for legal acts of humanitarian intervention as did the dispute resolution procedures outlined in the Covenant. These prohibited the League Council from dealing with any matter that, under international law, was within the jurisdiction of a member state. Article 15, paragraph 8 of the League Covenant read:

> If the dispute between the parties is claimed by one of them, and is found by the Council, to arise out of a matter which by international law is solely within the domestic jurisdiction of that party, the Council shall so report, and shall make no recommendation as to its settlement.

---

[40] Gong, *The Standard of 'Civilization' in International Society*, p. 58.

[41] J. Samuel Barkin and Bruce Cronin, "The State and the Nation: Changing Norms and the Rules of Sovereignty in International Relations," *International Organisation*, vol. 48, no. 1, 1994, pp. 121-122.

[42] C.A. Macartney, *National States and National Minorities*, Oxford University Press, London, 1934, pp. 273-4.

Similarly, the centrality of the non-intervention norm was reaffirmed by the formation of the Minorities Treaties. Infractions of the Treaties could only be addressed by Council recommendations and condemned by international public opinion. The rights of minorities thus depended in large part upon those that were extended to them by the presiding power.[43] The protection of individual human rights under the League was similarly poor. If the relevant issues were not covered by international law - and many were not - they were beyond the scope of the organisation.[44] Both of these factors, in addition to the restrictions of the Covenant, resulted in the League era being one in which the rights of states were again stressed above those of individuals in an effort to avoid the use of force in international politics. In consequence, an accepted doctrine of humanitarian intervention did not emerge in international politics. The continuing emphasis on order and stability in the state system, a lack of agreement between states about what "humanitarian intervention" actually meant, and its consequent potential for abuse by powerful states based on these differences in interpretation meant that the task of balancing human rights and state sovereignty remained a key issue during the formation of the United Nations.[45]

The United Nations

The centrality of non-intervention to international society in the twentieth century was reflected by the manner of its inclusion into the UN Charter. In the first chapter of the document, under the heading *Purposes and Principles*, Article 2(7) reads:

> Nothing contained in the present Charter shall authorize the United Nations to intervene in matters which are essentially within the domestic jurisdiction of any state or shall require the Members to submit such matters to settlement under the present Charter; but this principle shall not prejudice the application of enforcement measures under Chapter VII.

While most of the other norms which governed international society were tacitly accepted by states when they ratified the Charter as a whole, the United States, the USSR, Britain and China proposed that the norm of non-intervention should be stated more formally within the document, such was its perceived importance.[46] Accordingly the prohibition on intervention was moved forward from Chapter VIII of the original Dumbarton Oaks draft of the Charter, which had

---

[43] L.P. Mair, *The Protection of Minorities*, Christophers, London, 1928, p. 28.

[44] Murphy, *Humanitarian Intervention*, p. 59.

[45] David M. Kresock, "'Ethnic Cleansing' in the Balkans: The Legal Foundations of Foreign Intervention," *Cornell Journal of International Law*, vol. 27, 1994, p. 212.

[46] Antonio Cassese, *International Law in a Divided World*, Clarendon Press, Oxford, 1986, p. 129; M.S. Rajan, *United Nations and Domestic Jurisdiction*, Asia Publishing House, New York, 1961, p. 46.

dealt with the pacific settlement of disputes by the UNSC, eventually becoming Article 2(7) under the first chapter of the Charter.[47] The effect of this move was to circumscribe the powers and functions of the entire organisation rather than just affecting the operation of the Security Council.[48]

The article itself was intended to limit the jurisdiction of the new United Nations which, through the creation of the Economic and Social Council and other bodies, had a much wider scope than its inter-war predecessor, the League of Nations. The United States, in particular, argued that the wide jurisdiction of the General Assembly and the Economic and Social Council meant that the overall powers and authority of the new organisation needed to be clarified and steps taken to prevent the organisation deciding what pattern of social order it wanted and imposing this on states without their consent.[49]

In order to preserve the salience of Article 2(7), the United States, together with the three other sponsoring states, fought off a number of proposed revisions to its wording. For example, the proposal to replace the word "essentially" with "solely" was rejected by the US representative, John Foster Dulles, on the grounds that it would encompass too few of the crucial concerns of a state. The word "essentially" was seen as more expansive and thus more protective of a state's activities. This firm position on the wording of Article 2(7), together with its relocation in the Charter meant that in the context of the new organisation, "the scope of state jurisdiction was more strongly secured" than in the League of Nations.[50]

However, as indicated by the last sentence of Article 2(7), the prohibition on intervention in the Charter is not absolute. Where the Security Council identifies a threat to international peace and security under Chapter VII of the Charter, it is not bound by the restrictions of Article 2(7). The intention that lay behind this exception to the rule was to ensure that the Security Council retained the power to take such measures as its members deemed necessary to fulfil the organisation's primary objective: the maintenance of international peace and security. Importantly for the purposes of this study, the Charter does not define either the type or degree of threat which is necessary to make the exception to the non-intervention rule operative.[51] This creates the possibility of the Security Council members being able to redefine what they consider to constitute a threat to international peace and security.[52]

---

[47] "The United Nations Dumbarton Oaks Proposals for a General International Organisation", *The United Nations Conference on International Organisation*, United Nations Information Organisation, London, 1945.

[48] Rajan, *United Nations and Domestic Jurisdiction*, pp. 36-44.

[49] Ibid., p. 54.

[50] Bruno Simma, ed., *The Charter of the United Nations*, Oxford University Press, Oxford, 1994, p. 142.

[51] Rajan, *United Nations and Domestic Jurisdiction*, p. 94.

[52] Michael G. Schechter, "The United Nations in the Aftermath of Somalia: The Effects of the UN's Handling of Article 2(7) on the United Nations," in Edwin M. Smith and Michael G. Schechter, eds., *The United Nations in a New World Order*, The Keck Centre for International and Strategic Studies, 1994, pp. 56-58. For example, in 1966 and 1968 the

Understanding the Centrality of Consent 13

Another provision within the UN Charter which also underlines the prohibition against intervention, though not as directly as Article 2(7), is Article 2(1). It states "the organisation is based on the principle of sovereign equality of all its members." The members of the UN agreed that a constitutive element of the principle of sovereign equality was mutual respect for each other's territorial integrity and political independence.[53] While Article 2(7) defines the relationship between the organisation and states in domestic matters, the principle of sovereign equality encapsulated in Article 2(1) similarly precludes any interference by a state or group of states in the affairs of another member of international society.

Since the adoption of the Charter, the norm of non-intervention has been reaffirmed by a declaration of the UN General Assembly. In 1965, its members adopted the Declaration on Non-intervention which stated, "No state has the right to intervene, directly or indirectly for any reason whatever, in the internal or external affairs of any other State." This was qualified by the inclusion of the caveat "nothing in the foregoing paragraphs shall be construed as affecting the relevant provisions of the Charter relating to the maintenance of international peace and security."[54] This caveat left the UN Security Council able to lawfully violate the principle of non-intervention in order to fulfil its Charter responsibilities.

Tension in the Charter

In addition to the Charter's goal of preserving international peace and security, it was also dedicated towards the promotion of fundamental human rights and

---

Council voted to impose mandatory economic sanctions against Rhodesia. These actions under Chapter VII of the Charter were taken as a result of Rhodesian white minority rule and the illegal declaration of independence from the UK (1966) and due to violations of human rights which constituted a threat to international peace and security (1968). In 1977 the members of the Council took similar action against the Republic of South Africa, imposing an arms embargo on the republic. Though the Council justified its action as a result of the "the situation in South Africa," the apartheid system with its integral human rights abuses is commonly regarded as the main motivating factor. See Kelly Kate Peace and David P. Forsythe, "Human Rights, Humanitarian Intervention, and World Politics," *Human Rights Quarterly*, vol. 15, 1993, p. 302.

[53] Leland Goodrich, Edvard Hambro, and Anne Patricia Simons, *Charter of the United Nations: Commentary and Documents*, 3rd Revised ed., Columbia University Press, New York, 1969. pp. 37-38. The report of the Technical Committee at the San Francisco Conference considered the term "sovereign equality" to include the following elements: that states are juridically equal, that each state enjoys the rights inherent in full sovereignty, that the personality of the state is respected as well as its territorial integrity and political independence, and that a state should, under the international order, comply with its international duties and obligations.

[54] UNGA Resolution 2131. *UN Document*, A/6014. 21 December, 1965.

14 *Understanding the UN Security Council*

freedoms. The fulfilment of this second cluster of values however is often at odds with the protection of state sovereignty.[55] The preamble to the Charter reads:

> We the peoples of the United Nations determined to save succeeding generations from the scourge of war, which twice in our lifetime has brought untold sorrow to mankind, and to reaffirm faith in fundamental human rights, in the dignity and worth of the human person, in the equal rights of men and women and of nations large and small...

This tension between ensuring international peace and security and the goal of furthering individual human rights represents a persistent tension in the UN Charter and the actions of the UN organisation. As Lori Damrosch argues, these two clusters of values interrelate in the objectives for conflict prevention or containment, as well as objectives of the realisation of autonomy.[56] Yet although both clusters form the key objectives of the UN, the inclusion of human rights provisions into the Charter during the Dumbarton Oaks negotiations occurred belatedly in the drafting process as a result of a proposal from the United States. Until that point, it had been agreed that the organisation would focus predominantly on the preservation of international peace and security, while economic and social co-operation would be fostered by a subsidiary body of the General Assembly. Following the US proposal that human rights be mentioned, and despite resistance from the USSR and Britain, pressure from non-governmental organisations and numerous states ensured that the proposed Charter was amended to include the promotion of human rights as a focal point of the organisation.[57]

Despite this late amendment and the over-riding emphasis within the provisions of the UN Charter against the use of force, advocates of a unilateral right of humanitarian intervention point to three reasons why such a right is permissible under the terms of the Charter. First they assert that Articles 1(3), 55 and 56 indicate the furthering of human rights is a primary purpose of the UN. When the UNSC fails to intervene to fulfil this objective, the right to do so is passed to the organisation's individual members. Second, they argue that a pre-Charter customary right of humanitarian intervention is revived when the Council fails to act to counter instances of human rights abuses. Third, the prohibition in Article 2(4) on the use of force except in self-defence is circumvented if the use of force does not affect the target state's political independence and territorial integrity in the long term.[58]

In state practice however, Article 2(4) has been interpreted expansively, supporting a comprehensive ban on the use of force.[59] Outside the scope of the

---

[55] For a discussion of the problems in furthering the dual goals of order and justice see Bull, *The Anarchical Society*, pp. 74-95.

[56] Damrosch, *Enforcing Restraint*, p. 8.

[57] Murphy, *Humanitarian Intervention*, p. 69.

[58] Michael L. Burton, "Legalising the Sublegal: A Proposal for Codifying a Doctrine of Unilateral Humanitarian Intervention," *The Georgetown Law Journal*, vol. 85, 1996, p. 427.

[59] Wil D. Verwey, "Humanitarian Intervention," in A. Cassese, ed., *The Current Legal Regulation of the Use of Force*, Martinus Nijhoff Publishers, Lancaster, 1986, p. 67.

Understanding the Centrality of Consent

15

United Nations, the prohibition on the use of force to intervene for humanitarian reasons has also been upheld by the recent case law of the World Court, particularly the "Military Activities in Nicaragua" case.[60] Recent attempts at protecting human rights through the mechanisms of the UN International Covenant on Human Rights or regional initiatives such as the European Convention on Human Rights have allowed one state to raise the issue of human rights abuses in another signatory state, but these protocols do not codify a right of unilateral humanitarian intervention.[61]

Indeed, the reluctance of states the rely on humanitarian justifications for instances of intervention, even when substantial evidence for such a claim exists, was a feature of international politics during the Cold War. In 1971, India intervened in what was then East Pakistan in response to wide violations of human rights carried out by the Pakistani government. In the United Nations, India argued that its actions were in response to the large-scale violations of human rights by the Pakistani authorities and were based on nothing but the "purest of motives." [62] However, this humanitarian justification was quickly rejected by India itself in preference for one based on the right of self-defence.[63] While the verbatim provisional records of the Security Council record India justifying her actions in terms of protecting the human rights of the Bangladeshi people, the official records of the Security Council instead record India as justifying her actions as self-defence against an attack by Pakistan.[64] As Akehurst argues, India most likely chose to amend its comments in the official records because the right of self defence provided a stronger legal basis for its actions. Indeed, many states in the Security Council and the General Assembly attacked India's initial humanitarian justification, arguing that the situation was an internal affair of Pakistan.[65]

In Africa, Tanzania chose to adopt a similar argument to justify its intervention in Uganda in 1979. Rather than arguing that its participation in the overthrow of the oppressive regime of Idi Amin could be justified in humanitarian terms, Tanzania instead chose to invoke its right of self-defence. It argued that the deployment of its troops into Uganda was in response to a prior Ugandan invasion

---

[60] Nigel S. Rodley, "Human Rights and Humanitarian Intervention: The Case Law of the World Court," *International and Comparative Law Quarterly*, vol. 38, 1989, pp. 327- 333.

[61] Nigel S. Rodley, "Collective Intervention to Protect Human Rights and Civilian Populations: The Legal Framework," in Nigel S. Rodley, ed., *To Loose the Bands of Wickedness*, Brassey's (UK) Ltd., London, 1992, p. 23.

[62] *UN Documents*, S/PV. 1606, 4 December, 1971 and S/PV .1608, 6 December, 1971. Analysts remain sceptical of the true rationale behind India's action. See, for example, Thomas M. Franck and Nigel S. Rodley, "After Bangladesh: The Law of Humanitarian Intervention by Military Force," *The American Journal of International Law*, vol. 67, 1973. pp. 292-294. See also Arend and Roberts, *International Law and the Use of Force*, p. 119.

[63] Franck and Rodley, "After Bangladesh: The Law of Humanitarian Intervention by Military Force," pp. 292-294. See also Arend and Roberts, *International Law and the Use of Force*, p. 119.

[64] Michael Akehurst, "Humanitarian Intervention," in Bull, ed., *Intervention in World Politics*. pp. 96-97.

[65] Ibid., p. 97.

16 *Understanding the UN Security Council*

of Tanzania, and that its action had simply coincided with an internal revolt against Amin.[66] Tanzania's actions were subsequently criticized at an Organisation of African Unity (OAU) summit as violating the norm of non-intervention.[67]

Vietnam's intervention in Cambodia in 1979 similarly demonstrated the unwillingness of UN member states to support a doctrine of humanitarian intervention. Despite the appalling human rights record of Pol Pot's Cambodian regime, the Vietnamese government denied its involvement in Pol Pot's ouster, arguing instead that the Cambodian people had themselves deposed him. Despite this implicit denial of its involvement, the majority of UN member-states argued that Vietnam had acted illegally by intervening in the internal affairs of Cambodia, even in view of the Cambodian regime's violation of human rights. No state made any attempt to justify Vietnam's action in terms of a doctrine of humanitarian intervention.[68]

From these examples two things become clear. First, during the Cold War states remained reluctant to rely on a doctrine of humanitarian intervention in order to justify their actions, even in cases where the basis for such a claim was substantial. Instead, states often preferred to justify their actions by invoking the more legally acceptable right of self-defence. Second, the majority of UN member states condemned any violation of the principle of non-intervention, even in the face of gross abuses of human rights.

The Renewed Impetus Toward Humanitarian Intervention

The collapse of the bi-polar order has served to refocus attention on both the international peace and security and human rights objectives of the UN. While the organisation was intended to preserve the security of the modern state system, many of these states routinely violate human rights - actions that sometimes threaten to destabilize surrounding regions. Indeed the very system that the UNSC's members have agreed to protect is under attack for two reasons: the allegedly shrinking relevance of sovereignty in the modern state system and the increasingly criticized moral foundation of the modern nation-state.

The Relevance of Sovereignty

First, the concept of sovereignty remains a hotly debated topic, despite its importance as an ordering feature of international politics. Perhaps the most settled notion of what it means is reflected by the definition formulated by F.H. Hinsley. He defined it as "the idea that there is a final and absolute political authority in the political community and no final and absolute authority exists elsewhere."[69] More recently, Alan James has suggested that sovereignty is simply

---

[66] Arend and Roberts, *International Law and the Use of Force*, p. 124.

[67] Akehurst, "Humanitarian Intervention," pp. 98-99.

[68] Ibid., p. 97.

[69] Hinsley, *Sovereignty*, p. 26.

Understanding the Centrality of Consent 17

constitutional independence of other states, a condition which is legal, absolute and unitary.[70] However, many international relations theorists criticize sovereignty as an inaccurate concept that fails to reflect the changing role and character of the state in international relations. In recent debate a great deal of the emphasis has been directed away from the static notion of sovereignty towards a more shifting, interpretative conception, or as Sikkink argues, "a set of intersubjective understandings and expectations about the legitimate scope of state authority, reinforced by practices."[71] Just as the idea of sovereignty originally reflected the transition from the medieval system to the early form of the international state system, this evolution continues today. Some theorists, such as Barkin and Cronin, argue, "it is often not appreciated fully that sovereignty is a social construct, and like all social institutions its location is subject to changing interpretations."[72]

Many theorists have been willing to accept the inconsistencies inherent in the static conception of sovereignty in order to have a starting point for the creation of international political theory. Critics of this approach, however, are increasingly finding the notion of sovereign equality to be ill suited to the realities of the post-Cold War world. This is in part because rapidly changing social, economic and political circumstances have uncovered previously hidden ambiguities in the concept.[73] Within the international system there are many varieties of states that have each undergone a highly individualized economic and political development process. This in turn has consequences for the sovereign reality in each. Unlike nineteenth century states which achieved sovereign status from having sufficient territorial authority and international presence to justify normal diplomatic interchange with the European powers, new constitutive rules of sovereignty which emerged during the decolonization period favoured weak quasi-states and divorced juridical statehood from the empirical qualities of historical state formation.[74] The result, Georg Sorenson argues, is three distinct types of state in the international system today, and each type is faced with different factors that affect their sovereign identity.[75] For example, despite the definition of sovereignty as absolute power, internal sovereignty has never been absolute in practice.[76] This in turn affects the ability of the state to adhere to the constitutive rules of international society, since its internal power may not be sufficient to ensure that its constitutive

---

[70] Alan James, *Sovereign Statehood*, Allen & Unwin Ltd., London, 1986, pp. 15, 39.

[71] Kathryn Sikkink, "Human Rights, Principled Issue-Networks, and Sovereignty in Latin America," *International Organisation*, vol. 43, no. 3, 1993, p. 441.

[72] Barkin and Cronin, *The State and the Nation*, pp. 107-130.

[73] Camilleri and Falk, *The End of Sovereignty?*, p. 236.

[74] Ibid., p. 182.

[75] Georg Sorenson, "An Analysis of Contemporary Statehood: Consequences for Conflict and Co-operation," *Review of International Studies*, no. 23, 1997, pp. 258-264. Sorenson distinguishes between Westphalian, post-colonial, and post-modern states depending on their levels of interdependence, monopoly of military power, and economic and political development.

[76] Sikkink, "Human Rights, Principled Issue-Networks, and Sovereignty in Latin America," p. 413. Sikkink uses the example of the Treaty of Augsburg and the Peace of Westphalia which limited the power of the sovereign to control his subjects religious practices.

18 *Understanding the UN Security Council*

parts adhere to the rule of international society. Additionally, while constraints on state behaviour have existed since the emergence of international law, the continued growth of global interdependence has served to refocus attention on the increasing breadth of the limitations that contemporary states confront. This limits their ability to exercise external sovereignty. Analysts point to the growth of interdependence in the world economy, the rapid pace of technological change, or global ecological concerns as further reasons why the static notion of sovereignty is unsuited to the modern state system.[77]

Normative Criticisms

In addition to scepticism about the continuing relevance of sovereignty to the current system of states, the moral basis of this system is also coming under increased scrutiny. Many international relations academics and practitioners believe that the norm of non-intervention inadequately reflects the growing importance of human rights considerations in international politics. Consequently, there has been renewed pressure towards expanding the scope for unilateral or multilateral intervention aimed at the enforcement of certain societal, internationally recognised humanitarian norms.[78]

One classic debate that is indicative of the growth in tension between state-system values and human rights values is that between Michael Walzer, David Luban and Charles Beitz. Walzer argues that the state is accorded rights of territorial integrity and political independence that circumscribe the extent to which it can be legally subjected to foreign intervention.[79] Luban disagrees with this limited prescription for intervention arguing instead that the concept of sovereignty does not account for why non-interference in the domestic affairs of other states is a moral duty. For him the moral standing of a state derives from the "legitimacy" of the social contract made between the state and its people. The frequent incongruity between the two suggests that a more appropriate basis for the norm of non-intervention lies in what he terms "socially basic human rights."[80] Beitz also disagrees with the prevailing treatment of states as autonomous sources of ends within the international system, morally immune from external interference. Instead he believes that individual persons should be regarded and respected as the source of ends in international politics and that "it is the rights and interests of

---

[77] Camilleri and Falk, *The End of Sovereignty?*, pp. 99-236.

[78] For a comprehensive review of the international ethics debate see Oliver Ramsbotham and Tom Woodhouse, eds., *Humanitarian Intervention in Contemporary Conflict*, Polity Press, Cambridge, 1996, pp. 57-61.

[79] Michael Walzer, "The Rights of Political Communities," in Charles Beitz, et al., *International Ethics*, Princeton University Press, Princeton, 1985, p. 194. Walzer admits only three possible cases in which the non-intervention norm can be legally disregarded; in specific instances of national secession, when the intervention is in response to a previous intervention by another foreign power, and when there are humanitarian abuses such as enslavement or massacre within a state.

[80] David Luban, "Just War and Human Rights," in Beitz, ed., *International Ethics*, p. 210.

Understanding the Centrality of Consent 19

persons that are of fundamental importance from the moral point of view, and it is to these considerations that the justification of principles for international relations should appeal." Consequently, Beitz believes that the principle of non-intervention should apply only to those states that conform to appropriate principles of domestic justice that protect the rights and interests of individuals.[81]

One of the most recent indications of this subjective and fluid interpretation of sovereignty was the report of the International Commission on Intervention and State Sovereignty. The report was a response to Kofi Annan's challenge to UN member state to resolve the tension between sovereignty and its consequent prohibitions on interventions and the need for the international community to respond to gross abuses of human rights.[82] After in-depth international consultations the Commission found that sovereignty was being increasingly interpreted as engendering not only external responsibilities to other sovereign state, but also internally to its own people and does not "include any claim of the unlimited power of a state to do what it wants to its own people."[83] As the sense gains pace that sovereign identity stems from internal as well as the more traditional external responsibilities, the tension between the norm of non-intervention and the need to halt gross abuses of human rights will gain in intensity.

The debate on non-intervention reflects a re-emphasis in international relations on humanitarian concerns. From the perspective of international law the state remains the source of sovereign authority within a society of other similarly attributed states.[84] States are still bound by the norm of reciprocity, but if the demands on internal sovereignty are changing, states will be sovereign equals only so long as they are seen by the rest of the international community to be fulfilling their domestic responsibilities. If, under pressure from the expansion of international ethics, the criteria for statehood are getting tighter, this may, in turn, have a corresponding effect on the principle of sovereign equality from a legal perspective. The result, as Robert Jackson argues, would be to make states accountable for the treatment of their people and to differentiate between states in terms of humanitarianism.[85] If states become judged on how good they are at exercising internal sovereignty this could also affect the extent to which their external sovereignty is respected. Together these changes may fundamentally affect how the concept of sovereignty in international society is understood and the extent to which it remains at the heart of the international system.

---

[81] Charles Beitz, *Political Theory and International Relations*, Princeton University Press, Princeton, 1979. p. 55.

[82] *The Responsibility to Protect*, Report of the International Commission on Intervention and State Sovereignty, Ottawa, December, 2001.

[83] Ibid., p. 8.

[84] Eli Lauterpacht, "Sovereignty-Myth or Reality?," *International Affairs*, vol. 73, no. 1, 1997, p. 144.

[85] Jackson, *Quasi-States*, p. 40.

20 *Understanding the UN Security Council*

Expressing the Humanitarian Impetus

The end of the Cold War was thought by some to create an opportunity to fulfil both Charter objectives of securing international peace and security and furthering human rights. Javier Pérez de Cuéllar, writing just prior to the end of his tenure as Secretary-General argued:

> It is now increasingly felt that the principle of non-interference within the essential domestic jurisdiction of states cannot be regarded as a protective barrier behind which human rights could be massively and systematically violated with impunity...[86]

Similarly, following his appointment as UN Secretary-General, Boutros-Ghali also stressed the need to fulfil the Charter's human rights goals. He wrote:

> The United Nations has not been able to act effectively to bring an end to massive human rights violations. Faced with the barbaric conduct which fills the media today, the United Nations cannot stand idle or indifferent. The long term credibility of our Organization as a whole will depend upon the success of our response to this challenge.[87]

Under this new, post-Cold War humanitarian impetus the Great Powers, in particular the Union of Soviet Socialist Republics (USSR) and the United States (US), became more amenable to the idea of using the United Nations as a tool with which to confront post-Cold War challenges to international peace and security and to protect human rights. In turn, a key tool which the UN possessed that could be directed toward these ends was the deployment of peacekeeping and collective enforcement operations. The Soviet Union had become more positive toward the opportunities presented by the UN and peacekeeping during the fall of 1998.[88] The United States, led by George Bush, was also optimistic that the UN's Blue Helmets could play a positive role in the international system.[89]

The UN and Peacekeeping

The vast majority of peacekeeping operations carried out during the Cold War were what are now commonly referred to as *traditional peacekeeping operations.*

---

[86] Javier Pérez de Cuéllar, "Report of the Secretary-General on the Work of the Organisation," *UN Document*, A/46/1, 1991.

[87] Boutros Boutros-Ghali, "Report of the Secretary-General on the Work of the Organisation," *UN Document*, A/47/1, 1992.

[88] See for example the letter from the Deputy Head of the Delegation of the USSR, "Comprehensive Review of the Whole Question of Peacekeeping Operations in All their Aspects," *UN Document*, A/43/629, 22 September, 1988 as cited in Augustus R. Norton and Thomas G. Weiss, "Superpowers and Peace-keepers," *Survival*, vol. 32, no. 3, 1990, p. 213.

[89] George Bush and Brent Scowcroft, *A World Transformed*, Vintage Books, New York, 1998, p. 303.

Understanding the Centrality of Consent

Traditional peacekeeping generally refers to specific tasks such as the monitoring of international state borders or zones of separation, monitoring troop withdrawals, supervising the demobilisation of forces, or investigating cease-fire violations. In order to complete these tasks peacekeepers adhere to a set of operating principles which include the non-use of force except in self-defence, impartiality, the host government's consent to UN involvement, and continuing support for the mission from the UNSC.[90]

The restrictions placed on UN collective action by Article 2(7) of the UN Charter mean that a host government must agree to the deployment of any peacekeeping operation on its territory. In theory this principle of consent works well. It ensures that the UN has the full co-operation of the host state helping to avoid local resistance. It also implies that issues will be resolved by negotiation and suasion, thus making the use of force counter productive and unnecessary.[91]

In practice however, consent can be difficult to acquire and hard to maintain during the course of an operation. In many post-Cold War conflicts, peacekeepers were deployed into civil wars with many parties and were called upon to implement complex mandates, which only served to exacerbate the problems of maintaining a solid consensual basis during an operation.[92] *Second generation peacekeeping operations*, as some call these new missions, include the provision of assistance in the organisation and verification of elections, humanitarian assistance, mine clearance and training, preventative troops deployments, disarming of paramilitary forces, and the establishment of secure conditions for the delivery of humanitarian supplies.[93] *Peace enforcement operations* are distinct from peacekeeping in that they are coercive operations authorized under Chapter VII of the Charter and "are essentially deterrent in nature, using force or its threat, to enforce compliance, restore peace and to achieve the conditions specified in the [UN] mandate." Such operations have no specific identified enemy except those parties who do not comply with the terms of the relevant UN mandate.[94] *Collective enforcement operations* are in effect war conducted under the auspices of the United Nations. Directed against a clearly identified enemy and using war-fighting techniques, these enforcement actions are normally authorized under Chapter VII,

---

[90] See William J. Durch, *The Evolution of UN Peacekeeping*, St. Martin's Press, New York, 1993, p. 3.

[91] F.T. Liu, *United Nations Peacekeeping and the Non-Use of Force*, Lynne Rienner Publishers, Boulder, 1992, p. 11.

[92] For an indication of the myriad problems confronted by recent peacekeeping operations see Roberts, *The Crisis in UN Peacekeeping*, Cedric Thornberry, "Peacekeepers, Humanitarian Aid, and Civil Conflicts," *Journal of Humanitarian Assistance*, http://www-jha.sps.cam.ac.uk/a/a017.htm, 15 September, 1995, and Gustav Hagglund, "Peacekeeping in a Modern War Zone," *Survival*, vol. 32, no. 3, 1990.

[93] Mats Berdal, *Whither UN Peacekeeping?*, Adelphi Paper 281, International Institute for Strategic Studies, London, 1993, pp. 1-9.

[94] *Peace Support Operations*, First Draft, Joint Warfare Publication, Camberley, 1997, pp. 2-3.

22 *Understanding the UN Security Council*

like the Gulf War, or under exceptional action by the General Assembly, as occurred in the Korean War.[95]

The conduct of peacekeeping operations had to be modified in order to meet the new challenges of the post-Cold War period. Recognising the increased variety of roles that peacekeeping mandates included, such as the delivery of relief supplies, Boutros-Ghali offered a novel definition of peacekeeping in June 1992: "the deployment of a United Nations presence in the field, *hitherto* with the consent of all the parties concerned, normally involving United Nations military and/or police personnel and frequently civilians as well."[96] This comment was novel in that the use of the word 'hitherto' suggested that future peacekeeping operations would not necessarily adhere to the principle of consent as rigorously as in past operations.[97]

The Secretary-General's suggestion was an attempt to devise a new means of overcoming the deficiencies of consent-based peacekeeping in new, intra-state conflicts. In many UN operations, reliance on consent left UN personnel vulnerable to obstruction from numerous belligerent parties, including armed gangs and militias. The very meaning of "consent" also began to change in response to the pressures of post-Cold War conflicts. Generally during the Cold War consent meant the formal agreement of a host government to a UN initiative. Given the increasing prevalence of intra-state conflicts in the early 1990s, consent also came to include the agreement of the main belligerent parties to a UN operation. Accordingly, the consensual basis of many operations was often sporadic and unpredictable.

As suggested by Boutros-Ghali, the use of coercion by UN troops in order to fulfil their mandates appeared to offer a solution to these new obstacles in peacekeeping operations. However, as the UN's experiences in the former Yugoslavia and Somalia were to demonstrate, this new variant of peacekeeping operation that moved beyond consent had its limitations when deployed in internal conflicts. UN action in the field seemed caught half-way between adhering to the principle of consent and using more proactive, coercive measures. It was a

---

[95] Ibid. p. 1-3. It is important to note that in the debate on peacekeeping doctrine, some analysts have used the term "peace enforcement" to refer to collective enforcement operations such as the Gulf War. See for example Charles Dobbie's definition of peace enforcement, "A Concept for Post-Cold War Peacekeeping," *Survival*, vol. 36, no. 3, 1994. p. 121. This confusion arises in part from the rapid development of peacekeeping doctrine and the emergence of peace enforcement operations as a separate category of operations distinct from war-fighting, collective enforcement operations.

[96] Boutros-Ghali, *An Agenda for Peace*, p. 4.

[97] Boutros-Ghali argued in an interview with Jocelyn Coulon that his new definition of peacekeeping, less reliant on consent, was intended to fulfil his vision of new peacekeeping troops, more proactive in the implementation of peace, authorised to use force against recalcitrant parties, under the authority of the UNSC. See Jocelyn Coulon, *Soldiers of Diplomacy: The United Nations, Peacekeeping, and the New World Order*, University of Toronto Press, Toronto, 1998.

transition criticized by some analysts as taking the organisation into dangerous territory without a clearly defined, effective doctrine.[98]

The Debate on Peacekeeping Doctrine

Given the problems encountered by consent-based peacekeeping in the post -Cold War period, both commentators and practitioners offered a wide variety of suggestions as to how such operations might be enhanced.[99] One key area of proposed enhancements focused on the 'grey area' of operations that lies between traditional forms of peacekeeping and collective enforcement operations. At the heart of this debate on how to improve UN operations in this 'grey area' is the principle of consent. Attitudes towards its role in peacekeeping doctrine and the role UN peacekeeping should play in conflict resolution efforts can be distilled into three contending positions.

The Restrictive Position

The restrictive position was offered by commentators who were united in the belief that the United Nations needs to restrict itself to either peacekeeping along traditional lines - operations which emphasise the non-use of force except in self defence, impartiality, the consent of the host parties and fulfil only traditional peacekeeping tasks - or collective enforcement operations. They argued that the UN is not suited to 'middle ground' operations that combine elements of peacekeeping, based on impartiality and consent, with enforcement elements.

Proponents of this restrictive position include Richard K. Betts, David Rieff, Stephen John Stedman, Duane Bratt, Thomas G. Weiss and Masahiko Asada. Betts suggested that some peacekeeping operations "have unwittingly prolonged the suffering where they meant to relieve it". He argued that, in cases such as Bosnia, "the West's attempt at limited but impartial involvement abetted slow motion savagery." This led him to advocate that the UN, in the absence of sufficient support from its member states, stay out of conflicts and let the "locals fight it out." The only other alternative, he maintained, is the deployment of collective enforcement operations.[100] Stedman similarly argued that the UN's

---

[98] John Gerard Ruggie, "Wandering in the Void," *Foreign Affairs*, vol. 72, no. 5, 1993. See also Adam Roberts, "The Crisis in UN Peacekeeping," in Chester A. Crocker and Fen Osler Hampson, eds., *Managing Global Chaos*, United States Institute of Peace Press, Washington D.C., 1996.

[99] Proposals for the enhancement of peacekeeping operations have ranged from the creation of a standing UN force to practical suggestions as to how current operations could be improved. See for example Brian Urquhart, "Beyond the 'Sheriff's Posse," *Survival*, vol. 32, no. 3, 1990 and Urquhart's "For a UN Volunteer Military Force," *New York Review of Books*, 10 June, 1993. See also Berdal, *Whither UN Peacekeeping?*.

[100] Richard K Betts, "The Delusion of Impartial Intervention," *Foreign Affairs*, vol. 73, no. 6, 1994.

24 *Understanding the UN Security Council*

involvement in internal conflicts needed to be more selective. Morality-driven intervention may cause more problems that it solves as foreign involvement and aid initiatives may only prolong the war instead of ending it. However, he did not discount the potential effectiveness of UN peacekeeping operations along traditional lines where there is agreement between the warring parties and reasonable command and control over those with weapons, or the potential UN role in mounting clear collective enforcement operations under Chapter VII.[101] Reiff argued that the illusory idea of the UN playing an effective leadership role in conflicts as terrible as Bosnia simply does not work. He consequently suggested "small, preventative deployments" and "classical peacekeeping, are almost all the United Nations can be expected to do successfully."[102] Asada argued that the application of peacekeeping and enforcement measures in conflicts such as Bosnia and Somalia were counter productive. Indeed he suggested that peacekeeping operations vested with peace enforcement power incurred 'a disastrous blow', and instead argued for the maintenance of a clear distinction between peacekeeping, based on traditional principles, and collective enforcement operations.[103] Bratt suggested that the UN's experience of "two-tier" peacekeeping operations, in which the UNSC authorises a second bolstered peacekeeping force to protect the main peacekeeping personnel from attack, failed. As an alternative, Bratt suggested that the most successful forms of peacekeeping operations in internal conflicts were those which adhered to the three principles of traditional peacekeeping: consent, impartiality, and the limited use of force.[104] In turn, Weiss suggested that there is a role to be played by the UN in countering blatant interstate aggression or intervening for humanitarian reasons, but only by means of 'subcontracting' to a coalition of states under collective enforcement provisions of the UN Charter. In the absence of such a coalition Weiss argued that conflicts should be left to the warring parties to settle. Peacekeeping operations, he suggested, should only be deployed along traditional lines.[105]

The problem with this restrictive position was that it failed to offer any alternative solution to the obvious short-comings demonstrated in peacekeeping operations during the post-Cold War period. As Ramsbotham and Woodhouse have argued, reliance on this "either-or" position was unwise as it "is by no means clear that enforcement delivers either quick or neat solutions, or that abstention is

---

[101] Stephen John Stedman, "The New Interventionists," *Foreign Affairs*, vol. 72, no. 1, 1993.

[102] David Rieff, "The Illusions of Peacekeeping," *World Policy Journal*, vol. 11, no. 2, 1994.

[103] Masahiko Asada, "Peacemaking, Peacekeeping, and Peace Enforcement: Conceptual and Legal Underpinnings of the U.N. Role," in Selig S. Harrison and Masashi Mishihara, eds., *UN Peacekeeping: Japanese and American Perspectives*, Carnegie Endowment for International Peace, Washington D.C. 1995.

[104] Duane Bratt, "Explaining Peacekeeping Performance: The UN in Internal Conflicts," *International Peacekeeping*, vol. 4, no. 3, 1997.

[105] Thomas G. Weiss, "Rekindling Hope in UN Humanitarian Intervention," in Walter Clarke and Jeffrey Herbst, eds., *Learning From Somalia: the Lessons of Armed Humanitarian Intervention*, Westview Press, Oxford, 1997.

Understanding the Centrality of Consent

morally or politically wise."[106] Thus, due to the limited applications of either traditional peacekeeping or collective enforcement, it became necessary to accept the need to develop a variant of peacekeeping operation that exists in the 'grey area' between consent-based traditional peacekeeping and collective enforcement actions.

The Consent-Centric Position

The development of such an alternative and expansive variant was supported by a group of commentators who believed that peacekeeping doctrine had to be modified in order to meet the challenges of post-Cold War peacekeeping while retaining its emphasis on consent. They argued that while the use of force is not altogether incompatible with peacekeeping, its use could only be directed towards the maintenance of the consensual basis of the operation. Such analysts included Mats Berdal, Adam Roberts, Charles Dobbie, Theo Farrell and Shashi Tharoor.

Dobbie has argued that without the consent of the belligerent parties "peace enforcement [by which he means collective enforcement action under Article 42] will probably represent the only realistic means of effective outside intervention." As a result he stressed the necessity for a peacekeeping operation to maintain a stable consensual basis at the operational level, while coping with tactical losses of consent through a limited use of force authorized by the UNSC under Chapter VII. Importantly, Dobbie did not view adherence to the principle of consent at the operational level and the use of force as mutually exclusive, but he did see peacekeeping and collective enforcement as distinct concepts, with no lateral movement, in terms of the use of force, from one to the other.[107] Berdal similarly argued that though consent in civil wars is unlikely ever to be absolute, the conscious promotion of it "separates peacekeeping from enforcement." For him "consent at the strategic and operational levels remains a requirement for effective peacekeeping" and "the distinction between peacekeeping and enforcement must be reasserted, with the tendency of combining the two into one operation must be rejected."[108] Farell agreed that it is necessary to clearly distinguish between peacekeeping, with its emphasis on consent, and coercive collective enforcement measures.[109] Adam Roberts found no reason why peacekeeping operations could not be expanded to meet the challenges of the post-Cold War world, and rejected the view that the UN should confine itself to either traditional peacekeeping or enforcement action. However, he argued that the distinction between

---

[106] Tom Woodhouse and Oliver Ramsbotham, *Peacekeeping: Terra Incognita: Here Be Dragons*, INCORE, Londonderry, 1996.

[107] Dobbie, "A Concept for Post-Cold War Peacekeeping," pp. 121-48.

[108] Mats R. Berdal, "Fateful Encounter: The United States and UN Peacekeeping," *Survival*, vol. 36, no. 1, 1994, and "Beyond Peacekeeping: Reflections on the Evolution of International Peacekeeping After the Cold War," a paper presented at the Japan Institute for International Affairs, Tokyo, June 1994.

[109] Theo Farrell, "Sliding into War: The Somalia Imbroglio and US Army Peace Operations Doctrine," *International Peacekeeping*, vol. 2, no. 2, 1995.

peacekeeping and coercive enforcement must not be blurred. He suggested that any combination of the two distinct approaches which "downgrades consent as a key criterion for action takes peacekeeping into dangerous territory," and that many of the proposals for a new, more forceful variant of peacekeeping were "excessively optimistic." He argued against the view of peacekeeping as a "flexible technique, whose legal basis, purposes and mode of operating can be radically adapted and [applied] to difficult situations for which it is not necessarily appropriate." However, he also argued that a peacekeeping force cannot be entirely dependent on the whim of every local leader and therefore thus does not preclude the limited use of force at the tactical level.[110] Tharoor similarly rejected the adoption of a "back to basics" approach to peacekeeping and the suggestion that the UN should confine itself either to traditional peacekeeping or collective enforcement operations. Yet in advocating the modification of peacekeeping doctrine to cope with the challenges of the post-Cold War world, he joined Berdal, Dobbie and Roberts in emphasising that even a new variant of peacekeeping could only work with the co-operation and trust of the host parties. He rejected proposals for "peace enforcement operations" which combine a basic peacekeeping approach with the use of force as a "very troubling concept" and considered such proposals to be the military equivalent of "having one's cake and eating it too."[111] Instead he welcomed Dobbie's emphasis on consent and similarly recognised the scope for a limited use of force in securing tactical level consent.[112]

This second "consent-centric" position was distinguished from the "restrictive" position by contending that consent-based peacekeeping was an effective technique which could be used to address the challenges of second-generation peacekeeping operations and did not need to be restricted only to traditional peacekeeping tasks. They did not reject the use of force within peacekeeping outright, but rather advocated its use only at the tactical level in order to maintain a stable consensual basis for a peacekeeping operation.

In practice, the short-term legacy of UN peacekeeping initiatives in the early 1990s appeared to have been a re-emphasis on consent. In his 1995 *Supplement to An Agenda for Peace*, Boutros-Ghali again altered his conception of peacekeeping, based largely on the UN's experience in Bosnia and Somalia. He re-emphasised the centrality of consent to the success of peacekeeping operations and argued, "the logic of peacekeeping flows from political and military premises that are quite distinct from those of enforcement…to blur the distinction between the two can undermine the viability of the peacekeeping operation and endanger its personnel."[113] This same approach also appeared to have been adopted by the

---

[110] Adam Roberts, *The Crisis in UN Peacekeeping*. See also Adam Roberts, "From San Francisco to Sarajevo: The UN and the Use of Force," *Survival*, vol. 37, no. 4, 1995.

[111] Shashi Tharoor, "Should UN Peacekeeping Go 'Back to Basics?," *Survival*, vol. 37, no. 4, 1995 and Shashi Tharoor, "United Nations Peacekeeping in Europe," *Survival*, vol. 37, no. 2, 1995.

[112] Tharoor, "Should UN Peacekeeping Go 'Back to Basics'?", p. 57.

[113] Boutros Boutros-Ghali, "Supplement to An Agenda For Peace," *UN Document*, S/1995/1, 3 January, 1995.

Understanding the Centrality of Consent   27

British Army. Its concept of "Wider Peacekeeping", strongly influenced by the thinking of Charles Dobbie, similarly reflected the centrality of consent. Though it allowed for the limited use of force to restore tactical level consent, the concept of "Wider Peacekeeping" held that a stable consensual basis at the operational level was vital to an operations success.[114] Similarly, the US Army, influenced by its experience in Somalia and mindful of the British approach, adopted a new peacekeeping doctrine which downgraded the use of force as an effective means of fulfilling a peacekeeping mandate and instead placed an emphasis on preserving the consent and co-operation of the host parties.[115]

The "Middle-Ground" Position

The development of peacekeeping doctrine during the 1990s was also shaped by proponents of a third position who attempted to fill the 'middle ground' between traditional peacekeeping and collective enforcement action by the UN. This third position stemmed primarily from Boutros-Ghali's original 1992 suggestion that peacekeeping operations need not be so reliant on a firm consensual basis. Accordingly, "middle ground" theorists advocated the development of peacekeeping operations in which consent was downgraded and the use of force more frequent. The key to such theories is the applicability of force within peacekeeping operations: where to use it, when to use it and how much to use. This in effect leads to a combination of peacekeeping and peace enforcement actions combined into one operation as in Bosnia or Somalia. Proponents of this position included F.T. Liu, John Mackinlay and Jarat Chopra, John Gerard Ruggie, Marrack Goulding, Richard Connaughton, Stephen Ratner, James Gow and Christopher Dandeker.

This position experienced some refinement as it proved most vulnerable to the experiences of peacekeeping operations during the first half of the 1990s. Originally in 1990, John Mackinlay suggested that one of the key problems facing peacekeeping operations was that "there exists no concept for the progressive escalation of the use of force which might connect their [peacekeepers'] comparatively passive role through to the techniques of war." He advocated a concept which "explains how a peacekeeper might use limited force in various situations."[116] Two years later, Mackinlay and Jarat Chopra, introduced their concept for "second generation multinational operations." They suggested that the growing span of tasks undertaken by UN peacekeepers could be depicted as a continuum; low intensity operations at one end, such as observer mission, while at the other end lay high risk, high intensity operations involving larger military contingents and an increased likelihood of violence. Importantly, in their concept

---

[114] Charles Dobbie, *Wider Peacekeeping*, British Army Field Manual, 4th Draft, Wiltshire, 1995.

[115] Department of the Army (US), *FM 100-23: Peace Operations*, Washington D.C., 1994. For an analysis of the transition in US peacekeeping approach see Farrell, "Sliding into War: The Somalia Imbroglio and US Army Peace Operations Doctrine."

[116] John Mackinlay, "Powerful Peacekeepers," *Survival*, vol. 32, no. 3, 1990.

28 *Understanding the UN Security Council*

the principle of consent as the *sine qua non* of peacekeeping becomes less absolute as one moved along the continuum: "A second generation force needs to be capable of exercising a wide range of military responses as situations escalate and de-escalate."[117] In the same year, F.T. Liu took a more conservative approach, stressing the need for peacekeepers to use force only in self defence, but he also suggested the creation of a "two-tier" force; the first tier comprised of troops operating according to traditional principles of peacekeeping and a second, more heavily armed tier operating according to a less restrictive definition of "self-defence" to be called in when the first tier encountered resistance from the host parties. The activation of this second tier would then cause the UNSC to consider the use of enforcement measures to further support the peacekeeping force.[118]

By 1994, after the failure of the second United Nations Operation in Somalia (UNOSOM II) and the UN's difficulties in Bosnia, Mackinlay's position was modified somewhat, placing a larger emphasis on how the UN's response to a conflict should be determined by the level of local consent present and reducing the continuum of action to three "UN Operational Levels."[119] Yet while Mackinlay's modified position placed more emphasis on the principle of consent, some analysts persisted with the idea that "middle ground" peacekeeping operations could move back and forth between traditional peacekeeping and collective enforcement operations, depending on the circumstances of the conflict. Connaughton argued, "consent and impartiality are too fragile to serve as a fulcrum around which a sensible doctrine can by built."[120] Ratner meanwhile stressed the need for consent as a fundamental principle of peacekeeping but then also suggested that certain circumstances would dictate that the UN implement its mandate "through assertive, perhaps coercive measures" and, in situations where consent has evaporated, the UN could switch to peace enforcement.[121] Like Ratner, John Ruggie's suggestion for the improvement of UN peacekeeping hinged on the use of force, rather than consent. He argued that "any successful use of force short of simply imposing a surrender must alter the decision calculus of the target unit for it to change its objectionable behaviour." While consent is highly desirable, for Ruggie it is not an absolute and "force may be used to deter or compel."[122] Goulding appeared to straddle both the "consent-centric" and "middle-ground" positions. On one hand, he argued that the members of the Security Council, rather than combining peacekeeping with enforcement methods, need to

---

[117] John Mackinlay and Jarat Chopra, "Second Generation Multinational Operations," *The Washington Quarterly*, vol. 15, no. 3, 1992.

[118] F.T. Liu, *United Nations Peacekeeping and the Non-Use of Force*, Lynne Rienner Publishers, London, 1992.

[119] John Mackinlay, "Improving Multifunctional Forces," *Survival*, vol. 36, no. 3, 1994.

[120] Richard Connaughton, "Time to Clear the Doctrine Dilemma," *Jane's Defence Weekly*, 9 April, 1994.

[121] Stephen R. Ratner, *The New UN Peacekeeping*, Macmillan Press Ltd. London, 1995, p. 40.

[122] John Gerard Ruggie, "The UN and the Collective Use of Force: Whither or Whether?," *International Peacekeeping*, vol. 3, no. 4, 1996.

Understanding the Centrality of Consent   29

take a clear decision about whether the UN will involve itself in a conflict along traditional peacekeeping lines or by means of collective enforcement. However, Goulding merits inclusion with the "middle-ground position" because he also suggested that it may be desirable to adopt a "half-way house" approach between peacekeeping and enforcement in which UN troops are authorized to use force in order to fulfill such tasks as the delivery of humanitarian aid or enforce respect of an agreed cease-fire.[123]

Gow and Dandeker argued that the UN's experience in Bosnia has demonstrated that force can be used in the context of a peacekeeping operation with beneficial results. A doctrine based on consent, like that advocated by Dobbie, they argued, "did not provide a basis for action" towards achieving peace in a complex conflict. Instead they favoured a "workable" concept for middle-ground operations because the key difference between traditional peacekeeping and second generation peacekeeping occurs at the strategic level. In the former, the initiative lies with the hostile parties while in second generation peacekeeping the international community can control the initiative, in part through the use of force.[124]

In a similar attempt to devise a "middle-ground" alternative between collective enforcement and consent-based traditional peacekeeping, Daniel and Hayes offered the idea of "inducement" operations. Authorized to use force under Chapter VII, such operations would seek to use force to reacquire a solid consensual basis when it is lost since "consent is the variable at which inducement is aimed."[125] Similarly, Kofi Annan, the current Secretary-General of the UN, has accepted the need for the UN to adapt its "product line" to a much-changed world in which "the prerequisites of traditional peacekeeping will not exist in the great majority of cases." Accordingly, he advocates the development of "coercive inducement" operations in which the consent of the host parties is gained by the use of positive incentives or the threat of coercion.[126] Daniel and Hayes have again recently continued the thinking along this line. They argue that in "coercive inducement" operations host party consent should be regarded as a dependent

---

[123] Marrack Goulding, "The Use of Force by the United Nations," *International Peacekeeping*, vol. 3, no. 1, 1996.

[124] James Gow and Christopher Dandeker, "Peace-support Operations: The Problem of Legitimation," *The World Today*, vol. 51, no. 8, 1995. Gow and Dandeker argue that the key for success in this concept, which they characterize as "strategic peacekeeping," relies on the notion of "legitimation" which stems from the impartial agency of the UN, the competent and effective conduct of UN forces and the social support provided by groups and institutions affected by the deployment so that it retains its legitimacy. See Christopher Dandeker and James Gow, "The Future of Peace Support Operations: Strategic Peacekeeping and Success," *Armed Forces & Society*, vol. 23, no. 3, 1997.

[125] Donald C.F. Daniel and Bradd C. Hayes, "Securing Observance of UN Mandates Through the Employment of Military Force," *International Peacekeeping*, vol. 3, no. 4, 1996.

[126] Kofi A. Annan, "Challenges of New Peacekeeping," in Olara A. Otunnu and Michael W. Doyle, (eds), *Peacemaking and Peacekeeping for the New Century*, Rowman & Littlefield Publishers, Inc., New York, 1998.

30 *Understanding the UN Security Council*

rather than independent variable. Thus coercive inducement, "aims to augment or firm up consent at the strategic and tactical levels" in order to limit destabilizing behaviours on the part of local belligerents in order to buy time for long-term improvement initiatives. Combining the use of force with an impartial mandate differentiates coercive inducement from collective enforcement operations wherein the UN does not act impartially.[127]

Berdal, Dobbie, Tharoor, Roberts and Farell, did not agree with the concept of "middle ground operations" differentiated both from consent-based peacekeeping and collective enforcement. They regarded the use of force within peacekeeping as a limited tool only to be used either in self-defence or in order to shore up the consensual basis of the operation at the tactical level. Consequently, they rejected the view that UN troops can use force at the operational or strategic level in a "peace enforcement" operation without undermining the impartial role normally taken by peacekeepers. Any use of force at the operational or strategic level would, they argued, change the nature of peacekeeping operation to that of collective enforcement, hence their desire to reassert a clear distinction between consent-based peacekeeping and collective enforcement.[128]

Proponents of "middle ground" theory have seemed to gain the upper hand in the recent debate on peacekeeping doctrine. Many states are responding to the challenges exposed by 1990s peacekeeping by developing a practicable middle ground option between traditional peacekeeping and collective enforcement operations under the framework of "peace support operations doctrine."[129] This term is used to cover both peacekeeping and peace enforcement operations, and is conceptually distinct from collective enforcement operations sanctioned by the UN. As described by a 1997 joint UK-Swedish manual entitled "Peace Support Operations," they are operations which are in "support of an impartial mandate and are conducted neither in support of, no against, any specified party. A Peace Support Operation (PSO) force is a third-party referee to a conflict rather than a participant in it."[130] The development of the doctrine of Peace Support Operations by the British, for example, was an evolutionary step from the previous Wider Peacekeeping approach that had assumed the general consent of the main belligerents to a UN peacekeeping operation.[131] By contrast, the new PSO doctrine takes a more probing analysis of the level of host party consent before determining

---

[127] Donald C.F. Daniel and Bradd C. Hayes with Chantal de Jonge Oudraat, *Coercive Inducement and the Containment of International Crises*, United States Institute of Peace Press, Washington, D.C., 1999.

[128] Dobbie, "A Concept for Post-Cold War Peacekeeping," and Berdal, "Beyond Peacekeeping: Reflections on the Evolution of International Peacekeeping After the Cold War."

[129] During the course of the 1990s there was a gradual convergence in the military doctrine of NATO, the WEU and many European states towards "peace support operations" doctrine. See Philip Wilkinson, "Sharpening the Weapons of Peace: The Development of a Common Military Doctrine for Peace Support Operations," *International Security Information Service Briefing Paper No. 18*, 1998.

[130] *Peace Support Operations*, pp. 1-3.

[131] Wilkinson, "Sharpening the Weapons of Peace", pp. 4-5.

Understanding the Centrality of Consent   31

whether to deploy a peacekeeping or a peace enforcement operation. The lifting of the "doctrinal fog" that hampered peacekeeping efforts in the early 1990s was great assisted by the development of PSO doctrine and has resulted in consensus among key western state including Britain, France and the United States in how to approach the challenges posed by complex, intra-state conflict that are typical of the post-Cold War period.[132]

The development of PSO doctrine which was in effect the result of practical lessons learned by the participating states in the operations of the 1990s was complemented by the release in August 2000 of a review of UN peace and security activities commissioned by Kofi Annan. The so-called "Brahimi Report" examined the UN's peacekeeping experiences of the 1990s and came to the conclusion that the consent of the local parties and the use of force only in self – defence should remain as the "bedrock principles" of peacekeeping. Where more forceful action is required, the report advocated that it be entrusted to "coalitions of the willing" authorized under Chapter VII of the Charter.[133] After a decade of new challenges, it had been learned that UN peacekeeping, a blurring of consent and the use of force were uncomfortable bedfellows.

Consent at the Strategic Level

The role of and importance of consent in peacekeeping is the central issue around which the debate on peacekeeping doctrine revolves. In the mid-1990s the influence of "Wider Peacekeeping" emphasised the importance of a stable consensual basis at the operational level. The more recent ideas on "coercive inducement" and "peace support operations doctrine" suggest that the locus of the consent issue lies instead at the strategic level. Indeed, there are three different possible levels at which to analyze the principle of consent. The first is the *tactical level*, which can be defined as the level of peacekeeping operations at which engagements with the local parties are planned and executed in order to accomplish the objectives assigned to tactical units within a peacekeeping force. For example, an issue of consent at the tactical level could involve a belligerent host military unit refusing to allow a UN patrol to pass through a road check point. This is distinct from the *operational level* at which peacekeeping operations are planned, conducted and sustained in order to achieve particular objectives within specific theatres or areas of operations. A peacekeeping force commander, for example, decides at the operational level to deploy his force in a particular area depending on the level of consent forthcoming from a host government. The methods with which he chooses to do so in turn depend on the authorization and mandate given to the force by the UN Security Council at the *strategic level*. At this third level the members of the UN Security Council determine multi-national and

---

[132] For an in-depth review of the emergence of PSO doctrine, see Peter Viggo Jakobsen, "The Emerging Consensus on Grey Area Peace Operations Doctrine: Will It Last and Enhance Operational Effectiveness?," *International Peacekeeping*, vol. 7, no. 3, 2000.
[133] *UN Document* A/55/305, 21 August, 2000.

organisational objectives, developing and using resources at their disposal to meet these objectives, whether they be humanitarian, military or otherwise. The UNSC members also define the limits and assess the roles to be played by UN peacekeeping operations in relation to inter or intra-state conflicts and the belligerent parties therein and the challenges of consent that stem from such conflicts. In so doing they are cognisant not only of past peacekeeping experiences but also of future implications or precedents their decision may have for the effectiveness and credibility of future UN peacekeeping operations.[134]

This book takes a broad approach to the issue of consent and the development of peacekeeping doctrine by analysing the issue of consent from the strategic level. Unlike the majority of the commentary on peacekeeping doctrine that has been focused at the operational and tactical levels of consent, an analysis of the strategic level is valuable for a number of reasons.

First, this tier of "macro" factors affecting consent includes the motivation of the UNSC members for either adhering to, or moving beyond consent in particular operations. Similarly, it considers other 'macro' factors such as influences from the Secretary-General, the UN Secretariat and the General Assembly that would not be incorporated into an analysis of consent at either the tactical or operational levels.

Second, in many 1990s peacekeeping operations the line between the three levels of consent was increasingly blurred and issues of consent at one level would have an immediate and significant impact at another level. For example, the withdrawal of tactical level consent following the US attempt to capture Aidid in October, 1993 had implications not only for that particular tactical mission, but also the UNOSOM II operation as well as UNSC attitudes towards peacekeeping operations in general. In effect, in many post-Cold War conflicts tactical issues of consent are also strategic issues of consent, suggesting that a strategic level analysis is most suited to examining this period.

Third, because the issue of consent at the strategic level is closely related to the UNSC's use of Chapter VII and its respect for Article 2(7), this study may shed light on the notion that the members of the UNSC become more interventionist at the expense of the sovereign rights of UN member states during the early 1990s. As new norms emerge which motivate the actions of the Security Council members, these norms can, in turn, be codified in international law through the decisions of the international community.[135] It is thus important to fully understand the motivations behind those decisions as they may indicate the emergence of new, humanitarian priorities among the members of the UNSC as they seek to ensure international peace and security.

---

[134] These definitions have been devised by adapting US Department of Defence military definitions of the tactical, operational and strategic levels of war and revising them so that they apply to peacekeeping operations in the context of the United Nations. See *Dictionary of Military Terms*, The United States Department of Defence, 1999.

[135] Murphy, *Humanitarian Intervention*, p. 20.

Analysing Consent

The following five chapters of this study will trace the historical evolution of the Security Council's practice relating to the principle of consent during the early 1990s. They will include an analysis of the UN Guards Contingent in northern Iraq (UNGCI), the UN Operations in Somalia (UNOSOM I and II and UNITAF), the UN Protection Force in Bosnia Herzegovina (UNPROFOR), the United Nations Assistance Mission for Rwanda (UNAMIR), and the UN Mission in Haiti (UNMIH). Each of these cases were selected for inclusion in this study for two main reasons; in each host state consent was a key issue and each case also involved a significant humanitarian element which the members of the Security Council had to consider. Taken as a group, this selection of cases also indicates the wide range of responses by the members of the UNSC towards the challenges of peacekeeping operations in the early 1990s. As such they offer the best opportunity to explore the challenges of consent and examine how the UNSC has responded to it. In the case of northern Iraq, for example, the members of the Security Council preferred to deploy UN personnel with the consent of the government of Iraq, and did not authorize the use of force to protect the Iraq Kurds. This case contrasts directly with the UNSC's decision to authorize UNITAF to use force if necessary to deliver relief supplies to the Somali people. Somalia, in turn, contrasts dramatically with the lacklustre response of the UNSC to the Rwandan genocide. UNPROFOR offers the chance to examine the Security Council's attempt to combine both consent based peacekeeping techniques with enforcement methods, while the Haitian case presented the Council with both legal and practical issues of consent stemming from the presence of two governments, one *de facto* and one *de jure*. This selection of cases will accordingly allow this study to more fully understand the issues presented by consent-based peacekeeping, how the members of the UNSC have opted to overcome them, and their reasons for doing so.

The understanding of the UNSC's approach to the issue of consent in the early 1990s then provides an ideal grounding with which to consider the manner in which they dealt with Iraq in 2002 and 2003 in decisions taken just prior to the second Gulf War in the penultimate chapter. Were the concerns and motives of the Council's member consistent with those a decade earlier? What factors were central to the debate on disarming Iraq of its Weapons of Mass Destruction (WMD) and left the Security Council deadlocked and impotent?

The final chapter of the study will be a comparison and discussion of the case studies in order to assess the implications for sovereignty and the international order brought on by the changing responses of the UNSC members to the challenges of consent. It will also highlight possible consequences of recent UNSC decisions for future peacekeeping operations, the principle of non-intervention and the likely use of Chapter VII authority by the UNSC members in future international conflicts.

Other potential cases for this study that have not been examined include the UN Protection Force in Croatia and the UN Transitional Assistance Authority in Cambodia (UNTAC). In each of these cases, there was little, if any, consideration given by the members of the UNSC to the possibility of authorizing the peacekeepers to use force in order to implement their mandate. Thus, the scope for analysing the instances in which the USNC was prepared to go beyond consent and why such decisions were taken was limited. Consequently these cases were not included in the study. Also not included were the UNSC response to the Serbian repression of Kosovar Albanians or the response of the international community towards East Timor. As much as Iraq, these two cases were a function of the prior attitudes and approaches that the UNSC members had developed during the early 1990s and therefore this study focuses much more intensely on the 1991-1995 period as the formative years for UNSC decision making in the post-Cold War period.

The specific five-year period covered by the first five case-studies was also deliberately chosen in order to focus on the period in which the most significant opportunities, challenges and development of UN peacekeeping operations occurred. It provides the opportunity to see if the political rhetoric concerning the prospects for protecting human rights was replicated in practice and also offers the most relevant period of post-Cold War decision making with which to compare more recent decisions taken in the context of Iraq. The period begins with the Security Council's response to the Kurdish refugee crisis in northern Iraq, examining the expansion and consequent retrenchment of peacekeeping doctrine that arose out of the Somali case as well as the difficulties encountered by the UN in combining consent-based peacekeeping with coercive methods in Bosnia. By the end of this five-year period, peacekeeping doctrine had undergone a dramatic re-evaluation, but many of the challenges of the early 1990s still remain unresolved today.

Beyond Consent?

Assertions that the UNSC has demonstrated a increased propensity towards humanitarian intervention in the post-Cold War period appear to be supported by the fact there has been a dramatic increase in the number of Chapter VII resolutions adopted by the Security Council in the post-Cold War period (See Figure 1 below). This not only suggests an increased willingness to impose sanctions or authorize the use of force to cope with conflicts, but also could indicate that such measures were taken without the agreement of the state or states affected, since Chapter VII allows the UNSC to skirt the restrictions normally imposed on UN action by Article 2(7). However, looking merely at the number of Chapter VII resolutions and not at the circumstances behind their adoption provides a misleading impression of the UNSC's attitude towards host state consent and sovereignty.

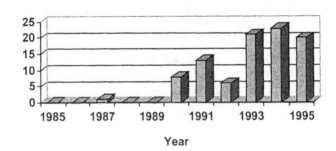

Figure 1 Number of Chapter VII Resolutions Adopted by the UNSC 1985-1995

In fact there is profound evidence that the members of the UNSC have continued to adhere to consent as a basis for UN operations despite their increased reliance on Chapter VII measures. This casts doubt on the assertion that there has been a shift within the UNSC away from consent and state sovereignty towards a new doctrine of humanitarian intervention, or that a new normative conception of state sovereignty is emerging that minimizes the protection afforded sovereign states by Article 2(7).[136] While the members of the Security Council have chosen, in particular, instances to interpret threats to international peace and security expansively this has occurred under exceptional circumstances of intra-state conflict.

This study will argue that while the Council was proactive in northern Iraq and Somalia, during both cases many of the UNSC members demonstrated concern that their actions be consistent with international law. Following significant problems encountered in Somalia, any " humanitarian intervention" enthusiasm within the UNSC was quickly tempered. In subsequent UN deployments, such as UNPROFOR and UNMIH, peacekeeping practice became even more squarely focused on consent. Chapter VII was normally used to create jurisdiction for the Security Council in cases where a sovereign authority was absent or under threat and also to bolster the self defence provisions available to UN troops. Only rarely was it used in order to permit the implementation of a particular mandate through the use of force, and when this occurred there was significant reluctance among members of the UNSC to do so, even in the face of flagrant abuses of human rights.[137] Any pursuit of 'humanitarian' objectives with authorization to use force

---

[136] Lori Fisler Damrosch, ed., *Enforcing Restraint: Collective Intervention in Internal Conflicts*, Council on Foreign Relations Press, New York, 1993. Damrosch argues that the recent history of international institutions demonstrates that collective international institutions seem under restraint and one of the main constraints is sovereignty. See p. 1.

[137] As Mandelbaum argues, in the early 1990s the international community demonstrated the pattern of "agreement in principle, but paralysis in action." Interventions would be launched under the auspices of the UN, but these would not be given adequate political or

usually coincided with the strategic interests of one of the P-5 members of the Security Council and it was this interest that galvanized any UN-mandated intervention. This same emphasis on non-intervention permeated the Security Council's consideration of the Iraqi crisis in 2002. As UNSC members were motivated by their strategic interests, the collision of these interests and the inherent conservatism of these leading sovereign states towards violating long established norms of the international political system left the Security Council deadlocked and impotent.

---

material support to fulfil their objectives. See Michael Mandelbaum, "The Reluctance to Intervene," *Foreign Policy*, no. 95, Summer, 1994.

Chapter 2

Northern Iraq 1991

The peacekeeping experiences of the Cold War established consent as a fundamental principle that facilitated UN involvement in conflicts around the globe. With the end of the Cold War the demand for UN peacekeeping initiatives dramatically increased, but the inadequacy of traditional peacekeeping principles in the face of new, post-Cold War challenges led to pressure from within the UN to improve the effectiveness of peacekeeping doctrine. Much of this pressure stemmed from post-Cold War optimism within the UNSC that it could take measures to protect international peace and security as well as take steps to further individual human rights. However, the members of the UNSC immediately encountered difficulties in simultaneously attempting to fulfil both of these objectives. In northern Iraq the UNSC had to respond to a humanitarian crisis that endangered regional stability, but which also involved the internal affairs of a sovereign state. Consequently, the UNSC's response to this crisis indicates the degree to which attitudes of members of the UNSC towards consent, non-intervention and sovereignty were changing with the onset of the post-Cold War era.

The international community's response to the humanitarian crisis in northern Iraq in the spring of 1991 represents an important milestone for the UN Security Council in the post-Cold War period. The massive exodus of Iraqi Kurdish and Shiite refugees from inside Iraq towards the Turkish, Kuwaiti and Iranian borders was met with an international response that suggested an emerging humanitarian emphasis in the behaviour of states. The Security Council's response to the crisis appeared to indicate a more active role for the world body in defending human rights. At the same time a number of western states including France, the United States and Britain, chose to deploy troops and air support to assist the stranded refugees, regarding their actions as consistent with the objectives of the Security Council.

These initiatives sparked a renewed debate on the legality of humanitarian intervention, with some commentators arguing that the crisis in northern Iraq marked a new era of collective humanitarian intervention under the authority of the United Nations, in which the sovereign rights of states were increasingly dependent on their internal actions.[1] The Secretary-General of the United Nations was prompted by these events to similarly suggest that "it is now increasingly felt that the principle of non-interference with the essential domestic jurisdiction of States

---

[1] Jarat Chopra and Thomas G. Weiss, "Sovereignty Is No Longer Sacrosanct: Codifying Humanitarian Intervention," *Ethics and International Affairs*, vol. 6, 1992.

38 *Understanding the UN Security Council*

cannot be regarded as a protective barrier behind which human rights could be massively or systematically violated..."[2] Some analysts, however, were more cautious in suggesting that the Council's actions with regard to northern Iraq indicated an emerging post-Cold War chapter in humanitarian intervention.[3]

This chapter will argue that the Council's decisions with regard to northern Iraq, and the subsequent transition from the coalition intervention to the deployment of the UN Guards Contingent in Iraq (UNGCI), reveal a significant reluctance among many of the Council's members to take any action that violated Iraq's sovereign rights. There was a great deal of pressure among the intervening coalition states, the non-coalition membership of the Security Council, and the UN Secretariat to act in accordance with the UN Charter. This meant respecting the restrictions posed by Article 2(7). Similarly, a close reading of the UNSC resolution on which the coalition intervention was based does not suggest that the Security Council was breaking new ground by authorizing intervention in order to protect human rights. Its action was based instead on the traditional concern of countering a perceived threat to international peace and security. What is significant about this case, however, is the Council's decision to characterize the flows of Kurdish refugees as a threat to international peace and security, brought on by the Iraqi government's repression of the Kurdish people.

The consequent emphasis on international law and respect for Iraqi sovereignty led to the consent-based deployment of the UN Guards. In this case, the principle of consent created three different opportunities; it allowed the UN into Iraq to assist the refugees, supported by the members of the Security Council; it allowed the coalition states to meet the political objectives of limiting the deployment time of their troops while also withdrawing from Iraq secure in the knowledge that the Iraqi government's ability to persecute the Kurds was reduced; finally, it allowed the Iraqi government to influence the nature of the UN humanitarian program in Iraq.

The Development of the Humanitarian Crisis

Following the Gulf War, the vulnerability of the Iraqi Baath regime combined with expectations of support from the west led to an uprising within Iraq. Disaffected army units and significant portions of the civilian population joined in the rebellion, which spread throughout the country, particularly in predominantly Kurdish areas of northern Iraq and Shiite areas of the south. By 19 March 1991, the majority of Iraqi Kurdistan, including the cities of Dohuk and Kirkuk, came under the nominal control of the rebels. In spite of this, the rebellion was short lived. Due to the residual Iraqi troop deployments in the south of the country, as well as the fact that the Shiite uprising was not as well organized as its northern

---

[2] Javier Pérez de Cuéllar, "Report of the Secretary-General on the Work of the Organisation," *UN Document*, A/46/1, 1991.

[3] See Mayall, "Non-intervention, Self-determination, and the 'New World Order,'" and Roberts, "Humanitarian War: Military Intervention and Human Rights."

Northern Iraq 1991

counterpart, it was more easily contained by the Iraqi government.[4] The city of Baghdad was not swept up in the tide of disaffection against President Hussein and there was no external support for the uprising from any of the western coalition states. The Iraqi rebels had been expecting US support for their efforts. A speech made by President Bush, transmitted in Iraq by the *Voice of America*, appeared to encourage the overthrow of the Baath regime and hinted at US support for the rebels.[5] This support never materialised and Bush later claimed that his comments were misinterpreted.[6] Without it, army units loyal to Saadam Hussein soon clamped down on the rebels using heavy artillery and helicopter gunships to punish the inhabitants of those areas that had joined in the uprising. The result was a massive exodus of Kurdish refugees north towards the borders of Iran and Turkey and the flight of Iraqi Shiites south towards Kuwait.[7]

The history of the Iraqi Kurds in the years immediately preceding the Gulf War had been particularly harsh. In 1987-88 Saddam Hussein pursued an exceptionally brutal campaign against the Kurds, using chemical weapons on Kurdish villages, killing an estimated five thousand Kurdish civilians and injuring

---

[4] Although the Iraqi government's crack down on both the Kurdish and Shiite uprisings elicited an interventionary response from the coalition states, this chapter is primarily concerned with the former. The Iraqi government's repression of the Shiites in the south was extreme but did not result in the same degree of involvement on the part of the allies as occurred in the north. The 1992 establishment of a no-fly-zone - the purpose of which was to limit the ability of the Iraqi government to use aircraft to attack Shiite rebels and allow the allies to monitor the situation - did not result in any coalition or UN deployment. The UN was barred from this area in October 1992 and there was no consideration given to deploying UN Guards in the south. Though the coalition states warned that they regarded Iraq's actions in the south as a violation of resolution 688 there was no supporting UNSC resolution to this effect. The allies chose primarily to base their actions in the south on international law. As Douglas Hurd argued: "We operate under international law...not every action that a British Government or an American Government or a French government takes has to be underwritten by a specific provision in a UN resolution provided we comply with international law. International law recognises extreme humanitarian need...We're clear, the French are clear, the Americans are clear on a strong legal as well as humanitarian ground in setting up this no fly zone." See Murphy, *Humanitarian Intervention*, and Marc Weller, ed., *Iraq and Kuwait, The Hostilities and Their Aftermath*, Cambridge International Documents Series, vol. 3, Grotius Press, Cambridge, 1993, p. 723.

[5] In a speech made before the American Academy for the Advancement of Science, US President Bush said "...there's another way for the bloodshed to stop, and that is for the Iraqi military to take matters into their own hands to force Saddam Hussein, the dictator, to step aside." Bush was subsequently pilloried in the press for not supporting the Kurdish uprising after giving this encouragement to rebel. As quoted in Helena Cook, *The Safe Havens in Northern Iraq*, Human Rights Centre, University of Sussex, 1995, p. 35.

[6] See "The President's News Conference", 16 April, 1991, Weekly Compilation of Presidential Documents, vol. 27, no. 16, as quoted in Marc Weller, *Iraq and Kuwait*, p. 717.

[7] See "Guess Who's Still Running Iraq," *The Economist*, 6 April, 1991 and "That Slippery Slope," *The Economist*, 13 April, 1991.

40 *Understanding the UN Security Council*

thousands more.[8] Fearing a repeat of such persecution, many Kurds abandoned their homes in the face of the renewed threat from President Hussein. On 16 March 1991, Hussein had warned the Kurds that they were, "repeating the same fateful error...and facing the same fate as those who came before."[9] Two weeks after the crackdown by Iraqi forces had begun, there were approximately 500,000 refugees either in Turkey or along the Iraq-Turkey border. This was in addition to the estimated 1,400,000 that had fled eastwards into Iran.[10]

The initial response of both the United States and Britain to this crisis occurred according to traditional norms of state interaction. President Bush declared the Kurdish exodus an "internal affair of Iraq" in which the US would not become involved. Similarly, British policy immediately following the end of *Operation Desert Storm* favoured staying out of the Kurdish issue.[11] But the growing humanitarian urgency of the situation, combined with the growing pressure on the Turkish border, forced the Americans and British to re-evaluate their positions.[12] The French agreed with the legal assessment that to intervene to assist the Kurds would constitute illegal interference in Iraq's internal affairs, but they suggested that they would attempt to change the law to allow such an intervention. Meanwhile, in the first week of April, 1991, both France and the UK decided that they could no longer sit on the sidelines and began unilateral aid deliveries to the Kurds in northern Iraq.[13]

Resolution 688

The gravity of the situation was brought to the attention of the Security Council by Turkey on 2 April, 1991 and by Iran on the following day. Fearing that they would be unable to cope with the influx of such large numbers of refugees, both countries requested an immediate meeting of the Security Council to consider the humanitarian crisis.[14] Both states expressed concern that the refugee flows could potentially threaten wider regional stability. Similarly, France suggested that the Security Council's consideration of the crisis was crucial since the flight of refugees potentially constituted a threat to international peace and security.[15] In part, this reflected a growing desire on the part of the French to advance the

---

[8] Barbara Stapleton, *The Shias of Iraq*, a Report to the Parliamentary Human Rights Group, March, 1993.

[9] Saddam Hussein as quoted in "The Backwash in the Gulf," *The Economist*, 23 March, 1991, p. 77.

[10] Cook, *The Safe Havens in Northern Iraq*, p. 35.

[11] Jane E. Stromseth, "Iraq's Repression of its Civilian Population: Collective Responses and Continuing Challenges", in Damrosch, *Enforcing Restraint*, p. 78.

[12] Mary Ellen O'Connell, "Continuing Limits on UN Intervention in Civil War," *Indiana Law Journal*, vol. 67, p. 905.

[13] Sean D. Murphy, Humanitarian Intervention, p. 170.

[14] *UN Documents*, S/22435, 3 April 1991 and S/22436, 4 April, 1991.

[15] *UN Document*, S/22442, 4 April, 1991.

doctrine of *droit d'ingérence*, or the right to intervene in sovereign states in order to protect basic human rights.[16]

The Iraqi Revolutionary Command Council sought to pre-empt the involvement of the UN in the Kurdish crisis by issuing an edict stating that it aimed to preserve the cultural variety present in Iraq. Consistent with this aim, it had pardoned all Iraqi Kurds for any crimes they had committed except in the cases of murder, rape or theft.[17] Unsurprisingly, this did not allay international concerns, and because of a growing awareness of the plight of the Kurds through western media reports, the Security Council held its emergency meeting on 5 April, 1991.

In the UNSC chamber, France initially proposed a resolution in which the Council was asked to display its "profound concern in the face of the exactions being committed against civilian populations in Iraq," but the proposal found insufficient support in the Council to be passed.[18] Undeterred, the French put forward a second draft resolution criticising the actions of the Iraqi government and demanding that it allow humanitarian access to international agencies in order to assist Iraqi civilians. The proposal was accepted by the members of the Council, by a vote of 10 to 3, with 2 abstentions, as resolution 688. The resolution reads, in part, as follows:

The Security Council,
Mindful of its duties and its responsibilities under the Charter of the United Nations for the maintenance of international peace and security,
Recalling Article 2, paragraph 7, of the Charter of the United Nations,
Gravely concerned by the repression of the Iraqi civilian population in many parts of Iraq, including most recently in Kurdish populated areas, which led to a massive flow of refugees towards and across international frontiers and to cross boundary incursions, which threaten international peace and security in the region...

1. Condemns the repression of the Iraqi civilian populations in many parts of Iraq, including most recently in Kurdish populated areas, the consequences of which threaten international peace and security in the region;
2. Demands that Iraq, as a contribution to remove the threat to international peace and security in the region, immediately end this repression and expresses the hope in the same context that an open dialogue will take place to ensure that the human and political rights of all Iraqi citizens are respected;
3. Insists that Iraq allow immediate access by international humanitarian organisations to all those in need of assistance in all parts of Iraq and to make available all necessary facilities for their operations...[19]

---

[16] "France Says World Must Re-examine 'Non Interference' Code," *Reuters,* 4 April, 1991. See also Philippe Moreau Defarges, "Assistance Politique, Ingérence Humanitaire," *Défense Nationale (Paris)*, vol. 49, no. 2, 1993.
[17] Statement issued by the Iraqi Revolutionary Command Council, 4 April, 1991 as quoted in *UN Document*, S/22452, 5 April, 1991.
[18] "France Steps Up the Pressure," *The Independent*, 4 April 1991.
[19] UNSC Resolution 688, 5 April, 1991.

The significance of the resolution lay in the fact that the members of the Security Council were willing to classify the refugee flows created by Iraqi persecution as a threat to international peace and security. This placed the issue within the competence of the Security Council, and potentially allowed its members to use their authority, including Article 42 measures, to counter the threat posed by the refugee flows.

During the debate on resolution 688 there were three distinct positions identifiable among the Council members. The first was held by those states that argued that the flagrant violation of basic human rights by the Iraqi government in persecuting the Kurds could not be left unchecked by the international community. States holding this view included France and Britain. For example, the French position was based on the UN Charter's emphasis on fundamental human rights and the dignity and worth of the human person. The French took the position that due to the scale of the tragedy, the actions of the Iraqi government could not be ignored. Mr. Rochereau de la Sablierè, the French representative argued,

> Violations of human rights such as those now being observed become a matter of international interest when they take on such proportions that they assume the dimension of a crime against humanity. That is indeed what is happening in Iraq.[20]

The most common position held by supporters of resolution 688 expressed concern for the rights of the Kurdish people, but justified the Security Council's involvement due to the international ramifications of the refugee flows. This position was taken by the United States, the USSR, Austria, Ecuador, Zaire, Côte d'Ivoire, and Romania. The comments of the Ecuadorian representative provide a concise summary of this position:

> It might have been perhaps a question of internal jurisdiction in Iraq, if the situation had not gone beyond the borders of the country...this is a situation that goes beyond the sphere of the internal affairs of a State; it is a situation which is affecting international relations and may become a threat to peace...It might be said that, even assuming that the measures I have just set out are taken, the Security Council would not be the body competent to take them...This would be so - I repeat - if we were dealing solely with a case of violation of human rights by a country within its own frontiers; however, once again I say that this is a situation which affects international peace and security, and I therefore believe that the Council is competent to take a stand and to act by taking steps to put an end to this situation.[21]

Taken as a group, the states in favour of the resolution felt strongly that the combination of flagrant human rights violations by the Iraqi state, substantial refugee flows, and the potential repercussions for regional security made the situation a legitimate concern of the Security Council. Within this package of concerns however, it was argued that the concern for international peace and security was the primary reason behind the decision of most states to support the

---

[20] *UN Document*, S/PV. 2982, 5 April, 1991.
[21] Ibid.

resolution. These states, consequently, stressed their respect for the sovereignty of Iraq, and the need for the Council to act in accordance with the UN Charter. The preamble of resolution 688 takes note of Article 2 (7) in order to recognise these concerns.[22]

Opponents of the draft resolution, including Yemen, Cuba and Zimbabwe believed that the Kurdish refugee problem was an internal affair of Iraq. They did not accept the argument that the situation posed a threat to international peace and security and therefore they felt that even the Security Council's consideration of the matter was a violation of the UN Charter. These states argued that the humanitarian situation should be addressed only by the relevant UN humanitarian agencies or by the General Assembly with the consent of the Iraqi government. They did not accept the rationale that human rights concerns justified action by the Security Council. As the representative of Zimbabwe argued,

> We recognise that a serious humanitarian situation has arisen as a result of these developments. However, this is in our view essentially an internal matter, as defined in paragraph 7 of Article 2 of the Charter. It is our view that addressing this situation in the manner suggested by the draft resolution would be inconsistent with the clear parameters of the Council's competence as provided for in the Charter...The humanitarian situation emanating from the present circumstances causes us great concern...However, we believe that the serious humanitarian situation and the question of refugees can be adequately addressed by the appropriate organs of the United Nations...While we realise that the humanitarian dimensions affect neighbouring States, we do not believe that this in any way makes the internal conflict in Iraq an issue that the Council should be seized of.[23]

The two states that abstained on the vote, India and China, did so expressly because of concerns about the protection of Iraq's sovereign rights. Though China is normally is a staunch defender of Article 2(7) it was not prepared to cast a negative vote and scupper the resolution. India, concerned about respect for the sovereign rights of Iraq, questioned the jurisdiction of the Council in the matter and suggested that resolving the situation should be left to other organs of the United Nations. The abstentions of India and China can also, in part, be explained by the other political factors present at the time: India had only just arrived on the Council and was in the process of negotiating a series of key bilateral economic agreements with the United States. Similarly, China was seeking "Most Favoured Nation" (MFN) status within the US Congress and was thus reluctant to raise American ire by vetoing the resolution.[24] Importantly, China was unwilling to allow Chapter VII to be mentioned in the resolution. When it was not, the Chinese were then prepared, with the added incentive of MFN status, to allow the resolution to pass.[25]

---

[22] The inclusion of this reference occurred after France received a request from India to do so. The first draft resolution was amended accordingly. Confidential interview.

[23] *UN Document*, S/PV. 2982, 5 April, 1991.

[24] Ninan Koshy, "The United Nations, the US and Northern Iraq," *Economic and Political Weekly*, vol. 31, no. 4, 1996, p. 2762.

[25] Confidential interview.

44 *Understanding the UN Security Council*

The one reality that was accepted by all of the Security Council members was that they were discussing a contentious issue and they accepted that the Council was stretching the boundaries of its normal jurisdiction. For this reason, there was a strong desire among supporters of the resolution to ensure that the actions of the Security Council would be in response to the strategic and humanitarian immediacy of the situation and would not establish a precedent that in future cases could be used for political purposes. The general feeling among the Council members was that any action taken in response to the Kurdish situation was an exceptional response to an exceptional set of circumstances.[26]

The adoption of resolution 688 set in motion two separate initiatives designed to alleviate the suffering of the Kurdish refugees as well as reduce the pressure on the borders of Turkey and Iran. The first came as a result of the western coalition expanding their relief deliveries to the Kurdish refugees inside northern Iraq while the second multi-lateral initiative occurred under the auspices of the UN.

The Western Coalition Initiative

The American, French and British initiative to help the Kurds occurred largely in response to three factors: growing domestic pressure in the West to aid the refugees; the sense among policy makers that the situation was an unresolved consequence of the coalition action during the Gulf War; and pressure from the Turkish government to remove the destabilizing presence of refugees gathered on its border.[27] On 4 April, John Major, the British Prime Minister, announced £20 million in relief aid to the Kurds and on 5 April, US President Bush announced that the United States had begun *Operation Provide Comfort* - relief flights into northern Iraq. Over the course of the next two weeks this aid effort was expanded. The delivery of supplies was augmented by land convoys and large groups of refugees were encouraged to move to areas more easily accessed by aid agencies. By the end of 23 April, a total of 875 relief flights had been flown, in addition to deliveries of supplies by truck and helicopter, totalling nearly 6,000 tons of relief supplies. Death rates among the refugees dropped from approximately 500-1000 per day at the height of the crisis to 60 per day by the end of April.[28]

Iraq protested against both the adoption of resolution 688 and the subsequent intervention of the coalition states into its northern sector. On 8 April, the Permanent Representative of Iraq to the UN complained to the President of the Security Council that the resolution was biased since it was adopted despite the Council having been informed that Iraq was willing to receive a fact finding

---

[26] Roland Dannreuther, *The Gulf Conflict: A Political and Strategic Analysis*, Adelphi Paper no. 264, Brassey's, London, 1992, p. 65.

[27] Peter Viggo Jakobsen, "National Interest, Humanitarianism or CNN: What Triggers UN Peace Enforcement After the Cold War?," *Journal of Peace Research*, vol. 33, no. 2, 1996, p. 208.

[28] Lawrence Freedman and David Boren, "'Safe Havens' for Kurds in Post-War Iraq," in Rodley, *To Loose the Bands of Wickedness*, p. 51.

mission from the UN.[29] He also protested against the American and British decision to begin relief flights into northern Iraq without the permission of the Iraqi government. The Iraqi Permanent Representative argued that such action constituted direct interference in the internal affairs of Iraq and therefore violated international law.[30]

Although the coalition relief operation gradually improved the condition of the refugees, a political solution to the Kurdish problem that had precipitated the crisis remained elusive. The attention of policy makers in the west refocused on devising a long-term solution to the Kurdish problem that would protect the refugees from future oppression by the Iraqi government.[31] Crucial factors that had to be considered in any such plan not only included the interests of the refugees, but also the sovereign rights of Iraq and the strategic concerns of neighbouring Turkey.

Turkey's strategic concerns were manifest in its response to the exodus of Kurds who gathered along its borders in the spring of 1991. Turkey had previously made pre-emptive attacks across the border into Iraq during the late 1980's in order to strike at Kurdish separatist camps. Since the refugees were considered to inevitably include some Kurdish separatists, Turkey was not prepared to allow the establishment of refugee camps inside its own border from which the Kurdish Workers' Party (PKK) could continue their attacks against Turkish targets.[32] Such were their concerns about the potential impact of a reinvigorated Kurdish political movement that Turkey asked the United States not to contact Kurdish opposition parties in Iraq during the Gulf War. The US agreed to this request in order to gain valuable Turkish co-operation during the conduct of the war.[33] Turkey had also allowed similar camps to be set up inside its border in the later 1980's following Saddam Hussein's persecution of the Kurds and, of the 60,000 Turkey gave refuge to then, more than half remained in the camps in 1991.[34] Turkish authorities did not want the same pattern to occur with the new influx of refugees. Though they had demonstrated an increased commitment to Western values including human rights with the signing of the Conference on Security and Cooperation in Europe (CSCE) Paris Charter in 1990 and were anxious to further solidify their co-operative relationship with Western Europe and the United States, the new Kurdish exodus from Iraq came just at the initial stages of this Turkish process of liberalisation. The Turkish response in a time of crisis was to revert to traditional policies.[35]

---

[29] *UN Document*, S/22460, 8 April, 1991.

[30] *UN Document*, S/22459, 8 April, 1991.

[31] Lois B. McHugh and Susan Epstein, "Kurdish Refugee Relief and Other Humanitarian Aid Issues in Iraq," *Congressional Research Service Issue Brief*, The Library of Congress, 31 May, 1991, p. 11.

[32] Freedman and Boren, "'Safe Havens' for Kurds in Post-War Iraq," p. 49.

[33] "The Kurds' Bid for Freedom," *The Economist*, 30 March, 1991, p. 67.

[34] "On Misery Mountain," *The Economist*, 13 April, 1991, p. 68.

[35] Freedman and Boren, "'Safe Havens' for Kurds in Post-War Iraq," p. 49.

46 *Understanding the UN Security Council*

Confronted by the human exodus from Iraq, Turkey initially assisted the fleeing refugees by providing humanitarian supplies and allowed limited numbers of them into camps inside Turkey. However, it was loath to allow the continuing stream of refugees across its border. On 3 April Turkish authorities closed the border with Iraq in order to prevent what the Turkish government worried would become additional long term camps.[36] It sought to avoid providing any type of permanent sanctuary to the Kurds and used a geographic rationale to argue that the refugees should be moved to more accessible areas further inside Iraq and away from the unsanitary and harsh mountain camps.[37]

The coalition states were also under pressure to assist Turkey because of its position as a key NATO ally in the Middle East that had provided substantial assistance to the Gulf War coalition.[38] This relationship, combined with Turkey's decision to close the border, forced western policy makers to come to the conclusion that if something was to be done to assist the refugees, it would have to occur within Iraq itself. Accordingly, the western coalition members were forced to seek some formula by which the Kurdish refugees could remain in Iraq, but be free from continued persecution by the Iraqi government. The solution that emerged was the creation of safe areas within northern Iraq where the refugees would be protected by coalition forces.

The Safe Areas

On 8 April, at the Luxembourg summit meeting of the European Community (EC), John Major proposed the creation of UN protected "safe enclaves" in northern Iraq for the Kurds.[39] Within the EC, the proposal was met with enthusiasm and $185 million for refugee aid. But when the EC supported Major's suggestion Iraq vehemently protested. The Iraqi Prime Minister, Saddam Hammadi, stated that it was a "suspicious proposal that Iraq categorically rejects and will resist with all means."[40]

The proposal was not as well received in Washington as it had been in EC capitals.[41] The attention of the US was focused on ensuring that the relief efforts

---

[36] "As Kurds Press Borders, Iran And Turkey Appeal for Aid," *International Herald Tribune*, 5 April, 1991.

[37] "Ankara to Relocate Refugees as Allied Airdrops Continue," *International Herald Tribune*, 15 April, 1991.

[38] Murphy, *Humanitarian Intervention*, p. 172. Turkish authorities claimed that by closing the oil pipeline to the port of Ceyhan, Turkey lost US$750,000 a month, part of estimated overall loss of approximately US$20 billion during the four years that the economic embargo was in place against Iraq. See Mahmut Bali Aykan, "Turkey's Policy in Northern Iraq, 1991-95," *Middle Eastern Studies*, vol. 32, no. 4 October, 1996, p. 353.

[39] John Major, *John Major: The Autobiography*, HarperCollins Publishers, London, 1999, p. 243.

[40] As quoted in "Iraq Denounces EC Call for Kurdish Haven as a Conspiracy," *The International Herald Tribune*, 10 April, 1991.

[41] Major, *John Major*, p. 243.

Northern Iraq 1991

continued unmolested by the Iraqi government and remained limited to that objective alone. Marlin Fitzwater, the White House spokesman, stated that the safe area idea was worthy of further consideration as a possible solution to the Kurdish dilemma, but the US was reluctant to deploy any US ground forces in northern Iraq.[42] Bush did not want to commit the US to any lasting military engagement with no foreseeable exit strategy. He was reluctant to move beyond the terms of the UN resolution which had originally authorised the coalition action in the Gulf as he did not want to renege on his pledge made to the American public that the Gulf War would not become another Vietnam.[43] Politically, Bush was also reluctant to stray from the relative political safety of a policy of relief flights, which had the support of most Americans, to a riskier policy in which US troops were deployed in northern Iraq.[44]

However, US policy underwent a remarkable transformation during the second week of April. After continued pressure from members of the EC, the emergence of support for the enclave idea within Congress, and the realisation that the plight of the Kurds was worsening due to adverse weather conditions, Bush announced on 16 April that American troops would be deployed into northern Iraq in order to establish relief camps for the Kurdish refugees.[45] In general terms, the coalition was motivated by a feeling of responsibility for the plight of the refugees, negative publicity surrounding the lacklustre response of the west to the Kurdish exodus, and also a good chance of success at reversing the humanitarian catastrophe in the short term.[46] More practically, it had become apparent that the refugees would need to be provided with protection once they moved from the exposed mountain terrain down to the valley where the majority of the relief aid was more easily distributed.

As they promoted this new strategic initiative, the coalition members sought to frame it as consistent with international law and sanctioned by the UN. The British recognised that their suggestion had the potential to be construed as illegal intervention in the territory of a sovereign state. It was an accusation that they had anticipated even before John Major's suggestion concerning the safe havens. At a press conference following his statement to EC leaders in Luxembourg on 8 April, Major expressed the British belief that the creation of the safe havens was authorized by resolution 688. He stated, "As to whether we need a new Security Council resolution [to authorise the creation of safe havens], we do not believe so. We believe the rubric exists within 688 to avoid the need for a separate resolution

---

[42] Freedman and Boren, "'Safe Havens' for Kurds in Post-War Iraq," p. 53.

[43] "Thousands of Iraqi Refugees Flee to Turkish Tent City," *The Times*, 1 April, 1991.

[44] In a Washington Post-American Broadcasting Corporation (ABC) News poll conducted during the first week of April, 7 out of 10 Americans said they approved of the way Bush was handling the Kurdish situation. "45% in Poll Favour Rebel Aid," *The International Herald Tribune*, 6-7 April, 1991. 45% of those polled thought the US should assist the rebels to overthrow Saddam Hussein.

[45] "Quick Gulf Exit? Not So Fast," *The International Herald Tribune*, 18 April, 1991.

[46] Peter Viggo Jakobsen, "National Interest, Humanitarianism or CNN," p. 208.

48   *Understanding the UN Security Council*

but clearly we will need to discuss that in New York."[47] The British also sought to deflect criticism of their action by suggesting that the creation of safe havens was not incompatible with respecting the sovereignty of Iraq. In a parliamentary debate on 15 April, Foreign Secretary Douglas Hurd argued that the purpose of the safe havens was "to create places and conditions in which the refugees can feel secure. We are not talking of a territorial enclave, a separate Kurdistan or a permanent UN presence. We support the territorial integrity of Iraq."[48]

American policy was also presented as being justified by the terms of resolution 688 and US policy makers stressed that it was not directed at interfering in Iraq's sovereign rights, but rather was aimed at alleviating the humanitarian crisis. At a news conference on 16 April when he announced the creation of the safe areas in *Operation Safe Haven*, Bush stated:

> Consistent with United Nations Security Resolution 688 and working closely with the United Nations and other international relief organisations and our European partners, I have directed the US military to begin immediately to establish several encampments in northern Iraq where relief supplies for these refugees will be made available...
>
> ...let me reassure them [the refugees] that adequate security will be provided at these temporary sites by US, British and French air and ground forces, again consistent with United Nations Security Council Resolution 688...
>
> ...the relief effort being announced here today constitutes an undertaking different in scale and approach. What is not different is basic policy. All along, I have said that the United States is not going to intervene militarily in Iraq's internal affairs.[49]

Bush was quick to point out the short-term nature of the policy and stressed that it was not going to result in US forces being indefinitely deployed in the area. He emphasized that the US aim was to turn the sites over to the UN as soon as possible after their establishment and that the United States had no intention of occupying Iraqi territory or becoming involved in its domestic turmoil.[50] This emphasis on the humanitarian nature of the operation and the expressed respect for Iraqi sovereignty was adopted in part to reduce the potential for Iraqi resistance to the coalition initiative, and also to appease the members of the Security Council who had expressed reservations about the coalition action.

The sensitivity of the western coalition states to the accusation that their actions were in violation of international law is also demonstrated by the

---

[47] Statement by the UK Prime Minister: A Safe Haven for the Kurds, 8 April, 1991, UK Foreign and Commonwealth Office Press Office, as quoted in Weller, *Iraq and Kuwait*, p. 714.

[48] UK House of Commons Parliamentary Debate, as quoted in Weller, *Iraq and Kuwait*, p. 717.

[49] US Presidential News Conference, 16 April, 1991, Weekly Compilation of Presidential Documents, vol. 27, no. 16 as quoted in Marc Weller, *Iraq and Kuwait*, p. 717.

[50] "Allied Troops to Help Kurds," *The Financial Times*, 17 April, 1991. As will be seen later in the chapter, the UN at this stage had not been consulted about assuming control of the Allied camps.

terminology that they chose to use during the operation. John Major, in a change from his original announcement, stressed that the camps being established were "safe areas" and not "enclaves." The term "safe area" was thought to lack the same sense of permanence engendered by the term "enclave" and therefore would not imply that Western policy was supporting the emergence of a Kurdish state within Iraq. Similarly, by avoiding any suggestion of permanence, the coalition states hoped to indicate that they had only short-term, humanitarian objectives. [51]

The politically thorny issue of Kurdish separation was also assiduously avoided by the allies. They went to great lengths not only to stress that they had no intention of meddling in Iraqi internal politics beyond assisting the refugees, but also took practical steps to limit the amount of political momentum that was given to Kurdish separatists by *Operation Safe Haven*. One such example was Bush's decision to order the Iraqi military to cease all military activities north of the 36th parallel on 10 April. This decision was taken not only to reduce the potential for direct conflict between Iraqi and coalition forces, but also because it implicitly discouraged claims of Kurdish separation. This was because the separatists claimed the strategically important oil town of Kirkuk, yet it is located below the 36 parallel and therefore remained under Iraqi control. [52]

Given that the refugees could not be moved into Turkey, the decision to create the safe areas was also due to the practical necessity of moving the refugees to areas where it was easier for aid agencies to deliver supplies to them. The temporary camps that had been established in the mountains had limited road access, often clogged with mud, and were exposed to the worst of the elements, consequently hampering airdrops. Accordingly, the plan involved US, British and French forces establishing a series of camps from which significant quantities of supplies could be delivered to those in need. In co-operation with US forces, British, French, and Dutch troops were deployed into northern Iraq with further assistance later provided by Italian, Canadian and Australian forces. The coalition troops also helped in setting up the camps, moving refugees and supplies into the appropriate areas, as well as serving to deter the Iraqi military from making attacks on the returning refugees. [53]

When President Bush announced that coalition forces would establish the safe areas in Iraqi territory, the Iraqi Minister of Foreign Affairs protested the deployment of these forces in the Zakhou region of Iraq in a letter to the UN Secretary-General:

---

[51] Freedman and Boren, "'Safe Havens' for Kurds in Post-War Iraq," p. 57.

[52] Ibid., p. 53.

[53] The original plan was to establish six 'zones of protection', with each servicing approximately 60,000 refugees each. The US planned to deploy five to ten thousand troops in order to build, run, and guard the camps. See "US Troops Survey Sites in Iraq for Safe Havens," *The Financial Times*, 18 April, 1991.

50   *Understanding the UN Security Council*

> ...the Government of Iraq is opposed to this measure [the establishment of the safe areas] since it would constitute a serious, unjustifiable and unfounded attack on the sovereignty and territorial integrity of Iraq...[54]

In order to rid themselves of the coalition troops, Iraqi authorities sought to have the UN take over the administration of the camps, but without any type of military force operating under the UN flag. Their strategy was to involve the UN in order to appease international demands for humanitarian action and thereby make the presence of coalition troops redundant, while simultaneously preventing the deployment of a UN police or peacekeeping force by withholding their consent to either type of force. In effect, the coalition camps would just be incorporated into the UN humanitarian program. However, when it came to the possibility of having UN security forces deployed on its territory, the Iraqi perception was that the suggestion of a UN police force in Iraq was an American initiative that sought to exploit the UN for American purposes. It was for this reason that Iraq did not accept the rationale that, by agreeing to UN forces in place of coalition troops, they would be ridding itself of the coalition presence. They saw the US as using the UN and therefore regarded a UN force as minimally different from coalition forces.[55]

Beyond the Charter?

The actions taken by the allies in creating a no-fly zone north of the 36th parallel and establishing safe havens in northern Iraq were originally justified in the terms of resolution 688. However, the two main interpretations of resolution 688 used at the time to provide legal justification for the actions of the US, France, and the UK do not stand up under closer scrutiny. The lack of any subsequent resolutions adopted by the Security Council on the situation in northern Iraq provides a third indicator that the Council as a whole was reluctant to impinge on Iraqi sovereignty.

    First, it is difficult to find a basis for the coalition intervention in the wording of resolution 688. The resolution makes no explicit reference to either Chapter VI or VII of the UN Charter, but does use the phrase "threat to international peace and security." This suggests that the UNSC considered the matter under Chapter VII of the Charter. The position of the US, France and the UK suggests they interpreted the resolution as based on Article 42, given the fact that the resolution *demanded* that Iraq stop its repression of civilians and allow access to international humanitarian organisations. Yet the problem with this interpretation is that the Council chose not to use its customary wording *"determines* a threat to international peace and security."[56] Article 39 requires such a determination to be made before Article 42 can be invoked. Instead the members of the UNSC used an alternative phrasing - "the consequences of which threaten international peace and security" - which was a deliberate obfuscation of the customary phrasing in order

---

[54] *UN Document*, S/22513, 21 April, 1991.

[55] *UN Document*, S/22599, 14 May, 1991.

[56] Murphy, *Humanitarian Intervention*, p. 197.

Northern Iraq 1991 51

to preclude the resolution being based under Article 42.[57] The Council's decision not to formulate resolution 688 in the normal manner, with no clear determination made that the situation constituted a threat to international peace and security, therefore suggests it cannot be viewed as falling under Article 42.[58] This interpretation is supported by comments made by Anthony Aust, Legal Counsellor for the British Foreign and Commonwealth Office before a Foreign Affairs Committee of the House of Commons on 2 December, 1992:

> Resolution 688, which applies not only to northern Iraq but to the whole of Iraq, was not made under Chapter VII. Resolution 688 recognised that there was a severe human rights and humanitarian situation in Iraq and, in particular, northern Iraq; but the intervention in northern Iraq "Provide Comfort" was in fact, not specifically mandated by the United Nations...[59]

This was also the view of the Secretary-General and his decision not to support the coalition intervention dealt a significant blow to its perceived legality. Since resolution 688 had expressly called on the Secretary-General to use "all the resources at his disposal," if Pérez de Cuéllar had chosen to support the coalition intervention, the legal basis for it would have been greatly strengthened. However, he did not and instead urged the allies to consult with Iraq before deploying forces in order to help the Kurds.[60]

As demonstrated earlier, US officials publicly took the position that resolution 688 provided adequate authorization for the coalition intervention, and therefore they did not formally attempt to seek additional authorization from the Security Council. White House spokesman Marlin Fitzwater summed up the American position by saying that it was a cardinal rule that "if you don't need it don't ask."[61] But President Bush nevertheless recognised the shortcomings of resolution 688 in terms of any possible future intervention by the UN in northern Iraq.[62] This inadequacy of the resolution potentially complicated the coalition aim of turning over the camps to UN administration. It was this realisation that prompted him to comment "I just wish that 688 could be sufficient" when talking with the Secretary-General. Bush was frustrated by the fact that in lieu of additional authorization from the Security Council, any potential UN action was dependent upon the consent of the Iraqi government.[63] Similarly, Bush's

---

[57] Confidential interview. Though the difference between the two phrases appears small, among the members of the Security Council, the decision to use the alternative phrasing was a deliberate action taken to demonstrate that the Council was not acting under Article 42 and serves to indicate that the Council was divided on the issue.

[58] Murphy, *Humanitarian Intervention*, p. 198.

[59] "The Expanding Role of the United Nations and its Implications for UK Policy," Minutes of Evidence, *House of Commons Foreign Affairs Committee*, 2 December, 1992.

[60] Pérez de Cuéllar, *Pilgrimage For Peace*, pp. 275-76.

[61] Fitzwater as quoted in "UN Chief Urges Consultation with Iraq," *The International Herald Tribune*, 18 April, 1991.

[62] Pérez de Cuéllar, *Pilgrimage For Peace*, pp. 277-8.

[63] Ibid.

52 *Understanding the UN Security Council*

suggestion that the US seek another resolution to authorize the coalition intervention, and the subsequent decision not to do so, suggests that the Americans recognised that it was not politically feasible in the Security Council. Two of the permanent members of the Council, namely the Soviet Union and China, had both indicated that they would not support a further resolution on the situation in northern Iraq, and certainly not one that was adopted under Chapter VII.[64] Soviet Foreign Ministry spokesman Vitaly Churkin expressed serious reservations concerning the creation of a safe haven in northern Iraq as it would mean taking away part of Iraq's sovereignty without Iraq's consent, and would therefore be against the UN Charter.[65]

The coalition members also tried to justify their action by linking resolution 688 with the provisions of the Gulf War cease-fire as set down in resolution 687. The terms of this latter resolution were clearly adopted under Chapter VII of the Charter and therefore were not bound by the restrictions of Article 2(7). The hope was that the actions of the coalition, consistent as they were with the humanitarian aims of resolution 688, could be justified if there was a perception that resolution 688 was clearly linked to the enforcement provisions of resolution 687. In the debate on the proposed resolution 688, the representative of Germany stated that the aim of resolution 687 to restore peace and security in the region could only be achieved if domestic peace in Iraq was present, thus equating the implementation of 687 with that of 688.[66] Similarly, John Major linked the two resolutions when he first suggested the creation of the safe havens on 8 April, following the EC summit. The safe haven idea was one of four 'action points' designed to deal with the refugee situation in Iraq and "build on Security Council resolutions 687 and 688."[67] His perception of the situation, as evidenced by this comment, was that resolutions 687 and 688, as well as the proposal for the safe havens, were part of a continuum with the action taken to cope with the humanitarian situation in northern Iraq representing the last part of that continuum.

There also seemed to be an attempt made by the United States to view resolution 688 and the terms of the Gulf War cease-fire in the same light. In a joint statement made by the Turkish Foreign Minister and the US Secretary of State, James Baker it was noted that "the plight of the refugees - as the Security Council resolution says a threat to international peace and security - has thus become another important issue in the full implementation of the cease-fire resolution."[68] The supposed link between 687 and 688 was again highlighted by a US diplomat before the sub-committee on Europe and the Middle East of the House Foreign

---

[64] Nicholas J. Wheeler, "Pluralist or Solidarist Conceptions of International Society: Bull and Vincent on Humanitarian Intervention," *Millennium*, vol. 21, no. 3, 1992, p. 483.

[65] "Bush Faces Renewed Pressure Over Kurds," *The Financial Times*, 13-14 April, 1991.

[66] *UN Document*, S/PV. 2982, 5 April, 1991.

[67] Koshy, "The United Nations, the US and Northern Iraq," p. 2762.

[68] Ibid. p. 2763.

Affairs Committee in Washington who said "behind UNSC resolution 688 are the enforcement provisions of 687..."[69]

Yet in the preamble of resolution 688 the Council decided not to cite any other prior resolution. This would suggest that the Security Council as a whole did not regard resolution 688 as linked to resolution 687. Additionally, resolution 687 makes no mention of the persecution of the Kurds, nor does it set down in the terms of the cease-fire any reference to human rights or require a change in Iraqi government policies with regard to human rights.[70] While the legal basis for the coalition intervention is more substantial when reference is made to resolution 687 than that provided by resolution 688 alone, the attempt to link the two resolutions is most likely explained as a way of garnering domestic and international political support for the actions of the coalition by attempting to portray it as intimately linked to the successful resolution of the war in the Gulf. Most commentators agree however, that the terms of resolution 687 were effectively considered at an end once Iraq had legally accepted the terms of the Security Council's cease-fire embodied in resolution 687.[71] This also makes it difficult to justify the view that 687 and 688 were linked.

An argument has also been made that the coalition action can be justified by a combined reading of resolution 688 and resolution 678 which authorized the coalition to use all necessary means "to restore international peace and security in the area," and provided the legal basis for the Gulf War.[72] It suggests that the actions taken by the western coalition in countering the Iraqi government's persecution of the Kurds, and removing the threat to international peace and security caused by the refugee flows, were consistent with both resolutions. Legally, it was justified because resolution 678 was explicitly adopted under Chapter VII of the Charter. However, the two main problems with this argument are, as with the supposed linkage between 688 and 687, the failure of the Security Council members to refer to any prior UN resolution in the preamble of resolution 688, and the fact that resolution 687 established a cease-fire between the coalition and the government of Iraq, in effect ending the authority given to the coalition states by resolution 678.[73]

Despite these attempted justifications for the coalition intervention into northern Iraq, it is clear that the intervention occurred without the authorization of the UN Security Council.[74] While the exact basis of resolution 688 in the Charter

---

[69] Comments of John H Kelly, US Asst. Secretary for Near Eastern and South Asian Affairs in a statement before the Sub Committee on Europe and the Middle East of the House Foreign Affairs Committee, 17 June, 1991 as quoted in Koshy, "The United Nations, the US and Northern Iraq," p. 2763.

[70] Koshy, "The United Nations, the US and Northern Iraq," p. 2762.

[71] Howard Adelman, "Humanitarian Intervention: The Case of the Kurds," International Journal of Refugee Law, vol. 4, no. 1, 1992, p. 21

[72] UN Security Council Resolution 678, 29 November, 1990.

[73] Sean Murphy, *Humanitarian Intervention*, p. 185.

[74] Though beyond the scope of this chapter, there has been some suggestion made that the unilateral intervention of the allied forces during *Operation Provide Comfort* and *Operation Safe Haven* (as distinct from the UN humanitarian operation) may be legal according to

54   *Understanding the UN Security Council*

is still of matter of debate within international legal circles, it is nevertheless clear that the resolution was not formulated under Article 42 of Chapter VII.[75] The absence of any decision taken explicitly under Chapter VII in resolution 688, meant that it had no more legal significance than a Chapter VI resolution.[76] While it can be argued that though the UNSC did not explicitly *authorize* the coalition intervention, its adoption of resolution 688 did serve to *legitimize* the intervention. It is also important to recognise that the intervention resulted from the actions of three liberal, western members of the UNSC. In contrast, the actions agreed on by the UNSC members, while important, were specifically circumscribed in their scope.[77]

The UN Initiative

While the coalition members sought to justify their intervention under resolution 688, the second initiative that arose as a result that resolution occurred under the auspices of the United Nations. The UN agencies sought to work with the Iraqi authorities in establishing a series of humanitarian centres within the country. Pérez de Cuéllar appointed Prince Sadruddin Aga Khan to oversee the UN humanitarian program for Iraq. A plan was developed whereby a series of humanitarian centres would be established throughout Iraq along with a number of relay stations to assist the refugees on the return journey to their homes. As Iraq still retained its sovereign authority, the humanitarian efforts of the UN occurred only with the consent of the Iraq government.

A Memorandum of Understanding (MOU) was drafted between the United Nations and the Iraqi government on 18 April, 1991, which set out detailed conditions surrounding the UN's humanitarian efforts in Iraq. The MOU gave the UN permission to use airlifts to transport relief supplies and also covered issues such as the staffing of the UN humanitarian centres and the type of aid that would be provided to those in need. It also identified the groups targeted for aid provision, as well as the role of Iraqi officials and international NGOs in the

---

customary norms of international law governing the rights of victors over a defeated country following the conclusion of a conflict. This was offered as an alternative justification for the allied action by the US. See Adelman, "Humanitarian Intervention," and Roberts, "Humanitarian War."

[75] A senior official involved in the northern Iraq intervention stressed that resolution 688 emerged as a result of what was politically desired by the allies, and politically possible within the UNSC. While steps were taken to ensure it was consistent with the Charter, the exact location of the resolution in the articles of the Charter was not foremost in the minds of those involved. Confidential interview with author. There is strong argument to be made for the location of resolution 688 in either article 40 or 41 of the UN Charter. See Murphy, *Humanitarian Intervention*, pp. 197-198.

[76] Confidential interview with author.

[77] For the suggestion that resolution 688 legitimised the coalition intervention, see Murphy, *Humanitarian Intervention*, p. 195.

humanitarian effort.[78]   The Iraqi government's primary concern was that the provisions of the MOU or the language used in it did not infringe upon its sovereignty or imply acceptance of resolution 688 which the Iraqi government had rejected.[79]

Despite having signed its own agreement with the Iraqi government aimed at assisting the refugees, the UN came under intense pressure to support the establishment of the coalition camps. On two separate occasions, Bush requested Pérez de Cuéllar to publicly support the Western action as being consistent with resolution 688; once before the public announcement of the intervention, and again in a letter to the Secretary-General the following day. French Prime Minister Michel Rocard also told the Secretary-General in Paris that he expected full UN backing for the coalition effort to set up the refugee camps. However, for Pérez de Cuéllar, resolution 688 did not provide sufficient authorization for the Western action, and he therefore took the position that the intervention was a violation of Iraqi sovereignty.[80]   Effectively, the Secretary-General was forced to straddle a political fence; on one side he could not support the intervention since he believed it to be inconsistent with the Charter, while from a humanitarian perspective he did not object to the measures taken by the coalition.

The coalition members also wanted UN support for their camps, since it would then be easier to turn them over to a UN security force once they were established. This would allow the coalition forces to be withdrawn without further endangering the refugees. However, the Secretary-General informed President Bush that just as resolution 688 did not provide the UN with sufficient authority to deploy a peacekeeping or police force to patrol the planned security zone without Iraqi consent, for this same reason it was also not possible to transform part of the coalition force into a 'blue helmet' force under the authority of the UN. Through his interpretation of the Charter and resolution 688, the Secretary-General insisted that Iraqi consent be obtained before a peacekeeping force could be deployed. He also pointed out two further complicating factors that hindered the deployment of a UN force. First, the General Assembly would have to approve the financing of a mission, and without a sound legal basis, the Assembly would object to it. Second, member states would be less likely to commit troops to the force if Iraq was likely to oppose its deployment.[81]

As a result of this position, attempts were made by the United Nations throughout the month of April to obtain Iraq's agreement to the deployment of a UN peacekeeping force. In the discussions between Iraqi authorities and Prince Sadruddin prior to the signing of the MOU, the Prince broached the possibility of a UN peacekeeping operation to assist the humanitarian program. The Iraqis rejected the idea of a UN peacekeeping or police force outright. Following the establishment of the humanitarian centres as provided for in the MOU, the possibility of deploying a peacekeeping force to provide security in the camps was

---

[78] *UN Document*, S/22513, 22 April, 1991 annex.

[79] Pérez de Cuéllar, *Pilgrimage For Peace*, p. 275.

[80] Ibid., p. 276.

[81] Ibid.

56   *Understanding the UN Security Council*

again raised by Prince Sadruddin on behalf of the Secretary-General. Once again the answer was no.[82]

The parallel efforts of the UN Secretariat and the coalition to bring relief to the Kurdish refugees worked independently of each other from early April until the UN adopted responsibility for the relief centres on 18 May. At times the separate initiatives also worked at cross-purposes. Privately, there was an increasing irritation within the UN Secretariat towards the coalition states, since it was felt that they were glossing over the UN Charter and its restrictions on intervention, as well as ignoring the general sentiment within the international community against intervention in Iraq.[83] This feeling was compounded by the impression among UN personnel that the coalition was co-opting UN policy initiatives. For example, President Bush informed the UN Secretary-General of the impending US deployment on 16 April, just before the same announcement was made publicly. When the Iraqi authorities learned of the US decision, they postponed the signing of the Memorandum of Understanding with the UN concerning its operation of relief centres throughout Iraq. At a news conference in Geneva on 19 April, Sadruddin drew attention to the fact that there were no arrangements between the coalition and the UN concerning the transfer of the camps from coalition to UN jurisdiction once they were established. He was reportedly irritated by American and British statements that the camps would be turned over to the UN as soon as possible after their establishment, despite the lack of any consultation on such a transfer.[84]

The UN Guards

The concept of using UN Guards to protect UN personnel and equipment emerged out of political necessity from John Major's original suggestion of a UN police force to protect the safe areas. A key consideration of the British in devising their plan had been pragmatism. The British saw President Bush's suggestion of transforming the coalition force into a UN force as likely to be vetoed by either the USSR or China in the Security Council. Deploying a UN police force or UN observer mission based on consent was a way around Chinese or Soviet objections.[85] This plan was refined over the course of the next two weeks. It was thought that a force without full military status would be less likely to incur Iraqi opposition and would also not need further authorisation from the Security Council in addition to resolution 688. The military shortcomings of such a deployment were to be bolstered by providing coalition air cover for the UN force.[86]

---

[82] Ibid., p. 278.

[83] G. Welhengama, "New Developments of International Law Through the Second Phase of the Gulf Crisis - An Analysis," *The Liverpool Law Review*, vol. 13, no. 1, 1991, p. 118.

[84] "Prince Calls for Aid Funds," *The Independent*, 20 April, 1991.

[85] "The Missing Link in the Major Plan," *The Independent*, 11 April, 1991.

[86] "EC Backs British Plan for UN to Police Northern Iraq," *The Independent*, 29 April, 1991.

Despite the political considerations incorporated into the British plan, it was adamantly rejected by the Iraqis. This left the initiative largely in the hands of the UN Secretary-General, who was confronted not only with pressure from the coalition to devise a solution whereby they could withdraw their troops, but also with Iraqi intransigence concerning the deployment of a peacekeeping or police force. As a result, Pérez de Cuéllar and his Executive Delegate were forced to improvise. During discussions with Iraqi authorities on 18 May, and having been given the second Iraqi rejection of a peacekeeping force, Prince Sadruddin asked whether the Iraqis would consider allowing the use of UN Guards for security purposes in and around the humanitarian centres.[87] Prince Sadruddin's idea was that the Guards would be able to patrol the relief camps to protect UN workers as well as the employees of the numerous NGOs participating in the relief effort. Their presence in the camps, combined with a limited observation role throughout northern Iraq, would also help to reassure the Kurdish refugee population and encourage them to return to their homes.[88] Since the primary role of the Guards would be limited to providing security to the camps and to the foreign personnel in them, the Iraqi government accepted Prince Sadruddin's proposal.

The pressure on Iraq to accept the UN Guards had also been increased by a number of other factors. First, Britain and France announced that they would use their positions within the Security Council to veto any proposal to relax the economic sanctions on Iraq.[89] This announcement came after Iraq had requested that the UN sanctions committee release $1 billion of Iraq's frozen assets and allow it to sell $950 million of oil in order to buy a variety of humanitarian supplies such as food and medicine.[90] Second, President Bush stated publicly that he was prepared to recommend that China be given MFN trading status with the United States, linking his decision to China's co-operation during the Gulf War. Seemingly unrelated to the situation in northern Iraq, this announcement nevertheless served to increase the pressure on Iraq to accept a UN force as it reduced the likelihood of China vetoing a US sponsored resolution for a Chapter VII authorized UN force. Bush had threatened to put such a proposal before the Security Council if Iraq did not agree to admit a UN security force.[91] The proposed resolution would have sought enforcement powers for the coalition under

---

[87] The Guards are individuals normally employed by the United Nations to provide security on UN property in New York, Geneva, Vienna, and Nairobi - properties where local police forces have no jurisdiction. The Guards are under the administration of the Secretary-General and are regular staff members of the UN Secretariat. They are financed from the regular UN budget, can be deployed only under the authority of the Secretary-General, and are limited both in number and in function.

[88] Pérez de Cuéllar, *Pilgrimage For Peace*, p. 278.

[89] "Allies Insist Iraq Admits UN Police," *The Guardian*, 11 May, 1991.

[90] "Hope Against Hope for Iraq's Kurds," *The Economist*, 4 May, 1991, p. 69.

[91] "Bush is Ready to Press UN to Police Iraq," *The International Herald Tribune*, 17 May, 1991.

58 *Understanding the UN Security Council*

Chapter VII of the Charter and would have created a force over which Iraq had no influence, unlike a consent-based UN police or peacekeeping operation.[92]

On 25 May, 1991 the Iraqi Minister of Foreign Affairs formally signed the agreement pertaining to the deployment of the UN Guards contingent in northern Iraq. This agreement subsequently became an annex to the MOU signed on 18 April in which the UN assumed responsibility for the operation of the relief centres in Iraq. The annex agreement detailed the arrangements for the areas in which the Guards would be deployed and the number of Guards that could be deployed in each area from a total strength of 500. They were to have complete freedom of movement, facilitated by suitable ground vehicles as well as transportation by helicopter, and were authorized to carry side arms. The Iraqi government in turn agreed to provide logistical support for them, including appropriate facilities in Baghdad as well as liaison officers to facilitate the Guards' work with Iraqi authorities.[93]

The Iraqi decision to finally agree to the UN presence was the result of three main considerations. The first was that the members of the coalition stood firm in their determination to ensure that some type of security force was left in Iraq to supervise the camps and provide the refugees with some measure of security. Saddam Hussein may have recognised that if he continued to frustrate the UN aid and security initiatives, he risked Britain or the US seeking another resolution to complement resolution 688 which would allow the coalition forces to assert greater control in northern Iraq.[94]

The second consideration was the fact that the coalition used the threat of continued sanctions on the Iraqi government in order to induce Iraqi acceptance of the UN Guards. On 10 May, John Major announced that the economic sanctions imposed during the Gulf war would remain in place until Saddam Hussein was removed. This policy was supported by both parties in the US Congress. Senator Bole Dole argued that the US should use the threat of continued sanctions as a means of forcing President Hussein to accept a UN force.[95] Faced with the prospects of prolonged economic hardship, the Iraqis agreed to the deployment of the UN Guards. In so doing, they were able to strengthen their argument that they were co-operating with the United Nations and also press for the sanctions to be removed sooner rather than later.

The third consideration was that the independent relief efforts of the UN and the allies worked to Iraq's advantage by giving it a means of avoiding prolonged occupation of its north by coalition forces. It was through the United Nations, which would operate only on a consensual basis, that Iraq would be able to minimise the foreign presence on its soil. It was with these three considerations in

---

[92] This US threat of seeking another resolution authorised under Chapter VII for the allied action can only be viewed as a means of increasing Iraqi uncertainty and pushing them further in the direction of accepting the Guards, since it was politically unlikely that any such resolution would have passed through the Security Council.

[93] *UN Document*, S/22663, 31 May, 1991.

[94] "Britain Calls on UN to Set Up Mission," *The Daily Telegraph*, 12 April, 1991.

[95] "UN's Kurd Relief Plan Starts," *The Independent*, 13 May, 1991.

mind that on 22 April, the Iraqi authorities requested the UN to assume responsibility for the operation of the coalition-established relief centres:

> ...Because the measures taken by the United States forces and the forces co-operating with them constitute a flagrant violation of Iraq's sovereignty and territorial integrity, and bearing in mind our opposition to the creation of the centres under United States control inside Iraqi territory and our belief that the agreement which our Government concluded with your representative on 18 April, 1991 has made it possible to define all relief operations in Iraq in an integrated and balanced manner, particularly those targeted to Kurds who are Iraqi citizens in such a way as to avoid the realisation of the alleged objectives of the United States centres and to remove any justification for the establishment of such centres...[96]

Immediately following the verbal agreement obtained by Prince Sadruddin to the deployment of UN Guards, ten volunteer Guards from the UN offices in Geneva were sent to the newly opened humanitarian centre in Dohuk. The Guards also assumed responsibility for three nearby transit camps that had been established by the coalition forces. As they did so, the coalition troops were withdrawn. The Iraqi authorities in the region co-operated with the UN efforts and the humanitarian centres and refugees in them went unmolested. The presence of the Guards, the respect of the Iraqi authorities for them, and the constantly improving humanitarian situation eventually led to renewed confidence among the refugees. Many of them soon left the camps and returned to their homes.[97] This was despite the fact the agreement covering the role of the Guards was such that they could only protect UN personnel engaged in relief efforts and not Iraqi nationals.

The original MOU and its annex covering the deployment of the UN Guards was renewed on 24 November, 1991 for another seven months until 10 June, 1992. The presence of the Guards was reinforced by the presence of *Operation Poised Hammer* in neighbouring Turkey, which served as a deterrent against further Iraqi government attacks on the refugees. The duration of the second MOU was characterized by continued Iraqi government co-operation with the UN as the international organisation tried to implement its humanitarian program for Iraq. This relationship was to change as the renewal date for the second MOU approached. The Iraqi government delayed its renewal of the MOU and ceased adhering to its terms. As a result, after 1 July, 1992 the humanitarian program in Iraq slowly began to grind to a halt as UN personnel suffered increased harassment, and visas and travel permits were not extended by the Iraqi government. As a result the number of UN Guards in the country dropped from

---

[96] *UN Document*, S/22513, 22 April, 1991. See also *UN Document*, S/22531, 24 April, 1991.

[97] Pérez de Cuéllar, *Pilgrimage For Peace*, p. 279.

60 *Understanding the UN Security Council*

the nearly 400 that had been deployed in April 1992 to just over 100 by the end of the summer.[98]

The Security Council protested Iraq's obstruction of the humanitarian effort and delay in renewing the MOU, and also highlighted its concern for UN personnel engaged in Iraq.[99] Eventually, on 22 October, 1992 the third MOU between the UN and the Iraqi government was signed covering a six-month period until 31 March, 1993. This third renewal however, represented a retrenchment on the part of the Iraqi government in terms of the degree of co-operation it was prepared to extend to the UN humanitarian initiative. The numbers of UN Guards agreed to in the new MOU was only 300 (representing a reduction of 200 from the original agreement), restrictions were placed on the size of the contingent's headquarters in Baghdad, and the Iraqi government tried to restrict the deployment of the Guards to northern Iraq, with no specific clause included in the agreement authorizing their deployment in the south. This was in contrast to the original MOU that had not placed any restrictions on where the humanitarian program's initiatives, or its Guards, could be deployed.[100] There was a tacit understanding that the Guards would only be deployed in the three northern governates in Iraq where the government did not exercise actual authority and therefore the activities of the Guards did not infringe on their interests.[101]

The Iraqi government's co-operation with the UN Guards ebbed and flowed along with the degree of international attention focused on northern Iraq. In the immediate aftermath of the crisis, co-operation was high, but only a year later Iraq dragged its feet on renewing the MOU. One key factor inducing co-operation was the presence of *Operation Poised Hammer* in Turkey. This 5000 strong Rapid Reaction Force (RRF) combined with air support served to provide the refugees with some measure of security in addition to the largely symbolic presence provided by the UN Guards. However, the RRF was withdrawn in September 1991, leaving only the air contingent to patrol the skies north of the 36th parallel. Deployed at Incirlik airbase in Turkey, its presence was contingent on the agreement of the Turkish government and had to be formally renewed every six months. After December 1992, the Turkish government reserved the right to revoke its agreement to the presence of *Operation Poised Hammer*, and it also became more critical of the coalition's use of air power in the region.

---

[98] Comments made by Mr. Jan Eliasson, Under Secretary-General for Humanitarian Affairs and Emergency Relief Co-ordinator for Iraq before the Security Council, *UN Document,* S/PV. 3139, 23 November, 1992.

[99] *UN Document*, S/PV. 3112, 2 September, 1992.

[100] Jane E. Stromseth, "Iraq's Repression of its Civilian Population," p. 96. This omission did not seriously hamper the efforts of the Guards. The humanitarian program in the south was gradually brought to an end due to improved conditions and therefore the presence of the UNGCI in the south was no longer required. Maria Keating, UN Humanitarian Affairs Advisor, Office of the Iraq Program, interview with author, 21 June, 1999.

[101] Yohannes Mengesha, Principal Officer, Office of the Deputy Secretary-General, DHA. Interview with author, New York, 18 June, 1999.

Northern Iraq 1991   61

These constraints on the degree of protection and monitoring which the coalition force was able to provide the Kurdish refugees and the UN Guards had an impact on the degree of co-operation which the Iraqi government was prepared to extend to the UN. As the coalition presence dwindled, so too did the level of Iraqi government co-operation with the UN. Because the UN Guards were deployed on the basis of consent, the Iraqi government could dictate to a large degree the nature of their deployment which it did once international attention was focused elsewhere in the world. The fact that the Guards were deployed into areas that the Iraqi government in practice exercised little control over, with only side arms and in limited numbers means that the UNGCI was not regarded by the Iraqi government as a threat to its interests.[102]

The third MOU between the UN and the government of Iraq continued to govern the relations between the two parties and the deployment of the UNGCI through the end of 1995. Co-operation between the UN and the Iraqi government was positive during this period.[103] In December 1995, there were more than eighty Guards deployed in three governates in northern Iraq; Erbil, Suleimaniyah and Dohuk. A number of attacks on UNGCI personnel and UN vehicles occurred in 1993 and 1994, as well as a bomb attacks on a UNGCI patrol in December, 1995. Though responsibility for the attacks was never determined, the majority occurred close to the lines of confrontation between Kurdish factions, and not in Iraqi government controlled areas.[104]

Conclusion

For the purposes of this study it is important to recognise that while the coalition responded to the humanitarian crisis in northern Iraq in the spring of 1991, their actions were not authorized by the UN Security Council. Nor can this episode be regarded as an indication that the members of the Security Council responded to the Kurdish exodus by authorizing a forcible military intervention into Iraq at the expense of Iraq's sovereign rights. The significance of resolution 688 lies in the fact that it insisted that the Iraqi government allow international humanitarian agencies access to all the Iraqi civilians in need and also condemned the Iraqi government's repression of its civilian population. To this end the Security Council was commenting on, and expressing its disapproval of, the behaviour of the Iraqi government. This meant that the members of the Council were concerning themselves with matters which normally are considered to fall "essentially within the domestic jurisdiction" of a state. However, in the case of Iraq, the Council members drew a clear connection between internal actions and external ramifications - the justification for their action stemmed from the exodus of Kurdish refugees which threatened to overwhelm the neighbouring states of

---

[102] Ibid.

[103] Maria Keating, interview with author.

[104] "DHA Review of the United Nations Guards Contingent in Iraq (UNGCI)," Iraq Programme, *Department of Humanitarian Affairs*, New York, 15 August, 1997.

Turkey and Iran. By characterizing the movement of refugees as a threat to international peace and security, the members of the Security Council arrogated to themselves the authority to consider the matter and take any appropriate measures they thought necessary to counter the threat. In this case, the extent of the measures that could be agreed upon within the Council was the expression of censure and demands for rectification as found in resolution 688.

A unique combination of political circumstances made the adoption of resolution 688 possible. Not least of these was the publicly voiced contention from some Western members of the Security Council that the UN lay at the beginning of a new era in which human rights should be increasingly promoted.[105] When the support of these countries was combined with those who agreed with the characterization of refugee flows as a threat to international peace and security, the adoption of resolution 688 became possible. But this was as far as most UNSC states were prepared to go, and even this step has to be regarded in the context of a post-war scenario in which the terms of the cease-fire meant that the UN was already deeply involved in the "internal affairs" of Iraq.[106]

While political intervention by the Council was possible, active UN military intervention or clear Chapter VII authorization for the coalition intervention did not occur. The actions and attitudes of the Council showed the extent to which they were still very much concerned about respecting Article 2(7), and that the consent of Iraq was necessary for any action to be taken by the UN in the absence of Chapter VII agreement within the Council. This centrality is demonstrated by the interpretation made by the Secretary-General of resolution 688, the frequency with which Article 2(7) was reaffirmed by both supporters and non-supporters of the resolution in the debate on it, and also the fact that the coalition states were keen to adhere the laws governing intervention to the furthest extent possible - either by getting a resolution clearly under Chapter VII, or ultimately pressuring the Iraqi government to consent to the UN Guards.

Following the Gulf War, Iraq was not in a strong position to militarily oppose the intervention of the coalition forces into its northern territories. As a result, it was largely through political means that Iraqi authorities attempted to obstruct the creation of the safe areas. Iraq sought to use the United Nations as a means of preventing the coalition states from deploying into Iraq, relying on the in-built restrictions of the UN Charter to prevent the organisation from acting in a manner that was inconsistent with Iraq's wishes. Generally, the Iraqi strategy can be seen as encouraging and accepting UN involvement in order to placate the humanitarian concerns of the international community, bring about the withdrawal of the coalition forces, while also trying to prevent the deployment of any UN police or peacekeeping force. Though Iraq agreed to the establishment of United Nations humanitarian centres, its consent as expressed in the MOU must, to some extent, be regarded as being elicited under duress. Faced with the coalition relief effort in its northern territory, and the assembled coalition air force at bases in Turkey providing backup to the relief effort in *Operation Poised Hammer*, the Iraqi

---

[105] *UN Document*, S/PV. 3046, 31 January, 1992.

[106] Sean D. Murphy, *Humanitarian Intervention*, p. 194.

government had little choice but to opt for the less intrusive presence of the UN humanitarian operation. But what is perhaps even more significant for the purposes of this study is the fact that although it had suffered military defeat at the hands of the coalition and was operating under the threat of *Operation Poised Hammer*, the Iraqi government was still able to negotiate firmly with the UN as to the nature and function of the relief effort throughout Iraq authorized by resolution 688.[107] This was primarily due to its rights as a sovereign state protected by the UN Charter, and the willingness of other states to respect these rights.

The case of northern Iraq thus serves to demonstrate the continued centrality of the principle of consent to the Security Council. It allowed the UN organisation to deploy a security presence into Iraq despite the fact that the Security Council was not prepared to authorize military intervention under Chapter VII of the Charter. The principle of consent also created a situation in which the government of Iraq was willing to agree to the deployment of the UN Guards because it, as host government, retained some ability to shape the nature of the deployment. This limited the scope of the UN initiatives but the organisation was nevertheless able to provide some measure of protection to the refugees, while simultaneously appeasing concerns within the UNSC that the sovereignty of Iraq not be violated.

---

[107] Ramsbotham and Woodhouse, *Humanitarian Intervention in Contemporary Conflict*, p. 82.

Chapter 3

Somalia

Soon after the UNSC's adoption of resolution 688 and its decision to classify the flow of Kurdish refugees as a threat to international peace and security, another humanitarian crisis emerged in Somalia. Like the case of northern Iraq, it also tested the newly declared humanitarian priorities of the UNSC members.[1] However, Somalia proved to be the watershed of post-Cold War peacekeeping operations. The Security Council members had to cope with a failed state in which the national government had collapsed and civil order had disintegrated. This situation created new issues of consent with which the members of the UNSC had to cope. For example, the lack of a sovereign government in Somalia meant that UN had to determine which local authority it was most appropriate to negotiate with. A second problem of a consent-based approach was revealed when the United Nations Operation in Somalia (UNOSOM I) proved ineffective in the anarchic atmosphere of Somalia. The UNSC had then to decide how it would attempt to overcome this lack of local consent in order to effectively deliver humanitarian aid to the Somali civilian population. To this end, the UNSC rejected consent in preference for what were expected to be more effective methods based on the threat and use of force. However, this transition beyond consent also proved to be fraught with difficulty. On the whole, Somalia tested the UNSC's ability to respond to the challenges of peacekeeping in anarchic, intra-state conflicts in the face of severe humanitarian need. The difficulties of moving beyond consent towards a reliance on the threat and use of force proved to be a traumatic failure for the UN organisation. It prompted a re-emphasis within the Security Council on consent-based peacekeeping methods, but also dampened the ability of the UN to respond to subsequent humanitarian crises.

The UN Becomes Involved

In response to the worsening humanitarian and political situation in Somali in December 1991, the outgoing Secretary-General of the United Nations, Javier Pérez de Cuéllar, decided to dispatch his Under Secretary-General for Special Political Affairs, James Jonah, to gain a first hand understanding of the prevailing conditions in the country. Jonah subsequently led a team of UN officials to Somalia in early January 1992 with the aim of encouraging political reconciliation among the fighting clans and securing unimpeded access for humanitarian relief

---

[1] See Chapter 1.

Somalia   65

efforts to those areas most in need.[2]   Upon arriving in Somalia, Jonah was confronted with myriad political and humanitarian challenges, not least of which was the ongoing battle for control of Mogadishu by the two primary clan leaders, Mohammed Farah Aidid and Ali Mahdi Mohamed.[3]   The failure of either man to consolidate power in Somalia following the ouster of Somali President Siad Barre had been one of the primary causes of Somalia's descent into anarchy.

Both Aidid and Ali Mahdi belonged to the United Somalia Congress (USC), a political movement formed in Rome in 1989 in order to bring about the overthrow of the Barre regime.   Despite this common aim, its members were not politically united but divided into three factions; one operating covertly in Mogadishu, the original faction in Rome and a military wing based in Ethiopia. The military wing was led by Aidid, who had defected from his post as Somalia's Ambassador to India in order to lead it.   Ali Mahdi, who was supported by the Rome USC faction, resented Aidid's intrusion onto the USC political scene.   When Aidid was declared chairman of the USC at a hastily organised USC Congress at Mustahil, near the Somalia-Ethiopia border, the Rome USC faction and Ali Mahdi disputed the validity of the Congress and refused to recognise Aidid's claim to the chairmanship.[4]

When Siad Barre was driven from Somalia on 27 January 1991, the chairman of USC Mogadishu, Hussein Omar Bod, appointed Ali Mahdi interim President of Somalia for twenty eight days.   Aidid was not consulted about Ali Mahdi's appointment but did not consider it endorsed by the USC as a whole, since only 4 out of a total of 105 USC central committee members had attended the meeting at which the appointment was made.   Faced with the more immediate threat of a counter attack by Barre's remaining military forces, Aidid opted to temporarily ignore the political challenge from Ali Mahdi and concentrate on consolidating the military victory over Barre.[5]

On 5 June, Ali Mahdi and Aidid signed an agreement that removed the distinctions between the three UNSC factions and created a united political movement.   This obliged Ali Mahdi to consult with the USC on key policy issues in his role as President.   One month later a USC congress appointed Aidid as its Chairman.   At the national level, Aidid was to be responsible for the formation of the Somali national army and Ali Mahdi was to form a new national government.[6] This arrangement lasted for only three months until Aidid refused to continue

---

[2] *The Blue Helmets*, 3rd Ed., UN Department of Pubic Information, New York, 1996, p. 288.
[3] In a early sign of the nature of Somali politics and of the difficulties the UN would face, the humanitarian airlift was temporarily suspended when Jonah flew to Mogadishu because Aidid's forces began to shell the airport.   This was to force Jonah's plane to divert to a second airport, controlled by the SNA, where Aidid could meet the UN envoy personally. See "UN Under Attack for Somalia 'Bungling,'" *The Independent*, 16 January, 1992.
[4] John Drysdale, *Whatever Happened to Somalia?*, Haan Associates, London, 1994, pp. 15-16.
[5] Ibid., p. 29.
[6] John Drysdale, "Foreign Military Intervention in Somalia: The Root Cause of the Shift from UN Peacekeeping to Peacemaking and its Consequences," in Walter Clarke and Jeffrey Herbst, eds., *Learning From Somalia*, Westview Press, Oxford, 1997, p. 119.

Understanding the UN Security Council

recognising Ali Mahdi as President, accusing him of exceeding his mandate, failing in his obligations to the USC Central Committee, and violating the 1960 Somalia constitution. This constitution had formed the cornerstone of the national reconciliation process.[7] War between Aidid and Ali Mahdi subsequently broke out on 17 November, 1991 and the fighting was primarily focused on gaining control of Mogadishu.

Jonah's mission to Somalia could not therefore be simply focused on negotiating improved humanitarian access with the host government since one had not yet been formed and a number of local actors, primarily Aidid and Ali Mahdi, were fighting for control. This meant that Jonah's first attempt at involving the UN in the ongoing dispute was fraught with political implications: to deal primarily with Ali Mahdi risked raising the ire of Aidid and yet Ali Mahdi had been declared interim President. Jonah was forced to develop an *ad hoc* political strategy since throughout 1991 the UN's activities in Somalia had primarily occurred through its relief agencies and had been focused on the delivery of humanitarian aid, with no thought given to greater political involvement.[8] Indeed, the members of the Security Council had been reluctant to become involved.[9] One former UN official has described the attitude of the UNSC to the Somali conflict at this time as "shamefully casual."[10]

As a result of his first trip to Somalia, Jonah reported to the new Secretary-General, Boutros Boutros-Ghali, that there was near unanimous support among the Somali factions for UN assistance in bringing about national reconciliation and the establishment of a cease-fire in Mogadishu. Aidid's was the lone voice of dissent. This positive reaction to Jonah's mission, coupled with the receipt of a letter from Ali Mahdi's appointed Prime Minister, Omer Arteh Qhalib, requesting the Security Council to devise a strategy for cementing peace in Somalia, resulted in the issue being placed on the agenda of the Security Council on 23 January 1992.[11] Omer Arteh Qhalib's request had been sought by members of the Security Council in order to overcome Chinese objections to the UNSC becoming involved in the internal affairs of Somalia.[12] Jonah recommended the deployment of an armed peacekeeping force in Somalia, to which Aidid responded by stating that his faction, the Somali National Alliance (SNA), was not interested in any outside military intervention.[13]

In response to the request of Omer Arteh Qhalib and the recommendations made by Boutros-Ghali, the members of the Security Council expressed concern that the situation in Somalia could constitute a threat to international peace and

---

[7] Drysdale, "Foreign Military Intervention in Somalia," p. 120.

[8] John Hirsch and Robert Oakley, *Somalia and Operation Restore Hope*, United States Institute of Peace Press, Washington D.C., 1995. p. 17.

[9] Elizabeth Lindenmayer, interview with author, 17 June, 1999.

[10] Confidential interview.

[11] *UN Document*, S/23445, 20 January, 1992.

[12] Confidential interview.

[13] Mohammed Dirye Abdullahi, *Fiasco in Somalia: US-UN Intervention*, Africa Institute of South Africa, 1995, p. 11.

Somalia 67

security.[14] Based on this characterisation of the conflict, they then decided to establish an arms embargo on Somalia, doing so under the Chapter VII provisions of the UN Charter. In addition, they asked the Secretary-General to increase the humanitarian assistance provided by the UN to Somalia and appoint a co-ordinator to oversee its delivery. These decisions were outlined in resolution 733.[15] Importantly, the resolution did not adopt Jonah's recommendation for a peacekeeping force primarily because the United States was not prepared to meet the increased financial costs of a new operation. The US was also concerned about the legality of an intervention without the invitation of the main host parties.[16]

Boutros-Ghali forwarded copies of resolution 733 to both Ali Mahdi and Aidid. Ali Mahdi subsequently confirmed his acceptance of the resolution, but Aidid's position was less clear. In a letter to the Secretary-General, Aidid expressed certain questions about the text of the resolution and asked that the Council reconsider the matter, without expressly indicating either his support or disapproval of the resolution.[17] The Secretary-General also invited the two main belligerents to consultations at the UN Headquarters in New York in order to discuss the establishment of a cease-fire in Mogadishu, as requested by the Security Council in paragraph 3 of resolution 733. The UN position on the Somali parties that were to be involved in these talks was simply to include the two main factions involved in the conflict around Mogadishu. The consultations did not imply official recognition of any particular faction. The talks were partially successful when both parties committed themselves to a cessation of hostilities and cease-fire within Mogadishu. However, the representatives of Ali Mahdi expressed their doubt that any cease-fire arrangement would hold without an international supervisory mechanism.[18]

Consultations between the UN and the two main factions continued in Mogadishu on 29 February, along with representatives from the Organisation for African Unity (OAU) and the League of Arab States (LAS). Intending to consolidate on the progress made in New York, the joint UN-OAU-LAS delegation included a UN military advisor whose role was to assist the parties to work out the details of the cease-fire and discuss the modalities for a possible UN monitoring role. In a report to the Security Council, Boutros-Ghali stressed that this planned monitoring role consisted of the deployment of a small number of unarmed observers in order to verify and supervise the cease-fire. Ali Mahdi expressed his satisfaction with these arrangements and even went so far as to request the presence of a UN peacekeeping force to monitor it as well as assist with

---

[14] The Council was motivated in part by news that there had been a dramatic increase of the number of Somali refugees fleeing to Kenya and consequently threatening the stability of that country. "Refugees Threaten Kenya," *The Times*, 7 February, 1992.

[15] UNSC Resolution 733, 23 January, 1992.

[16] Hirsch and Oakley, *Somalia and Operation Restore Hope*, p. 38.

[17] *UN Document*, S/23693, 11 March, 1992. Boutros-Ghali's report makes no mention as to the specific details of Aidid's concerns about the resolution and the author has not been able to discover what these concerns were through interviews with individuals involved.

[18] Ibid.

68 *Understanding the UN Security Council*

disarmament and the delivery of relief supplies. Aidid's agreement to the proposed UN observer mission was more difficult to obtain but, eventually, both he and Ali Mahdi signed an agreement on the implementation of the cease-fire on 3 March. Although Aidid insisted that the observers wear civilian clothing with UN berets and armbands for identification, he nonetheless formally agreed to the UN Military Observer (UNMO) deployment before representatives of the UN, the OAU and the LAS. The agreement stated that the two leaders:

> Hereby agree to take immediate steps, personally as well as through the persons under my command, for the implementation of measures aimed at stabilising the cease-fire by means of a United Nations monitoring mechanism.[19]

In response to the limited political progress that had been made between the two main belligerents, the Security Council issued resolution 746, urging the parties to respect their commitments as well as assist the Secretary-General in coping with the dire humanitarian situation.[20] In the debate among the members of the Security Council prior to their adoption of resolution 746, there was agreement that the nature of the conflict in Somalia, with its severe humanitarian repercussions and the lack of a central government, required the involvement of the United Nations. The two primary reasons advanced by members of the Council for action were the threat posed by the conflict to regional security and the severe humanitarian effects of the conflict. As the representative of India, Mr. Gharekhan argued:

> There is no single political authority today in Somalia with which the world community can interact and to which it can turn for a resolution of this problem. The people of Somalia, innocent men, women and children caught in a horrendous web of internecine warfare, cry out for help. The sheer magnitude of the problem and its continuation constitute a threat to the peace and security of the region, as mentioned in the draft resolution before us. The Somali situation is thus *sui generis* and, as the Secretary-General points out, has eluded conventional solutions. The principles drawn from the United Nations Charter, which the Security Council must always build upon in its consideration of the issues before it, have nevertheless to be applied in this case also. But as the Secretary-General himself concludes, new avenues and innovative methods commensurate with the humanitarian and political situation at hand need to be explored to facilitate a peace settlement. [21]

Like India, many members of the Council, while recognising the lack of a government in Somalia, nevertheless believed that the involvement of the UN should remain consistent with the principles of the UN Charter. This included undertaking actions that were consistent with Somalia's identity as a sovereign state. As the representative of Organisation of the Islamic Conference (OIC) argued before the Council:

---

[19] Ibid.

[20] UNSC Resolution 746, 17 March, 1992.

[21] *UN Document*, S/PV .3060, 17 March, 1992.

Somalia 69

[the members of the OIC] have affirmed their commitment to the restoration and preservation of the unity, sovereignty, territorial integrity and political independence of Somalia. In view of the dangers inherent in the present situation in Somalia, it is necessary that the international community as a whole reiterate its commitment to these principles.

Similarly, the representative of China, Mr. Li Daoyu stated:

It is our hope and belief that United Nations activities in Somalia will be conducted in accordance with the purpose and principles of the Charter of the United Nations, with full respect for Somalia's independence and sovereignty, so as to make due contributions to the early restoration of a just and lasting peace in Somalia.[22]

Even at this early stage of the United Nations involvement in Somalia, there were indications that the UN, as an organisation, was responding to the internal conflict among the factions on two levels. The first was pragmatic and was evidenced by the decision of the Secretary-General and Jonah to pursue negotiations with the two main belligerents so as to secure as cease-fire that would, in turn, facilitate the delivery of humanitarian supplies. This approach was dictated by the realities on the ground. The second level was the disposition of the Council to continue to regard Somalia as a member state of the United Nations despite the absence of a central government. The necessity of such an approach was stressed in the UNSC debate and was demonstrated by the efforts made to obtain the official request for UNSC involvement from Omer Arteh Qhalib, despite the fact he was living in Saudi Arabia.

Consistent with resolution 764, a UN technical team was dispatched to Somalia and began detailed negotiations with both Aidid and Ali Mahdi on the UN role in supervising the cease-fire. Unlike Ali Mahdi, Aidid stressed his opposition to any UN peacekeeping force or other form of UN military presence. He was suspicious of any type of UN deployment since he believed that it would strengthen the position of Ali Mahdi, just as Jonah's diplomatic visit to Mogadishu in December 1991 had, in Aidid's view, demonstrated UN support for Ali Mahdi's claim to the Presidency. This had been caused by Jonah's public announcement that Ali Mahdi had agreed to the deployment of UNMOs and the UN's support for this position.[23]

Despite the differing positions of the two faction leaders, both signed an agreement on 27 March allowing the deployment of UNMOs to monitor the cease-fire as well as the deployment of UN security personnel to protect UN employees and safeguard UN humanitarian initiatives in Mogadishu. Ali Mahdi again encouraged a more expansive role for the UN, suggesting that a force of up to 4500 personnel be deployed, together with air and armour support, to stabilize the security situation in and around Mogadishu.[24]

---

[22] Ibid.

[23] Drysdale, "Foreign Military Intervention in Somalia," p. 120.

[24] *UN Document*, S/32829, annex I and II, 21 April, 1992.

70 *Understanding the UN Security Council*

Based on the agreement reached between the UN technical team and the two main factions in Mogadishu, the Secretary-General recommended to the Security Council members that they authorize the deployment of a contingent of UN military observers in order to monitor the cease-fire and a security force to provide a military escort for humanitarian relief convoys. For the security personnel, Boutros-Ghali suggested:

> Their task will be to provide the United Nations convoys of relief supplies with a sufficiently strong military escort to deter attack and to fire effectively in self-defence if deterrence should not prove effective. [25]

Like the UNMOs, the security personnel were to wear national uniforms with UN insignia. The recommended size of the unit was 500 personnel, but this would only be confirmed after consultation with the two parties. Similarly, the appointment of the Force Commander, and the nations from which the troops would be contributed were both issues which, the Secretary-General noted, could only be finalised following consultations with the two local factions. [26]

The Security Council members decided to follow the Secretary-General's recommendations and authorized the deployment of the United Nations Operation in Somalia (UNOSOM) on 24 April. [27] The Security Council requested Boutros-Ghali to immediately deploy the 50 UNMOs, and its members agreed in principle to establish as soon as possible a UN security force consistent with the Secretary-General's report following further consultations with the parties in Mogadishu. The Secretary-General was also authorized by the members of the Security Council to appoint a Special Representative to oversee UNOSOM. On 28 April, Mohammed Sahnoun was asked by Boutros-Ghali to take up this position.

The first, and what would prove to be the most difficult, task that confronted Sahnoun upon his arrival in Mogadishu on 4 May was negotiating the deployment of the UN observers and security personnel. Aidid was still wary of any involvement by the UN. Though he had been somewhat reassured as to its impartiality following his March consultations with Robert Gallagher, the Canadian UN official who led the technical team, Aidid still felt that the presence of UN military personnel would bolster Ali Mahdi's claim to the Presidency. Negotiations between Sahnoun and Aidid's faction began on 9 May and continued over the course of the next five weeks, initially focusing on the deployment of the military observers. Aidid insisted that the observers wear only blue berets and arm bands over civilian clothing to identify them as UN personnel. He also wanted to reduce the number of observers, below the fifty authorised by resolution 751. [28] Finally, on 21 June Sahnoun was able to convince Aidid to agree to the

---

[25] *UN Document*, S/23892, 21 April, 1992.
[26] Ibid.
[27] UN Security Council Resolution 751, 24 April, 1992.
[28] Drysdale, *Whatever Happened to Somalia?*, p. 50.

Somalia 71

deployment of all fifty observers clothed in their national military uniforms with UN insignia.[29]

The agreement was however, short-lived. On 25 June a Russian aircraft with UN markings was found to be carrying currency and military equipment from Nairobi to Ali Mahdi's faction in Mogadishu. Though the aircraft had been previously under charter to the World Food Programme (WFP), the UN claimed that the contract had expired and the UN markings had simply not been removed from the aircraft. Aidid was unconvinced and consequently suspended his agreement for the deployment of the UN observers. The three UNMOs, who had already arrived in Mogadishu, were served with an expulsion notice by the SNA.[30] The situation was only resolved after Sahnoun got the agreement of Ali Mahdi not to put the currency into circulation. The SNA and Aidid then agreed to allow the UNMO deployment to resume, a process that was finally completed in July 1992, three months after the adoption of resolution 751.[31]

After dealing with the crisis over the military observers, Sahnoun then focused on negotiating the deployment of the UN security personnel to protect the aid effort in Mogadishu. He met with Aidid and three other chairmen of the SNA and was eventually able to secure their agreement for the deployment of 500 UN personnel for the purposes of ensuring the security and safety of aid workers on 12 August. The SNA specifically distinguished between the security personnel and normal UN peacekeepers, since they would not agree to the deployment of the latter. The agreement was also altered to refer to "security personnel" rather than "security force," the former title being more acceptable to Aidid. The security personnel were only to be stationed in the port, airport and along transit routes to relief storage and distribution centres. Importantly, Sahnoun drafted a hand-written addition to the agreement at the insistence of the SNA, stating that the number of security personnel deployed could only be increased with the consent of the local parties.[32] Aidid had apparently been aware of a report to the Security Council written by Boutros-Ghali on 22 July in which he recommended to the Council that the number of personnel in the security force (the deployment of which was still to be negotiated) be increased to cope with the deepening humanitarian crisis in Somalia.[33]

Though the members of the Council opted not to adopt this recommendation of the Secretary-General in the next resolution pertaining to Somalia, resolution 767, they nonetheless warned the parties of their intent to ensure the general stabilisation of the situation in Somalia.[34] Paragraph 4 of the resolution reads:

---

[29] *UN Document*, S/24179, 25 June, 1992.

[30] "UN Men Ordered Out," *The Guardian*, 7 July, 1992. Despite the expulsion notice, the three observers were ordered by New York to remain in Somalia.

[31] *The Blue Helmets*, p. 291.

[32] Drysdale, *Whatever Happened to Somalia?*, p. 52, and Drysdale, "Foreign Military Intervention in Somalia," p. 124.

[33] Drysdale, "Foreign Military Intervention in Somalia," p. 123.

[34] UNSC Resolution 767, 24 July, 1992.

72 *Understanding the UN Security Council*

> Calls upon the parties, movements and factions in Somalia to co-operate with the United Nations with a view to the urgent deployment of the United Nations security personnel called for in paragraphs 4 and 5 of its resolution 751 (1992), and otherwise assist in the general stabilisation of the situation in Somalia. In the absence of such co-operation, the Security Council does not exclude other measures to deliver humanitarian assistance to Somalia.

The 500 Pakistani UN security personnel were deployed in Mogadishu on 14 September, 1992. However their effectiveness was to be undermined by the decision of the Security Council to authorize an increase in the strength of UNOSOM by 3000 personnel in resolution 775.[35] This expansion was consistent with the recommendations made by the Secretary-General in his July report to the Council, and the rationale for it was the increasing severity of the famine that was striking the fertile, river areas of Somalia and aggravating the humanitarian crisis. However, neither Sahnoun or Aidid had been consulted about the increase and both were informed of the actions by the Security Council by way of a public BBC radio broadcast.[36] Aidid was enraged as the authorization was in violation of the agreement made between Sahnoun and the SNA on 12 August that specifically stated that any increase in the number of UN personnel required the consent of the local parties. Sahnoun, undermined by New York, felt the announcement untimely and made without proper consultation.[37]

Aidid used the opportunity presented by resolution 775 to further frustrate the deployment of the UNOSOM personnel. Prior to the adoption of the resolution, one of his key advisors, Mohammed Ahmed Noor stated: "We cannot allow foreigners. Bringing in foreign troops is an infringement of the sovereignty of the people of Somalia."[38] Sahnoun sought to negotiate the deployment of the enlarged contingent of UNOSOM personnel throughout most of the Somali countryside, but this merely served to heighten Aidid's suspicions about the UN's true intentions. The expansion of the UN into areas, such as Bosaso and Berbera, where there was no humanitarian emergency, suggested to him a more subtle UN political agenda.[39] Aidid responded to Sahnoun's request by insisting that the UN Pakistani security personnel in Mogadishu train and equip a new Somali police force in the city. Sahnoun accepted Aidid's rationale that this police force could eventually serve as a replacement once the UN security personnel departed. Aidid refused to agree to the deployment of additional security personnel to the city of Kismayo until the police force had been recruited and commenced its training.[40]

At the same time, the language used by the UNSC in its resolutions on Somalia was becoming increasingly aggressive. Resolution 767, for example, clearly determined the Somali situation "to constitute a threat to international peace

---

[35] UNSC Resolution 775, 28 August, 1992.

[36] Hirsch and Oakley, *Somalia and Operation Restore Hope*, p. 26.

[37] Mohammed Sahnoun, *Somalia: The Missed Opportunities*, United States Institute of Peace Press, Washington D.C., 1994, p. 53.

[38] "Somalia Force Opposes UN Aid Plan," *International Herald Tribune*, 8-9 August, 1992.

[39] Drysdale, *Whatever Happened to Somalia?* p. 62.

[40] Drysdale, "Foreign Military Intervention in Somalia" p. 125.

and security" under Article 39, unlike earlier resolutions that had only implied that Article 39 might be invoked in the future.[41] It is likely that such a characterization of the situation was made by the members of the UNSC in order to place pressure on the Somali factions through the possibility of action under Chapter VII. Such action was only possible if the situation was characterized as a threat to international peace and security. In reality, the implications of the Somali conflict for wider regional and international security were limited.[42]

During this time, Sahnoun was coming under increasing criticism from the UN Secretariat. At a donor's conference in Geneva on 12 October 1992, Sahnoun stated that the complexity and sensitivity of the political and military situation in Somalia was such that it would be impossible for UN security personnel to function effectively without the co-operation and support of local Somali forces.[43] In order to simplify the deployment of the expanded number of UNOSOM personnel at various ports throughout the country, Sahnoun had attempted to find a consensus among the faction leaders, including Ali Mahdi and Aidid. This strategy was in part intended to ease concerns among the local parties that the UN was intent on establishing a military occupation of the country. As part of this approach, Sahnoun tended to overlook much of Aidid's anti-UN posturing in order to secure his co-operation on the ground. Because of this, Sahnoun was criticised within UN headquarters as giving Aidid an implicit veto over further troop deployments in Mogadishu and insufficiently defending the credibility of the UN organisation.[44]

Sahnoun also adopted this strategy because he realised that in the face of continued intransigence from Aidid, it was likely that the Security Council would take action under Article 42 of the UN Charter. Sahnoun advised Aidid to this effect in three separate meetings in September 1992, but Aidid remained unimpressed. There was a growing frustration within both the UN Secretariat and the Secretary-General's Office with Aidid. This consequently increased pressure towards the adoption of more forceful UN strategy in Somalia. Faced with this growing pressure and feeling as though he had lost the confidence of the Secretary-General, Sahnoun resigned from his position.[45]

The desire of the UN Secretariat and, in particular, of the Secretary-General to adopt a more pro-active approach to the situation in Somalia as a means of coping with the demands of the worsening humanitarian crisis, was in part

---

[41] Mark R. Hutchinson, "Restoring Hope: UN Security Council Resolutions For Somalia and an Expanded Doctrine of Humanitarian Intervention," *Harvard International Law Journal*, vol. 34, 1993, p. 628. UNSC Resolution 767, 24 July, 1992. Resolutions 746 (17 March, 1992) and 751 (24 April, 1992) had both expressed the UNSC's concern "that the continuation of the situation in Somalia constitutes a threat to international peace and security."

[42] James Mayall, ed., *The New Interventionism*, 1991-1994, Cambridge University Press, Cambridge, 1996, p. 3.

[43] Sahnoun, *Somalia: The Missed Opportunities*, p. 27.

[44] Hirsch and Oakley, *Somalia and Operation Restore Hope*, pp. 29-30.

[45] Drysdale, "Foreign Military Intervention in Somalia," p. 126.

74 *Understanding the UN Security Council*

evidenced by two factors. One was the publication of Boutros-Ghali's *An Agenda for Peace*, with his revised definition of peacekeeping. By suggesting a shift towards a more robust form of peacekeeping, less beholden to consent, he hoped that the UN could fulfil a more expansive role in securing international peace. The situation in Somalia thus presented the United Nations and its Secretary-General with a situation in which the lack of consent from the local parties was delaying the deployment of UN security personnel to assist with the delivery and protection of humanitarian relief. It provided the ideal opportunity to put into practice the new, post-Cold War version of peacekeeping which was less centred around consent.[46] Yet this new approach was produced despite a lack of experience and understanding in dealing with internal conflicts, particularly ones in which there was no existing host government with which to negotiate and the mission objectives were largely humanitarian.[47]

The Secretary-General was also frustrated by the lacklustre response of many UN member states to the UN's appeal for financial and material assistance for Somalia. In particular he felt, along with representatives of the OAU and LAS, that the response of the UN Security Council members to the Somali crisis was insufficient.[48] He believed the UNSC was focusing too much on the situation in Bosnia at the risk of ineffectiveness in Somalia.[49] These two factors meant that Boutros-Ghali and other senior officials in New York were not willing to have the implementation of the operation's mandate effectively held hostage by Aidid, particularly once the members of the Council began to devote more resources and attention to the crisis.

The implementation of UNOSOM's mandate, including a 100-day action plan to cope with the humanitarian crisis and put the country back on the road to economic self-sufficiency, was hampered due to disagreements with local factions as to the UN's role. In one case, the Pakistani UN contingent deployed at the airport came to an arrangement whereby they would take control of the airport area, replacing a militia subclan of the Hawadle who had been protecting the facility. This was a necessary move in order to open up the airport to humanitarian flights, but it worked contrary to the interests of the SNA. When the agreement was announced on the BBC, Aidid, who had had no warning of the deal, was outraged. He interpreted the UN's actions as an attempt to undermine his authority and threatened to remove the Pakistanis and UNOSOM from Somalia.[50] Aidid also

---

[46] Coulon, *Soldiers of Diplomacy*, p. 8.

[47] Elisabeth Lindenmayer, interview with author, 17 June, 1999. See also Ioan Lewis and James Mayall, "Somalia," in James Mayall, ed., *The New Interventionism*, p. 109.

[48] Hirsch and Oakley, *Somalia and Operation Restore Hope*, p. 37.

[49] *UN Document*, S/24333, 21 July, 1992.

[50] Terrence Lyons and Ahmed I. Samatar, *Somalia: State Collapse, Military Intervention and Strategies for Political Reconstruction*, The Brookings Institution, Washington D.C., 1995, p. 75. The Hawadle clan which controlled the airport leaned towards Ali Mahdi in Mogadishu politics. They had made an agreement with the SNA on 12 August to guarantee the security of the airport in return for a portion of the landing fees. When repeated fire fights and looting of overland convoys worsened around the airport, the UNOSOM

warned that any forcible deployment of UNOSOM would be met with violence and as if to reinforce this threat, Pakistani troops at the airport came under SNA gun fire and mortar barrages. Additionally, relief ships attempting to enter into the port of Mogadishu were shelled by Aidid's forces. This increased tension between the SNA and the UN was the first task to be confronted by Ismat Kittani, an Iraqi diplomat who was appointed as the new Special Representative of the Secretary-General on 8 November.

In response to the SNA hostility towards the UN, a spokesman of the Secretary-General issued a public statement, on 27 November, to the people of Somalia in an attempt to dispel concerns that the UN was attempting to force its control of the country. In highlighting the humanitarian aims of UNOSOM the spokesman stated:

> In undertaking this task, the United Nations can only succeed with the consent and support of the Somali people. The purposes and methods of the United Nations under Mr. Kittani's leadership will remain unchanged as set forth by the Security Council.[51]

Yet the atmosphere in Somalia continued to deteriorate, with increased attacks on civilian aid workers throughout the country and the looting of relief supplies which had come to form the new backbone of an alternative Somali economy controlled by the militias. Boutros-Ghali wrote to the President of the Security Council on 27 November, informing the members of the Council of these developments. In the final paragraph of his letter, Boutros-Ghali suggested that under the then prevailing circumstances, the operation of UNOSOM was "exceedingly difficult." Therefore, he argued that in further considering the matter he would "not exclude the possibility that it may become necessary to review the basic premises and principles of the United Nations effort in Somalia."[52] In effect, he was asking for a re-appraisal of the UN's reliance on local consent to implement its aid initiatives.

In response to the Secretary-General's letter, the members of the Security Council met in informal discussions on 25 November. They believed that the situation was intolerable and expressed doubt that the methods then being employed by UNOSOM would be sufficient to bring the situation under control. During the consultations, there was strong support for the Boutros-Ghali's view that the situation demanded that the possible use of Chapter VII measures be used in the context of Somalia, and he was therefore asked by the Council to compile a set of recommendations for the Council to consider.[53]

In response to the Council's request, the Secretary-General identified five options that he believed would most adequately meet the aim of ensuring the

---

commander struck a deal with the Hawadle which allowed his UN troops to take over the airport while still giving the Hawadle revenue from landing fees.

[51] *UN Document*, S/24859, 27 November, 1992.

[52] Ibid.

[53] *UN Document*, S/24868, 30 November, 1992.

76 *Understanding the UN Security Council*

delivery of relief supplies to those in need in Somalia.[54] The first option was to continue the deployment of UNOSOM, intensifying efforts to complete the deployment of security personnel as authorised by resolution 775. In this scenario, the operation would continue along traditional peacekeeping lines, adhere to the principle of consent and not deploy without the agreement of the local factions. However, Boutros-Ghali discounted this option as not sufficient to meet the humanitarian needs of the country. The second option involved withdrawing the military component of UNOSOM entirely and leaving the aid agencies to negotiate independently with the local factions. This option was similarly discounted due to the expectation that the aid effort, without UN protection, would be severely circumscribed by the anarchic atmosphere of Somalia.

Working from the assumption that more forceful measures were required to cope with the situation, three more options were identified. The third option involved UNOSOM undertaking a show of force in Mogadishu in order to create suitable conditions in that city for the delivery of relief supplies. However, the weakness of such a strategy lay in the fact that while it might be effective in Mogadishu, its effect on militia groups in other parts of the country was likely to be limited. The Secretary- General argued therefore that such a show of force by UNOSOM would need to occur countrywide and would thus stretch the organisational capacity of the UN organisation. The fourth option involved a countrywide collective enforcement operation undertaken by a group of Member states under the authorization of the Security Council. The fifth option would be force an enforcement operation to be carried out under the command and control of the United Nations.

The growing demand in New York for more action and less talk due to the impotence of UNOSOM and the continuing humanitarian crisis, coincided with a growing awareness of the situation in Somalia among members of the Security Council, in particular the United States. While Boutros-Ghali was preparing his list of options for the members of the Security Council, he met with Lawrence Eagleburger, then US Acting Secretary of State. Eagleburger conveyed to the Secretary-General the willingness of the United States to lead a multi-national enforcement operation, under the auspices of the United Nations, with the aim of delivering humanitarian supplies to the Somali people. The Secretary-General, though expressing his preference for forceful action to be taken under the command and control of the UN, recognised the limitations of the organisation and therefore recommended that a group of member states be authorized to undertake the necessary action in Somalia.[55]

UNITAF

The members of the Security Council met on 3 December 1992 to consider the recommendations put forward by the Secretary-General. The draft resolution that

---

[54] Ibid.
[55] Ibid.

the Council members considered represented a significant expansion of the UN's role in the post-Cold War world. It proposed the use of military force to intervene in a UN member state in order to resolve a humanitarian crisis that threatened tens of thousands of lives. The gravity of the situation, both in terms of the situation in Somalia and the proposed expansion of the UN's role in ensuring international peace and security, was not lost on the members of the Council. There were a number of themes that emerged from the discussion of Council members. Many of them, for example, found it appropriate to characterize the growing humanitarian consequences of the famine as an ever-increasing threat to international security. They argued that the Council's role in dealing with such threats, as set out in the UN Charter, made it imperative that they act to counter the crisis. There was also firm support for the Secretary-General's opinion that, having tried to resolve the crisis through traditional means and mechanisms such as negotiation with the local factions, the failure of such measures dictated the adoption of an alternative approach.[56] As the representative of Zimbabwe Mr. Mumbengegwi argued:

> Patient negotiations by the Special Representative of the Secretary-General over a long period of time have shown that the humanitarian imperatives of the Somali crisis cannot be met through conventional methods. The various faction leaders have, for reasons best known to themselves, displayed varying degrees of indifference to the suffering of their own people.

The representative of Russia agreed:

> Obviously, under such circumstances, it is essential that additional and urgent steps should be taken by the United Nations and the international community as a whole...The Russian delegation is convinced that at the present juncture, resolution of the crisis requires the use of international armed forces under the auspices of the Security Council to ensure the delivery and safe keeping of the humanitarian assistance and its distribution to the country's starving population.

Members of the Council were also acutely aware that intervening in Somalia broke new ground in terms of the action taken by the Security Council towards a UN member state. The Ecuadorian representative notably suggested that the sovereignty of the state lay with the Somali people, because of the collapse of the Somali government:

> In Somali there is no Government that can be the interlocutor of the United Nations for the purpose of agreeing upon a humanitarian assistance operation. But the Somali people - solely sovereign in respect of its destiny - is our interlocutor, and we are heeding its call.

By characterizing the UNSC actions as taken in order protect the Somali people, the implicit argument was that Council was defending the sovereign identity of the

---

[56] The comments made by the UNSC members on resolution 794 are found in *UN Document*, S/PV .3145, 3 December, 1992.

state of Somalia. An important criterion for Council members was the fact that the crisis threatened not only the political rights of the Somali people, but also their basic human rights. For this reason, some UNSC members such as France argued that resolution 794 was the Council's next step in a series of actions that demonstrated an increased determination within the Council to expand the role of the United Nations in protecting international peace and security and furthering human rights. Mr. Merimée of France welcomed the resolution as creating a new prerogative for the Security Council:

> We consider this decision, reached after very careful consideration, to be of major importance. For us, the commitment is part of the principle of establishing access to victims and of the right to emergency humanitarian assistance, which my country has so often stressed in recent years...By this resolution the United Nations has demonstrated its capacity to adapt to new challenges and is acting directly in line with the proposals put forward in the Secretary-General's report "An Agenda For Peace".

Members of the Council also expressed the belief that the burden of expectation was on the UN Security Council to cope with the Somali situation. To this end, the representative of Morocco applauded the actions of the Council:

> By authorizing this urgent and exceptional operation, the Security Council is responding to the expectations of the international community as a whole, particularly those of the Arab, African and Muslim communities to which my country belongs.

The view that the Council and its actions were under international scrutiny was accurate. Indeed certain members of the Council itself were attentive to their potential long-term implications and thus attempted to limit the degree of precedent that would be created by the Security Council's action in regard to Somalia. For this reason some Council members made a point of stressing that the adoption of resolution 794 was a unique response to a unique situation. The representative of Zimbabwe noted:

> It is those considerations that have convinced my delegation that the question of Somalia is a unique situation that warrants a unique approach. However, any unique situation and the unique solution adopted create of necessity a precedent against which future, similar situations will be measured. Since the situation in Somalia is the first of its kind to be addressed by the Council, it is essential that it be handled correctly.

Similarly, traditionally conservative and sovereignty-defending China cautioned that:

> the military operation authorized by the draft resolution is an exceptional action in view of the unique situation in Somalia, and its purpose is to create promptly a secure environment in a short period of time for the humanitarian relief effort in Somalia. Once such an environment is created, the military operations should cease.

China had in fact been opposed to the idea of a western-led, UN intervention into Somalia, but due to a political miscalculation found themselves unable to oppose it in the Security Council. They had assumed that African resistance to such a proposal would prevent it from getting beyond the planning stage, and had accordingly agreed to defer to the African position on the issue. However, when the African states supported the US proposal, the Chinese were bound to go along with it.[57]

With resolution 794, the Security Council decided that in addition to the authorized deployment of the UNOSOM, they would endorse the recommendations made by the Secretary-General and accept the offer of the United States to lead an operation to Somalia in order to secure the delivery of relief supplies. Under Chapter VII, the members of the Council authorized "the Secretary-General and member states co-operating to implement the offer [of the US] to use all necessary means to establish as soon as possible a secure environment for humanitarian relief operations in Somalia."[58] Significantly, resolution 794 represented the first time that the members of the UNSC had characterized an internal humanitarian crisis as a threat to international peace and security, thus justifying action under Chapter VII of the Charter.[59]

The most important and supportive member of the Council for the new Chapter VII action authorized by resolution was the United States. In fact, in an unprecedented move, the first draft of resolution 794 had been written in the Pentagon, by US policy makers.[60] After having watered down resolution 733 at the outset of the UN's involvement in Somalia in order to restrict its peacekeeping commitments, the US had come full circle and was now prepared to lead a multi-national enforcement mission.

This political about-face by the Bush administration came about through a variety of factors. In part its motivation stemmed from growing Congressional pressure. In early July, 1991 Senator Nancy Kassebaum had travelled to Somalia to witness first hand the scenes of state collapse and humanitarian need. As a result of her visit, legislation was introduced calling for the deployment of UN forces - without the approval of the Somali factions if necessary - in order to meet the humanitarian needs of the country.[61] Within one week, the resolution had been adopted by both houses of Congress.[62]

In August 1992, the United States had also chosen to expand its direct involvement in Somalia by volunteering to use its air lift capacity to transport the first contingent of UNOSOM troops to Mogadishu. Similarly, the US Agency for International Development (USAID) had, by the end of August, provided some

---

[57] Sir David Hannay, interview with author, 29 November, 1999.

[58] UNSC Resolution 794, 3 December, 1992.

[59] Ioan Lewis and James Mayall, "Somalia," in Mayall, ed. *The New Interventionism*, p. 94.

[60] Walter Clarke, "Failed Visions and Uncertain Mandates," in Clarke and Herbst, eds., *Learning From Somalia*, p. 9.

[61] Harry Johnston and Ted Dagne, "Congress and the Somali Crisis," in Clarke and Herbst, eds., *Learning From Somalia*, p. 192.

[62] US Congressional Resolution 132, 10 August, 1992.

80 *Understanding the UN Security Council*

$149 million of relief assistance during the previous two years.[63] It was not until increasing media reports and an emotive cable from the US ambassador in Kenya on the perceived worsening situation in Somalia, that President Bush considered the issue.[64]

By November, there was increasing pressure on the White House from within the State Department for the deployment of a major UN force to distribute relief supplies. The Pentagon proposed that in the event of such an effort, the US should lead a multi-national operation, as during the Gulf War, with the intention of the unified force being replaced by a UN operation as soon as the situation had been stabilized.[65]

Following consultations between the Joint Chiefs of Staff, the US Central Command, and officials from the Departments of State and Defence, a proposal emerged to use Chapter VII authorization to cope with the near anarchy in Somalia that would confront any US-led coalition effort.[66] During this planning stage, the issue of Somali consent for the operation was not considered since the Somali government had collapsed, and the main issue for the US was whether or not the mission was "doable."[67]

The continuing crisis in Somalia eventually led the Bush administration to approach the UN with its offer to lead an international effort to assist the Somali people. On 3 December, President Bush announced that the United States would lead *Operation Restore Hope* and ensure the delivery of relief supplies to the Somali people.[68]

The US willingness to become engaged in the Somalia crisis was not initially replicated in European capitals. When asked by Boutros-Ghali for assistance, Germany cited constitutional restrictions that prevented it from contributing combat troops to any international force. France argued that it already had too many overseas commitments. Both Britain and Italy declined, Britain citing that it had already committed a significant number of peacekeeping forces to Bosnia. It

---

[63] "US Food Airlift Boosts Somali Aid Effort," *The Financial Times*, 15-16 August, 1992.

[64] Jeffrey Clark, "Debacle in Somalia," *Foreign Affairs*, vol. 72, no. 1,1993, p. 119. For an interesting examination of the media's role in increasing public awareness of the Somali crisis see Jonathan Mermin, "Television News and American Intervention in Somalia: The Myth of a Media-Driven Foreign Policy," *Political Science Quarterly*, vol. 112, no. 3, 1997. The US Ambassador in Kenya was Smith Hempstone. In reality, the US relief airlift, Operation Provide Relief was largely effective and the death rates in the most severely affected parts of Somalia were beginning to fall. See Michael Maren, *The Road To Hell*, The Free Press, New York, 1997, pp. 204-209.

[65] John R. Bolton, "Wrong Turn in Somalia," *Foreign Affairs*, vol. 73, no. 1, 1994, p. 58.

[66] Hirsch and Oakley, *Somalia and Operation Restore Hope*, pp. 42-43. The Powell Doctrine, named after Colin Powell, Chairman of the US Joints Chiefs of Staff, stated that for US military involvement in any situation there had to be a 'doable' mission and the overwhelming threat or use of force, as was used in the Gulf War.

[67] John Hirsch, interview with author, 4 August, 1998.

[68] For a detailed outline of the Bush administration's arrival at the decision to lead UNITAF see "Anatomy of a Decision: How Bush Made Up His Mind to Send Troops to Somalia," *The International Herald Tribune*, 7 December, 1992.

Somalia 81

was only after the US decision to lead a Unified Task Force (UNITAF) that Italy and France agreed to send troops, having in effect had their hand forced by the unexpected American willingness to lead an international coalition.[69] UNITAF would eventually come to involve some thirty-seven thousand troops from twenty contributing countries, deployed over some forty percent of the Somali countryside.[70]

UNITAF-Somali Relations

Relations between the local Somali factions and UNITAF were a significant improvement on those that had existed between UNOSOM and the local parties. Primarily this was due to the decision of the United States to engage the parties and negotiate the role of the force while simultaneously deploying a significant military presence into Mogadishu and throughout the country. The US representative on the Security Council indicated that, although resolution 794 authorized members of UNITAF to use "all necessary means" to ensure the delivery and protection of relief supplies, the US attitude to the actual use of force was more flexible: "our mission is a peaceful one, and we will endorse the use of force only if and when we decide it is necessary to accomplish our objectives."[71]

The over-riding objective of the US operation was to achieve to delivery of relief supplies, while minimising any potential casualties. Accordingly, they adopted a policy that stressed a limited period of deployment and a limited degree of political involvement in the Somali problem.[72] This restricted approach was ironic in that much of the food problem facing Somalia had been solved prior to UNITAF's deployment, and in December 1992 what Somalia most needed was political reconciliation - exactly what the US was not prepared to become involved in.[73] In effect, the Bush administration restricted the rules of engagement of the US forces in Somalia to such a degree that they operated much along the lines of a traditional Chapter VI peacekeeping force, rather than adopting a more confrontational strategy, as authorised by resolution 794.[74] This desire to avoid long term political engagement and short term military confrontation led the

---

[69] "Europe as Super Power? An Ambition, Not a Reality," and "Into Africa With Generous Intentions and Skimpy Experience," *International Herald Tribune*, 10 December, 1992.

[70] *The Blue Helmets*, p. 296.

[71] *UN Document*, S/PV .3145, 3 December, 1992.

[72] Walter Clarke and Jeffrey Herbst, "Somalia and the Future of Humanitarian Intervention," *Foreign Affairs*, vol. 75, no. 2, 1996, p. 78.

[73] *Operation Restore Hope: A Preliminary Assessment*, African Rights, May 1993. p. 1. The contention that death rates had begun to fall by the time UNITAF was deployed is also supported by Maren, *The Road To Hell*, pp. 204-209.

[74] The limited 'doable' mandate of UNITAF, the limited period of its deployment, and its ability to utilise overwhelming force were all the result of pressure from Colin Powell and his reluctance to become engaged in Somalia. John Hirsch interview with author, 4 August, 1998, New York.

United States to focus more on protecting their troops rather than identifying and fulfilling strategic goals.[75]

The Americans went to great lengths to ensure that the Somali factions were aware of their intentions, both in terms of delivering relief supplies and protecting their personnel.[76] Days before the dramatic landing of US Marines on the beaches of Mogadishu, US Special Envoy Robert Oakley, a former US Ambassador to Somalia, had met with the key faction leaders, including Aidid and Ali Mahdi, reaching an agreement whereby the UNITAF deployment would not be opposed. Aidid in fact found the involvement of the United States in Somali much preferable to the involvement of the United Nations. This acceptance of the US was partly due to the urging of one of his key advisors, Osman Ato, who had close ties with US business and US officials in Nairobi. Aidid withdrew his medium to heavy weapons from Mogadishu and deployed them across the Ethiopian border before the arrival of the US Marines in order to keep them out of UNITAF's reach.[77] He even publicly welcomed UNITAF's deployment in Somalia and stated that he had no confidence in the ability of the UN to conduct the peace process, calling on the US to take the place of the international organisation. He called the efforts of Boutros-Ghali "too meddling, too divisive and too secretive to produce any positive result..."[78]

Yet the cause of Aidid's obstruction of UNOSOM's deployment had been his fear that the UN favoured Ali Mahdi's claim to the Somali Presidency. Aidid was also suspicious of the UN as a whole, because it was led by Boutros-Ghali who, as Egyptian Foreign Minister, had supported the Barre government. Aidid was concerned that Boutros-Ghali would again seek to support Barre under the auspices of the UN. For these reasons, Aidid's fear was not of an intervention *per se*, just of a UN led intervention. Thus, because he believed that the US led *Operation Restore Hope* would not adversely affect his political standing in Mogadishu or Somalia, Aidid did not object to the deployment of UNITAF.[79]

Disarmament was one of the key issues of contention between the United States and the UN. When the United States had originally made its offer to lead the UNITAF operation, it was only prepared to ensure the unimpeded flow of

---

[75] Clarke, "Failed Visions and Uncertain Mandates in Somalia," pp. 4, 10.

[76] Sometimes the good intentions of the Americans had unintended results. Among the leaflets dropped to reassure the Somali people as to the good intentions of UNITAF was one written in Somali which read "The Slave Forces have come here to help you..." It was intended to read "The World Forces have come here to help you." It turned out that the translation had been completed by a US Serviceman who had been born in Somalia, but had moved to American at an early age. See Keith B. Moore, *Illustrated Catalogue of UNITAF Aerial Leaflets Used in Support of Operation Restore Hope, Somalia*, Blatter Catalogue, April 1995.

[77] Lyons and Samatar, *Somalia*, p. 87. Ethiopia was sympathetic to Aidid's cause, having provided him with space in which to train his USC military wing prior to the overthrow of Barre.

[78] "Warlords' Anti-UN Stand Threatens Somali Talks," *International Herald Tribune*, 6 January, 1993.

[79] Drysdale, "Foreign Military Intervention in Somalia," p. 129.

Somalia 83

humanitarian supplies to those areas most in need.[80] President Bush reminded the UN Secretary-General of this the day after the Security Council members had authorized the deployment of UNITAF. He also stressed his expectation that a UN operation to take over from UNITAF.[81]

In an attempt to minimise the risk to its troops, the United States was not willing to disarm the militias and thus left the power of the factions leaders intact. Other UNITAF contributors, however, successfully pursued a strategy of disarmament. The Australian contingent in Baidoa implemented an aggressive 'street by street' disarmament policy and promoted a sustainable law and order system. Regarding Somalia as a collapsed state with no effective government, the Australians took the view that there was no sovereign authority upon which the disarmament process could infringe.[82] French forces deployed in Hoddur also adopted a ground up approach, termed "control by immersion," working in small groups and spreading themselves across their areas of responsibility.[83] They confiscated any heavy weapons or armed trucks they found, and improvised a registration process for small arms, significantly improved the security situation in and around Hoddur.[84]

In order to ensure that the principle of consent would remain the main basis upon which UNITAF could operate tactically, both the US and the UN had to involve the militia leaders in the political reconciliation process. This policy, expressed through Robert Oakley's deliberate negotiations with the local factions in order to reduce the potential for friction between UNITAF and the Somali militias, formed a template for subsequent US and UN negotiations. These conferred a degree of legitimacy on military factions that were, in fact, hard pressed to deliver on their political commitments, such as the formation of any new, transition government.[85] This engagement with local militia leaders was the result of a decision taken in December, 1992 by US officials who deliberately reserved places for them in plans for a proposed interim governing authority. The faction leaders reciprocated by allowing UNITAF to deploy and distribute humanitarian assistance. The United Nations, which co-ordinated the political reconciliation process, played a secondary role in this overall strategy of local

---

[80] "Disarming the Thugs," *International Herald Tribune*, 14 December, 1992.

[81] Bush as quoted by John R. Bolton, "Wrong Turn in Somalia," p. 60.

[82] Robert G. Patman, "Disarming Somalia: The Contrasting Fortunes of United States and Australian Peacekeepers during United Nations Intervention, 1992-1993," *African Affairs*, vol. 96, 1997. Patman's analysis provides an interesting study of the contrasting approaches and results of both UNITAF contributors.

[83] Christine O'Connell, *France and the United Nations in Somalia*, M.Phil Thesis, University of Oxford, 1996, p. 77.

[84] Gérard Prunier, "The Experience of European Armies in Operation Restore Hope," in Clarke and Herbst, eds., *Learning From Somalia*, pp. 139-140.

[85] Lewis and Mayall, "Somalia," p. 123.

accommodation. Fourteen main militia groups recognised by the UN went on to play a major role in subsequent political reconciliation efforts.[86]

In discussions with US prior to the deployment of UNITAF, senior United Nations officials had rejected the idea that *Operation Restore Hope* would eventually become a UN peacekeeping operation, arguing that it would be a corruption of traditional peacekeeping principles as it relied too much on the use of force.[87] Boutros-Ghali was also concerned by the fact that the limited mandate of US forces would leave significant responsibilities to the follow on, UN-led operation.[88] Once UNITAF was deployed, UN officials tried to persuade the United States to take a proactive approach to solving Somalia's problems, including tackling the thorny issues of disarming the militias and promoting political reconciliation.[89] In a report to the Security Council shortly after the deployment of UNITAF, Boutros-Ghali suggested that before any transition could be made from the enforcement operation to a more traditional UN-led peacekeeping force it was necessary for UNITAF to both take action to control and neutralise the heavy weapons of the factions and also disarm the gangs threatening the humanitarian operations.[90] This objective was never adopted by the American contingent in UNITAF.[91]

The failure of UNITAF as a whole to adequately disarm the Somali factions eventually led to a drastically worsened security atmosphere through many parts of the country. Boutros-Ghali had hoped that a follow-on Chapter VI UN peacekeeping operation would be all that was necessary in order to consolidate the gains made by UNITAF.[92] Instead the UN found itself confronted by a situation in which there was little consent at either the tactical or operational levels for international initiatives, casting doubt on the potential effectiveness of a consent-based peacekeeping approach in the wake of UNITAF.

UNOSOM II

Boutros-Ghali had anticipated that the UN would have to undertake a variety of complex tasks upon UNITAF's withdrawal, but the role he envisaged was based on the assumption that UNITAF would have "brought about an effective cessation of hostilities throughout the country and [would] have established the secure

---

[86] Lyons and Samatar, *Somalia*, p. 46. During the initial Addis meeting it was the militia leaders who took centre stage. Leaders of Somali civil society such as intellectuals, elders and business leaders were kept on the periphery.

[87] Hirsch and Oakley, *Somalia and Operation Restore Hope*, p. 45.

[88] John Hirsch, interview with author, 4 August, 1998.

[89] Jonathan T. Howe, "Relations between the United States and the UN in Somalia," Clarke and Herbst, *Learning From Somalia*, p. 175.

[90] *UN Document*, S/24992, 19 December, 1992.

[91] US officials held the belief that UNITAF had always been planned in the expectation that it would be followed by a robust, UN enforcement mission. John Hirsch, interview with author, 4 August, 1998.

[92] Marrack Goulding, interview with author, 6 July, 1999.

Somalia 85

environment called for in resolution 794."[93]   However, as the exact plans for the transition from UNITAF to UNOSOM II began to solidify, it quickly became apparent that Boutros-Ghali's assumptions about UNITAF's achievements would be incorrect.   Consequently the responsibilities of the UN operation were far greater than he had originally anticipated.   Indeed, the required scope of the operation was far beyond what he had envisaged for UN peacekeeping in *An Agenda for Peace*.[94]   The reality of the situation on the ground and the continuing desire within the UN to ensure that UNOSOM II built upon the success of UNITAF led the Secretary-General to recommend that the Security Council authorize an expansive, UN-led enforcement operation. Like UNITAF, it would be based on Chapter VII of the Charter and not be contingent on the consent of the local factions:

> It is clear to me that the effort undertaken by UNITAF to establish a secure environment in Somalia is far from complete and in any case has not attempted to address the situation throughout all of Somalia. Moreover, there have been, especially recently, some disheartening reverses. Accordingly, the threat to international peace and security which the Security Council ascertained in the third preambular paragraph of resolution 794 (1992) is still in existence. Consequently, UNOSOM II will not be able to implement the above mandate unless it is endowed with enforcement powers under Chapter VII of the Charter.[95]

The members of the Council met formally on 26 March 1993 to consider the report of the Secretary-General.   There were three primary motives behind the decision to authorize a newly configured UNOSOM operation with resolution 814.[96]   First, many of the Council's members believed that resolution 814 represented the next necessary step towards the Council's goal of establishing Somali sovereignty. As the representative of Morocco argued:

> The Security Council's adoption under Chapter VII of the historic resolution 794 (1992) on 3 December 1992 was a firm and appropriate response to a situation unprecedented in the annals of the United Nations...
> Despite all these positive developments, the improvement noted in the field remains relative and is not irreversible, as mentioned by the Secretary-General in his report. The problem of security has not been fully resolved and disarmament is far from being complete...
> UNOSOM II will be called upon to undertake the enormous task of rebuilding the country, restoring its political institutions and renewing its economy. This operation, the first of its kind ever undertaken by the United Nations, clearly illustrated the important role which this Organisation, henceforth the very embodiment of international solidarity, can play in crises of this kind.

---

[93] *UN Document*, S/24992, 19 December, 1992.

[94]Ian Johnstone, interview with author, 17 June, 1999.

[95] *UN Document*, S/25354, 3 March, 1993. In this report Boutros-Ghali subtly avoids mention of the fact that his efforts to get the US to disarm the Somalis had failed.

[96] The statements made during this debate are recorded in *UN Document*, S/PV .3188, 26 March, 1993.

86 *Understanding the UN Security Council*

Second, the goal of "rebuilding the country" also resonated throughout many of the UNSC member's statements. They recognised that the actions taken in relation to Somalia were "creating history" by restoring a member state of the international community. As the member for Djibouti, Mr. Olhaye argued:

> Clearly, in Somalia we have witnessed a political and social collapse manifested in human and material destruction. But the underlying perception remains, the sense of "nationhood". Perhaps our role is at bottom to provide a secure basis for its re-emergence institutionally.

This position was supported by Madeleine Albright, the representative of the United States who stated:

> It is now time for the United Nations to complete the work begun by the Unified Task Force. By adopting this draft resolution, we will embark on an unprecedented enterprise aimed at nothing less that the restoration of an entire country as a proud, functioning and viable member of the community of nations. This is a historic undertaking.

Third, many of the UNSC members believed that any effective UN operation would require authorization under Chapter VII of the UN Charter. This would serve to create jurisdiction for the Council in a state where there was no sovereign authority and it would also permit the use of enforcement measures. The need for the latter was based on two factors: the need to maintain security and continue relief and reconciliation initiatives and also to improve the security situation throughout other parts of Somalia where UNITAF had not deployed. These concerns were highlighted by the representative of France:

> The events of the last few weeks have confirmed, in particular, that satisfactory security conditions have not yet been restored...the factions still have large quantities of arms at their disposal, and serious incidents are still occurring, such as, for example, the recent resumption of confrontations between factions at Kismayo. We are also concerned about the risk of a deterioration in the north of the country arising particularly from the Task Force's absence from the area. In such circumstances, it is essential that UNOSOM II should have the necessary mandate and resources, in the first place in order for it to carry out its mission in a situation that remains unstable, and in the second to take the necessary steps to improve security.

Similarly, the representative of Spain stated:

> The United Nations recognises that it is impossible to limit itself to ensuring the distribution of humanitarian assistance and that it is also necessary to support the process of rehabilitation and national reconstruction in Somalia. Both tasks can only be undertaken feasibly if security is guaranteed throughout the entire territory of Somalia. This is the main mission of UNOSOM II and the reason why United Nations forces will continue to act in accordance with Chapter VII of the Charter...

Somalia 87

Even China, the permanent member traditionally the most reluctant to allow the use of Chapter VII in the context of a UN operation, agreed with its use in the case of UNOSOM II. But it still sought to ensure that enforcement measures were only used when necessary and that the Council's response to the situation in Somalia should not have a bearing on future crises faced by the UN. As its representative argued:

> Authorizing UNOSOM II to take enforcement action under Chapter VII of the Charter in order to implement its mandate has made it the first operation of its kind in the history of United Nations peacekeeping. It is our understanding that this authorization is based on the needs of the unique situation in Somalia and should not constitute a precedent for United Nations peacekeeping operations. At the same time we believe that UNOSOM II should act prudently in carrying out such enforcement action. Once the situation in Somalia improves, UNOSOM II should promptly resume its normal peacekeeping operations.

Based on these positions the members of the Security Council authorized the deployment of UNOSOM II under Chapter VII of the Charter until 31 October, 1993. The resolution reaffirmed the consensus among members of the Council that in the continued absence of a national government the sovereign authority in Somalia lay with the Somali people. The preamble to resolution 814 stated that the Council acted while 'recognising that the people of Somalia bear the ultimate responsibility for national reconciliation and reconstruction of their own country.'[97] For the first time the members of the Council cited the violation of international humanitarian law as a key factor which created a threat to international peace and security and thus allowed the use of Chapter VII to authorize the UNOSOM II deployment.[98]

The United States advocated that the UN operation adopt a broad range of objectives. In fact, like resolution 794, the first draft of resolution 814 was written in the Pentagon and consequently encapsulated many of the objectives that the US had for the UN operation.[99] There was also only limited contact between those in the field and the officials who helped to assemble the UN's report on the situation in Somalia. This created a disjuncture between the terms of the resolution and the true needs and realities in Somalia.[100] Despite the expansive mandate of the UN-led operation, including the tasks of disarmament, demining, political reconciliation, humanitarian assistance, and economic regeneration initiatives, the US was eager to withdraw its military units as soon as possible. Only a Quick Reaction Force (QRF) of Americans was left to support the UN force, along with some temporary logistics units.[101]

The contribution of the QRF and the logistics units did represent a change from the original US plan of complete withdrawal that had been the intention of the

---

[97] UN Security Council Resolution 814, 26 March 1993.

[98] Hutchinson, "Restoring Hope," p. 632.

[99] Clarke, " Failed Visions and Uncertain Mandates in Somalia," p. 9.

[100] John Hirsch, interview with author, 4 August, 1998.

[101] Howe, "Relations Between the United States and the UN in Somalia," p. 176.

88 *Understanding the UN Security Council*

Bush administration.[102]   This change in US policy had been brought on by two factors. First was the arrival of the Clinton administration in the White House which, by way of a policy of assertive multilateralism, demonstrated increased enthusiasm for UN peacekeeping operations. The UN's operation in Somalia was one theatre in which they could demonstrate this new commitment and consequently led to pressure on the UN to adopt such an expansive mandate for UNOSOM II in resolution 814.[103]   This same enthusiasm for peacekeeping operations also led to a re-evaluation of US participation in UNOSOM II and which prompted the change in contribution from that originally planned by the Bush administration. Similarly, though UNOSOM II was originally conceived as a Chapter VI traditional peacekeeping operation within UN circles, this was modified so that it could be conducted according to the Powell Doctrine, based on the overwhelming threat and use of force. US pressure to adopt this approach in UNOSOM II created a shift beyond the terms of peacekeeping and into peace enforcement under Chapter VII of the Charter.[104]

It was a shift that was reluctantly agreed to by the UN Secretariat whose eagerness to extract as much political and material commitment as possible from the US outweighed concerns about the change in peacekeeping doctrine.[105]   One strategy for retaining increased US support during the operation was the decision to appoint American Admiral Jonathan Howe as the Special Representative of the Secretary- General (SRSG) as well as ensuring that the deputy force Commander was also an American.[106]   The role of Howe as SRSG assisted the UN's aim of securing American engagement since Howe had been chosen for the job by the Clinton administration and was constantly in touch with both New York and the Pentagon during the course of the operation.[107]

UNOSOM II – Somali Relations

While the details of the transition from UNITAF to UNOSOM II were being worked out between New York and Washington, political reconciliation initiatives among the local parties in Somalia went ahead. The most significant of these was

---

[102] Bolton, "Wrong Turn in Somalia," p. 62.

[103] Hirsch and Oakley, *Somalia and Operation Restore Hope*, p. xix.

[104] Ibid., pp 46-47. This change had initially begun under US Secretary of Defence Dick Cheney and US Chairman of the Joint Chiefs of Staff Colin Powell during the Bush administration, and was carried over in the Clinton administration which took the decision to continue the US participation in a UN-led Chapter VII operation.

[105] Ibid., p. 111.

[106] Allegedly the pressure to ensure that Americans were included in the UNOSOM II set up was such that the original deputy to Force Commander Lt.-General Levik Bir (a senior non-US officer) allegedly faked a heart attack in order to get out of Mogadishu and out of the US political firing line. He was subsequently replaced by an American. See John Drysdale, *Whatever Happened to Somalia?*, p. 7.

[107] Hirsch and Oakley, *Somalia and Operation Restore Hope*, p. 154. See also Elizabeth Drew, *On the Edge: The Clinton Presidency*, Simon & Schuster, New York, 1994, p. 320.

Somalia 89

the Addis Ababa conference on National Reconciliation that met on 15 March 1993.[108] The lack of sovereign authority continued to create problems for UNOSOM II in terms of deciding which parties to include in the political process. The talks continued to be dominated by the factions. While some of the civil society representatives attempted to influence the course of the talks, the UN, led by Deputy Special Representative Lansana Kouyate of Guinea, allowed them to be marginalized while seeking a pragmatic agreement with the factions. Kouyate believed that the March conference provided an opportunity to create a "bottom-up" political structure that would eventually marginalize the militia leaders though it was they who would initially be required to negotiate the agreement. Howe, who viewed the conference as reinforcing the power of the warlords, opposed this approach. He refused to meet with them in an attempt to reduce their perceived legitimacy.[109] However, such initiatives, including the establishment of District Councils, were viewed by Aidid as an attempt to marginalize him.[110] These problems of fostering the emergence of a sovereign authority in Somalia resulted in the operation adopting a two level strategy of consent; ground level negotiations based on pragmatism, combined with a strategic approach based on the Chapter VII authority until such time as a stable government emerged to assume the sovereign responsibilities of the Somali state.

Despite the limited political progress, the security situation in Somalia, particularly within Mogadishu, deteriorated following the departure of the bulk of the US forces in May 1993.[111] UNOSOM II had to cope with inadequate command and control, logistical and military capabilities while attempting to implement a mandate that was more expansive and politically sensitive that the one that had faced UNITAF. UNOSOM II also created problems for itself as the result of a conceptual carry over of ideas from traditional peacekeeping operations based on consent and the use of force only in self-defence. There was no clear agreement among troop contributing nations as to what the rules of engagement were. Somalis were greeted with varying degrees of forceful response depending on which national contingent they were dealing with.[112] In general, the UN forces went to great lengths to avoid using force, despite the fact that the operation had been authorized under Chapter VII and despite the continual threat of violence from the SNA, other factions and rogue gangs.[113]

---

[108] *The Blue Helmets*, p. 299.

[109] Lyons and Samatar, *Somalia*, p. 54.

[110] John Hirsch, interview with author, 4 August, 1998.

[111] See for example "UN Forces Face Danger as Somalis Turn Against Them," *The Independent*, 30 June, 1993.

[112] One post-operation analysis of UNOSOM II highlighted the failure of individual troop contingents to respond consistently to the direction of the Force Commander as a fundamental cause of the operation's failure to create a secure environment in Somalia. See *Comprehensive Report on Lessons-Learned From United Nations Operation in Somalia*, Friedrich Ebert Stiftung, Life and Peace Institute, Norwegian Institute of International Affairs in co-operation with the Lessons Learned Unit, DPKO, December 1995. p. 15.

[113] Hirsch and Oakley, *Somalia and Operation Restore Hope*, p. 113.

The Somali factions exploited the apparent vulnerability of UNOSOM II and the confusion surrounding rules of engagement as they began to restart their internal disputes. In response to this renewed fighting and the increasing lawlessness on the streets of Mogadishu, the UN adopted a more forceful approach to the factional fighting. In effect the move beyond consent at the strategic level that had occurred in resolution 814 was implemented at the operational and tactical levels. As the UN troops attempted to carry out their new mandate, tension in the city increased and there were increased clashes between UN troops and Somali militias. On 5 June, 25 Pakistani UN troops were killed and more than 50 wounded when they were ambushed by members of Aidid's militia. This event was to lead to a rapid increase in the predominance of military activity within UNOSOM II, as UN policy became more focused on disarming the factions as a precondition of effective political and economic rehabilitation.

This more forceful role had also been encouraged by the members of the Security Council who reaffirmed their support for the use of Chapter VII enforcement measures to bring those responsible for the 5 June attack to justice. Resolution 837 condemned the attacks on the UN troops which were "launched by forces apparently belonging to the United Somali Congress (USC/SNA)." The third operative paragraph of the resolution re-emphasised "the crucial importance of the disarmament of all Somali parties." Significantly, the fifth substantive paragraph read:

> Reaffirms that the Secretary-General is authorized under resolution 814 (1993) to take all necessary measures against all those responsible for the armed attacks referred to in paragraph 1 above [the USC/SNA], including against those responsible for publicly inciting such attacks, to establish the effective authority of UNOSOM II throughout Somalia, including to secure the investigation of their actions and their arrest and detention for prosecution, trial and punishment.[114]

It was a decision taken on the basis that failure to act would encourage other attacks on UN personnel in Somalia and in other peacekeeping operations deployed across the globe.[115] The decision to re-emphasise the authority of UNOSOM II to use force, and to mandate it to take action against those responsible for the attack on the Pakistani soldiers was to result in the active pursuit of Aidid.

It was a step that was taken with the full support of the Council's members. In the debate prior to its adoption and statements made following the vote, the members of the Council were united in both their condemnation of the attack and the manner in which UNOSOM II should respond. The representative of Pakistan, for example, argued that "For the United Nations, and for the Security Council in particular, it is imperative that we act in a manner which will swiftly bring to justice the perpetrators of this murderous defiance of the Council's authority," while Madeleine Albright of the US argued that "These actions threaten

---

[114] UNSC Resolution 837, 6 June, 1993.
[115] Clarke and Herbst, "Somalia and the Future of Humanitarian Intervention," p. 80.

international peace and security and must be dealt with accordingly." Mr. Ladsous of France argued that "What has taken place in Somalia is unacceptable and requires from the Council the strongest possible reaction. The resolution that we have just adopted is fully in accord with this objective," while the Council's representative of Russia stated, "We voted with satisfaction for the strong resolution just adopted with regard to the crime committed in Somalia."[116]

Yet the decision of the Council to single out Aidid was to considerably harm the relationship between UNOSOM II and the SNA. Throughout the summer of 1993 the situation in Mogadishu and throughout Somali continued to deteriorate.[117] On 12 July, having received intelligence that Aidid was meeting his militia commanders at a secret location, UNOSOM II helicopters attacked the supposed meeting place without warning, killing a number of Aidid's clan elders. It was subsequently discovered that the meeting had been held to discuss the possibility of renewing dialogue between the Haiweye clan and the UN. However, due to the rash action of the UN, the incident deepened the resentment within the Haiweye towards the UN operation and the clan members decided to coalesce behind Aidid.[118] A promising opportunity for political reconciliation between the UN and the Haiweye had been lost.

In response to the UNOSOM decision to arrest him, Aidid broadcast the following statement on Somali radio:

> The US-UNOSOM have falsely accused me and [the] SNA. They are misleading world opinion and trying first of all to eliminate USC/SNA and their leaders and me by ordering my arrest. But such unjust actions cannot succeed because from the humanitarian role they have transformed themselves to politicians interfering in the country with military operations, which is against the UN Charter and Resolutions.[119]

The efforts of UNOSOM II to apprehend Aidid continued until 3 October, 1993 when a force of elite US commandos, brought in especially to assist in the hunt for Aidid, were engaged in a gun battle with SNA militia in Mogadishu. Eighteen US soldiers were killed and eighty wounded while more than two hundred Somalis were killed.[120] UNOSOM II was confronted with its second major military disaster in four months. Anger and frustration at the apparent transformation of what had been a humanitarian mission into a war-fighting operation that was causing significant losses of life on both sides led to a re-examination of international motives in Somalia.

---

[116] These comments are recorded in *UN Document*, S/PV.3229, 6 June, 1993.

[117] See for example "UN Helpless to Keep Guns Off Streets of Mogadishu," *The Daily Telegraph*, 12 July, 1993.

[118] Hussein M. Adam, "Somalia: A Terrible Beauty Being Born," in I. William Zartmann, ed., *Collapsed States*, Lynne Reiner Publishers, London, 1995, p. 85.

[119] Ruhela, Satys Paul, ed., *Mohammed Farah Aidid and His Vision of Somalia*, Vikas Publishing House PVT Ltd., New Delhi, 1994. p. 171.

[120] *The Blue Helmets*, p. 301. For an detailed analysis of the 3 October incident see Mark Bowden, *Black Hawk Down*, Bantam Press, New York, 1999.

Re-evaluation and Retrenchment

Faced with an unworkable policy towards Somalia, UNOSOM II underwent a shift in emphasis away from the pursuit of Aidid and disarmament towards enhanced political reconciliation efforts. The members of the Council recognised that a limited UN enforcement operation could not function effectively in the face of local opposition. The first step in this process was a Security Council resolution withdrawing the order to arrest Aidid. With it the UNSC states recognised the failure of their decision to move UNOSOM II beyond consent. They requested:

> that the Secretary-General, under his authority in resolution 814 (1993) and 837 (1993), pending the completion of the report of the Commission, suspend arrest actions against those individuals who might be implicated but are not currently detained pursuant to resolution 837...[121]

On 9 October, the USC/SNA declared a unilateral cease-fire, ending its attacks on UN personnel. The United States decided to focus on force protection rather than mandate implementation, reinforcing its QRF with M1A1 Tanks and Bradley fighting vehicles. Simultaneously Clinton announced that all US forces would be withdrawn from Somalia by 31 March, 1994. Sweden, Belgium, and France similarly announced their decisions to withdraw from UNOSOM II, unwilling to stay without a significant American presence in the country.[122]

As the size of UNOSOM II began to be dramatically reduced by these withdrawals, there was a re-emphasis of the existing operation on the principle of consent and a recognition of the limits of using force. Resolution 886 extended the operation's mandate until 31 May, 1994 and recalled "that the highest priority of UNOSOM II continues to be to support the efforts of the Somali people in promoting the process of national reconciliation and the establishment of democratic institutions."[123] In adopting this resolution the UNSC had not chosen to reduce UNOSOM II to a traditional peacekeeping operation based officially on consent or reduce the size and mandate to the force to focus on the maintenance of humanitarian supply routes. These had been two alternative options identified by the Secretary-General.[124] However, it was clear that consent and not coercion would be the preferred means of implementing the extended mandate. Mr. Hato, the representative of Japan argued, "Japan is of the view that the United Nations Operation in Somalia (UNOSOM II) should to try to avoid coercive methods as far as possible...," while the Brazilian representative stressed, "...the United Nations cannot impose peace in Somali or anywhere else if the parties involved are not

---

[121] UNSC Resolution 885, 16 November, 1993. For the debate see *UN Document*, S/PV .3315, 16 November, 1993.
[122] Boutros Boutros-Ghali, *Unvanquished*, I.B. Tauris Publishers, London, 1999, p. 119. See also "France Criticised US Conduct in Somalia," *International Herald Tribune*, 8 October, 1993.
[123] UNSC Resolution 886, 18 November, 1993.
[124] *UN Document*, S/26738, 12 November, 1993.

Somalia 93

willing to make peace themselves."[125] Despite its official authorization to use force, UNOSOM II did not do so pro-actively and came to resemble a more traditional peacekeeping operation in its operating principles.

Over the next three months, the willingness of the international community to continue its support for Somali reconciliation dwindled considerably. The Secretary-General could not find adequate replacements for the impending withdrawal of the US, Belgian, French, and Swedish contingents on 31 March, 1994 and UNOSOM II had adopted a much more defensive posture within Somalia as its main aim was to avoid further casualties. In his report to the Council on 6 January, 1994 Boutros-Ghali drew the Council's attention to the three options for UNOSOM II that he had identified in his previous report. Due to the change in circumstances, he noted that it had become impossible for the Council to authorize a continuation of the operation in its current guise as the UN could not find adequate reinforcements from among the UN member states. Accordingly, he recommended that the Council authorize the continuation of UNOSOM II along the lines of traditional peacekeeping operation, relying on the co-operation of the host parties for disarmament initiatives, but retaining the capacity to use force in self-defence.[126] In reality, this simply formalised the practices that had been unofficially used in UNOSOM II following the adoption of resolution 885.

Considering the Secretary-General's report, the members of the Council decided to adopt his recommendations in resolution 897.[127] However, while reducing the *modus operandi* of UNOSOM II to that of a traditional peacekeeping operation, they authorized the change in its mandate under Chapter VII of the UN Charter. The reason for this was provided in the resolution's final pre-ambular paragraph:

> Determining that the situation in Somalia continues to threaten peace and security and having regard to the exceptional circumstances, including in particular absence of a government in Somalia...

This characterization served to justify the Security Council's involvement in the conflict, but was not used to give UNOSOM II the authority to use force beyond that necessary to defend itself. The Security Council members believed that the contributions of the international community to Somalia had been unprecedented, but in the face of continued fighting between the Somalia factions and the limited progress made towards political reconciliation, the onus for further progress now lay firmly with the Somali people themselves.

The decision of the Council to continue the deployment of UNOSOM II in the guise of a traditional peacekeeping operation stemmed in part from the belief of some Council members that the UN could not simply abandon the Somali people. As the Nigerian representative stated:

---

[125] *UN Document*, S/PV .3317, 18 November, 1993.

[126] *UN Document*, S/1994/12, 6 January, 1994.

[127] UNSC Resolution 897, 4 February, 1994.

94 *Understanding the UN Security Council*

It appears to our delegation that for the credibility of our Organisation and in the higher interest of the Somali people, UNOSOM II cannot simply fold up and exit from Somalia. To do so would, among other things, mean that all the soldiers and other who paid the supreme sacrifice on behalf of the international community had indeed died in vain and that United Nations involvement in Somalia was a "mission impossible." [128]

Some members held the opinion that the weakness of adopting Chapter VII measures had be revealed. For the Chinese, the experience in Somalia had revealed the problems of the use of force and the lack of consent:

The experiences and lessons of the United Nations Operations in Somalia (UNOSOM II) have shown that the fundamental and effective way to settle the Somali question is by peaceful means. Resort to coercive military actions will only serve to complicate matters. The second option recommended by the Secretary-General is also in conformity with this principle in its advocacy of non-use of coercive measures to achieve disarmament by the Somali parties themselves.

Confronted with the failure of the UNOSOM II mandate in Somalia, the Council members opportunely stressed the responsibility of the Somali people in sorting out their own affairs, demonstrating that the international good will present in early 1992 was no more. In the opinion of the UK government:

The rebuilding of Somalia cannot be in the hands of UNOSOM II or of the international community: it must be, and it is, in the hands of the Somali people. The international community will continue to help them in their efforts to re-establish viable national institutions and rebuild their country. But it cannot do the job for them.

It was however, the comments of the representative of the Czech Republic who most accurately summed up the action taken by the Council with resolution 897:

UNOSOM II has to stay until a political solution is found lest all the dramatic improvements in the daily life of so many Somalis unravel in the chaos which would prevail otherwise. Yet we no longer have the wherewithal to disarm even the worst of the thugs and bandits, which is a precondition to attaining the necessary political solution. We are trying to square a circle: in our view, resolution 897 (1994), puts UNOSOM II's work in a hold pattern.

Indeed, UNOSOM II did adopt a holding pattern and for the next nine months the operation was gradually reduced to a limited peacekeeping operation, withdrawn from outlying posts within Somalia to UN compounds where its personnel could be better protected. The security situation throughout the country continued to deteriorate, but UNOSOM II made no effort to halt the decline, as it

---

[128] The comments of the Security Council members on resolution 897 are recorded in *UN Document*, S/PV .3334, 4 February, 1994.

no longer had the mandate nor the means to do so.[129] From an initial authorized deployment size of approximately 28,000 personnel in March 1993, the number of troops deployed under UNOSOM II as of 2 February 1995 was 7,956. Though efforts were still made to deliver humanitarian supplies and political reconciliation was encouraged through support for the regional and district councils, the role of UNOSOM II was increasingly limited until its eventual withdrawal on 28 February, 1995.

Conclusion

The involvement of the United Nations in Somalia represents a turning point for the Security Council in the post-Cold War period. The breakdown of the Somali state and its humanitarian crisis presented the Council with a clear humanitarian imperative in a state where there was no sovereign authority. When they originally decided to authorize the deployment of the UN security personnel to Somalia in resolution 751, the members of the Security Council were concerned that the humanitarian crisis constituted a threat to international peace and security. They decided to respond with UNOSOM I in order to counter that threat as well as demonstrate that UN could fulfil both of the primary objectives of the UN Charter. In so doing, however, members of the Council were keen to adhere to the principles of the Charter. This was stressed by both China and India prior to the adoption of resolution 746. This conservatism is also reflected in the basis of UNOSOM I on consent. However, this traditional policy led to difficulties in identifying the appropriate parties with which to negotiate the deployment of the UN operation. In practice, Sahnoun was forced to negotiate with the primary political factions in Mogadishu. However, the lack of co-operation from key factions, particularly the SNA, demonstrated the problems of such a consent-based approach.

Increasingly frustrated by the intransigence of the Somali factions, the members of the UNSC and the UN Secretariat reconsidered the principles upon which the UN was operating in the country. Capitalizing on the US offer to lead the international effort to deliver humanitarian aid, the UNSC invoked Chapter VII in order to allow the coalition the use of force when necessary. Such action was justified as a unique response to a unique situation. The humanitarian imperative had minimised earlier concerns about intervention and there was no opposition within the Council to the flexible interpretation of the situation as a threat to international peace and security to create jurisdiction for the Council to cope with the crisis under Chapter VII. In legal terms, this invocation of Chapter VII made it unnecessary to seek consent from the Somalia government, had it existed. However, in practical terms local consent at the tactical level was still essential in order to allow UNITAF to implement its mandate with minimal casualties. This emphasis on consent prevented American forces from attempting to disarm the

---

[129] "UN Impotent as Anarchy Takes Over," *The Daily Telegraph*, 2 September, 1994.

96   *Understanding the UN Security Council*

Somali factions for fear of sustaining casualties, but as the experience of the Australian and French contingents demonstrated, adherence to consent did not preclude a more proactive, and ultimately successful, approach to disarmament.

The UNSC members similarly believed that UNOSOM II required Chapter VII authorization. It provided the Council with jurisdiction in a country without a sovereign government and its also permitted members of the UN operation to use force in order to implement their mandate. This was intended to compensate for the continued lack of consent at the tactical level, but the decision to go beyond consent at the strategic level had severe consequences at the tactical level. The political sensitivity of UNOSOM II's mandate put it into direct conflict with the objectives of the SNA. Following the deaths of 25 peacekeepers, the UNSC decided to use its authority to pursue Aidid as the man responsible for the UN deaths. The Security Council had effectively then gone beyond consent officially at both the strategic and tactical levels and the implications of this for UNOSOM II were enormous. The pursuit of Aidid cost more lives and the members of the Council were quickly forced to re-evaluate their overall approach to Somalia and particularly the role of consent in UNOSOM II.

The result of this re-evaluation was to re-emphasise the consensual basis of the operation. Though Chapter VII authorization was still used by the Council on resolutions concerning Somalia this was only due to the continued absence of any government. For UNOSOM II, its mandate was revised and the use of force was authorized only in self-defence. Gradually the force was reduced both in size and scope until its eventual withdrawal in early 1995. The Security Council members stressed the ultimate responsibility of the Somalia people to solve their own problems. The appetite for a new UN role in the post-Cold War era appeared to have waned considerably. The Clinton administration released in May, 1994 its Presidential Decision Directive 25 (PDD 25), outlining the circumstances in which the US would, in future become involved in peacekeeping operations. It highlighted problems of command and control, financial concerns and also stipulated that any future such involvement with the UN must be in the direct interest of the US.[130] It also incorporated elements of the Powell Doctrine into US plans for any future use of American military forces in UN peacekeeping operations.[131] This policy review was largely the result of American experiences in UNITAF and UNOSOM II.

The UN intervention in Somalia was viewed by the members of the Security Council as strengthening the principle of state sovereignty. By taking action to neutralise the threat to international peace and security that emanated from the Somali conflict, as well as working to restore a viable Somali government, the Council sought to shore up a crumbling sovereign state. Its action was also an attempt to protect the non-derogable human rights of the Somalia people, by

---

[130] *Clinton Administration Policy on Reforming Multilateral Peace Operations (PDD 25)*, Press Release, Bureau of International Organisational Affairs, US Department of State, 22 February, 1996.

[131] Kenneth J. Campbell, "Once Burned, Twice Cautious: Explaining the Weinberger-Powell Doctrine," *Armed Forces and Society*, vol. 24, no. 3, 1998.

assuming the sovereign responsibility to protect these rights that normally would have been the job of the national government. Yet while the uniqueness of the Somali situation was used to justify the circumvention of one of the most fundamental structuring principles of the international order, the Council's decision to go beyond one of its own fundamental principles of peacekeeping operations proved to be a step too far. Though non-adherence to the principle of consent was possible at the strategic level due to the absence of a Somalia government, the decision of the Council members to authorize the use of force under Chapter VII of the Charter led to the direct conflict between UNOSOM II and the SNA. This confrontation on the ground ultimately led to the failure of UNOSOM II and a harsh legacy that would affect the conduct of future peacekeeping operations.

Chapter 4

Haiti

October 1993 was not a good month for UN peacekeeping. On 3 October, 17 US soldiers were killed in Mogadishu in UNOSOM II. Later in the same month the advance deployment of peacekeepers from the United Nations Mission in Haiti (UNMIH) was effectively forestalled by an angry mob in Port-au-Prince. The ability of the UN to constructively address situations of internal conflict seemed limited by the reliance of peacekeeping on the consent and co-operation of the host parties and the reluctance of UN member states to use coercion in the wake of the Somalia imbroglio. Yet thirteen months later, in January 1995, the situation had come full circle. UNMIH was successfully deployed into a permissive environment following on from a UN-authorized, multi-national enforcement operation called *Operation Uphold Democracy*. It was a novel situation created by the existence of a *de facto* Haitian government in Port-au-Prince as well as an internationally recognised government in exile in the United States led by Jean Bertrand Aristide. In terms of consent, the members of the Security Council had to not only obtain the support of Aristide in order to make their actions legal, but also have the practical co-operation of the *de facto* government in order to allow UN initiatives to be feasible. It was also a novel situation given the motivations of the international community. As its name suggests, *Operation Uphold Democracy* was ostensibly justified as restoring the legitimate, democratically elected government of Aristide to power. However, the eventual deployment of the US-led Chapter VII operation also had much to do also with US strategic concerns and domestic political pressures on the Clinton administration. The following chapter examines the UNSC's actions in Haiti, particularly its members' motives for authorizing the use of enforcement measures to restore Aristide and their response to the challenges of consent.

Background

The history of Haiti immediately prior to the deployment of *Operation Uphold Democracy* to restore Aristide to power involved an abortive national transition to democracy. In 1986, the Haitian dictator Jean Claude Duvalier fled from Port-au-Prince to exile in France after growing political unrest. The impetus for this unrest came from elements within the Haitian military and Catholic church. Duvalier was replaced by the Conseil National de Gouvernment (CNG), a combination of military officials and civilians led by General Henri Namphy. Under the CNG limited political and human rights initiatives were undertaken, including the creation of an electoral commission, the separation of the police from the military, and the organisation of national elections in November, 1987. These elections were preceded by growing violence throughout the country, including the continued operation of the Tontons Macoutes (a paramilitary force created under Duvalier and loyal to the government) and death squads attempting to intimidate local grass-roots political organisations. Though the CNG was supported by the military and the Catholic church, there was growing opposition to the continuing violence in the country. This focal point of this anti-violence movement was a community-based Catholic organisation, the Ti-Legliz, led by Aristide.[1]

In the lead up to the election, political violence against voters increased to such an extent that the electoral commission declared that the elections had failed. The commission itself was subsequently dissolved by the CNG. In September, 1988 a new leader of the CNG emerged, General Prosper Avril, who requested that the Organisation of American States (OAS) and UN assist the Haitian government in organizing new national elections. Consequently, a new set of elections was organized in December 1990, with support from both international organisations.[2]

National elections were held on 16 December 1990, and saw the overwhelming endorsement of Aristide as Haitian President, with an estimated 66.4 percent of the vote. Haiti appeared to have put its long history of political dictatorship firmly in the past. The election of Aristide represented the culmination of long-standing efforts to establish the principle of democratic legitimacy.[3] Such hopes were, however, short-lived. Aristide held power for only eight months, a period characterized by violence against paramilitary groups by Aristide supporters, an ironic about-face on the original anti-violence platform of the Ti-Leglize. There were also reports of political intimidation by Aristide's supporters against other political parties and legislation was passed without Parliamentary consideration. Aristide's attempts at political and economic reform increased the hostility of the Haitian elite and Haitian military towards his government.[4] Eventually, on the evening of 29 September, a military coup led by General Raoul Cédras, arrested Aristide and wrested control of key government buildings. Aristide was permitted to flee to Venezuela the next evening and Haiti's brief fling with democracy came to an end.

---

[1] David Malone, *Decision-Making in the UN Security Council: The Case of Haiti, 1990-1997*, Clarendon Press, Oxford, 1998, p. 45.

[2] Anthony P. Maingot, "Haiti and Aristide: The Legacy of History," *Current History*, February, 1992, p. 67. Avril resigned following a mass anti-government demonstration and pressure from the United States. In his place, and pending the holding of national elections, Ertha Pascal-Trouillot was selected as President in keeping with the 1987 Haitian Constitution. Pascal-Trouillot's Presidency was backed by General Hérard Abraham who controlled the military.

[3] Anthony P. Maingot, "Sovereign Consent versus State-Centric Sovereignty," in Tom Farer, ed., *Beyond Sovereignty?*, p. 189.

[4] Maingot, "Haiti and Aristide," p. 68.

On the Outside Looking In

The coup was met with dismay by the international community, particularly given the fact that both the OAS and the UN had played key roles in organizing and supervising the elections. In addition, the members of the OAS had recently adopted the "Santiago Commitment to Democracy and Development and the Renewal of the Inter-American System" in June.[5] Less than three months later, a democratic government in the Caribbean basin had been overthrown. After being informed of the coup by the Haitian representative to the UN, and in the wake of OAS condemnation of it, the members of the Security Council met on 30 September to discuss the crisis.[6] Immediately, their consultations became concerned with the restrictions imposed on their actions by Article 2(7) of the Charter.[7] If the coup was an internal affair of Haiti, then the Security Council could only involve itself with the consent of the Haitian government. This was a problem in itself as there were two Haitian governments; the *de jure*, democratically elected government of Aristide and the *de facto* government of the military junta. Without the consent of the appropriate governmental authority, the only means by which the UNSC could legally involve itself in the situation was by formally determining that the situation was a threat to international peace and security, thus justifying UNSC action under Chapter VII of the Charter.

It was felt by a majority of the UNSC members that their discussion of the coup was in fact a violation of Article 2(7) as the coup was considered an internal matter in the sovereign affairs of Haiti. The opposition to the UNSC's consideration of the matter was led by China, India and Cuba, preventing the Council from issuing any resolution on the coup.[8] Nevertheless, the Secretary-General issued a statement expressing dismay at Aristide's overthrow and the setback for democracy. This statement was supported in a personal capacity by the President of the Security Council, French Ambassador Merimée, who issued a statement of support for Aristide's return.[9] Though a number of UNSC states were opposed to becoming involved in the matter, Aristide was given the unprecedented opportunity to address the Council during its formal session on 3 October. This apparent shift in position came about as a result of OAS, French and American pressure to support Aristide. Nevertheless, China, Cuba and India indicated their continued resistance to UNSC involvement. Cuba, while condemning the

---

[5] OAS-AG/RES. 1080 (XXI-0/91), 5 June, 1991.

[6] The unprecedented convening of the Council in the wake of the coup was likely due to the prior, decisive action of the OAS. See Diego Arria, "Diplomacy and the Four Friends of Haiti," in Georges A. Fauriol, ed., *Haitian Frustrations*, The Centre for Strategic and International Studies, Washington D.C., 1995, p. 93.

[7] Justin Morris, "Force and Democracy: UN/US Intervention in Haiti," *International Peacekeeping*, vol. 2, no. 3, 1995, p. 402.

[8] Ibid. The US, France and Canada tried to get a resolution put before the Council condemning the coup, but Cuba, Ecuador, India and the other non-aligned states on the Council would not support it. See also Arria, "Diplomacy and the Four Friends," p. 94.

[9] *UN Document*, SC/5311 HI/5, 1 October, 1991.

overthrow of Aristide, was also keen to prevent the Council's future involvement in the issue because of the implication that the Haitian situation threatened international peace and security.[10] Neither the representative of China, nor the representative of India opted to address the Council. India had toned down its opposition to the Council's involvement in the matter as it assumed the Presidency of the Council for the month of October.

All other UNSC members, including the Soviet Union, expressed their support for Aristide's government. However, because of the opposition of some UNSC members to the Council's involvement in the issue no substantive action could be taken. Instead, the President of the Security Council made a brief, but unusually substantive statement at the 3 October meeting.[11] He directed his comments to Aristide:

> The grave events that have taken place in your country deserve to be strongly condemned. They represent a violent usurpation of legitimate democratic authority and power in your country. We urge and call for the immediate reversal of the situation and for the restoration of the legitimate Government of Haiti...we support the efforts of the Organisation of American States to bring about the restoration of legitimate authority in Haiti...[12]

Because of these concerns about being involved in the affairs of a sovereign state, the majority of Council members remained reluctant to deepen the Council's involvement in the Haitian situation. As a result, initiatives aimed at restoring Aristide to power were left largely in the hands of the OAS and, to a lesser degree, the UN General Assembly.[13]

On the same day that the UNSC met, the members of the OAS convened an emergency meeting at which they asserted that they regarded Aristide to be the legitimate Haitian head of state.[14] Later, on 6 October a Special Mission of OAS Heads of Government travelled to Haiti and met with the coup leaders and a variety of political groups in order to determine whether Aristide could be restored, and if so, by what means. On 8 October, the OAS met again in Washington and adopted a resolution that urged OAS member states to impose a trade embargo on Haiti and created a civilian mission to support the development of democracy and respect for human rights in Haiti. These initiatives were supported by a UN General Assembly Resolution that called for the reinstatement of the legitimate government of Haiti.[15]

---

[10] Sir David Hannay, interview with author, 29 November, 1999. See also the comments of the Cuban representative, *UN Document*, S/PV .3011, 3 October, 1991.

[11] Malone, *Decision-Making*, p. 63.

[12] *UN Document,* S/PV .3011, 3 October, 1991.

[13] Malone, *Decision-Making*, p. 63. Malone suggests that a number of Latin American states did not support a UNSC role in Haiti, leading many non-aligned states to take a similar position against UNSC involvement.

[14] OAS-MRE/RES 1/91, 3 October, 1991.

[15] UN General Assembly Resolution A/RES/46/7, 11 October, 1991. As the effects of the voluntary OAS sanctions were beginning to be felt in Haiti during the closing few months of

102   *Understanding the UN Security Council*

During this time, UN involvement in the Haitian situation was confined to the General Assembly, with the Security Council remaining on the sidelines. This was due to two main reasons. First, there was no impetus from any member of the Council to push for the Council as a whole to become engaged in the matter. The US, whose interests were most involved, was not willing to raise the issue within the Council. Second, neither the OAS nor the Group of Latin American and Caribbean countries at the United Nations (GRULAC) sought UNSC involvement in the Haitian situation in the immediate aftermath of the coup.[16]

The Role of the United States

With regard to US policy on Haiti, the key issue was not whether the return of Arisitide was most effectively brought about by the use of consensual or coercive measures, but rather whether his restoration served US interests. As the most powerful nation in the Caribbean basin, the US did not place the restoration of Aristide high on its political agenda in the immediate aftermath of the coup. Concrete measures that would have placed real pressure on the *de facto* regime, such as breaking diplomatic ties or freezing private assets of coup leaders, were not pursued.[17] While the Bush administration did publicly denounce the coup in order to deter further military coups against other civilian governments in Latin America the US also began to criticize Aristide's human rights record.[18] It partly blamed the coup on Aristide and the inflammatory speeches he had made encouraging vigilante mobs which in turn led to increased human rights abuses.[19] Part of the US reluctance to actively promote the restoration of Aristide came from its close relationship with the coup leaders.[20] In short, the Bush administration remained

---

1991, they were soon to be undermined by a change in US policy. Confronted by an influx of Haitian refugees to the United States, the Bush administration sought to find a long term solution to the refugee problem by securing some degree of political stability in Haiti itself. Despite statements publicly supporting the legitimate government of Aristide, the Bush administration opted to modify its participation in the OAS embargo in early February 1992, excluding certain products and supplies needed to maintain US-owned assembly industries in Haiti. The Bush policy can be viewed as two-faced; publicly denouncing the coup, while deliberately keeping the economic embargo weak so as to not damage US business interests and returning Haitian refugees into the arms of the military regime. For details see: Kati Doyle, "Hollow Diplomacy in Haiti," *World Policy Journal*, vol. 11, no. 1, 1994; Alex Dupuy, *Haiti in the New World Order*; and Irwin P. Stotzky, *Silencing the Guns in Haiti*, University of Chicago Press, London, 1997.

[16] Malone, *Decision-Making*, p. 76.

[17] Doyle, "Hollow Diplomacy in Haiti," p. 51.

[18] Kim Ives, "The Coup and US Foreign Policy," in James Ridgeway, ed., *The Haiti Files: Decoding the Crisis*, Essential Books/Azul Editions, Washington, 1994, pp. 88-90.

[19] Alex Dupuy, *Haiti in the New World Order*, Westview Press, Oxford, 1997, p. 137.

[20] Cédras had been trained by the US military as had Henry Namphy and Prosper Avril, who governed the country following the departure of Duvalier. Contacts between the *de facto* regime and US officials from both the US embassy in Port-au-Prince and USAID remained

Haiti 103

sceptical of Aristide and, while denouncing his overthrow, was content to deal instead with the coup leaders and their wealthy Haitian backers over whom the US had some leverage. As one senior UN official described US Haiti policy during this time:

> Two lines about Haiti co-existed at the time. There was the line about the "return to democracy," which was for public consumption. And then there was a second line, spoken privately within the administration. And the Haitian military knew it perfectly well.[21]

Even the arrival in the White House of the Clinton administration, which had criticized Bush's policy of *refoulement,* chose to maintain that same policy once in office.[22] Clinton's reneging on his campaign pledge caused him to be pilloried in the press. The New York Times attacked the new administration, arguing that Clinton's change "is an unconscionable about-face...Mr. Clinton's real worry appears to be political fallout in Florida in reaction to a flood of poor black Haitians..."[23] This indeed appeared to be the concern of the new administration. As one transition official who assisted in taking over Haitian policy from the Bush administration commented, "The main goal [for the Clinton administration] is to keep Haitians in Haiti."[24]

International Involvement

The reluctance of some UNSC members to allow the Security Council to get involved in efforts to restore the *de jure* government of Haiti led to the formation of the Group of Friends on Haiti, including France, Canada, Venezuela, and the United States. The main objective of the Group of Friends was to find a means of overcoming the reservations of most Security Council states to becoming involved in the Haitian question. This was complemented by an OAS request that the UN participate in the OAS civilian mission being sent to Haiti. Additionally, the General Assembly adopted a resolution on 24 November that encouraged greater

---

strong. This favourable position of the coup leaders contrasted sharply with the antipathy with which US officials greeted Aristide's emergence onto the political scene in Haiti. He was seen as a "radical firebrand" who threatened the established relationship between the US and the Haitian elite. See Amy Wilentz, "Love and Haiti," *New Republic*, 5 July, 1993, p. 18.

[21] As quoted in Doyle, "Hollow Diplomacy in Haiti," p. 52.

[22] Refoulement was the policy of returning refugees intercepted on the high seas to Haiti. "US Circle Haiti to Block Mass Exodus of Refugees," *International Herald Tribune*, 16-17 January, 1993.

[23] New York Times editorial as printed in "Haiti: Short-term Cruelty," *International Herald Tribune*, 18 January, 1993.

[24] As quoted in "Clinton is Offered 2-Part Haiti Plan," *International Herald Tribune*, 7 January, 1993.

104 *Understanding the UN Security Council*

UN-OAS co-operation towards Haiti and also condemned the violation of human rights occurring under the *de facto* government.[25]

Boutros Boutros-Ghali was keen to involve the UN in the Haitian issue. He had kept abreast of OAS initiatives during 1992, and on 11 December appointed Dante Caputo as his Special Envoy for Haiti. Boutros-Ghali's initiative was complemented by the decision of the OAS, on 13 December, to explore the possibility of using the Security Council's help to bolster the economic embargo on Haiti. Shortly thereafter, Aristide requested the deployment of a joint UN-OAS human rights monitoring team to Haiti. It was a request welcomed by both the Bush administration and the incoming Clinton administration, both of which believed that it would encourage Haitians to remain in Haiti.[26] Haitian Prime Minister Mark Bazin of the *de facto* government and Caputo signed an agreement, authorizing the deployment of the International Civilian Mission in Haiti (MICIVIH). It was deployed on 5 March, 1993 throughout Haiti and was mandated by the General Assembly to verify, in conjunction with the OAS contingent, respect for human rights in Haiti as well as take steps to promote human rights.[27] The peculiar state of Haitian politics left these initiatives requiring consent from two Haitian governments. Legally, Aristide's approval was required but the *de facto* authorities control of Haitian territory meant that their consent was also necessary for practical reasons.

In May 1993 Lawrence Pezullo, the US Envoy to Haiti appointed by Clinton, and Caputo presented the *de facto* regime with a proposal to deploy UN police monitors in order to monitor the activities of the Haitian military. The plan envisaged the monitors deployed together with the Haitian police in order to build confidence within the civilian population, monitor the performance of the Haitian military and train new civilian police. The US was keen to have its military personnel in Haiti in order to deter another coup, but Aristide was wary of US assistance to the Haitian military. By incorporating the US personnel into the UN contingent, under the authority of the UN special envoy, the plan became acceptable to Aristide. The mission would assist in the training of the Haitian police and assist with the "professionalization" of the Haitian military.[28] However, the proposed mission was flatly rejected by the *de facto* regime which questioned the motives and objectives of the deployment. They were wary of Canadian and French involvement in the police contingent, as both countries were supporters of Aristide.[29] Its leaders stated that they would fight any foreign attempt at invading Haiti.[30] The UN's initiatives were, in effect, caught in a "consent trap." In order to have Aristide's support for the mission, the police contingent had to come under UN auspices. However, a UN, as opposed to US, mission was unacceptable to the *de facto* authorities. Consequently, the UN police monitors were not deployed.

---

[25] Malone, *Decision-Making*, pp. 74-75.
[26] "Aristide Asks UN to Help Cut Exodus," *International Herald Tribune*, 14 January, 1993.
[27] UN General Assembly Resolution 47/20B, 20 April, 1993.
[28] Ian Martin, "Haiti: Mangled Multilateralism," *Foreign Policy*, no. 95, 1994, pp. 77-78.
[29] Ibid.
[30] "Haitian Army Vows to Fight West's Plan," *The Guardian*, 17 May, 1993.

The First Use of Chapter VII in Haiti

Faced with the prospect of Aristide's continued exile, the international community began to increase the pressure on the *de facto* regime. On 7 June, 1993 the President of the Security Council received a letter from the Permanent Representative of Haiti to the UN (representing Aristide's government) requesting that the Council adopt a resolution making the OAS sanctions against Haiti mandatory for all UN member states.[31] This request came in the wake of an OAS meeting at which OAS Foreign Ministers had urged the strengthening of the embargo.[32]

In response to the Haitian request, the members of the Council adopted resolution 841 on 16 June 1993. Acting under Chapter VII and stating "in these unique and exceptional circumstances, the continuation of this situation threatens international peace and security in the region," the Security Council implemented a mandatory embargo on all petroleum and petroleum products, military arms and equipment and imposed a freeze on all assets held by the *de facto* authorities in Haiti held in foreign states.[33] The resolution had been sponsored by three states of the Group of Friends including France, the US and Venezuela. However, characterizing the situation as a threat to international peace and security had been an issue of substantial debate within the Group and had delayed the formulation of the resolution.[34] Even in the formal debate within the Security Council on the draft resolution, only two states drew attention to the threat posed to international peace and security by the Haiti situation. Canada, for example, briefly highlighted the consequences for regional security brought on by Haitian instability, but did so only after providing a lengthy justification for Aristide's return on the basis of his democratic credentials. It was only the Venezuelan representative who made a substantiated argument for why the situation threatened international peace and security, characterizing the potential flood of "hundreds of thousand of Haitians, in terrified flight to other countries" as an indubitable threat to the peace and security of the Caribbean basin.[35]

Most other members of the Council stressed the need for the Council to act in order to restore the legitimate, democratic government of Aristide and indeed the emphasis of the entire debate centred around the issues of democratic legitimacy and the need to enforce the rule of law rather than the threat to regional security. Some states expressed their reluctance to invoke Chapter VII. Brazil, which would emerge as one of the states most suspicious of UNSC Chapter VII action with regard to Haiti, characterized the situation in Haiti as "unique and exceptional," due to the request for UNSC assistance from Aristide and the actions taken (unsuccessfully) by the OAS and the General Assembly. China characterized the Haiti situation as an internal affair of a UN member state, but alluded to Aristide's

---

[31] *UN Document S/25958*, 7 June, 1993.

[32] Malone, *Decision-Making*, p. 84.

[33] UNSC Resolution 841, 16 June, 1993.

[34] Arria, "Diplomacy and the Four Friends of Haiti," p. 94.

[35] *UN Document*, S/PV .3238, 16 June, 1993.

106 *Understanding the UN Security Council*

request, the involvement of the OAS and General Assembly and the uniqueness of the situation as reasons why it voted it favour of the resolution. The Chinese representative was careful to point out that its vote in the affirmative did not affect its "consistent position" of reluctance at UNSC involvement in internal matters of member states.[36] Indeed, such was the level of reluctance to invoke Chapter VII in this instance that the UNSC President, on the specific request of the Council members, made an unusual statement following the adoption of resolution 841, stressing its unique and exceptional nature.[37]

Behind the scenes much political legwork was undertaken in order to ensure that the resolution would be passed. An exception was made in the resolution to allow the importation of propane gas for cooking purposes as a result of French concerns. The French, however, failed to get the other members of the UNSC to authorize a naval blockade of Haiti. Both Brazil and Venezuela were opposed to such an initiative based on long-standing Latin American concerns about intervention into the internal affairs of states.[38] Nevertheless, Aristide's consent for the embargo had served to overcome many of the previous concerns among the Security Council membership that the UNSC should not get involved in the Haitian situation for fear of infringing on Haitian sovereignty.

The Governors Island Agreement

The strong action taken by the Security Council had an immediate affect on the *de facto* government in Haiti. On 21 June Cédras agreed to meet with Caputo in New York on the condition that the imposition of the sanctions be postponed. They were not, but Cédras nevertheless agreed to proximity talks with Aristide on Governors Island in New York on 27 June.[39] For Cédras the negotiations held the appeal of legitimizing his authority, despite the violent take over from Aristide.[40] By 3 July, both men had signed an agreement which included seven key provisions: the nomination of a new Prime Minister by Aristide, and the appointee's confirmation by the Haitian Parliament; suspension of the UN/OAS sanctions following the new Prime Minister's assumption of office; the reform of the armed forces and the creation of a new police force with UN/OAS assistance; an amnesty granted to the coup leaders; the resignation of Cédras and the appointment, by Aristide, of a new Commander in Chief of the Haitian military; Aristide's return to Haiti on 30 October, 1993; the verification of the agreement by the OAS and the UN.[41]

---

[36] Ibid.

[37] Ibid.

[38] New York Times editorial as printed in "Haiti: Brazil Doesn't Help," *International Herald Tribune*, 19-20 June, 1993. See also Arria, "Diplomacy and the Four Friends," p. 94.

[39] Cédras and Aristide never met face to met during the negotiations. David Malone, interview with author, 17 December, 1999.

[40] Ives, "The Coup and US Foreign Policy," p. 98.

[41] *UN Document*, S/26063, 12 July, 1993.

Aristide was reluctant to sign the agreement and only did so after intense pressure from Boutros-Ghali and United States officials.[42] His main concern was that the agreement did not adequately guarantee the terms of his return to Haiti. Boutros-Ghali informed the Council of his intention to consult with Aristide on the deployment of UN personnel to assist with the establishment of the new police force and the modernisation of the military.[43] Following the signing of the Governors Island Agreement (GIA), Haiti's prospects looked good: a plan had been developed to allow the peaceful transfer of power from the illegal military regime to the democratically elected government, and the OAS and UN had demonstrated considerable co-operation in negotiating the GIA, suggesting that the international community was committed to Haiti's development.[44]

The GIA was also significant in that it brought together the *de jure* and *de facto* Haitian governments under one common framework. This framework provided the international community with the consent of each Haitian government for the restoration of Aristide.[45] Unlike the previous plan for UN police monitors to deploy in Haiti which had failed due to a lack of consent from the *de factos*, the GIA provided a mutually-agreed transition process which appeared to have removed UN initiatives from the "consent trap."

On 24 July, Aristide sent a letter to the UN Secretary-General in which he outlined a proposal for the UN to assist the Haitian government in the reform of its military and police forces as prescribed in the GIA. Aristide suggested, as a result of earlier consultations with Boutros-Ghali, that a total of 1160 UN personnel would be required to assist with both tasks. It was expected that they would serve under a commander appointed by the UN Secretary-General, but operate in respect of the Haitian Constitution and Haitian sovereignty. The letter stated that they would only be issued with side arms for their personal protection and would not be authorized to use force to control violence.[46] Following Aristide's letter, Boutros-Ghali proposed to the Security Council the creation of a United Nations Mission in Haiti (UNMIH). He recommended that the mission consist of 567 civilian police monitors to provide guidance and advice to the Haitian military elements in control of law and order, as well as assist with the establishment of a police academy and the training of new police officers. He also recommended the deployment of 60 military trainers and 500 engineers to assist with the modernization of the Haitian

---

[42] Between the time that Cédras signed and Aristide finally put pen to paper, eleven hours had elapsed and the exiled Haitian President had received no fewer than three phone calls of encouragement from Tony Lake, Warren Christopher and the US vice-president, Al Gore. Malone, *Decision-Making*, p. 87. The Clinton administration's strategy towards Haiti and Aristide was focused around the key goal of forcing him to make political concessions to his political opponents in Haiti, accepting the end of his Presidential term in 1996 (which included his years in exile) and accepting the liberal economic policies recommended international financial institutions in exchange for US support for his return to Haiti. See Dupuy, *Haiti in the New World Order*, p. 138.

[43] Malone, *Decision-Making*, p. 87.

[44] Martin, "Haiti: Mangled Multilateralism," p. 73.

[45] Sir David Hannay, interview with author, 29 November, 1999.

[46] *UN Document*, S/26180, 28 July, 1993.

108 *Understanding the UN Security Council*

armed forces, the building of new military barracks, the repair of roads and the drilling of wells. The Secretary-General requested that the troops be deployed for an initial period of six months.[47]

The members of the Security Council partially adopted the recommendations of the Secretary-General with resolution 862 on 31 August, 1993, authorizing the deployment of an advance team of 30 UN personnel to make an assessment of requirements for the possible deployment of UNMIH. Concern about the cost and financing of the peacekeeping operation, as well as concern about how its mandate was to be fulfilled, prevented the members of the Council from adopting the recommendations of Boutros-Ghali in full.[48]   However, the consensual basis for the deployment remained secure and shortly after the advance team reported back to the Secretary-General he was able to recommend its full deployment to the Council. He wrote that it was essential for the parties to adhere to and implement the GIA in order to establish and maintain stability in Haiti.[49]

Growing tensions and violence in Haiti led to renewed pressure to carry out a rapid deployment of UNMIH.   The President of the Security Council made a statement on 17 September deploring the upsurge in violence in Haiti and stated that the members of the Council would hold the *de facto* authorities responsible for the safety of UN personnel and for any violation of the terms of the GIA. The Council also threatened that the continued failure of the *de factos* to implement the GIA would lead to the re-imposition of the sanctions of resolution 841.[50]

The deployment of UNMIH was eventually authorized by resolution 867 on 23 September, 1993. There were two main motivations behind the decision of the Council to adopt this resolution. The first, consistent with the rationale behind resolution 841, was the emphasis on the restoration of democracy. For example, the representative of Spain suggested that the deployment of UNMIH would "bring to the people of Haiti the help they need to restore democracy and democratic institutions." Similarly, the United States representative stressed that "today the United Nations takes another important step towards the restoration of democratic government to Haiti."[51]   But linked to this was the notion that civil order was

---

[47] *UN Document*, S/26352, 25 August, 1993.

[48] See operative paragraph four of Resolution 862, 31 August, 1993, and Malone, *Decision-Making*, p. 90.

[49] *UN Document*, S/26480, 21 September, 1993.

[50] *UN Document*, S/26460, 6 October, 1993.

[51] *UN Document*, S/PV .3282, 23 September, 1993. While the Clinton administration was publicly calling for the return of Aristide to Haiti, senior Conservative politicians in Washington had protested US support for the exiled Haitian President. Senator Bob Dole, Henry Kissinger, Jesse Helms, Elliot Abrams and Dick Cheney all spoke out against Aristide. Following Clinton's attempt to increase pressure on the de facto regime, he was undercut by growing scepticism in Congress. A profile of the Haitian President by the CIA's senior Latin America analyst concluded that Aristide had psychological problems, accusations that subsequently turned out to be baseless, but were aimed at turning public support away from the exiled leader. See Karin von Hippel, "Democratisation as Foreign Policy: The Case of Haiti," *The World Today*, January 1995, p. 12 and Constable, "Haiti: A Nation in Despair," p. 114.

Haiti 109

promoted through respect for democratic principles. Again, in the words of the US representative, "the establishment and maintenance of civil order by democratic means is essential to the future of Haiti, and helping that to occur is a central purpose of the United Nations mission." The Japanese representative similarly linked the two themes: "Japan strongly hopes that the responsible authorities will take immediate measures...to maintain public order and expedite the process of recovery and a return to democratic, constitutional order in Haiti."[52] Interestingly, not one of the seven representatives whose chose to comment on the adoption of resolution 867 drew attention to the supposed threat posed by Haitian instability to regional security.

Loss of *De Facto* Consent

An advance team of UNMIH personnel arrived in Port-au-Prince on 11 October aboard the USS *Harlan County*. However, in the days immediately prior to its landing, the political atmosphere in Haiti deteriorated. Although possessing the approval for UNMIH from the *de facto* regime as well as from Aristide, the Front Révolutionnaire pour l'Avancement et le Progrès Haitien (FRAPH), a pro-government group, declared a general strike against UNMIH.[53]

As the *Harlan County* prepared to enter Port-au-Prince to deploy the first contingent of UNMIH personnel, it found its arranged docking berth occupied and a group of agitated demonstrators crowding the dockyard. Wielding small weapons, threatening foreign diplomatic personnel, including the US Charge d'Affaires, the demonstrators proclaimed they would turn Haiti "into another Somalia."[54] In response to this opposition, the *Harlan County* received orders from the White House not to discharge the UNMIH personnel, and return to its base at Guantánamo Bay, Cuba. The Central Intelligence Agency (CIA) and Pentagon officials at the White House had advised that US lives were in danger. However, it later emerged that the leader of the FRAPH, Emmanuel Constant, had organised the demonstration with the tacit approval of the CIA, and had assured the agency that no American lives would be endangered.[55]

Apparently falling foul of inter-agency disagreement within the US government as to the desirability of UNMIH, the credibility of the international community was nevertheless damaged by the *Harlan County* incident. Its resolve towards re-installing the legitimate, democratic government of Aristide had proven thin in the face a small demonstration by armed gangs. It was a reaction that was undoubtedly conditioned by the recent tragedies in Somalia and the deaths of the Pakistani and US soldiers deployed in UNOSOM II.[56] It nevertheless

---

[52] These comments are recorded in *UN Document,* S/PV .3282, 23 September, 1993.

[53] Malone, *Decision-Making*, p. 91.

[54] Boutros-Ghali, *Unvanquished*, p. 108.

[55] Malone , *Decision-Making*, p. 92.

[56] Pamela Constable, "Haiti: A Nation in Despair, a Policy Adrift," *Current History*, vol. 93, no. 581, 1994, p. 112.

110 *Understanding the UN Security Council*

demonstrated that consent-based peacekeeping in the case of UNMIH meant near absolute tactical consent on the ground as well as strategic consent from the *de jure* and *de facto* governments.

To its credit, the Security Council acted quickly in response to the *Harlan County* incident. On 13 October it adopted resolution 873, re-imposing the sanctions originally authorised by resolution 841.[57] However, the violence in Haiti continued. On 14 October the new reform-oriented, US trained Haitian Justice Minister, Guy Malary, was assassinated. His murder was viewed as a challenge from the Haitian military and the civilian right wing elite to the international community.[58] It was a challenge that was declined as, on the same day, Canada announced the withdrawal of its UNMIH personnel from Port-au-Prince. Shortly thereafter, the Canadians were followed by UNMIH's American personnel.[59] Similarly, on 16 October, the majority of MICIVIH was withdrawn.[60]

In response to the rapidly deteriorating situation, and the ever diminishing prospect of his return to Haiti, Aristide wrote to Boutros-Ghali requesting that the sanctions on Haiti be further strengthened due to the failure of the coup leaders to implement the GIA.[61] The Security Council agreed to these measures in resolution 875, on 16 October, and imposed a naval blockade around Haiti. The members of the Council cited their outrage at the murder of Malary, and noted the need for the enhanced embargo in order to protect the prospect of democracy in Haiti. Once again, China voted in favour of the resolution, qualifying its support as based on the "unique and exceptional nature" of the Haitian case.[62] Russia viewed the recent incidents in Haiti as a challenge to the international community from the *de facto* government which required "the expression of the Security Council's determination to complete the political settlement in Haiti." Brazil also overcame its reservations towards Chapter VII action by the UNSC with regard to the Haitian situation because its "uniqueness and exceptional character" and the fact that the action of the Council was taken in response to a "formal and explicit request by the legitimate Government of Haiti. Brazil regarded that request as "essential for the Security Council to act as it did."[63]

In effect, the *de facto* government's failure to implement the GIA meant that it lost any standing that it may have previously had in the eyes of the Security Council members. This helped to solidify support within the UNSC behind

---

[57] UNSC Resolution 873, 13 October, 1993.

[58] Constable, "Haiti: A Nation in Despair," p. 109.

[59] The withdrawal of the advance Canadian contingent was brought on by the failure to deploy the troops on board the *USS Harlan County*. Louise Fréchette, interview with author, 17 December, 1999.

[60] Malone, *Decision-Making*, p. 92.

[61] *UN Document*, S/26587, 15 October, 1993.

[62] China was also keen to avoid "blocking" UNSC action on issues of concern to other members of the UNSC, preferring instead to act only in cases where Chinese interests were involved. Louis Frechette, interview with author, 17 December, 1999.

[63] The comments of the UNSC members are recorded in *UN Document*, S/PV .3293, 16 October, 1993.

Haiti 111

Aristide.[64] Despite the invocation of Chapter VII, no member of the Council highlighted the threat posed to international peace and security by the Haitian situation. Instead the main emphasis throughout the debate on the resolution was the promotion of democracy in Haiti and the protection of human rights.[65] Accordingly, the Council members appeared to flexibly interpret the phrase "international peace and security" so as to arrogate themselves the authority to act under Chapter VII and promote the restoration of the Aristide government.[66]

Following the re-imposition of sanctions and the withdrawal of most UN personnel from Haiti, the effort to restore Aristide remained confined to diplomatic initiatives. The *de facto* authorities appeared to have successfully called the bluff on the international community and the pressure on them to implement the terms of the GIA was limited. The sanctions, which had been reapplied by the members of the Council on 13 October, appeared to be ineffective as the porous border with the Dominican Republic allowed the Haitian military to easily obtain gasoline and oil supplies.[67] The levels of violence in Haiti continued to grow, and many of those killed were supporters of Aristide. The few remaining MICIVIH observers in Port-au-Prince reported that much of the violence was carried out by members of FRAPH or attachés with links to the *de facto* government.[68]

Renewed political efforts by the Clinton administration to remove Haiti from the political radar increased the likelihood of the proposals for a strengthened UNMIH mandate being accepted by the Council. These were brought on by three main factors. First was Aristide's criticism of the US policy of turning Haitian refugees back to Port-au-Prince as they attempted to flee to Florida. Aristide also threatened to rescind the 1981 agreement between Haiti (signed by Duvalier) and the United States which allowed the US to legally intercept and repatriate Haitian refugees.[69] Second was the decision of the Congressional Black Caucus, traditionally key supporters of Clinton and an integral part of his Democratic coalition, to publicly criticize his Haitian policy and call for the replacement of

---

[64] Sir David Hannay, interview with author, 29 November, 1999.

[65] *UN Document*, S/PV .3293, 16 October, 1993.

[66] Louis Fréchette, interview with author, 17 December, 1999.

[67] Constable, "Haiti: A Nation in Despair," p. 109.

[68] *The Blue Helmets*, p. 620. A few administrative personnel had remained in Port-au-Prince following the withdrawal of most MICIVIH employees in October, 1993.

[69] Dupuy, *Haiti in the New World Order*, p. 157. During this period Aristide pursued a two pronged strategy. First he negotiated with the political elite in Haiti in order to reduce their suspicions of his return. Second, he increasingly sought to convince Washington that without his return, the problems of the Haitian refugees and the economic instability of the state would continue to plague the Clinton administration. While his assumption that the US government wanted to restore stability to Haiti in order to limit the flow of refugees to the US was correct, this objective did not necessarily mean the restoration of a democratic government as US government actions later in the crisis demonstrate. See also Joseph S. Tulchin, "The Formulation of US Foreign Policy in the Caribbean," The Annals of the American Academy of Political and Social Science, no. 533, 1994, p. 185.

112 *Understanding the UN Security Council*

Pezullo.[70] The third factor was increasingly negative publicity for the administration on the Haiti issue.[71]

On 6 May, 1994, the members of the Security Council decided to increase the pressure on the *de facto* Haitian government by furthering tightening the sanctions already in place. Resolution 917, adopted on 6 May, 1994, restricted air travel into and out of Haiti, took steps to confine the coup leaders, Haiti military officers and their families in Haiti by denying them travel to other countries, and expanded the freeze on Haitian financial assets to include those held by anyone connected with the Haitian military, the perpetrators of the 1991 coup or the *de facto* regime. The resolution also further restricted the import or export of commodities or products to or from Haiti.[72]

The tightening of sanctions and the specific restrictions imposed on the coup leaders and their families had a minimal impact on pressuring them to accept the terms of the GIA.[73] Defying the pressure of the international community the *de facto* government appointed a "provisional President," Emile Jonassaint, on 11 May.[74] This flew in the face of the international efforts to restore Aristide to the country as its legitimate President, and was met with condemnation from the Security Council.[75] Yet due to strong opposition from many Latin American countries to the use of force to restore Aristide, international efforts to this end remained confined to diplomatic and economic measures.[76]

The situation in the country continued to deteriorate throughout the summer of 1994. It emerged that during a two month period earlier in the spring nearly 21,000 refugees had fled from Haiti and it was suspected that 300,000 were soon to be following.[77] The cost of caring for the Haitian refugees held at Guantanamo Bay military base in Cuba was $14 million per month.[78] On 9 June, the Group of

---

[70] "White House Urged to Act Over Haiti," *The Financial Times*, 24 March, 1994.

[71] Malone, *Decision-Making*, p. 104. Six members of Congress chained themselves to the fence of the White House in protest of the US Haitian policy and brought a further wave of negative publicity down on the Clinton administration. This was exacerbated by the decision of Randall Robinson, an advocate of US Black interest in foreign policy, to launch a hunger strike to protest the US policy. As a concession to the Black Caucus, Pezullo resigned and in his place William Gray III was appointed as Special Advisor on Haiti.

[72] UNSC Resolution 917, 6 May, 1994.

[73] The regime leaders, anticipating the US imposed financial restrictions, had long before transferred their funds to accounts where they could not be frozen. As a result, such financial restrictions were ineffective. See Harold Hongju Koh, "The Haiti Paradigm in United States Human Rights Policy," *The Yale Law Journal*, vol. 103, 1994, p. 2432.

[74] *The Blue Helmets*, p. 62.

[75] *UN Document*, S/PRST/1994/24, 11 May, 1994.

[76] "Latin American Reject Use of Force to Unseat Haitian Military," *International Herald Tribune*, 14-15 May, 1994.

[77] The reality of the Haitian refugee flow is a subject of debate to this day. Some analysts argue that the estimated numbers of refugees were greatly exaggerated. See for example John Canham-Clyne, "Selling out Democracy," in *The Haiti Files*, pp. 112-113. Regardless of whether or not this was the case, the important thing is that there was a *perception* within the US that a wave of refugees was coming.

[78] von Hippel, "Democratisation as Foreign Policy," p. 13.

Friends wrote to the President of the Security Council expressing their continued concern at the situation in Haiti and their determination "to promote the full redeployment" of UNMIH once conditions improved. To this end they suggested that the mission be reconfigured and strengthened.[79] On the same day, an OAS resolution made a similar recommendation.[80]

In late June, Boutros-Ghali informed the members of the Security Council that the *de facto* government had not made any move toward implementing the GIA. He also reported that Jonassaint's appointment had been condemned by the Haitian Prime Minister, Robert Malval, as well as by the main Haitian political parties. Joinassaint had taken steps to reduce the public liberty of the Haitian people by declaring a state of emergency, and human rights violations were reported to have increased sharply, particularly against supporters of Aristide. Similarly, Boutros-Ghali reported that the humanitarian situation continued to deteriorate, with relief efforts hampered by the poor security situation and the limited stocks available to humanitarian agencies.[81] Later that same month, the Secretary-General suggested that because the situation had deteriorated to such an extent, the members of the Security Council would perhaps have to consider altering the mandate under which UNMIH would be deployed once political progress towards implementing the GIA recommenced. With the continued intransigence of the military government and the violent tactics of the attachés the deployment of a consensual, non-coercive peacekeeping mission into Haiti no longer seemed appropriate. In the interim, he suggested that the mandate of the operation be again extended.[82]

With resolution 933 the members of the Security Council opted to extend the mandate of UNMIH until the end of July, 1994 and also requested the Secretary-General to report back to them on the possible expansion and deployment of UNMIH following the departure of the military leadership. The Council members noted their concern about the deteriorating humanitarian situation in Haiti and continued to classify the Haitian situation as a threat to international peace and security.

Though the resolution was adopted unanimously, Brazil appeared hesitant towards moving the efforts of the international community away from sanctions and towards the strengthening of UNMIH. Its representative argued that the sanctions should be given longer to work and any bolstering of UNMIH should occur "within the framework of a multilateral effort aimed at helping the legitimate government." The Russian representative also questioned the rethinking of UNMIH's deployment, expressing concern about the financing, strength, and length of a potentially revised mission.[83] However, Russian support for the resolution came about as a result of political horse-trading. The Russians had

---

[79] *UN Document*, S/1994/686, 9 June, 1994.
[80] OAS Resolution MRE/RES.6/94, 9 June, 1994.
[81] *UN Document*, S/1994/742, 20 June, 1994.
[82] *UN Document*, S/1994/765, 28 June, 1994.
[83] *UN Document*, S/PV .3397, 30 June, 1997.

114 *Understanding the UN Security Council*

threatened to veto the resolution because of a lack of American support for Russian proposals for a peacekeeping operation in Georgia.[84]

In another act of defiance to the wishes of the international community, the *de facto* government expelled the recently re-deployed MICIVIH personnel from Haiti on 11 July.[85] In response, the members of the Security Council issued a statement in which they considered the action of the *de facto* government as "a serious escalation in the defiant stance of Haiti's illegal *de facto* regime towards the international community," and suggested that "this provocative behaviour directly affects the peace and security in the region."[86] Though the *de factos* did not have the legal authority to demand the withdrawal of the UN civilian mission they nonetheless remained in control of Haitian territory. Consequently, MICIVIH personnel left Port-au-Prince on 13 July.

Towards a Multi-National Force

Consistent with the UNSC's request in resolution 933, Boutros-Ghali submitted his proposal for a strengthened UNMIH on 15 July 1994.[87] It focused on coping with the transitional period following the departure of the *de facto* government and leading up to the restoration of the legitimate government. The main tasks envisaged for UNMIH during this period were ensuring the security of the international presence, ensuring public order, protecting key installations and protecting senior government officials. Importantly, the Secretary-General raised the possible need for a new UNMIH mandate to be authorized under Chapter VII of the Charter in order to permit the operation to use force. Such methods, he noted, would be required to fulfil basic tasks of ensuring law and order and bringing any transitional violence under control. To this end, Boutros-Ghali recommended the deployment of 15,610 troops, deployed in two phases. The first phase would be directed at securing public order, combating violence and assisting the legitimate government. The second phase would be directed towards the implementation of the GIA. The expansion and revision of the mandate, he noted, would require the consent of the legitimate authorities.[88] This plan, despite its use of Chapter VII, remained predicated on the voluntary departure of the military

---

[84] David Malone, "Haiti and the International Community: A Case Study," *Survival*, vol. 39, no.2, 1997, p. 138. The Russian decision to initially oppose resolution 933 was linked to Russia's experience supporting the French operation in Rwanda and the failure of the Russians to seek a similar agreement from the French in return for Russian support for *Opération Turquoise*.

[85] "Haiti Ousts Observers From UN and OAS," *International Herald Tribune*, 12 July, 1994. The MICIVIH mandate had been renewed by the UN General Assembly on 8 July, 1994. UNGA Resolution A/48/L.57.

[86] *UN Document*, S/PRST/1994/32, 12 July, 1994.

[87] *UN Document*, S/1994/828, 15 July, 1994.

[88] Ibid.

Haiti 115

authorities from Haiti and did not consider the use of force to bring about the departure of those authorities.

Despite this concrete proposal, Boutros-Ghali was sceptical of the UN's ability to deploy the revised UNMIH force quickly enough. He also doubted that the mission would be given adequate resources by UN member states. These concerns led him to advise the Council against the expansion of UNMIH. Instead, he suggested two alternative approaches. In the first the UNSC, at the request of the legitimate government, would authorize a group of member states to implement the tasks envisaged for UNMIH. In the second a UN-authorized coalition of members states would, again at the request of the legitimate government, implement the tasks envisaged in phase one of the deployment before transferring responsibility for the implementation of the phase two tasks to a Chapter VI authorized UNMIH.[89] In both options the multi-national Chapter VII authorized forces were predicated on a prior request from the legitimate government of Aristide. Because of this request, the use of Chapter VII in either option would not take the Security Council beyond the consent of the *de jure* host government.

The UN seemed to be moving towards the potential use of force in Haiti but only in relation to the maintenance of public order following the departure of the *de facto* regime. However, the United States had begun to consider means of forcing the *de factos* the leave Haiti. In early July, it emerged that the US had been secretly planning the seizure of Haitian airfields and ports. While this plan was ultimately abandoned, the emphasis on coercion remained, sparked mainly by the decision of the OAS and Friends to urge a re-evaluation of UNMIH's mandate, the continued intransigence of the *de factos* and renewed domestic political pressure. The decision of the *de factos* to order out the remaining MICIVIH personnel on 11 July was another key factor pushing the White House towards the adoption of coercive methods to reinstall Aristide.[90]

During the last week of July, 1994 the US compiled a draft UNSC resolution advocating the restoration of Aristide that was circulated to the GRULAC states. Only Argentina supported the US proposal. Brazil and Venezuela both wanted an explicit request from Aristide before they would support the resolution.[91] Consent from the exiled Haitian President for any attempt by the Security Council to adopt coercive measures with regard to Haiti thus became crucial. Yet it was a problematic issue. A year earlier, when Aristide had agreed to the deployment of MICIVIH and the UN police monitors, he had been criticized by a wide variety of Haiti's popular organisations who argued that:

> You gave the OAS and UN authorization to send "civilian observers" into the country, and even though it was strong medicine and a hard blow, we never officially protested because we always believed that you knew what you were doing and that there was a line you would not cross.

---

[89] Ibid.

[90] Malone, *Decision-Making*, p. 107.

[91] Ibid. p. 109.

116   *Understanding the UN Security Council*

> ...we cannot understand your silence and the silence of your government in this affair...We hope that you will immediately take an official public position that is crystal clear in denouncing and condemning this plan [to deploy UN police monitors].[92]

Aristide believed that by the terms of the 1987 Haitian Constitution he was barred from calling for a foreign invasion of Haiti.[93] Were he to do so, he believed that he would be undermining his legitimacy as President by acting contrary to the Constitution.

Legally, if the Council chose to act under Chapter VII, they did not require Aristide's consent. Politically, however, Aristide's request for UN action to deploy a MNF to Haiti was crucial to getting such a resolution passed in the Security Council. Without his consent, the resolution would have likely faced a Chinese veto and fierce opposition from Latin American states.[94]

Eventually on 29 July, under great pressure from both the UN and US, and probably recognising that the MNF represented his best chance to return to power, Aristide sent a letter to the President of the Security Council requesting "prompt and decisive action" by the international community. This first letter was rejected by the Group of Friends as insufficiently explicit. Consequently, the next morning, Boutros-Ghali received a second letter from the Permanent Representative of Haiti to the UN, Fritz Longchamp, which expressed the consent of the *de jure* Haitian government to the proposed UNSC resolution.[95]

On 31 July the members of the Security Council met to discuss the proposals of the Secretary-General and the draft resolution presented by the Group of Friends. The resolution was not unopposed and its critics, including Mexico, Cuba, Uruguay, Venezuela and Brazil had three key problems with its terms.

First, they did not accept that the situation in Haiti constituted a threat to international peace and security.[96] Consequently, they felt that the proposed use of Chapter VII to authorize the resolution was unjustified. Although they had been willing to go along with the characterization of the situation as a threat to international peace and security in order to implement the economic embargo, they were not willing to make a similar characterization in order to authorize the use of force. Instead they expressed their preference for a continued reliance on other methods, such as prolonged sanctions, to remedy the situation. Mexico, for example, doubted the timing of the resolution and regretted "that the Security Council has decided that it is necessary to have recourse to the use of force to resolve the crisis in Haiti." The Cuban representative argued that the characterization of the situation in Haiti was something "new and removed from the precepts established by the Charter of the United Nations concerning the

---

[92] As quoted in Ives, "The Coup and US Foreign Policy," p. 97.
[93] "UN Backs Use of Force to Remove Haiti Junta," *The Financial Times*, 1 August, 1994.
[94] Zhou Fei, interview with author, 15 December, 1999.
[95] Aristide apparently never openly accepted the MNF intervention in order to be able to disclaim responsibility for it. See Boutros-Ghali, *Unvanquished*, p. 153.
[96] *UN Document*, S/PV .3413, 31 July, 1994.

Haiti 117

authority of the Security Council." Similarly, Uruguay did "not believe that the internal political situation in Haiti projects externally in such a way as to represent a threat to international peace and security."[97] Second, the critics wanted Aristide's restoration to power be explicitly mentioned in the preamble of the resolution as an objective of the UNSC.[98] A third concern of the GRULAC states was the role of the United States and their reluctance to see a US-led, UN sanctioned intervention in the Caribbean.[99]

Given the problems with characterizing the conflict as a threat to international peace and security, the supporters of the resolution instead focused on the need to re-establish the legitimate government of Haiti and relieve the humanitarian crisis. Canada argued that its "commitment to restoring democracy in Haiti is unwavering." The US characterized the rationale underlying the resolution as a simple choice between right and wrong, "in favour of democracy, law, dignity and relief from suffering long endured and never deserved" or not. France similarly focused on the need to restore Aristide rather than the need to counter a threat to international peace and security. It was only the Argentinean representative who linked the maintenance of international peace and security, the consolidation of democracy and the promotion of human rights as the inter-related objectives of the resolution.[100]

The draft resolution was adopted by a vote of twelve in favour, none against, with two states (Brazil and China) abstaining. Both New Zealand and Russia stated that the request of Aristide for Security Council action on Haiti was a key consideration in their support for the resolution.[101] Brazil's reservations were explained as due to the speed with which the decision to authorize the use of force had occurred. The Brazilians wished more time for consideration of the resolution's potential implications, and also to allow more time for sanctions to take their toll on the *de facto* regime. China explained its abstention as due to the fact it did not believe the Council was justified in its use of force in the context of Haiti. It argued "resolving problems such as that of Haiti through military means does not conform with the principles enshrined in the United Nations Charter and lacks sufficient and convincing ground."[102]

The debate also included statements that suggested that some UNSC members believed that the Council's action served to restore the true sovereign authority in Haiti. The Argentinean representative argued that the solution to the

---

[97] Ibid.

[98] Ian Williams, "No Free Hand in Haiti," *New Statesman & Society*, 29 July, 1994, p. 10.

[99] Morris, "Force and Democracy," p. 405. However, the fact that the US was willing to act using the UN framework helped to mute Latin American objections to its lead role in the MNF. See Malone, "Haiti and the International Community," p. 137.

[100] Ibid. The characterisation of the situation as a threat to international peace and security appears to have been one of convenience. Sir David Hannay, for example, believes that Haiti did not represent a real threat to regional security, but because the international community wanted to resolve the situation, such a characterisation had to be made. Sir David Hannay, interview with author, 29 November, 1999.

[101] *UN Document*, S/PV .3413, 31 July, 1994.

[102] Ibid.

118 *Understanding the UN Security Council*

problems in Haiti "requires respect and support for the sovereignty of the Haitian people, which was seized and usurped by those who unlawfully hold power." The Haitian representative similarly argued that helping to remove the *de facto* government and restore Aristide was a demonstration of the Council's respect for Haitian sovereignty: "by stating the consent of the Government of President Aristide to the draft resolution before the Council, we are calling on the international community, through you, Mr. President, to join with us in defending our national sovereignty." [103]

Resolution 940 authorized:

> ...member states to form a multinational force under unified command and control and, in this framework, to use all necessary means to facilitate the departure from Haiti of the military leadership, consistent with the Governors Island Agreement, the prompt return of the legitimately elected President and the restoration of the legitimate authorities of the Government of Haiti, and to establish and maintain a secure and stable environment that will permit implementation of the Governors Island Agreement, on the understanding that the cost of implementing this temporary operation will be borne by the participating Member States...

It extended the mandate of UNMIH by six months, envisaging that the peacekeeping operation would take over from the Multi-National Force (MNF) following the creation of "a secure and stable environment." The resolution also explicitly authorised the MNF to use all necessary means to facilitate the departure of the military leadership from Haiti, an issue which the 15 July report of the UN Secretary-General had avoided. [104]

In the hours immediately after the Security Council's adoption of resolution 940, the *de facto* regime declared a state of siege. President Jonassaint called the Council's action "arbitrary, iniquitous and in violation of international rights." [105] In an attempt to bring about the peaceful deployment of the MNF authorized by resolution 940, Boutros-Ghali dispatched a UN official to meet with the *de facto* authorities in the hopes of discussing the implementation of the resolution. The *de facto* authorities refused to meet with the UN envoy. [106]

There was certainly little effort made to deploy the MNF quickly. Indeed the Clinton administration hoped that the threat of invasion, combined with ongoing sanctions would finally force the *de facto* regime to accede to the demands of the international community. The US desire to get the resolution through the Security Council had primarily been about domestic political realities and the approach of mid-term elections. The Clinton administration was eager to maintain its key support base within the Black Caucus, particularly given the fact that, apart from the Haitian issue, the administration faced two crucial domestic issues, on health

---

[103] Ibid.

[104] UNSC Resolution 940, 31 July, 1994 and *UN Document*, S/1994/828, 15 July, 1994.

[105] "Haiti Declares State of Siege After UN Vote on Force," *The Financial Times*, 2 August, 1994.

[106] *The Blue Helmets*, p. 623.

care and crime, being debated in Congress in the later summer of 1994 for which it needed the Caucus' support.[107]

In the interim, domestic US opposition to the possible implementation of resolution 940 was growing. According to opinion polls, between 66 and 73 per cent of US voters opposed military action in Haiti, while 78 per cent felt that Clinton should have asked Congress for permission to invade Haiti.[108] This compounded internal divisions within the Clinton administration on the efficacy of intervention and the potential results of continued sanctions.[109]

Awaiting the implementation of resolution 940, the *de facto* regime remained defiant. On 28 August, 1994 Father Jean-Marie Vincent, a key supporter and friend of Aristide was murdered by attachés. Responding to this killing, and perhaps wanting to pre-empt further Congressional opposition to military action in Haiti, Clinton issued an ultimatum to the *de facto* Haitian regime. He stated that the US had to intervene in Haiti "to protect our interests, to stop the brutal atrocities that threaten tens of thousands of Haitians, to secure our borders and to preserve stability and promote democracy in our hemisphere..."[110] The White House tried desperately to get rid of the increasingly defiant military regime. Pressure from the refugee outflow caused it to look to other options beyond sanctions in order to remedy the situation. Intervention under the terms of resolution 940 was viewed as a last resort. One such initiative was the $12 million financing of a covert operation by the CIA to finance the overthrow of the coup leaders by 'friendly' elements within the Haitian military.[111] The commitment of the US to the re-instalment of a democratic regime seemed weaker than its desire to simply install a regime that was more amenable to US interests. When such initiatives failed, the primary option remaining was action under the terms of resolution 940.

Presenting the regime with a last chance to avoid the forcible intervention of the MNF, Clinton despatched former US President Jimmy Carter, Senator Sam Nunn, and the Chairman of the Joints Chiefs of Staff, Colin Powell, to meet with the *de facto* authorities. When faced with the imminent arrival of US troops and offered a dignified and 'honourable' exit, including an amnesty, the key *de facto*

---

[107] Ian Williams, "US Dithers on Haiti," *New Statesman & Society*, 12 August, 1994, p. 10.

[108] Lori Fisler Damrosch, "AGORA: The 1994 US Action in Haiti," *The American Journal of International Law*, vol. 89, 1995, p. 59.

[109] Morris Morley and Chris McGillion, "'Disobedient Generals and the Politics of Redemocratization: The Clinton Administration and Haiti," *Political Science Quarterly*, vol. 112, no. 3, 1997, p. 379. There was also an internal US debate raging on constitutional objections to the deployment of US troops by the US President without the agreement of Congress. In August 1994, the US Senate passed a resolution declaring that in order for the United States to use force in Haiti, Congressional approval was required. Clinton stated in September, 1994 that he would not request authorisation from Congress to deploy troops to Haiti and by mid-September a furious debate raged in Washington and on Capitol Hill. See Gaddis Smith, "Haiti: From Intervention to Intervasion," *Current History*, vol. 94, no. 589, 1994, p. 58 and Malone, *Decision-Making*, p. 111.

[110] Clinton as quoted in Dupuy, *Haiti in the New World Order*, p. 159.

[111] Morely and McGillion, "Disobedient Generals," p. 380.

120 *Understanding the UN Security Council*

authorities agreed to leave Haiti and ordered their troops not to oppose *Operation Uphold Democracy.*[112] On the eve of the invasion, the US also achieved another of its key goals - Aristide's assurance that he would not seek another term in office beyond 1996.[113] Interestingly, US negotiations with the *de factos* cut right to the heart of the questions on legitimacy and sovereignty even at the last minute. Jonasaint agreed not to oppose the deployment of US forces, but insisted that he, as President, would sign the formal agreement on the peaceful occupation of Haiti. As Jonasaint was not recognised by the US as Haitian President, Colin Powell had to telephone the White House in order to get approval for Jonassaint to sign the document.[114]

Operation Uphold Democracy

Having secured the agreement of the *de facto* authorities not to oppose the deployment of the MFN, the first elements of *Operation Uphold Democracy* were deployed to Haiti on 19 September, 1994. Nine days later, on 27 September, the United States reported to the UNSC President that 12,000 MFN personnel had been deployed in Haiti with operations being conducted in the cities of Port-au-Prince, Jacmel, Gonaives and Cap Haitien. In addition it reported that all key military ports and installations had been secured. The report stated that the force was firmly on its way to establishing a stable and secure environment across Haiti.[115] In its second report on the fulfilment of resolution 940 and the activities of the MNF, the US informed the President of the Security Council that the situation in Haiti was relatively quiet, with few acts of violence. The MNF also had begun to reduce the number of troops deployed from its peak of 21,000, as well as to implement disarmament programs against the FRAPH and attachés and throughout the Haitian public.[116]

On 10 October, the Haitian Parliament passed legislation granting amnesty to key *de facto* authorities, whereupon Cédras resigned as Commander in Chief of the Haitian armed forces as called for in the agreement negotiated by Carter.[117] Five days later, with the coup leaders having left the country, Aristide returned to Haiti to resume his functions as President.[118] Welcoming Aristide's return to Haiti, the

---

[112] Malone, *Decision-Making*, p. 112.

[113] Jean-Germain Gros, "Haiti's Flagging Transition", *Journal of Democracy*, vol. 8, no. 4, 1997, p. 94.

[114] "Carter Reveals Countdown to High Noon in Caribbean," *The Guardian*, 20 September, 1994.

[115] *UN Document*, S/1994/1107, 28 September, 1994.

[116] *UN Document*, S/1994/1148, 10 October, 1994.

[117] Normally in international law, agreements signed under duress are not considered binding. However, as the MNF was authorised by the Security Council, the agreement the *de factos* signed following the Nunn/Powell/Carter mission was considered legitimate. Confidential interview with author.

[118] "Haitians Stay Calm as Aristide Resumes Power," *The Financial Times*, 17 October, 1994.

Transition to UNMIH

As envisaged in resolution 940, preparations for the transfer from the MNF to the UNMIH peacekeeping operation continued throughout the rest of 1994 and early 1995. The member states of the MNF informed the UNSC President that, consistent with resolution 940, a stable and secure environment had been established in Haiti.[120] In response, the Security Council state adopted resolution 975, declaring that the MNF had met its objectives and authorizing the Secretary-General to take the necessary steps to ensure a smooth transition from the MNF the UNMIH.[121] Eventually, on 31 March, 1995 the official transition from the MNF to UNMIH took place in Port-au-Prince.

Conclusion

The military coup against Aristide in 1991 resulted in the formation of two Haitian governments; the *de jure*, led by Aristide in exile in the United States, and the *de facto* in power in Haiti. For the United Nations to become involved in supporting the return of Aristide, the organisation had to obtain the consent of both Haitian governments to any peace-making or peacekeeping initiatives. The consent of the *de facto* government was needed for practical reasons. From a political standpoint, many UNSC members believed that the coup was an internal affair of Haiti in which the UNSC should not become involved. These reservations precluded any UNSC involvement in the issue for nearly two years. When the UN did become engaged in Haiti, the hazards of having to weave through such a delicate political minefield were demonstrated by the fate of the proposed UN police monitors mission in May 1993. For the mission to be acceptable to Aristide, US advisors had to be incorporated into a UN force. The *de facto* government was wary of the UN and flatly rejected the proposed mission. However, the consent of the *de factos* was a practical necessity given their control of Haitian territory.

The intransigence of the *de factos* towards a gradual transfer of power back to the Aristide government prompted the international community to place increased pressure on them. The imposition of the economic and military embargo, made possible only by Aristide's request for it, pressured the *de factos* into signing the GIA. This agreement was significant in that combined the 'sovereign' consent of both the *de factos* and the *de jure* Haitian governments under a common framework and clearly identified a transition process for the restoration of Aristide, including the deployment of UNMIH. However, when the

---

[119] UNSC Resolution 948, 15 October, 1994.

[120] *UN Document*, S/1995/55, 19 January, 1995.

[121] UNSC Resolution 975, 30 January, 1995.

122 *Understanding the UN Security Council*

advance elements of the peacekeeping mission were greeted with hostility in Port-au-Prince, it became clear that the *de factos*, allegedly with prompting from the CIA, had reneged on their commitment to implement the GIA. The decision to withdraw the *Harlan County* without discharging its cargo also underscored the reluctance of the United States to deploy peacekeeping troops without near absolute consent on the ground in the wake of Somalia.

Continued defiance on the part of the *de facto* authorities, despite additional pressure from the international community to implement the terms of the GIA, led to more vocal calls for the restoration of Aristide. In practice, the situation in October, 1993 compared to that before the GIA had been signed was not different - Aristide's internationally recognised government was still in exile, and Haiti was controlled by the *de facto* military regime. But what brought on the increased pressure from the international community had been the failure of the *de factos* to implement the GIA. Their inability to live up to their international commitments consequently further decreased their standing in the eyes of the sovereign members of the international community.[122]

Despite international condemnation of the *de factos* actions, only limited steps were taken to restore Aristide in the wake of the *Harlan County* incident. Although recognising the *de factos* as an illegitimate government, the international community appeared hesitant to take any form of action other than the reluctant imposition of Chapter VII economic sanctions in order to bring about Aristide's restoration. This situation changed as political repression in Haiti began to increase and, more significantly, the outflow of Haitian refugees became an issue of considerable importance in US domestic politics. Clinton had to counter the growing political issue of the Haitian refugees and the growing opposition within his own party, led by the Congressional Black Caucus, against his policy on refugees. Aristide's return was intended to achieve this. Consequently, it would be inaccurate to believe that the main motivating factor for the US was the desire to restore democracy to Haiti.[123] Instead it wanted to install a government that would be more able to cope with the economic and social ills of the country, ills which impinged on US interests. As Maingot has argued, it was " a rare case where the law of necessity works towards a moral end."[124]

Given this injection of US political commitment to restoring Aristide, there were still reservations among the Latin American members of the Security Council towards using force to remove the *de facto* regime. There were two main objections among members of the UNSC to using Chapter VII in relation to Haiti. First, not all members of the Council believed that the conflict presented a threat to

---

[122] As outlined in Chapter One, the ability of states to honour international treaties or obligations is a key component of sovereign status. See Jackson, *Quasi-States*, p. 35.

[123] It is difficult to believe that two short years after having abandoned its "moral" Presidential election promise not to repatriate Haitian refugees in exchange for the more politically expedient policy followed by its Republican predecessor, the Clinton administration would again shed this realist approach in favour of the 'restoration of democracy' mantra. See Doyle, "Hollow Diplomacy in Haiti," p. 52.

[124] Maingot, "Sovereign Consent Versus State-Centric Sovereignty," p. 199.

Haiti 123

international peace and security. Second, the Latin American members of the UNSC and of GRULAC did not like the idea of a UN-authorized, US-led intervention into the Caribbean basin. Consequently, Aristide's consent to any resolutions involving Chapter VII authorization for UN or UN authorized forces became crucial to overcoming these concerns and getting such proposals through the Security Council.

This was particularly the case with resolution 940 which authorized the MNF to use all necessary means to facilitate the departure of the *de facto* military regime from Haiti. Aristide's agreement to the dispatch of international force to remove the *de factos* served to overcome reluctance within the Council to authorizing forcible military intervention. Russia, New Zealand, and Argentina all made it clear that their support for resolution 940 stemmed from Aristide's request for action by the international community.[125] The nature of this support indicates a desire among some UNSC members that the restrictions imposed on Council actions by Article 2(7) not be overcome solely through the invocation of Chapter VII, but instead be negated by the request of the legitimate Haitian government. This emphasises the continued importance of the non-intervention norm in UNSC decision-making.

Even after the adoption of resolution 940, there was limited pressure placed on the *de factos* to remove themselves from power. The US considered using the terms of resolution 940 to resolve the Haitian issue only as a last resort. The consent of the *de factos* to any multi-national intervention remained of paramount importance primarily because of their ability to inflict casualties on American troops. Consequently, when an intervention under the terms of resolution 940 was finally accepted to be the only option left open to the Clinton administration, it despatched the Carter/Nunn/Powell mission to effectively "induce" the consent of the *de factos* to the invasion.

While the consent of both Aristide and the *de factos* was crucial to bringing about the restoration of a democratic regime to Haiti, the degree to which the actions of the Security Council members were purely motivated by the "democratic imperative" is less clear. The UNSC's action in Haiti is now often viewed or portrayed as deliberate action taken in order to restore a democratic government in Haiti.[126] While this indeed was the end result, the members of the Council were by no means united to this end. The United States in particular, while publicly pronouncing its desire for Aristide's return, seemed to have the main objective of supporting a Haitian government, democratically elected or otherwise, that could return stability to the country and stem the flow of refugees to the coast of Florida.

---

[125] This same factor had also allowed Venezuela and Brazil to overcome their resistance to the idea of *Operation Uphold Democracy* during informal consultations on the proposed intervention.

[126] Strobe Talbott, "Democracy and the National Interest," *Foreign Affairs*, vol. 75, no.6, 1996, p. 58. Note Talbott's characterisation of US action in Haiti as "President Clinton's desire to defend democracy and his obligation to protect American borders combined to justify the use of military force" emphasising the defending of democracy first.

124   *Understanding the UN Security Council*

In short, the US wanted a regime that suited its interests.[127] In the end, this turned out to be Aristide's government. But the notion of sovereignty and of sovereign government that guided the US action reflects a traditional conception of sovereignty, a conception of a government, elected or not, that is able to control the country, its people, and enter into relations with foreign states.[128] It so happened that in the case of Haiti, the government perceived to be best able to do this was Aristide's.

For this reason, the UNSC's action in Haiti offers a lesson that has more to do with the power of the United States in the Council and the willingness of the P-5 to trade political support on issues of particular national interest than it does on the notion that the Council members were moving into a new era in which support for democracy, human rights and the protection of international peace and security were synonymous.[129] Nor does it suggest any new, emerging conception of sovereignty or sovereign authority guiding the actions of the UNSC members. What the Haitian case does demonstrate, however, is the fact that the members of the Security Council are willing to apply the term "threat to international peace and security" to a particular situation where such a threat may, in reality, be minimal, but where they wish to arrogate to themselves the authority to become involved in the situation under Chapter VII of the UN Charter.

---

[127] Morely and McGillion, "Disobedient Generals," p. 383.

[128] Michael J. Glennon, "Sovereignty and Community After Haiti: Rethinking the Collective Use of Force," *The American Journal of International Law*, vol. 89:58, 1995, p. 71.

[129] Richard Falk, "The Haiti Intervention: A Dangerous World Order Precedent for the United Nations," *Harvard International Law Journal*, vol. 38, no. 2, 1995, pp. 354, 356.

Chapter 5

Rwanda

The humanitarian tragedy which struck the small African state of Rwanda in the spring of 1994 provides a painful yet telling insight into the attitudes of the Security Council members towards consent and peacekeeping in the wake of UNOSOM II. During the deployment of the United Nations Assistance Mission in Rwanda (UNAMIR), the Security Council kept the force firmly based on traditional peacekeeping methods. Even in the face of direct attacks on UN personnel and the systematic killing of Rwandan civilians, the members of the UNSC were initially unwilling to authorize the use of force under Chapter VII to counter the violence. In fact, they responded to the Rwandan genocide by reducing the size of UNAMIR. This decision directly relates to the central questions considered in this thesis. Rwanda presents a clear case where the Council's members were reluctant to abandon the principle of consent in preference for enforcement measures under Chapter VII, even when presented with a clear humanitarian case for doing so. It was only well into the crisis that the Council was shamed into reluctantly authorizing a Chapter VII intervention led by France, a former patron of Rwanda. The rationale behind the UNSC's adherence to consent and the decisions taken in response to the Rwandan genocide are the focus of the following chapter.

Background

The UN's initial involvement in Rwanda came in the form of the United Nations Observer Mission Uganda-Rwanda (UNOMUR). Deployed in June 1993, this mission was intended to monitor the border between Uganda and Rwanda in order to verify that no military supplies were being transported across it. Rwanda had accused the Ugandan government of supplying weapons and other war material to the Rwandan Patriotic Front (RPF), a rebel movement which had been at war with the Rwanda government since 1990. The RPF was comprised primarily of Rwandan Tutsis who were exiled from Rwanda and had taken refuge in Uganda. They were dedicated to the overthrow of the Juvénal Habyarimanda regime and the return of both Tutsi and Hutu refugees to Rwanda.[1] UNOMUR was designed to supplement an existing OAU observer mission, the Neutral Military Observer

---

[1] Arthur Jay Klinghoffer, *The International Dimension of Genocide in Rwanda*, Macmillan Press Ltd., London, 1998, p. 14. See also Wm. Cyrus Reed, "Exile, Reform, and the Rise of the Rwandan Patriotic Front," *The Journal of Modern African Studies*, vol. 34, no. 3, 1996.

126 *Understanding the UN Security Council*

Group (NMOG I). Following political negotiations, the Rwandan government and the RPF signed the Arusha Agreement in August 1993. In it, the two parties agreed on the establishment of a transitional government, the integration of the government's Forces Armées Rwandaises: (FAR) and RPF armies, and the repatriations of refugees. The two sides called on the United Nations to provide a neutral international force to oversee the implementation of the peace agreement.[2]

UNAMIR I

Responding to the request of the Rwandan parties, Boutros-Ghali recommended to the members of the Security Council that a UN force be established in order to assist in ensuring the security of the capital city, Kigali, monitor the cease-fire agreement, monitor the security situation in the lead up to national elections and assist with mine clearance.[3] The Security Council members subsequently adopted the Secretary-General's recommendations and authorized the deployment of UNAMIR in resolution 872.[4] It appeared to be a case well suited to a Chapter VI traditional peacekeeping operation; there was a signed peace agreement, the UN had the co-operation and consent of the two main parties, and both parties appeared to respect the cease-fire agreement. To many in the UN, Rwanda appeared to offer an'easy' mission in the wake of the Somalia imbroglio.[5]

Co-operation with the RPF and the Rwandan government was positive and the deployment of UNAMIR progressed well in the lead up to the scheduled installation of the transitional government on 31 December 1993.[6] Juvénal Habyarimana was appointed President of the transitional government in early January 1994, but lack of agreement prevented the other provisions of the Arusha agreement from being implemented. In addition, February 1994 saw increased tension and political violence between the main parties.[7] This led to frustration among members of the Security Council culminating in a threat from the UNSC to withdraw the peacekeeping force if more rapid progress was not made.[8] For its part, the RPF was wary of a large UN presence because it believed that France, a key ally of the Rwandan government, was using the peacekeeping operation to protect its allies in Kigali. Consequently, the RPF sought to limit the size of the UN operation.[9]

---

[2] *UN Document*, S/25951, 11 June, 1993.

[3] *UN Document*, S/26488, 24 September, 1993.

[4] UNSC Resolution 872, 5 October, 1993.

[5] Howard Adelman and Astri Suhrke, *The International Response to Conflict and Genocide: Lessons From the Rwanda Experience*, Steering Committee of the Joint Evaluation of Emergency Assistance to Rwanda, 1996, p. 35.

[6] UNSC Resolution 891, 20 December, 1993 extended the mandate by six months and UNSC Resolution 893, 6 January, 1994 authorised the deployment of an additional UN battalion.

[7] *The Blue Helmets*, p. 345.

[8] UNSC Resolution 909, 5 April, 1994.

[9] Adelman and Suhrke, *The International Response to Conflict and Genocide*, p. 36.

Change of Context

UNAMIR was deployed in Rwanda with the consent of both main parties and was mandated to carry out a number of tasks while operating according to traditional peacekeeping principles. In the context of the Arusha peace agreement, this formula appeared to work well. However, the consensual basis of the operation appeared more solid than it was in reality. Brigadier-General Roméo Dallaire, the Canadian Force Commander of UNAMIR, has argued that the UN's assessment of the consensual basis of the operation was superficial "and did not clearly reflect that there was considerable opposition amongst the hard-liner government elements, and more importantly, their militia to the peace agreement."[10] Similarly, RPF officials believed that the Rwandan government's participation in the Arusha Process was a delaying strategy in order to give it time to more fully prepare for the planned genocide.[11]

The assassination on 6 April, 1993 of Habyarimana dramatically changed UNAMIR's operating environment. The assassination, most likely carried out by extremist Hutu elements within the FAR and the ruling party's *interahamwe* militia forces, immediately created the opportunity for these same elements to systematically begin the killing of Tutsis and moderate Hutus perceived to favour the RPF.[12] Coming as it did the day before the transitional government of the Arusha peace process was due to be installed (8 April) the assassination seemed well timed and well planned.[13] So too did the organized killing of Rwandan civilians. Extremist elements in the FAR and the government set up roadblocks throughout Kigali and initially focused on eliminating their political opponents, whether Hutu or Tutsi. Tutsi civilians were targeted simply because of their ethnicity.[14]

One target was the Prime Minister appointed to the transitional government, Agathe Uwilingiyimana. Although under the protection of a contingent of ten Belgian and three Ghanaian UNAMIR peacekeepers in her house, Uwilingiyimana asked for additional protection from the UN. When UN reinforcements were barred from getting through to her, she decided to leave her bodyguard and attempted to flee to a nearby UN compound, only to be caught *en route* and killed. The peacekeepers, surrounded and outgunned by the FAR, decided to lay down their weapons and not exercise their right of self defence as permitted under the

---

[10] Romeo Dallaire as quoted in "Dallaire's Story: UN Failed Rwanda," *The National Post*, 20 December, 1999.

[11] Ben Ruegangaza, interview with author, 21 March, 1999.

[12] For an analysis of the contending theories as to who assassinated Habyarimana see Gérard Prunier, *The Rwanda Crisis: History of a Genocide*, Hurst & Company, London, 1995, pp. 213-229.

[13] Helen M Hintjens, "Explaining the 1994 Genocide in Rwanda," *The Journal of Modern African Studies*, vol. 37, no. 2, 1999, p. 262.

[14] Adelman and Suhrke, *International Response to Conflict and Genocide*, p. 38. For a comprehensive account of the early days of the genocide and the breakdown of the Rwandan government see Philip Gourevitch, *We Wish To Inform You That Tomorrow We Will Be Killed With Our Families*, Picador, Oxford, 1998.

128 *Understanding the UN Security Council*

UNAMIR mandate. They were then taken to Camp Kigali, a military base in the city, where the ten Belgians were subsequently tortured and killed.[15] There could be no clearer sign that tactical consent on the ground to the continued presence of UNAMIR peacekeepers had been withdrawn. The Security Council quickly condemned the murders and demanded that the Rwandan parties desist from further acts of violence.[16]

The loss of consent seemed strategically directed at Belgian UN troops. The Rwandan Government had been furious with the Belgian government which stopped supplying arms to Rwanda as civil war broke out with the RPF in 1990, consequently sparking anti-Belgian broadcasts in the Rwandan media and accusations that they supported the RPF.[17] This led to the Belgians being specifically targeted as the Hutu extremists believed that casualties among the Belgian contingent would cause its withdrawal and effectively paralyse UNAMIR.[18]

Amid the confusion within Kigali, Dallaire attempted to mediate between the FAR commander and the RPF. An RPF battalion, stationed in Kigali under the terms of the Arusha peace process, had broken out of its barracks in order to repulse the FAR and *interahamwe* onslaught. The circumstances of the violence were not immediately clear. Many outside Rwanda believed it to be a resumption of civil war, an interpretation which hampered the ability of the Security Council to understand and respond to the crisis.[19] There was no attempt made by the remainder of the UNAMIR force to mount a rescue mission for the 10 Belgians and 3 Ghanaians since it was not clear where they had been taken. Also, as Dallaire

---

[15] For an account of the circumstances leading to the murder of the peacekeepers see Astri Suhrke, "Facing Genocide: the Record of the Belgian Battalion in Rwanda," *Security Dialogue*, vol, 29, no. 1, 1998. Though traditional peacekeeping entails the use of force in self-defence, the UNAMIR peacekeepers had been given a six-point outline of the Rules of Engagement (ROE). The ROE stressed that in an incident, UN troops were to display non-aggressive and co-operative behaviour. Authorisation from higher authority was to be obtained before using force in self-defence. During the stand-off, the surrounded Belgians were apparently given such authorisation. See also *Report of the Independent Inquiry into the Actions of the United Nations During the 1994 Genocide in Rwanda*, 15 December, 1999, pp. 10-12.

[16] *UN Document*, S/PRST/1994/16, 7 April, 1994.

[17] Omaar and de Waal, *Rwanda: Death, Despair and Defiance*, p. 674.

[18] The United Nations had been forewarned of this in the "genocide fax" sent to UN Headquarters by Dallaire who had obtained his information from an informant within the government. See Philip Gourevitch, "The Genocide Fax," *The New Yorker*, 11 May, 1998 and *Report of the Independent Inquiry into the Actions of the United Nations During the 1994 Genocide in Rwanda*, 15 December, 1999, p. 6. Dallaire had been ordered not to seize the weapons being stockpiled for the killings because such action was beyond the authority of the UNAMIR mandate. Boutros-Ghali, *Unvanquished*, p. 130.

[19] New Zealand Ambassador to the UN, Colin Keating stated "We were kept in the dark. The situation was much more dangerous than ever presented to the Council." As quoted in Linda Melvern, "Genocide Behind the Thin Blue Line," *Security Dialogue*, vol., 28, no. 3, 1997, p. 338.

later concluded, the balance of forces between the FAR and UNAMIR would have made any offensive action by the UN force 'suicidal.'[20]

Operating according to traditional peacekeeping principles left the force vulnerable once the extremist Hutu elements gained control and announced the formation of an "interim" government on 8 April. One of the two stable parties with whom the UN had agreed to the deployment of UNAMIR, namely the Rwandan government, was in turmoil. Deployed with a limited number of personnel, lightly armed, and dispersed throughout Kigali and the rest of the country meant that UNAMIR was not in a position to respond with force to the attacks of the FAR and *interahamwe* on civilians. They were however, able to offer limited protection to large groups of terrorised civilians at various gathering points throughout Kigali largely through their presence. Dallaire later argued that had he been given 5,000 troops with a mandate to use force, UNAMIR could have stopped the killings.[21]

Response of the Security Council

Though the chaos in Rwanda began on the 7 April, the UNSC did not take action in response to the situation until 20 April. Immediate international efforts were focused on the evacuation of expatriates from Kigali. To this end, the French, Belgian, and American governments launched separate rescue missions to remove their expatriates from Kigali. The French deployed 190 paratroopers, under the auspices *Operation Amaryllis* on 9 April, and the Belgians sent 250 troops the next day.[22] Belgium asked the UN to modify the UNAMIR mandate to allow the international troops extricating their nationals from Kigali to also take action to stop the mass killing. The French were vehemently opposed to the idea, as the RPF had made it clear that it would militarily oppose any French intervention. Paris was also concerned that any such intervention would be regarded as support for the interim government and create further friction with the RPF.[23] UNAMIR was instructed to assist with the evacuation of foreign nationals, but was ordered not to compromise its consensual basis of operation by acting "beyond its mandate."[24]

The members of the Council met with senior UN officials in informal sessions where they discussed the best available response to the dramatically

---

[20] Suhrke, "Facing Genocide," p. 41. The 3 Ghanaian peacekeepers were later released unharmed, adding credibility to the theory that the Belgians were deliberately targeted.

[21] Melvern, "Genocide Behind the Thin Blue Line," p. 339. This assessment was supported by RPF officials. Ben Ruegangaza and Major Thougene Rudasingwa, interviews with author, 21 and 23 March, 1999, respectively.

[22] For details of the Belgian and French operations see Prunier, *The Rwanda Crisis: History of a Genocide*, p. 234.

[23] Prunier, *The Rwanda Crisis: History of a Genocide*, p. 235.

[24] *Report of the Independent Inquiry into the Actions of the United Nations During the 1994 Genocide in Rwanda*, 15 December, 1999, p. 13.

130 *Understanding the UN Security Council*

changed situation. The Council members were told by Kofi Annan, then Under Secretary-General in the Department of Peacekeeping Operations, that in order for UNAMIR to continue operating it would need more resources and an enlarged mandate. Assistant Secretary-General Iqbal Riza, Annan's deputy, mooted the possibility of humanitarian intervention to protect civilians, but quickly dismissed the idea, because of the increased need for resources and risks that such an undertaking would entail.[25]

In response to the murder of its soldiers, the Belgian government announced on 13 April that it would withdraw its contingent from Rwanda by 20 April, an announcement that was greeted with enthusiasm by the Belgian public.[26] The Belgians were not willing to support the deployment of their peacekeepers under Chapter VI rules of engagement and called on the Security Council to suspend the activities of UNAMIR.[27] In the wake of this announcement, the government of Bangladesh also opted to withdraw its UNAMIR contingent to Nairobi.[28]

Boutros-Ghali wrote to the Security Council reporting that without the Belgians, UNAMIR would be hard pressed to carry out its responsibilities.[29] Consequently, he asked Dallaire to prepare plans for the withdrawal of the force in the event that no replacement contingent was found. Britain, France and the US objected to the insinuation that without the Belgians the operation would have to be shut down. However, they did not offer any reinforcements. Ironically, Albright proposed that a small force be kept in Kigali "to show the will of the international community" while options for changing the mandate of the force were considered.[30] On 13 April, Nigeria and the non-aligned states circulated a draft resolution to members of the Council authorising the strengthening of UNAMIR, but found no UN members willing to contribute to the envisaged force. The draft resolution was not even tabled before the Council.[31]

Reporting to the members of the Security Council on 20 April, Boutros-Ghali described how UNAMIR, in the wake of the death of the Rwandan President, had focused on negotiating with the parties in order to establish a cease-fire, protecting UN staff, civilians, assisting with the evacuation of non-Rwandan nationals, and providing humanitarian assistance to displaced persons. The Secretary-General

---

[25] Howard Adelman and Astri Suhrke, *The International Response to Conflict and Genocide: Lessons From the Rwanda Experience*, Steering Committee of the Joint Evaluation of Emergency Assistance to Rwanda, 1996, p. 42.

[26] Arthur Jay Klinghoffer, *The International Dimension of Genocide in Rwanda*, Macmillan Press Ltd., London, 1998, p. 89. See also *UN Document*, S/1994/446, 15 April, 1994.

[27] *UN Document*, S/1994/ 430, 13 April, 1994.

[28] Klinghoffer, *The International Dimension of Genocide in Rwanda*, p. 44. Dallaire regarded the Bangaldeshi contingent as an ineffective handicap for UNAMIR and supported their withdrawal. See L. R. Melvern, A People Betrayed: *The Role of the West in Rwanda's Genocide*, Zed Books, London, 2000, p. 165.

[29] Boutros-Gali apparently supported the idea of a UNAMIR pull-out if no troops were found to replace the Belgian contingent. See Melvern, *A People Betrayed*, p. 148.

[30] US Permanent Representative to the UN, Madeleine Albright as quoted in Boutros-Ghali, *Unvanquished*, p. 133.

[31] Adelman and Suhrke, *The International Response to Conflict and Genocide*, pp. 43-44.

then identified three alternative courses of action open to the Council. First, it could authorize the massive and immediate reinforcement of UNAMIR in order to "coerce the opposing sides into a cease-fire," under Chapter VII of the Charter. The second option involved the withdrawal of the bulk of UNAMIR from Rwanda, leaving only the Force Commander, necessary staff and troops in order to bring the opposing sides back into the Arusha peace process. The third option was to completely withdraw UNAMIR from Rwanda.[32]

The Security Council members were thus presented with a choice between vastly increasing the size and mandate of UNAMIR, or reducing it down to a skeleton force and having it continue to operate according to traditional peacekeeping principles. It was a stark choice for which the Secretariat was criticized in the Council since no option had been identified that would have authorized the reinforcement of UNAMIR in order to protect civilians but without Chapter VII authorization.[33]

In the lead up to the 20 April meeting of the Security Council, the Secretariat and the UNSC members were allegedly unclear as to what exactly was going on in Rwanda.[34] Primarily interpreting the renewed violence as continued civil war, rather than as a systematic genocide accompanied by civil war, they responded accordingly. Boutros-Ghali's report to the Council thus emphasised the need to establish a cease-fire between the two parties. It is also clear that he failed to recognise that the Rwanda government had in fact been overthrown from within, led by the Presidential Guard and Hutu extremists.[35] Instead he focused blame on "unruly elements" within the Presidential Guard.[36]

When the members of the Council met on 21 April to discuss the situation, the representative of Djibouti expressed a preference for an intermediate option between the deployment of an enforcement operation and the reduction of UNAMIR. He argued:

> We see not so much the need to coerce the combatants into a cease-fire and enforce law and order as the need to maintain minimum safety for innocent civilians and to offer some protection, while pushing for a return to negotiations.[37]

But despite expressing support for a more substantive response to the crisis in Rwanda, he ended his statement with a comment that reflected a negative conception of the possibility of enforcement action. He quoted the UN Special Representative in Rwanda, Roger Booh-Booh:

---

[32] *UN Document*, S/1994/470, 20 April, 1994. For an account of how these three options were arrived at see *Report of the Independent Inquiry into the Actions of the United Nations During the 1994 Genocide in Rwanda*, 15 December, 1999, pp. 14-16.

[33] Adelman and Suhrke, *The International Response to Conflict*, p. 42.

[34] Iqbal Riza, interview with author, 15 December, 1999.

[35] *UN Document*, S/1994/470, 20 April, 1994.

[36] Adelman and Suhrke, *The International Response to Conflict*, p. 42.

[37] *UN Document*, S/PV .3368, 21 April, 1994.

> We came to assist Rwanda, but we cannot impose any solution on the Rwandan people, who have to help us to help them.

The Council's objective consideration of the situation was not aided by the presence on the UNSC of the representative of the Rwanda government, Jean-Damascène Bizimana. He characterized the actions of the interim Rwandan government as attempts to restore law and order, protect civilians, and promote a resumption of the Arusha process. He also accused the RPF of launching the "wave of massacres" when in fact it was the work of his own government.[38]

The Council members chose to adopt the second option identified by the Secretary-General, and with resolution 912, authorized the reduction in UNAMIR's force level and reduced its mandate to acting as an intermediary between the two parties, while carrying out humanitarian relief to the extent feasible. The resolution was adopted unanimously.[39]

A large part of the reason behind the Council's decision to reduce the mandate of UNAMIR came about because none of the P-5 was willing to advocate the adoption of a more vigorous approach to coping with the crisis. Instead, the primary desire was to consolidate UNAMIR in the wake of the Belgian withdrawal and the operation's effective collapse.[40] The United States, still reeling from the loss of 18 soldiers in Somalia seven months earlier and concerned about the growing financial implications of UN peacekeeping operations, favoured the complete withdrawal of UNAMIR. The Pentagon was adamantly against any form of intervention into Rwanda and had little difficulty in quashing the limited support for such action that existed in the State Department's Africa Bureau. In particular, Rwanda did not meet the rigorous criteria for US involvement in a peacekeeping operation as set out by Presidential Decision Directive 25 (PDD-25), then being developed by the Clinton administration. Only intensive lobbying by Madeleine Albright in her own government kept UNAMIR in the field.[41]

France was similarly unwilling to become engaged in Rwanda, primarily because it was a key supporter of the Rwandan government. There had been close ties between French President Mitterand and Habyarimana, and between the sons of the two Presidents. Many officials from the Habyarimana regime took refuge in the French Embassy once the killings began.[42] France had also been a key arms supplier to the Rwandan government after the outbreak of war with the RPF, deploying military advisors and 680 troops to assist the Francophone Rwandan government and ensure that Rwanda remained a member of the Francophone

---

[38] *UN Document*, S/PV .3368, 21 April, 1994.

[39] UNSC Resolution 912, 21 April, 1994.

[40] Sir David Hannay, interview with author, 29 November, 1999.

[41] Holly J. Burkhalter, "The Question of Genocide: The Clinton Administration and Rwanda," *World Policy Journal*, vol. 11, no. 4, 1994, p. 48. PDD-25 was released one month after the genocide began.

[42] Prunier, *The Rwanda Crisis: History of a Genocide*, p. 236.

African community.[43] Britain argued that the provision of Chapter VII authority to bolster UNAMIR was not feasible given the lessons learned in Somalia.[44]

Over the course of the next four weeks, as more accurate information as to the scale of the killings became available, pressure increased on the members of the Council to reverse their decision to reduce UNAMIR presence in Rwanda. During this period of UNSC vacillation an estimated five to ten percent of the Rwandan population had been killed.[45] New Zealand, Argentina, the Czech Republic and Spain were all key sources of renewed pressure and played a large role in effectively 'shaming' the Council into taking more substantive action to help the people of Rwanda.[46] The UN had also been sharply criticized by the RPF which called for the resignation of Jacques-Roger Booh-Booh, the Special Representative of the Secretary-General, on the grounds of incompetence. The RPF also stated that it did not want more UN troops deployed to Rwanda since they gave the Rwandan people a false sense of security.[47] During this time Kagame believed only the RPF could halt the killings:

> All those claiming to be civilised had turned their backs. I knew that we were alone. We would have to sort out the problem. I developed contempt for those people in the world who claimed to stand for values of moral authority.[48]

On 29 April, the Secretary-General urged the Council to reconsider its decision to reduce the size of UNAMIR, and instead consider the possible use of force to end the massacres.[49] The next day, the President of the UNSC issued a statement condemning the "breaches of international humanitarian law in Rwanda" and demanding an immediate cease-fire between the RPF and the interim Government.[50] Four days later, Boutros-Ghali, increasing the pressure on the Council, characterized the killings in Rwanda as genocide and urged the Council members to act.[51]

In a separate report presented to the Council on 13 May, the Secretary-General submitted a plan for UNAMIR II, in effect a reinforcement of the existing

---

[43] Stephen D. Goose and Frank Smyth, "Arming Genocide in Rwanda," *Foreign Affairs*, vol. 73, no. 5, 1994, p. 89.

[44] *Report of the Independent Inquiry into the Actions of the United Nations During the 1994 Genocide in Rwanda*, 15 December, 1999, p. 16.

[45] Helen M Hintjens, "Explaining the 1994 Genocide in Rwanda," *The Journal of Modern African Studies*, vol. 37, no. 2, 1999, p. 241.

[46] Alex de Waal and Rakiya Omaar, *Rwanda: Death Despair and Defiance*, African Rights, London, 1994, p. 688.

[47] Prunier, *The Rwanda Crisis: History of a Genocide*, p. 276. Booh-Booh was eventually replaced by Pakistani Shaharyar Khan Mohammed.

[48] As quoted in Melvern, *A People Betrayed*, p. 189.

[49] *UN Document*, S/1994/518, 29 April, 1994.

[50] *UN Document*, S/PRST/1994/21, 30 April, 1994.

[51] Adelman and Suhrke, *The International Response to Conflict*, p. 49 Adelman and Suhrke state that Boutros-Ghali did not characterise the killings as genocide until 31 May, though *The Blue Helmets* records him using the terms publicly on 4 May, 1993.

UNAMIR operation, designed to provide safe conditions for civilians in Rwanda. In particular, UNAMIR II was to "establish access to sites where displaced and other affected persons are concentrated" and assure their protection. However, in order to carry out its tasks, UNAMIR II would not be given an enforcement mandate, but would be a highly-mobile, well armed and credible force, relying on deterrence to carry out its tasks. Importantly however, the plan did envisage an expanded interpretation of self-defence, allowing UNAMIR II to use force to defend itself against individuals or forces threatening protected sites and populations, and the means of delivery of relief supplies.[52]

In discussions of the Secretary-General's formal recommendations for UNAMIR II, a key provision that the United States insisted be incorporated into the resolution was an explicit reference to the need for the parties' consent to the deployment. The advisability of such a reference was questioned by other members of the Council, and the US suggestion was eventually toned down.[53]

On 16 May, the Security Council members chose to adopt the proposal of the Secretary-General in resolution 918, authorizing an increase in UNAMIR's contingent to 5,500 troops. Additionally, the expanded mandate for the force was also officially adopted. These modifications to the peacekeeping force, outlined in section A of the resolution, made no mention of Chapter VII. Section B of the resolution however, referred to Chapter VII in implementing an arms embargo on Rwanda. Section A of the resolution was adopted unanimously by the Council, while Section B was adopted by a count of fourteen votes in favour and one opposed.[54]

It was Rwanda itself that opposed the second part of resolution 918. Its representative argued before the Council that the embargo should instead be imposed on Uganda, which he accused of supplying arms to the RPF. While supportive of the deployment of UNAMIR II, the Rwandan government worried that if the force was deployed to protect civilians, since most of the civilians were in government territory, the presence of UNAMIR II would hinder the operations of government forces. Instead the Rwandan government called for the deployment of the peacekeepers as a buffer force, interposed between the opposing armies.[55] This position arose from the fact that government forces were on the defensive militarily from RPF advances and therefore the deployment of UN troops in order to stabilize the situation was consistent with the government's interests.[56]

---

[52] *UN Document*, S/1994/565, 13 May, 1994.

[53] *Report of the Independent Inquiry into the Actions of the United Nations During the 1994 Genocide in Rwanda*, 15 December, 1999, p. 18. The preamble to resolution 918 states "stressing the importance it attaches to the support and co-operation of the parties for the successful implementation of all aspects of the mandate." UNSC Resolution 918, 16 May, 1994.

[54] UNSC Resolution 918, 16 May, 1994.

[55] *UN Document*, S/1994/531, 3 May, 1994. See also the comments of the Rwandan representative in *UN Document*, S/PV .3377, 16 May, 1994.

[56] By the end of May, 1994 the RPF had control of nearly one half of Rwandan territory and government forces were withdrawing to the west and south. See *UN Document*, S/1994/640, 31 May, 1994.

Rwanda   135

In the chaos of the Rwandan crisis, there was no objection from other members of the Council about invoking Chapter VII, in order to authorize the arms embargo, without the consent of the Rwandan government. This was primarily due to a growing sense within the Council that the changing political circumstances in Rwanda and the actions of the interim Rwandan government left its representative status somewhat suspect. The representative of New Zealand, for example, argued that the Rwandan representative did not represent a state, but was the mouthpiece of a faction and therefore had no legitimacy and should not be seated in the Council.[57] The New Zealand position on the Rwandan representative's status makes it clear that the Council's understanding of the Rwandan crisis was much improved as compared with four weeks earlier. This is also demonstrated by the statement of the Czech representative, who accurately identified the Presidential Guard, assisted by loyal elements of the FAR and the militia, as being responsible for the genocide.[58] From a legal perspective, the members of the Council had explicitly determined that the Rwandan conflict constituted a threat to international peace and security in resolution 918 and therefore they were authorized by the UN Charter to ignore the protests of the Rwandan government.

The RPF, for its part, gave contradictory signals concerning the deployment of UNAMIR II. It was concerned that the force would either be ineffective like the existing UNAMIR operation or that it would get in the way of RPF attempts at defeating government forces. They originally informed Madeleine Albright on 4 May that they opposed the deployment of additional UN forces into Rwanda. However, just prior to the Council's adoption of resolution 918, the RPF indicated it would accept the new UN force, provided it did not come between RPF forces and those of the government.[59] The RPF remained adamantly opposed to the inclusion of French units in UNAMIR II.[60]

Minimising Risk

Although the members of the UNSC had gained a better understanding of the Rwandan situation by the middle of May, 1994, their desire to assist the Rwandan people remained limited. They were not concerned about interfering in the internal affairs of the Rwandan state since they were already suspicious of the Rwandan government's legitimacy. Instead their prime concern was minimising the risk involved in launching any initiative to aid the Rwandan people. Consequently, the consent of the local parties to any such initiative became a practical as opposed to legal issue. Concerns about risk meant that the options considered by the UNSC to respond to the genocide remained very conservative. For example, there was no willingness to extend Chapter VII authority to the mandate of UNAMIR II, though the mission had been given the ability to use force to in order to prevent

---

[57] *UN Document*, S/PV .3377, 16 May, 1994.

[58] Ibid.

[59] Adelman and Suhrke, *The International Response to Conflict*, p. 52.

[60] Ibid. p. 54.

136   *Understanding the UN Security Council*

obstructions to the fulfilment of its mandate.[61]   Only New Zealand and Djibouti argued that the Council should do more than simply expanding the force size of UNAMIR. Several of the Council members highlighted the "rapid" and substantial role that the Security Council was playing to end the Rwanda crisis.   The self-congratulatory tone of such statements gave the impression that the Council was taking extraordinary steps to assist the people of Rwanda. China, for example, argued that resolution 918 was a "reflection of the international community's good will and its sincere desire to create conditions for the early restoration of peace and security in [Rwanda]." The Brazilian representative stated "The Security Council has been seized of the matter since the resumption of the conflict, and had been continuously addressing the situation in order to be able to respond through concrete action."[62]

A number of UNSC members also stressed that the ultimate solution to the Rwandan crisis lay in the hands of the Rwandan people themselves, suggesting a very restrictive interpretation of the norm of non-intervention. Oman, for example, argued that it was hesitant to involve peacekeeping forces in internal disputes. Its representative argued that his delegation:

> ...would like to stress that the achievement of peace in Rwanda lies in the hands of the Rwandese parties themselves...it is crucial for both conflicting parties in Rwanda to demonstrate political will and a sincere desire to achieve a cease-fire...[63]

The explicit locating of responsibility for the end of the crisis with the two main Rwandan parties led a number of the UNSC members, including Pakistan, Oman and Russia, to portray the deployment of a peacekeeping operation as something that came only after a responsible demonstration of a local willingness to reconcile. Such statements make evident that they did not view the deployment of UNAMIR to be a means of stopping the slaughter of hundreds of thousands of innocent civilians. Pakistan warned that "the pressure to withdraw UNAMIR could...mount once again if the Rwandese parties fail to bring the hostilities and killings to an end within a reasonable period." Similarly, the Russian representative alluded to the possibility of withdrawing UNAMIR:

> if...the conditions necessary for continuing the peacekeeping operation do not come about in Rwanda, and if there is no progress towards a political settlement, the Security Council will have to give serious thought to what further action it should take.[64]

The United States was certainly not considering leading an intervention into Rwanda similar to its actions in Somalia. Of all the statements made within the Security Council during the discussion of resolution 918, those of the United States

---

[61] J. Mathew Vaccaro, "The Politics of Genocide: Peacekeeping and Rwanda," in William J. Durch, ed., *UN Peacekeeping*, p. 378.

[62] *UN Document*, S/PV .3377, 16 May, 1994.

[63] Ibid.

[64] Ibid.

were the most restrictive on the deployment of the expanded UNAMIR. Though characterizing the actions of the Council in adopting resolution 918 as going to "extraordinary lengths," the US called for the viability of the mission to be properly evaluated and suggested that the Secretary-General closely examine "a well-defined concept of operations; availability of resources; consent of the parties; progress towards a cease-fire; and the duration of the mandate."[65] His report had to be submitted and approved before the second phase of the resolution, involving the deployment of a new contingent of UNAMIR troops, could be implemented.

In addition, on 3 May, the Clinton Administration had issued PDD-25 and the restrictions of this presidential directive on US participation in UN peacekeeping operations were directly incorporated into resolution 918. American restrictions became UN restrictions.[66] When Boutros-Ghali first circulated concrete plans for a more robust UNAMIR, including the deployment of 4,000 peace enforcement troops, Madeleine Albright responded by arguing that the US had "serious reservations about proposals to establish a large peace enforcement mission which would operate throughout Rwanda..."[67] The US had originally favoured a plan to send a small peacekeeping force with a limited mandate along Rwanda's borders in order to create a zone of protection. This directly contrasted with a UN Secretariat plan to deploy additional troops in Kigali.[68] The US, with no troops of its own involved, finally agreed with the UN plan and by 13 May it appeared as though UNAMIR II was becoming a reality. However, the US backtracked and demanded that only 850 troops be initially despatched, with the remainder deployed at an unspecified later date. Additionally, it was not willing to consider the use of force by UNAMIR II troops except in cases of self-defence.[69] Pressure on the US from within the Security Council forced it to abandon this plan, but led to the phased implementation plan for UNAMIR II.[70]

The US demands slowed the potential deployment time of the full UNAMIR II force since the Council had to consider the report of the Secretary-General and approve it before the second phase of the deployment could proceed. In a situation where thousands were being killed every day, any such delay was, literally, deadly. This was noted by the Nigerian representative:

> ...we are unhappy with the import of operative paragraph 7 of the present resolution, which would seem to imply that the second phase of UNAMIR's deployment will be dependent on a number of conditionalities, including a further decision or action by the Council.[71]

---

[65] Ibid.

[66] Boutros-Ghali, *Unvanquished*, p. 135.

[67] As quoted in Ibid., p. 135.

[68] Omaar and de Waal, *Rwanda: Death, Despair and Defiance*, p. 689.

[69] Burkhalter, "The Question of Genocide," p. 50.

[70] de Waal and Omaar, *Rwanda: Death Despair and Defiance*, p. 690.

[71] *UN Document*, S/PV .3377, 16 May, 1994.

138 *Understanding the UN Security Council*

The comments of many UNSC members in the debate on resolution 918 make evident the prevailing attitude that in absence of a demonstrated desire on the part of the local parties to end the hostilities, UNAMIR would be withdrawn. In effect, the members of the Council were asking for the main parties to create a situation suitable for a consent-based peacekeeping mission, rather than the UNSC members proactively responding to the situation on a scale similar to that taken during the Somali famine in 1991-92. The members of the Council were clearly reluctant to assume the risk of intervening in Rwanda, even with Chapter VII authorization. Instead, they sought near total consent on the ground from the Rwandan parties in order to allay the risks posed by UN involvement in the conflict. While such a position was entirely unsuited to the ongoing situation in Rwanda, the informal consultations among the UNSC members nevertheless indicated that they considered the consent of the Rwandan parties to be a fundamental requirement on which any UN response to the crisis was formulated. As Chinmaya Gharekhan, Special Representative of the Secretary-General on the Security Council, reported to Boutros-Ghali:

> There is no support from any delegation for a forceful or enforcement action. They all emphasised that whatever action is contemplated could be implemented only if both the Rwandese parties agree to it and promise their co-operation.[72]

From Chapter VI to Chapter VII

It was not until three weeks after the adoption of resolution 918 that the Security Council finally authorized the deployment of UNAMIR II's second and third phases, the bulk of the force, with resolution 925.[73] The true reluctance of the UN members to support substantive action in Rwanda without the total consent and co-operation of the host parties became evident as the Secretary-General began looking for troop contributions towards UNAMIR II. While a number of African nations were willing to contribute soldiers, they often required their troops to be equipped properly, or transported to and from the theatre of operations. Western states, in contrast, were not willing to contribute troops for UNAMIR II, though in some cases they were willing to match up with a troop contributing nation and help to finance its deployment. Ultimately such complications severely restricted the ability of the UN to deploy the full complement of UNAMIR II troops on schedule.[74] Of the 5,500 troops authorized by resolution 918, by early June only 354 fully equipped soldiers had been volunteered to the new force, despite the

---

[72] as quoted in *Report of the Independent Inquiry into the Actions of the United Nations During the 1994 Genocide in Rwanda*, 15 December, 1999, p. 28.

[73] UNSC Resolution 925, 8 June, 1994.

[74] One example of the United States not helping to speed the deployment of UNAMIR concerned the leasing of 50 APCs to the UN for use by the Ghanaian UN contingent. For details, see de Waal and Omaar, *Rwanda: Death Despair and Defiance*, pp. 691-92.

Secretariat having approached over 50 states for support.[75] Adding to the difficulties was the RPF's refusal to allow the inclusion of French troops in the expanded UN force.[76] Consequently, Boutros-Ghali reported that he was not able to provide the UNSC with a firm deployment schedule for the force. He wrote, "…none of those Governments possessing the capacity to provide fully trained and equipped military units have offered so far to do so for the implementation of the Security Council's resolutions to deal with the situation in Rwanda." As of 18 June, the UNAMIR force deployed in Rwanda totalled 503, including troops and military observers.

In light of an expected delay of at least three months in deploying UNAMIR II, Boutros-Ghali raised the possibility of the UNSC taking up a French offer to lead a Chapter VII authorized, multi-national force to provide protection for threatened civilians and Internally Displaced Persons (IDPs) in Rwanda.[77] Chapter VII authorization had been requested by the French in order to "provide a legal framework for their intervention."[78]

The French offer was greeted with some hesitation by other members of the Security Council. France had long been a supporter of the Habyarimana government, and with the outbreak of civil war in 1990, had invoked the terms of a 1975 bilateral technical military assistance accord in order to intervene on the side of Habyarimana to bolster his government and provide arms to the FAR. French troops assisted with the training of the FAR and helped to man checkpoints and carry out patrols.[79] One French shipment of arms to the government was intercepted by UNAMIR forces on 22 January, 1994 as it was in violation of the Arusha Accords. There were also reports, adamantly denied by the French government, that another shipment of French arms arrived in Kigali on 9 April, two days after the assassination of the Rwandan President.[80]

This legacy of French support for the Rwandan government meant that the supposedly "humanitarian" objectives of the proposed French intervention were viewed with suspicion by other members of the UNSC. In a UNSC debate on a draft resolution authorizing the deployment of a Chapter VII, French-led operation into Rwandan to protect the civilian population, these concerns were highlighted. During this debate the most common concern among both supporters and opponents of the resolution was that the operation be conducted in an impartial manner and that it have the consent and co-operation of the two main parties in Rwanda. Unsurprisingly, this was a difficult condition to fulfil. For its part, the

---

[75] Vaccaro, "The Politics of Genocide," p. 384.

[76] Adelman and Suhrke, *The International Response to Conflict*, p. 54.

[77] *UN Document*, S/1994/728, 20 June, 1994.

[78] As quoted in *Report of the Independent Inquiry into the Actions of the United Nations During the 1994 Genocide in Rwanda*, 15 December, 1999, p. 21.

[79] Mel McNulty, "France's Role in Rwanda and External Military Intervention: A Double Discrediting," *International Peacekeeping*, vol. 4, no. 3, 1997, p. 30. France had also assisted the FAR during early engagements with the RPF. See Gourevitch, *We Wish To Inform You*, p. 89.

[80] Adelman and Suhrke, *The International Response to Conflict*, p. 39.

140 *Understanding the UN Security Council*

interim government supported the intervention by French forces - no surprise, given the legacy of French support for the Habimyndara regime. In the debate on the proposed French-led intervention, named *Opération Turquoise*, the Rwandan representative urged the other members of the Security Council "to give their full support to the proposed humanitarian operation and to participate in a speedy settlement of the bloody conflict in Rwanda."[81] By contrast, the RPF did not support to the deployment of *Opération Turquoise*. Upon hearing of French plans to intervene, an RPF delegation was sent to Paris to reiterate the RPF's opposition to *Opération Turquoise* directly to Alain Juppé. The delegation threatened that French troops would be opposed by force if necessary.[82] In an official communiqué issued on the same day as the Security Council was debating the French offer to lead an MNF into Rwanda, the RPF called the proposal "intentionally dangerous" and designed to protect the perpetrators of the genocide. It publicly repeated its threat to oppose any French intervention with all means.[83]

Recognising the need for a substantial response to the Rwandan crisis, and the opposition of the RPF to the French intervention, many supporters of the resolution stressed the need for French impartiality. The US representative argued "...we encourage the force upon its arrival, and through its actions, to demonstrate its impartiality and even-handedness in dealing with the parties in Rwanda." The Russian position was even firmer on the issue of consent, as it predicated its support for the resolution on the impartial, neutral manner of the intervention. Its representative argued "...to ensure the success of this operation, we believe it of paramount importance to obtain the agreement of both the Rwandan parties."[84] The Russian and American support for the French intervention was, at least in part, the result of the informal agreement among the three powers to offer each other mutual support on the use of Chapter VII in their respective areas of interest.[85] The British representative stressed that "it will be vital that those forces deploying to Rwanda act and are seen to act with clearly demonstrable impartiality and in no sense become involved in the fighting between the military forces of the parties..." A failure to adopt an impartial stance, he argued, could heighten the risks not only to French troops, but also UN troops with UNAMIR. The Czech representative also stressed his government's preference that despite the Chapter VII authorization of the resolution, "consent be secured from the two warring parties prior to the multinational force's deployment." Similar concerns were expressed by the representative of Oman.[86]

Despite the overwhelming humanitarian imperative for UNSC action in response to the Rwandan crisis, some states opposed the resolution. Nigeria took the position that any response to the Rwandan crisis should be subsumed within the

---

[81] *UN Document*, S/PV .3392, 22 June, 1994.

[82] Major Thougene Rudasingwa, interview with author, 23 March, 1999. Rudasingwa led the RPF delegation to Paris.

[83] BBC Summary of World Broadcasts, Part II, AL2028, 22 June, 1994.

[84] *UN Document*, S/PV .3392, 22 June, 1994.

[85] See Malone, *Decision Making*, p. 117.

[86] *UN Document*, S/PV .3392, 22 June, 1994.

Rwanda 141

United Nations instead of a UN-authorized multi-national force. Other concerns about the French proposal stemmed from concern about the consent of the host parties for the operation. China argued that because the French MNF could not guarantee the co-operation of the host parties, effective measures to address the conflict should be taken in the context of UNAMIR. The New Zealand representative doubted that the proposed MNF would adequately protect Rwandan civilians and was also concerned that failure of the French to secure the co-operation of the Rwandan parties to its intervention would dramatically heighten the security risks faced by UNAMIR. Brazil also highlighted the potential effects of the MNF on UNAMIR and stated that the opposition of the RPF to the proposed resolution was a key factor preventing its support for the resolution.[87]

The French sought to allay these concerns within the Council about its motives in volunteering to lead the MNF by stating:

> The goal of the French initiative is exclusively humanitarian: the initiative is motivated by the plight of the people, in the face of which, we believe, the international community cannot and must not remain passive. It will not be the mission of our soldiers in Rwanda to interpose themselves between the warring parties, still less to influence in any way the military and political situation. Our objective is simple: to rescue endangered civilians and put an end to the massacres, and to do so in an impartial manner.[88]

The proposed resolution only narrowly passed. Spain, the Czech Republic, Argentina, Oman, Russia, the UK, and the United States all expressed a similar position that though the French led operation was not an ideal option, they would nevertheless support the resolution.[89] Together with the affirmative votes from France, Djibouti, a member of the Council which was entirely economically dependent on France, and Rwanda (whose seat was still held by a representative of the interim government) the resolution was passed with ten votes in favour, and none against. Five states, including China, Brazil, New Zealand, Nigeria and Pakistan all abstained.[90] In practice, France was the only state with the military capability and the political will to intervene in Rwanda and this dearth of

---

[87] Ibid.

[88] Ibid.

[89] Within the Council, there had been an informal agreement reached with the French as to their objectives once deployed in Rwanda and that *Operation Turquoise* would be a-political. Iqbal Riza, interview with author, 15 December, 1999. Members of the Council also saw the French intervention as serving to cushion the transfer of power to the RPF and protect Hutu civilians from possible revenge attacks, although this had the additional effect of affording the perpetrators of the genocide a degree of protection. Sir David Hannay, interview with author, 29 November, 1999.

[90] *UN Document*, S/PV .3392, 22 June, 1994. See also Omaar and de Waal, *Rwanda: Death, Defiance and Despair*, pp. 677-78. The resolution was passed as UNSC Resolution 929, 22 June, 1994.

142 *Understanding the UN Security Council*

alternatives led other members of the UNSC to reluctantly support the French offer.[91]

As *Opération Turquoise* was authorized under Chapter VII, the UNSC was not bound by the Charter to respect RPF demands though in practice considerable effort was expended to limit possible friction between the RPF and French forces. After pressure from the United States, and faced with a *fait accompli* from the UNSC in the form of resolution 925, the RPF withdrew its objections to *Opération Turquoise* just prior to its deployment.[92]

Opération Turquoise

The deployment of *Opération Turquoise* occurred on 23 June, 1994 into south-western Rwanda. The choice of deployment site served to reinforce the French claims that they were motivated simply by humanitarian aims, and were not seeking to support the Rwandan government under the guise of *Opération Turquoise*.[93] There was a deliberate attempt made to keep French and RPF forces apart and the French were very conscious of ensuring that *Opération Turquoise* was not regarded as a biased intervention.[94] In order to prevent the French deployment helping the government cause, the RPF concentrated on speeding its advance to Kigali in order to pre-empt the possibility of a reinvigorated government force, using the French presence, consolidating its military position. The plan worked and the security situation in Rwanda had been transformed by the consolidation of power by the RPF in the first two weeks of July.

The French intervention was not entirely free of political machinations. When the French decided to create a safe zone, it was criticized as providing perpetrators of the genocide with shelter from pursuing RPF fighters. In practice, *Opération Turquoise* did provide the necessary cover for many of those responsible for the genocide to escape into eastern Zaire, as the RPF were barred from entering the safe area.[95] The commander of the French intervention, General Jean-Claude Lafourcase, tried to distinguish between militia soldiers responsible for the killings and Rwandan government forces, a futile attempt to exonerate the latter from any blame.[96] After the RPF consolidated power and routed the interim government from Kigali, the French government informed the UN on 11 July that French forces would begin their withdrawal by 31 July, earlier than originally planned. The interim government had been forced from the country and had fled

---

[91] Michel Duval, interview with author, 16 December, 1999.

[92] Ben Ruegangaza, interview with author, 21 March, 1999. The RPF agreed not to oppose the French deployment provided that it remained confined within its stated zone of operation in the province of Butare. When French paratroopers passed over the provincial boundary, there were engagements between RPF and French forces.

[93] Prunier, *The Rwanda Crisis: History of a Genocide*, pp. 284-285, 291.

[94] Ibid., pp. 284-286.

[95] Ben Ruegangaza, interview with author, 21 March, 1999.

[96] Omaar and de Waal, *Rwanda: Death, Defiance and Despair*, p. 706.

Rwanda 143

to Zaire while the RPF had gained control of the country and formed a Government of National Unity (GNU). It also declared a unilateral cease-fire, effectively ending the civil war. The French government completed its withdrawal from Rwanda on 21 August, and UNAMIR II troops assumed responsibility for the humanitarian protection zone.[97]

With the formation of the GNU and the declaration of the cease-fire, UN efforts became focused on dealing with the immense humanitarian crisis brought on by the flight of Rwandan civilians to Zaire. Many Rwandan Hutus feared reprisal attacks following the victory of the Tutsi-dominated RPF, while the fleeing interim government forces coerced thousands of Rwandan civilians to flee into exile with them. UNAMIR focused on the core tasks of helping to resettle returning refugees from the north-west while also ensuring security in the south-west "safety zone". The GNU also asked for UNAMIR's assistance in establishing a national police force.[98]

Loss of Consent and Withdrawal

UNAMIR finally deployed its full complement of troops as authorized by resolution 925 during October, 1994. On 25 November, the GNU was officially installed in Kigali. For the following eight months UNAMIR concentrated on assisting with the maintenance of general security, delivering humanitarian supplies, and assisting IDPs and refugees return to their homes. Eventually, in early June, 1995, the GNU informed the Secretary-General that it wished to reconsider the mandate of UNAMIR in Rwanda. Accordingly, Boutros-Ghali suggested that the focus of the force be shifted from peacekeeping to confidence building. He reported that there had been incidents of harassment of UNAMIR by elements of the Rwandan Patriotic Army, the new national army, including denying the UN force access to certain parts of the country as well as to Kigali airport. He also reported that in consultations with the UN, the Rwandan government had insisted that any renewal of the UNAMIR mandate would entail a "sharp reduction both in the scope of UNAMIR's tasks and in troop levels." Initial proposals of the Secretary-General to limit the tasks of UNAMIR and reduce its force complement to 2,330 were viewed by the new government as insufficient.[99] Boutros-Ghali emphasised that it was necessary to carry out UNAMIR's tasks "with full respect for the Government's sovereign authority."[100]

Following further consultations between the UN and the Rwandan government, the Security Council decided, in resolution 997 of 9 June, 1995, to authorize a reduction in UNAMIR's size to 1,800 troops and adjusted its mandate

---

[97] *The Blue Helmets*, p. 354.

[98] Ibid., pp. 354-55.

[99] Major Thougene Rudasingwa, interview with author, 23 March, 1999. Rudasingwa argued that UNAMIR II was completely ineffective as it stayed confined primarily to its barracks in Kigali.

[100] *UN Document*, S/1995/457, 4 June, 1995.

144 *Understanding the UN Security Council*

to focus on assisting with the return of refugees, the provision of humanitarian aid, training the national police force, and contributing to the security of UN personnel in Rwanda.[101] Despite this shift in the size and mandate of the force, the Rwandan Foreign Minister informed Boutros-Ghali that his government would not agree to the continued deployment of UNAMIR beyond 8 December, 1995. The new Rwandan government based its position on the belief that the presence of a UN peacekeeping operation no longer met its national "priority needs" which it identified as repatriating refugees and rebuilding the country's infrastructure. "The security of Rwanda," the Foreign Minister wrote, "is the responsibility of the Government of Rwanda and UNAMIR plays no role in it."[102] The GNU took particular offence to comments made by Boutros-Ghali in press conference when he stated:

> Concerning Rwanda, again the position is very clear. If a Government says that it does not want United Nations forces, you have two choices: either you pull out or you decide to maintain the forces on the basis of Chapter VII. Here is the problem.

The GNU characterized the UNSC resolution 1029 as a:

> final renewal, not a postponement of the problem [of UNAMIR's mandate]. Could it be his intention to recommend an extension of UNAMIR or propose the maintenance of UNAMIR on the basis of Chapter VII? How could that be contemplated in view of the sovereignty of Rwanda and the imperative to ensure the co-operation of the Government of Rwanda?[103]

The new government was also unhappy with reports by UN monitors that accused RPF forces of human rights violations, the UN's provision of funds for Hutu refugees at the expense of rebuilding Rwandan infrastructure, and the controlling manner of UNAMIR which, it was felt by the government, infringed on its sovereignty.[104]

On 1 December, the Secretary-General informed the UNSC of the need to withdraw the force. Faced with the withdrawal of consent from the host government and the financial burdens of the peacekeeping operation there was little opportunity to make case for continuing the operation.[105] Accordingly, the Security Council members adopted resolution 1029 which extended the mandate of the force until 8 March, 1996 in order to give it sufficient time to withdraw. The last units of UNAMIR were withdrawn on 19 April, 1996.

---

[101] UNSC Resolution 997, 9 June, 1995.

[102] *UN Document*, S/1995/1018, 8 December, 1995.

[103] *UN Document*, S/1995/1055, 22 December, 1995.

[104] Arthur Jay Klinghoffer, *The International Dimension of Genocide in Rwanda*, Macmillan Press Ltd., London, 1998, p. 70.

[105] *UN Document*, S/1995/1002, 1 December, 1995.

Conclusion

The conservatism that the members of the Security Council demonstrated during the Rwanda crisis differs drastically from the earlier enthusiasm that characterized the deployment of UNOSOM II in Somalia just over a year earlier. Yet a difference in humanitarian need between the two cases is not the reason behind the UNSC's response in each. The killings in Rwanda during April and May, 1994 have been since judged by international lawyers to be the third example of genocide carried out in the twentieth century.[106] Instead, what can explain the Security Council's conservatism in the Rwanda case is the attitudes of its members towards risk and the consequent emphasis on the principle of consent as a means of allaying that risk. The deaths of American soldiers deployed in support of UNOSOM II drastically changed the US attitude towards peacekeeping as exemplified by PDD-25. These restrictions are clearly visible as having been incorporated into resolution 918, where American, self-imposed restrictions became UN restrictions due to the power that the US wielded within the UN organisation. As one UN official commented at the time, "the ghost of Somalia hovers over the whole Rwanda operation."[107] The fact that none of the other P-5 states with the exception of France were willing to take the lead in Rwanda, combined with the emphasis from within the UN Secretariat that UNAMIR remain consistent with its mandate also added to the impotence of the UN.

In the context of the Arusha peace process, consent based, traditional peacekeeping appeared to be an ideal confidence building mechanism. However, when the context of the conflict changed with the assassination of the Rwandan President, UNAMIR's mandate left it unable to respond to the widespread violence. This impotence was not due to a failure of peacekeeping doctrine, but rather resulted from a lack of Security Council support to provide the operation with the practicable means and mandate to protect Rwandan civilians and an inadequate assessment of consensual basis. In this situation where risk minimisation was at the forefront of policy decision, local consent from the government and the RPF gained in importance.

To a certain degree, UNAMIR II's foundation on the consent of the host parties precluded it from receiving sufficient personnel. The RPF's understandable opposition to the deployment of French troops within UNAMIR II severely hampered efforts to bolster the peacekeeping force, thus creating the need to deploy a MNF as a stop-gap measure in order to stabilize the situation until such time as UNAMIR II could be deployed.[108] RPF concerns were also considered

---

[106] Melvern, "Genocide Behind the Thin Blue Line," p. 333.

[107] Senior UN official as quoted in "The UN's Rwanda Failure," *New Statesman & Society*, 29 July, 1994, p. 4.

[108] This provides a partial explanation to the query expressed by the Independent Inquiry into the Action of the UN in Rwanda as to why the substantial deployment of troops under *Opération Turquoise* were not put at the disposal of UNAMIR II instead. See *Report of the*

Understanding the UN Security Council

when the Council eventually decided to authorize the deployment of *Opération Turquoise*. Once the rebel movement gained control of the country, established the GNU and set to work reconstructing the country, it assumed Rwanda's sovereign responsibilities. This meant that the interim government's representative at the UN was removed from his seat and replaced with an RPF representative.[109] More importantly however, the brevity of the RPF's hold on power did not lead the Security Council to question or disregard the new government's concerns about the prolongation of UNAMIR II's mandate in 1995. When Rwanda refused to agree to the extension of the mandate, the UNSC's members chose to accede to its wishes and withdrew UNAMIR II.[110]

However, respect for sovereignty and Article 2(7) does not explain the Council's inaction during April, 1994 when the genocide was at its height. The Council's members were willing to impose an arms embargo on Rwanda despite the protest of its then interim government because of the increasingly fragile status of that government. Similarly, the Council was willing to use Chapter VII to authorize *Opération Turquoise*. Clearly, the restrictions of Article 2(7) did not prevent the Council from taking very limited action under Chapter VII to counter the genocide. However, an unwillingness to assume military and political risk weighed more heavily in the minds of the Security Council members, consequently preventing them from deploying a timely and effective UN-led peace enforcement operation to save Rwandan civilians. Instead, the consent and co-operation of the two host parties, whether of sovereign status or not, was of fundamental concern among the UNSC's members when formulating their response to the genocide.

The Rwanda crisis represents a severe failure of the United Nations to adequately respond to one of the most extreme violations of international humanitarian law in the twentieth century. Additionally, the repercussions of the genocide in the form of refugee flows into Zaire demonstrated the consequence of the UNSC's inaction for international peace and security. The manner in which the Council did patch together a response in the form of *Opération Turquoise* has raised questions about the Council's use of its Chapter VII authority.[111] Why, for example, in the face of a threat to international peace and security did the Council members authorize the French operation under Chapter VII, while the UN-led operation already in Rwanda had only a Chapter VI mandate? Again, the answer appears to be an unwillingness on the part of the UNSC states to avoid putting UN

Independent Inquiry into the Actions of the United Nations During the 1994 Genocide in Rwanda, 15 December, 1999, pp. 38-39.

[109] No attempt was made to expel the interim government of Rwanda's representative on the UNSC, Jerome Bicamumpaka, until 16 July, 1994. Omaar and de Waal, *Rwanda: Death, Despair and Defiance*, p. 697

[110] The UNSC members, in particular the US, were also keen to reduce the financial burden of peacekeeping operations and therefore were even less likely to press for the prolongation of UNAMIR II in the field.

[111] See for example, Adelman and Suhrke, *International Response to Genocide*, p. 57 and Omaar and de Waal, *Rwanda: Death, Despair and Defiance*, p. 698.

troops at risk and a lack of political motivation to become involved in a conflict which did not threaten or involve the interests of any P-5 members apart from France. Indeed, the actions of the UNSC in Rwanda call into question the contention that the members of the Council were increasingly willing to take action to protect human rights in the post-Cold War period.

Chapter 6

Bosnia

In 1992, the United Nations Protection Force (UNPROFOR) was deployed into Bosnia-Herzegovina to cope with growing instability between Bosnian Serb, Muslim and Croat populations. Intended to assist the UNHCR to provide humanitarian assistance to civilians affected by the fighting, UNPROFOR was given a difficult mandate that relied on the consent and co-operation of numerous local belligerents for its implementation. As the conflict worsened, the members of the Security Council chose to authorize the use of air power to assist UNPROFOR to implement its rapidly expanding mandate. Yet this move towards the use of coercive methods as a substitute for coherent policy ignored the practical necessity of adherence to the principle of consent at the operational and tactical levels. Due to the vulnerability of UNPROFOR troops on the ground, the Security Council's decision to use force was not implemented strategically until the summer of 1995.

This chapter traces the decisions made by the UNSC members in Bosnia in response to the challenges of consent, beginning with a brief history of the operation until the summer of 1993. It then examines four key incidents that provide insight into the attitudes among the UNSC members to the challenges of consent faced by UNPROFOR and the tentative use of coercion as a means of overcoming these difficulties. The first was the decision of the Council to authorize the use of air strikes in order to assist UNPROFOR to carry out the humanitarian elements of its mandate. The second was the decision whether or not to use or threaten air strikes in defence of the safe areas of Tuzla, Srebrenica, Gorazde and Sarajevo. The third was the issue of the deployment of the RRF in the spring of 1995 to augment the defensive capabilities of UNPROFOR on the ground. The fourth and final instance examined in this chapter is the decision of the UNSC members to adopt a more coercive policy towards the Bosnian Serbs during *Operation Deliberate Force*, which relied on the use of force to bring the parties to the negotiating table and led to the Dayton Agreement in November 1995.

Background

Following the Croatian and Slovenian declarations of independence from Yugoslavia in June 1991, conflict broke out in Croatia between the Croatian government and radical Serb elements in Knin. Hostilities spread between paramilitary forces and local police contingents until Yugoslav National Army (JNA) forces were deployed in order to protect the significant Serb minority in

Croatia. At the request of the Yugoslav government, the Security Council imposed an arms embargo on the country with resolution 713, characterizing the situation as a "threat to international peace and security" and acting under Chapter VII of the UN Charter.[1] The federal Yugoslav government also requested that the UN establish a peacekeeping operation in Yugoslavia in order to contain the conflict. Accordingly the members of the Security Council approved the efforts of the Secretary-General toward establishing such an operation with resolution 721.[2] Following the signing of a cease-fire agreement on 23 November, the UNSC adopted resolution 743, authorizing the deployment of UNPROFOR in order to help consolidate the political progress.[3] UNPROFOR was originally authorized "to create conditions of peace and security required for the negotiation of an overall settlement of the Yugoslav crisis," ensure the demilitarization of UN designated protected areas (UNPAs) and protect civilians in those areas from attack. In addition, the force was to monitor the functioning of local police, control access to the UNPAs, assist refugees and IDPs to return to their homes, as well as verify the withdrawal of the JNA and irregular forces from Croatia.[4]

UNPROFOR in Bosnia

Following growing instability in Bosnia-Herzegovina, the members of the Security Council decided to create a separate Bosnia-Herzegovina command within UNPROFOR with resolution 776.[5] The Security Council's decision to do so recognised the gradual expansion of UNPROFOR into Bosnia that had occurred over the summer of 1992. Primarily, the force had been focused on re-opening the Sarajevo airport for humanitarian deliveries and reducing tensions between Bosnian Serb and Bosnian Muslim forces in the city. Following talks brokered by the UN, agreement was reached between the two opposing sides for the re-opening of Sarajevo airport. They also agreed that UNPROFOR would assume operational responsibility for it.[6]

The Security Council authorized the Secretary-General to deploy additional UNPROFOR units in order to secure Sarajevo airport and ensure the delivery of humanitarian assistance consistent with the 5 June Sarajevo Airport Agreement.[7] However, implementation of the Airport Agreement proved difficult in practice. A

---

[1] UNSC Resolution 713, 25 September, 1991.

[2] UNSC Resolution 721, 27 November, 1991. Letter from the Permanent Representative of Yugoslavia to the UN, Darko Silovic to the President of the Security Council which reads, "I have been instructed by my government to request the establishment of a peacekeeping operation in Yugoslavia..." *UN Document*, S/23240, 26 November 1991.

[3] UNSC Resolution 743, 21 February, 1992.

[4] The initial plan for UNPROFOR, as approved by the UNSC is contained in *UN Document*, S/23280, annex III.

[5] UNSC Resolution 776, 14 September, 1992.

[6] *UN Document*, S/24075, 6 June, 1992.

[7] UNSC Resolution 764, 13 July, 1992.

150   *Understanding the UN Security Council*

lack of consent and co-operation with UNPROFOR on the ground and the failure of the parties to establish a cease-fire throughout Bosnia temporarily prevented the Secretary-General from recommending to the Council that UNPROFOR be expanded to take on its supervisory role at the airport.[8] Indeed, Boutros-Ghali was sceptical that a UN peacekeeping operation in Bosnia would be successful since there was no durable political agreement between the main belligerents on which a force mandate could be based.[9]

As the conflict began to spread throughout the country, the UNSC was under increasing pressure to resolve the conflict and ameliorate its humanitarian consequences. On 13 August, the deteriorating conditions in Bosnia and pressure from the Bosnian government to address the situation led to the Council's adoption of resolution 770 under Chapter VII of the UN Charter.[10] Noting that the situation in Bosnia constituted "a threat to international peace and security" and "reaffirming the sovereignty of Bosnia-Herzegovina", the members of the Council called upon states "to take nationally or through regional arrangements all measures necessary to facilitate in co-ordination with the United Nations the delivery...of humanitarian assistance."[11] Despite the strong terms of the resolution, the members of the Council informally decided that the delivery of humanitarian assistance should be entrusted to UNPROFOR.[12]

The Secretary-General formalised this decision by recommending that the mandate of UNPROFOR be again expanded to include assisting UNHCR to deliver humanitarian supplies throughout Bosnia-Herzegovina and, where necessary, provide protection for the UNHCR relief convoys.[13] With his initial scepticism toward peacekeeping in Bosnia ignored by the members of the Security Council, Boutros-Ghali diligently sought to ensure that UNPROFOR was given the means and mandate necessary to ensure that it could fulfil the tasks set for it by the UNSC. Consequently, he recommended that the force be strengthened and its mandate expanded to provide protective support for UNHCR humanitarian convoys.[14] In order to do so, he stated that UNPROFOR would operate according to traditional peacekeeping rules of engagement and would be authorized to use

---

[8] *UN Document*, S/24333, 21 July, 1992. For details on the airport agreement and the subsequent difficulties faced by UNPROFOR in trying to implement it, see Lewis MacKenzie, *Peackeeper: The Road to Sarajevo*, Douglas & McIntyre, Toronto, 1993.

[9] Boutros-Ghali, *Unvanquished*, p. 40.

[10] Muhamed Sacirbey, interview with author, 14 December, 1999. See also UNSC Resolution 770, 13 August, 1992.

[11] Though the phrase "threat to international peace and security" was used in the formulation of the resolution, the conflict was apparently not seen as a threat to wider European security by many in the UNSC. Instead the primary concern was to stabilise the humanitarian situation while allowing the International Conference on the Former Yugoslavia (ICFY) to negotiate a wider peace. Dame Pauline Neville-Jones, interview with author, 26 November, 1999. This view was supported by both Lord Douglas Hurd and Sir Malcolm Rifkind in interviews with the author, 9 December and 23 November, 1999, respectively.

[12] *UN Document*, S/24540, 10 September, 1992.

[13] Ibid.

[14] Boutros-Ghali, *Unvanquished*, p. 40

Bosnia 151

force only in self-defence. However, the definition of self-defence was to include instances where UNPROFOR was prevented from carrying out its mandate.[15] The Security Council adopted these recommendations with resolution 776 and, consistent with the report of the Secretary-General, the resolution made no mention of Chapter VII.[16] The Council members were not prepared to authorize UNPROFOR to use "all necessary means" to ensure the delivery of relief supplies in contrast to its invocation of Chapter VII in resolution 770.

At this point UNPROFOR was envisaged and assembled as a consent-based peacekeeping operation. The UN troops were armed only with light weapons, had minimal armoured support and were dispersed through Bosnia with the relief convoys. As such, they were reliant on the consent and the co-operation of the host parties in order to implement the force mandate.[17] This dependency was ameliorated given the fact that the two main parties involved had agreed to co-operate with the delivery of humanitarian supplies at the London Conference on the former Yugoslavia, 27 August, 1992.[18] The leader of the Bosnian Serbs, Radovan Karadzic, welcomed the expansion of UNPROFOR's activities, suggesting that they would serve to build trust between the belligerent parties.[19]

Yet the legal status of the two parties differed. Bosnia-Herzegovina had been given membership in the United Nations on 22 May, 1992.[20] The United Nations however, refused to recognise the break away state of Repulika Srpska and in turn the Bosnian Serbs refused to recognise the authority of the United Nations.[21]

Safe Havens and Air Strikes

UNPROFOR's efforts during its first year in Bosnia were routinely obstructed by the local parties on the ground, predominantly the Bosnian Serbs.[22] This stemmed from the numerous quasi-independent paramilitary groups in operation and the

---

[15] *UN Document*, S/24540, 10 September, 1992.

[16] UNSC Resolution 776, 14 September, 1992.

[17] Adam Roberts, "Communal Conflict as a Challenge to International Organisation: The Case of Former Yugoslavia," *Review of International Studies*, vol. 21, 1995, p. 402. For an analysis of problems faced by UNPROFOR in the performance of its mandate see Barry Ashton, "Making Peace Agreements Work: United Nations Experience in the Former Yugoslavia," *Cornell International Law Journal*, vol. 30, 1997.

[18] See the preamble of UNSC Resolution 776, 14 September, 1992.

[19] "Karadzic Says Agreement Reached With UNPROFOR on Supervision of Artillery," *BBC Summary of World Broadcasts*, Part 2, EE/1476, p. C1/4, 3 September, 1992.

[20] UNGA Resolution 46/237, 22 May, 1992.

[21] Michael Rose, *Fighting For Peace*, Warner Books, London, 1998, p. 149. Due to the difference in status between the Bosnian Serbs and the Bosnian government, they were treated differently when visited by foreign representatives and there was never any consideration given to recognising the Republika Srpska as a sovereign state in any final political settlement. Lord Douglas Hurd, interview with author, 9 December, 1999.

[22] *The Blue Helmets*, p. 523.

152 *Understanding the UN Security Council*

failure of the Bosnian Serb leadership to exercise control over them.[23] In early 1993, this lack of co-operation with UNPROFOR and continued attacks on the civilian population placed the Security Council under increasing pressure to take more constructive measures in response to Bosnian Serb aggression. In order to protect humanitarian flights into Bosnia, the UNSC had adopted resolution 781 in October, 1992, banning all non-UN military flights in Bosnian airspace.[24] In response to repeated violations of this ban and the bombing, on 13 March 1993, of two Bosnian villages, the Council, again acting under Chapter VII, authorized UN members states to take "all necessary measures" to ensure compliance with the no fly zone.[25] It was another step in a process of 'creeping escalation' with which the UNSC was responding to the complexities of the Bosnian conflict.[26]

Radovan Karadzic called the new resolution "one more of the many deeply unjust actions against the Serbian people."[27] In order to avoid confrontation with the UNSC on the issue of military flights, the Bosnian Serbs consequently announced that they had instituted a voluntary ban on military flights over Bosnia and that the UN resolution was therefore "pointless."[28] The Bosnian government, vulnerable to superior Bosnian Serb air power, argued that the no fly zone, originally agreed to by both parties at the 1992 London Conference, was the responsibility of the UNSC to enforce.[29] The members of the UNSC and Boutros-Ghali were becoming increasingly frustrated by the political intransigence of the Bosnian Serbs. This led the UN Secretary-General to suggest that the failure of the Bosnian Serbs to withdraw from territory acquired through force would lead to the deployment of a UN peace enforcement operation.[30]

In practice, the members of the Security Council did not take such a dramatic step. Responding to Bosnian Serb paramilitary attacks on the city of Srebrenica, which caused a large number of civilian casualties and severely impeded the United Nations humanitarian relief operations in the area, the Security Council passed resolution 819. The resolution demanded that Srebrenica be treated as a "safe area" by the combatants and that Bosnian Serb paramilitary units withdraw from around the city.[31] Three weeks later, the Council adopted resolution 824 which expanded the safe area concept to the towns of Sarajevo, Tuzla, Zepa, Gorazde, and Bihac. This action was, in part, due to pressure from the Bosnian

---

[23] Bunce, "The Elusive Peace in the Former Yugoslavia," p. 716.

[24] UNSC Resolution 781, 9 October, 1992.

[25] UNSC Resolution 816, 31 March, 1993.

[26] Spyros Economides and Paul Taylor, "Former Yugoslavia," in James Mayall, ed., *The New Interventionism, 1991-1994*, Cambridge University Press, Cambridge, 1994, p. 69.

[27] As quoted in Marjan Malesic, "International Peacekeeping: An Object of Propaganda in Former Yugoslavia," *International Peacekeeping*, vol. 5, no. 2, 1998, p. 93.

[28] "Karadzic: Serbian Compromise makes UN Resolution on No Fly Zone 'Pointless,'" *BBC Summary of World Broadcasts*, Part 2, EE/1507, p. C1/1, 9 October, 1992.

[29] See *UN Documents*, S/24616, 5 October, 1992 and S/24622, 6 October, 1992.

[30] Boutros-Ghali, *Unvanquished*, p. 74.

[31] UNSC Resolution 819, 16 April, 1993.

Bosnia 153

government to assist in the protection of Bosnian civilians.[32] Once again the Council demanded that military attacks on these areas be stopped, Bosnian Serbs units withdraw from them, and humanitarian agencies be given unimpeded access to the new safe areas. Both resolutions creating the safe areas were adopted under Chapter VII of the UN Charter, but neither resolution provided UNPROFOR with additional means or authority to use force to implement its mandate. The operation therefore remained squarely based on the consent and the co-operation of the host parties.

Resolution 836

Following the creation of the safe havens, the Security Council passed resolution 836 which represented a new phase in the peacekeeping efforts in Bosnia-Herzegovina. Not only did the Security Council decide to authorize UNPROFOR to use all necessary means, including the use of force, in the performance of its mandate, but the Council also authorized member states of the United Nations to support the peacekeeping force by providing it with air power.[33] Drawing attention to the rights of Bosnia-Herzegovina as a member state of the UN and the Security Council's responsibility to protect Bosnia's sovereign identity, the fifth, ninth and tenth substantive paragraphs of resolution 836 read:

> The Council:...
>
> 5. Also decides to extend... the mandate of the United Nations Protection Force in order to enable it, in the safe areas referred to in resolution 824 (1993), to deter attacks against the safe areas, to monitor the cease-fire, to promote the withdrawal of military or paramilitary units other than those of the Government of the Republic of Bosnia and Herzegovina and to occupy some key points on the ground, in addition to participating in the delivery of humanitarian relief to the population as provided for in resolution 776 (1992) of 14 September 1992...
>
> 9. Authorises the Force, in addition to the mandate defined in resolution 770 (1992) of 13 August 1992 and 776 (1992) in carrying out the mandate defined in paragraph 5 above, acting in self-defence, to take the necessary measures, including the use of force, in reply to bombardments against the safe areas by any of the parties or to armed incursion into them or in the event of any

---

[32] UNSC Resolution 824, 6 May, 1993. See also the letters from the Bosnian government, requesting an emergency meeting of the Security Council with the regard to the situation in Zepa, *UN Document* S/25718, 4 May, 1993, and imploring the UNSC to take "whatever measures are necessary" to save Zepa and its people, *UN Document*, S/25730, 5 May, 1993.

[33] This was not the first time the Security Council had considered allowing UNPROFOR to use force to fulfil its mandate, but protecting the safe havens made the UNSC members willing to authorise it for the first time. In July 1991 Austria had suggested the UN consider possible military intervention in Bosnia to end the conflict, but the western UNSC members refused to support the proposal. See Sabrina Petra Ramet, "War in the Balkans," *Foreign Affairs*, vol. 71, 1991-92, p. 95.

154 *Understanding the UN Security Council*

> deliberate obstruction in or around those areas to the freedom of movement of the Force or of protected humanitarian convoys;

> 10. Decides that, notwithstanding paragraph 1 of resolution 816 (1993), Member States, acting nationally or through regional organisations or arrangements, may take, under the authority of the Security Council and subject to close co-ordination with the Secretary-General and the Force, all necessary measures, through the use of air power, in and around the safe areas in Bosnia and Herzegovina, to support the Force in the performance of its mandate set out in paragraphs 5 and 9 above;[34]

The resolution mentions three main concerns of the Security Council members that caused them to broaden the means and the mandate of UNPROFOR. First, the Council members were intent on protecting the sovereign identity of the state of Bosnia-Herzegovina and chose to explicitly reaffirm its sovereignty, political independence and territorial integrity. They also noted the responsibility of the UNSC to protect the character of the country as a member of the United Nations. Second, they decided to characterize the conflict as a threat to international peace and security, doing so under Article 39 of Chapter VII, thus allowing the authorization of the use of force under Article 42 of the UN Charter.[35] Third, they sought to halt the Bosnian Serb's continuing forcible acquisition of territory and ethnic cleansing. Resolution 836 noted that such practices were unlawful and expressed the UNSC's concern at the continuing hostilities in and around the designated safe areas. In a statement prior to the vote on the draft resolution the representative of Turkey, for example, stressed:

> [Turkey's] sole aim, from the beginning of the crisis, has been to help restore peace in Bosnia and Herzegovina and to secure its independence, sovereignty, territorial integrity and unity by rejecting the acquisition of territory through violence and force, and, in this case, genocide.[36]

The permanent members of the Council stressed that resolution 836 was adopted as an interim step in order to stabilize the military and political situation in critical areas of Bosnia-Herzegovina and protect civilians. In order to do so, they were willing to authorize the use of force under Chapter VII. As Yuliy Vorontsov, the Permanent Representative of Russia stated:

> The Russian delegation is firmly convinced that the implementation of this resolution will be an important practical step by the world community genuinely to curb the violence and to stop the shooting on the long-suffering land of the Bosnians. Henceforth, any attempted military attacks, shooting and shelling of the safe areas, and armed incursions into those areas, and any hindrance to the delivery of humanitarian assistance will be stopped by United Nations forces by using all

---

[34] UNSC Resolution 836, 4 June, 1993.

[35] See Chapter One.

[36] *UN Document*, S/PV. 3228, 4 June, 1993.

Bosnia 155

necessary measures, including the use of armed force. This will be an important factor for stabilizing the situation and in these areas and for lessening the suffering of the civilian population.[37]

In addition to helping to ease the humanitarian suffering of Bosnian civilians taking refuge in the safe areas, it was argued that resolution 836 also made an equitable political settlement more likely. According to the representative of France:

> The draft resolution addresses an immediate, vital humanitarian objective: ensuring the survival of civilian populations in the safe areas. It also addresses a paramount political objective: maintaining the territorial basis needed for the development and implementation of the Peace Plan for Bosnia and Herzegovina.[38]

Madeleine Albright, the US representative, capitalized on the willingness of the Council to invoke Chapter VII and stressed that the resolution was "an intermediate step - no more, no less" on the way to an equitable settlement and that the members of the Council had not ruled out "options for new and tougher measures, none of which is prejudged or excluded from consideration."[39]

Despite the political rhetoric voiced in the Council chamber and the appearance of resolution 836 as a substantial step towards protecting Bosnian civilians, in reality it was a very hesitant and weak policy. This was brought on by doubts as to its efficacy and a lack of intent among the members of the P-5 to implement it in practice. For example, officials within the UN Secretariat did not support the resolution as it further expanded the organisation's involvement in Bosnia without sufficient support from member states.[40] China repeated its traditional reservations towards the use of Chapter VII in the context of peacekeeping operations. Britain, which had voted in favour of the resolution, was concerned at the possibility that the safe area concept could lead to each safe area becoming a "protectorate" of the UN, something which would require a more binding commitment on the part of the UK and the other permanent members of the Security Council to defend. For this reason, Sir David Hannay, the British representative, urged his French and Russian counterparts to support resolution 836 which seemed to offer protection to the safe areas but did not involved any greater commitment on the part of UNPROFOR.[41]

In consequence, the safe havens concept was a short-term expedient policy that was intended to deter attacks on particular areas of vulnerability, but one which, in practice, was never intended to require defence by UNPROFOR.[42] The

---

[37] Ibid.

[38] Ibid.

[39] Ibid.

[40] Chris Coleman, interview with author, 17 June, 1999.

[41] Richard Caplan, *Post Mortem on UNPROFOR*, London Defence Studies Series No. 33, p. 8.

[42] Sir David Hannay, interview with author, 29 November, 1999. The interpretation that resolutions 824 and 836 allowed the use of air power to deter attacks on the safe areas and

156 *Understanding the UN Security Council*

main factor which precluded outright French and British support for the air strikes as a means to protect the safe areas was a reluctance to raise the military ante while British and French troops were on the ground participating in the peacekeeping operation.[43] In effect, the establishment of the safe areas created the expectation of security, which did not exist in reality.[44]

Other members of the UNSC questioned the true intentions and commitment of the P-5 to implementing the resolution.[45] Pakistan, for example, supported authorization of the use of force to protect the safe areas under Chapter VII, but did not believe that the resolution went far enough. The fear of the Pakistani government was that if further enforcement measures were not adopted, the safe areas would become part of a *status quo*, which could only benefit the Bosnian Serb aggressors. Venezuela, another ardent supporter of the safe-area concept, also believed the language of resolution 836 to be sufficiently imprecise as to allow the P-5 members the opportunity to avoid adequately protecting the safe areas.[46] As the Venezuelan representative argued:

> We note with profound concern that this conflict is seen by the major countries as being unrelated to their strategic interests...[f]or Venezuela, the draft resolution before the Council today has serious difficulties...It proposes an initiative that we find, on the one hand, incomplete in scope and, on the other, contrary to its own objectives. In this draft, the Council concentrates on those areas still under siege and attack, in an attempt to save them. This is well and good. However, it also makes it clear that it does so in the face of political reluctance to shoulder the same degree of responsibility for the broader and more meaningful goal of the fair and equitable distribution of territory between the various communities of the Republic of Bosnia and Herzegovina.[47]

The representative of Bosnia-Herzegovina, though supportive of the resolution, expressed dismay that suggested improvements to the draft resolution had not been incorporated into it. His government had wanted the designation of "safe-area" applied to a wider range of Bosnian communities, the removal of the arms embargo, and the incorporation of the safe-area concept into a wider strategy to confront Serb aggression and secure peace. The Bosnian government was also suspicious of the Council's commitment to ending the conflict:

> ...the lack of key elements promoting true peace and real safe areas make us very suspicious that the motivations behind the draft resolution most directly reflect a

---

not defend them was also supported by the Bosnian commander of UNPROFOR, General Michael Rose. See Rose, *Fighting For Peace*, p. 360.

[43] David Owen, *Balkan Odyssey*, Victor Gollancz Publishers, 1995, p. 136.

[44] Lord Douglas Hurd, interview with author, 9 December, 1999.

[45] There were also significant differences of interpretation between supporters of the resolution as to what it actually entailed as indicated by the comments of the New Zealand and American representatives, *UN Document*, S/PV .3228, 4 June, 1993.

[46] Caplan, *Post Mortem on UNPROFOR*, p. 8.

[47] *UN Document*, S/PV. 3228, 4 June, 1993.

Bosnia 157

continuing lack of will to confront the aggressor and an absence of commitment to the Republic and people of Bosnia and Herzegovina.[48]

The issue of the arms embargo, in particular, was a complex one. Originally applied by the UNSC in September 1991 under Chapter VII of the UN Charter at the request of the federal Yugoslav government, it was maintained on the territory of the former Yugoslavia even after the independence of Bosnia, Croatia, and Slovenia was accepted by the UN. Its continued imposition on Bosnia, despite the request of the Bosnian government to have it removed, appeared to suggest that the members of the Council were indeed ignoring the sovereign concerns of the host state. In fact, the Bosnians' desire to have the embargo removed was not absolute and they did not want the removal of the embargo if it meant the withdrawal of UNPROFOR.[49] The embargo itself was not entirely effective and the Bosnians were able to purchase military supplies primarily from eastern European states for delivery through Croatia. Arguing against it however was designed to achieve either of two objectives; allow the Bosnians to defend themselves or provoke international military intervention against the Bosnian Serbs.[50]

Despite the appearance of resolution 836 as part of a long-term political strategy towards solving the conflict in the former Yugoslavia, politically it was a stopgap measure. With the US rejection of the Vance-Owen Peace Plan (VOPP), a plan that had divided Bosnia into ethnic cantons but, in American eyes, rewarded ethnic cleansing, the international community was left scrambling for an alternative policy. The primary policy option put forward by the Clinton administration, termed "lift and strike," fulfilled the primary US objectives of avoiding the deployment of US ground forces into a potential Bosnian quagmire and not alienating the Yeltsin government in Moscow.[51] However, "lift and strike" was rejected by the Europeans who refused to endorse a policy which potentially endangered UNPROFOR troops as well as the UNHCR humanitarian programme. The inflexibility of this European position, combined with a change in Clinton's

---

[48] Ibid.

[49] The Bosnian government apparently agreed to stop asking for the lifting of the arms embargo in early 1995, provided that UNPROFOR was not withdrawn. Lord Douglas Hurd, interview with author, 9 December, 1999.

[50] Muhammed Sacirbey, interview with author, 14 December 1999.

[51] Elizabeth Drew, *On the Edge: The Clinton Presidency*, Simon & Schuster, New York, 1994, p.145. "Lift and strike" referred to the lifting of the arms embargo introduced by UN resolution 713 and undertaking air strikes to defend UNPROFOR. The arm embargo had banned the importation of all military equipment and weapons to Yugoslavia, yet there was pressure from both the UN General Assembly and the US Congress to lift the embargo in order to allow the ill-equipped Bosnian government to defend itself. Air strikes were seen as a corollary of lifting the embargo in order to provide cover for the Bosnian government army as it re-armed itself once the embargo was lifted. The General Assembly adopted resolution 47/121 (18 December, 1992) which urged the Security Council to exempt Bosnia-Herzegovina from the arms embargo so it could properly defend itself against the better armed Serbs. See also Owen, *Balkan Odyssey*, p. 142.

158 *Understanding the UN Security Council*

personal attitude towards the suitability of "lift and strike," resulted in its rejection as a policy option. Instead, air strikes emerged as the primary alternative.[52]

Yet the true stop-gap nature of resolution 836 was confirmed by the UNSC's response to Boutros-Ghali's report on how to best implement the resolution. He recommended that, in order for the safe areas to be adequately protected, it was necessary to deploy 34,000 additional UN troops to obtain "deterrence through strength." Instead, the members of the Security Council opted for the "light option" and chose to deploy only 7,600.[53] With such a limited reinforcement, Boutros-Ghali noted, " [since] UNPROFOR ground troops will not be sufficient to resist a concentrated assault on any of the safe areas, particular emphasis must be placed on the availability of a credible air-strike capability provided by Member States." He also stated that, even with reinforcement, UNPROFOR "assumed the consent and co-operation of the parties."[54]

Yet even after this report stressed the necessity of adhering to consent, the members of the Security Council continued to hint at adding further coercive elements to UNPROFOR. The US representative issued an indirect warning to the Bosnian Serbs stating, "the United States voted in favour of this resolution as an intermediate step that does not foreclose options involving tougher measures."[55] The Russian representative appeared supportive of this firm stance. While he stressed that the consent of the parties was vital to the success of the "safe areas," they could be protected by other tougher means:

> We share the Secretary-General's view that the implementation of the decision to set up safe areas must be predicated upon the consent and co-operation of all the Bosnian parties.
> These parties must clearly realise that if they refuse such co-operation this will involve the adoption of new, tougher measures, none of which is either pre-determined or ruled out.[56]

By perching precariously halfway between a firm, though more ineffective operation based on consent and the use of air strikes, the members of the Security

---

[52] Drew, *On the Edge*, p. 157. Drew relates that Clinton had read the book *Balkan Ghosts*, by Richard Caplan, which argues that the Balkan peoples have a historical legacy of infighting, and it was this that led Clinton to decide to drop "lift and strike." Out of the confusion of "lift and strike" and the Vance-Owen Peace Plan (VOPP) emerged the Joint Action Programme. This plan envisaged no long term political goal or settlement, but was mainly a half-hearted attempt to provided some protection for Bosnian civilians by emphasising the idea of "safe areas." Under pressure to demonstrate its political resolve in Bosnia, the US was extremely reluctant to deploy ground forces, consequently leading to a reliance on air power to protect the "safe areas". It was in this uncertain atmosphere that resolution 836 was adopted. See also Owen, *Balkan Odyssey*, p. 172 and Mats Berdal, "Fateful Encounter: The United States and UN Peacekeeping," *Survival*, vol. 36, no. 1, 1994, pp. 36-37.

[53] This limited expansion was authorised in UNSC Resolution 844, 18 June, 1993.

[54] *UN Document*, S/25939, 14 June, 1993.

[55] *UN Document*, S/PV. 3241, 18 June, 1993.

[56] Ibid.

Bosnia 159

Council revealed an approach to the conflict in Bosnia that was largely the result of a lack of policy direction. This in turn resulted from a lack of international political commitment to ending the fighting. The members of the Council were caught between implementing two very different types of intervention in Bosnia: one directed towards minimising the humanitarian impact of the fighting and a second aimed at preventing the acquisition of territory by force and the preservation of Bosnia's borders. The first objective was best achieved by consent-based peacekeeping methods, while the latter appeared to require a more forceful approach.[57] Ultimately, UNPROFOR came to reflect elements of both types of intervention.

The Council members also ignored what was feasible in terms of fulfilling UNPROFOR's mandate on the ground.[58] Consent still served as the foundation of UNPROFOR's activities because it was the only reasonably effective approach possible given the lacklustre political commitment of the Security Council. However, it also limited the ability of UNPROFOR to fulfil its mandate. The adoption of resolution 836 had set the stage for the use of air power to assist UNPROFOR in the performance of its mandate, but rather than representing a robust and firm statement of intent to use force and go beyond consent, the actual use of air power proved to be half-hearted and ineffective at protecting the safe areas or ending Bosnian Serb territorial conquests. This was primarily because it was recognised that any use of air power could take UNPROFOR into peace enforcement and therefore neither the UN nor the troop contributing states wanted to cross this line and potentially endanger UN personnel on the ground.[59]

Srebrenica and Tuzla

The limits of applying force in the context of a consent-based peacekeeping operation mandated to protect civilians and deliver humanitarian supplies were demonstrated in early 1994. At that time, there were two main problems faced by UNPROFOR. The first was the re-opening of Tuzla airport for humanitarian flights. The issue of the airport lay at the heart of the UN deployment in Bosnia - easing the humanitarian consequences of the conflict. Radovan Karadzic, the Bosnian Serb leader, had categorically refused to allow the re-opening of the airport before the conclusion of an overall peace settlement. The Bosnian Serbs believed that the airport was being used to smuggle weapons to the government forces.[60] The second main problem occurred in the city of Srebrenica where the Bosnian Serbs had opposed the replacement of Canadian soldiers with troops from

---

[57] Spyros Economides and Paul Taylor, "Former Yugoslavia," in Mayall, ed., *The New Interventionism*, p. 64.

[58] Pentagon planners had accepted that the use of air power alone would not be adequate to protect the safe areas. See Owen, *Balkan Odyssey*, pp. 172-73.

[59] Dame Pauline Neville-Jones, interview with author, 26 November, 1999.

[60] Boutros-Ghali, *Unvanquished*, p. 143.

160   *Understanding the UN Security Council*

the Netherlands since December 1993.[61] Yet, the issue of the troop rotation was a fundamental element of the UN deployment in the former Yugoslavia: the freedom of movement of its troops to which both the Bosnian government and Bosnian Serbs had agreed in the 18 November 1993 Geneva Agreement.[62]

Under instructions from Boutros-Ghali, his Special Representative Yasushi Akashi subsequently identified three options designed to resolve the issues, each of which depended on the level of consent forthcoming from the host parties. The first option saw the two objectives achieved through negotiation with the parties. The second option assumed that the local parties would not consent to either the troop rotation or the opening of the airport, but that they would not use force to prevent the UN from doing so. This created the possibility of the UN using a limited degree of force to achieve these two objectives. The third option envisaged a situation in which the parties disagreed with the UN objectives and used military force to try to prevent their achievement. In response, the UN would be required to rely on the use of air power and additional troops from member states to achieve the two objectives. In Akashi's view, the first two scenarios could be carried out within the existing UNPROFOR mandate, while the third would require additional Security Council authorization. In view of these options, Boutros-Ghali noted that since both cities were designated safe areas under Chapter VII, the UN was therefore not legally obliged to seek the consent of the parties involved to carry out any task that was consistent with the existing mandate of the force.[63]

However, the options available to the UN had to be qualified by the practical situation on the ground. The EU envoy David Owen recommended that air power could be used in the Tuzla case in the event that further diplomatic methods proved unsuccessful. However, he also noted that the very threat of air strikes compromised UN assurances that the reopened airport would only be used to airlift humanitarian supplies to the city. This, he argued, would only serve to heighten Bosnian Serbs' suspicions about the UN's motives and damage the negotiation process.[64] The UNHCR was similarly concerned that forcing the opening of Tuzla airport could endanger the Sarajevo airlift operation, a vital component of the UN's overall humanitarian operation in Bosnia. Boutros-Ghali consequently advised the UNSC members against using air strikes to open Tuzla airport or to force the troop

---

[61] "Generals Battling the Bureaucracy," *The Independent*, 31 January, 1994.

[62] Rose, *Fighting For Peace*, p. 34.

[63] *UN Document*, S/1994/94, 28 January, 1994.

[64] Owen, *Balkan Odyssey*, CD-ROM Reference Disk. COERU, 14 January, 1994. On the issue of Srebrenica, the Pale Serbs had effectively tried to delay UN efforts to replace the Canadian troops. French General Briquemont, commander of UNPROFOR, had written to Karadzic requesting that the troops rotation be allowed to occur. Karadzic replied that while he had no objection to this, the modalities of the rotations had to be sorted out beforehand with Bosnian Serb General Ratko Mladic. Karadzic repeated his agreement to the rotation in a meeting with Akashi on 10 January. The problem with with this arrangement was that General Mladic was "abroad" and could not be contacted. Therefore the rotation could not be carried out.

rotation in Srebrenica.[65] This position was supported by the UNPROFOR Bosnia Commander, General Sir Michael Rose.[66] The combined approach of threatening air strikes while simultaneously pursuing negotiations eventually helped to bring about the troop rotation, but negotiations on the re-opening of Tuzla airport endured for the duration of UNPROFOR's deployment.[67] However, these issues had demonstrated that even though UNPROFOR had the legal authority to use air power, it was not a practicable option.

"Close air support" vs. "Pre-emptive Strikes"

The Tuzla and Srebrenica issues highlighted a crucial difference in interpretation of "air strikes" between NATO and the UN which further hampered the ability of UNPROFOR to use its Chapter VII authority to fulfil its mandate. The Secretary-General, his Special Representative, and military commanders in UNPROFOR were concerned that the general use of air strikes against Bosnian Serbs targets would endanger UN personnel on the ground. Understandably, this was a key concern of UNPROFOR troop-contributors.[68] Accordingly their use of the term "air strikes" referred to the use of air power as close air support in defence of UN forces and directed against specific Bosnian Serb weapons installations that were targeting UN personnel.[69] This was the same interpretation of air strikes used by the Russians, and envisaged the use of force reactively in response to the actions of the host parties. The US however, did not want the potential use of air power circumscribed in any way. Consequently, they deliberately obfuscated the term in order to keep open the option of generalized air strikes, in the event that such action was needed in response to future Bosnian Serb activity.[70] Because the

---

[65] "Boutros-Ghali Opposes Bosnian Air Strikes," *International Herald Tribune*, 20 January, 1994.

[66] Rose, *Fighting For Peace*, p. 21.

[67] Though NATO members emphasising their readiness to carry out air strikes "in order to prevent the strangulation of Sarajevo, the safe areas and other threatened areas in Bosnia-Herzegovina," such statements were little more than repetitions of what had previously been said following the North Atlantic Council (NAC) meeting on 2 August, 1993. Declaration of the Heads of State and Government Participating in the Meeting of the North Atlantic Council, held at NATO Headquarters, Brussels, 10-11 January, 1994. Internal divisions, primarily between the US and France on air strikes, made their actual use unlikely. See "On Bosnia, Allies Agree Only to Bicker," *International Herald Tribune*, 22, 23 January, 1994. On the issue of the troop rotation in Srebrenica, the Bosnian Serbs agreed to the replacement of the Canadian contingent with UN troops from the Netherlands, a process which was completed on 10 March 1994.

[68] In early 1994, the Canadian government announced a review of its participation in UNPROFOR following an incident in which Canadian UN troops were taken hostage by Bosnian Serb forces. See "Canada to Review Peacekeeping Role in Bosnia," *Reuters News Service*, 4 January, 1994.

[69] Boutros-Ghali, *Unvanquished*, p. 86.

[70] Owen, *Balkan Odyssey*, p. 247.

162 *Understanding the UN Security Council*

Security Council members were not united behind the threat of using air strikes in order to assist UNPROFOR to carry out its mandate, a common political goal to which the employment of enforcement measures could be directed remained conspicuously absent among the P-5.[71] Consequently, the threat of resolution 836 to move UNPROFOR beyond consent was not implemented in practice until the fall of 1995.

Marketplace Mortar Attack

The extent to which the members of the UNSC were divided on the issue of consent and coercion in the context of UNPROFOR was further demonstrated in early 1994. On 4 and 5 February two mortar attacks on Sarajevo claimed a total of 68 civilian lives and wounded a further 160. These attacks were in direct violation of UNSC resolution 824 which had extended the designation of "safe area" to the city of Sarajevo. Karadzic claimed that the mortar attack was carried out by Muslim forces and intentionally designed to implicate the Bosnian Serbs.[72] Since the attack of 4 February was found to have come from a Bosnian Serb position, the Secretary-General informed the Security Council that he felt it necessary, due to the violation of resolution 824, to prepare for the use of air strikes against Bosnian Serbs positions in order to deter further attacks. He then wrote to the Secretary-General of NATO, Manfred Wörner, requesting the alliance's support and suggested that the:

> co-ordination of such air strikes would be elaborated through direct contacts between UNPROFOR headquarters and NATO's Southern Command, as has already been done in the case of close air support for the self-defence of United Nations personnel in Bosnia-Herzegovina.[73]

On 9 February, three days after Boutros-Ghali's request to Wörner, NATO's North Atlantic Council (NAC) issued a statement calling for both parties to remove their heavy weapons from a 20 kilometre exclusion zone around Sarajevo or place

---

[71] Spyros Economides and Paul Taylor, "Former Yugoslavia," in Mayall, ed., *The New Interventionism*, p. 72. See also *UN Document*, S/1994/50, 18 January, 1994. The US had wanted a firmer commitment from the NAC for the use of air strikes at a NATO meeting August 9, 1993, but the more sceptical Europeans pressed for an additional meeting of the NAC to decide on the specific use of air strikes in a particular case. NATO control over the use of air power was also limited by the insistence of Boutros-Ghali that he retain the authority to call for air support from the NATO alliance. See Drew, *On the Edge*, p. 278. The UN Secretary-General noted that while NATO forces had been authorised by the North Atlantic Council to provide UNPROFOR with close air support in situations of self-defence, further authorisation was required from the NAC to use air strikes for pre-emptive or punitive purposes. See *UN Document*, S/1994/94, 28 January, 1994.
[72] "Bosnian Serbs on Sarajevo Killing," *BBC Summary of World Broadcasts*, Part 2, EE/1918, p. C/1, 10 February, 1994.
[73] *UN Document*, S/1994/131, annex, 7 February, 1994.

them under the supervision of UNPROFOR. The NAC warned that if any heavy weapons were found within the exclusion zone after 20 February they would be subject to NATO air strikes.[74] The Bosnian Serbs responded to the NATO ultimatum by warning that they would "use all available means" to defend themselves against NATO attacks.[75]

The prospect of punitive NATO air strikes against the Bosnian Serbs concerned the Russians.[76] Their position was that the use of air power should only have involved close air support on the basis of prior consultations between the members of the Security Council and the Secretary-General before any decision was taken to request the assistance of regional organisations such as NATO. The basis of this position was a different interpretation of substantive paragraph ten of resolution 836 which read

> ...Member States, acting nationally or through regional organisations and arrangements, may take, *under the authority of the Security Council, and subject to close co-ordination with the Secretary-General and the Force*, all necessary measures, through the use of air power in and around the safe areas in Bosnia Herzegovina, to support the Force in the performance of its mandate...[emphasis added].

The Russian interpretation contrasted directly with that of Boutros-Ghali who interpreted the resolution as giving the UN Secretary-General *carte blanche* to use air strikes wherever he deemed necessary, whether for close air support or pre-emptive air strikes, without further recourse to the Security Council.[77]

---

[74] "Decisions taken at the meeting of the North Atlantic Council on 9th February, 1994," *NATO Press Release (94) 15*, 9 February, 1994. The NAC accordingly authorised its Commander-in-Chief, Allied Forces Southern Europe, Admiral Jeremy Boorda, to launch air strikes, at the request of the United Nations, against any weapons sites whether inside or outside the exclusion zone that were found to be responsible for attacks on Sarajevo. In its meeting of 9 February, the NAC had decided to accept the request of the Boutros-Ghali to launch air strikes against artillery positions in or around Sarajevo "which are determined by UNPROFOR to be responsible for attacks against civilian targets in that city." In coming to this decision, the NAC recalled its decision of 2 August, 1993 when it had originally agreed to assist the UN by providing air power to assist UNPROFOR in the performance of its mandate. But whereas the 2 August decision had limited the use of air strikes to provide protective air cover to UNPROFOR in the case of attack or in the case of wide-scale interference with humanitarian assistance, the 9 February, 1994 decision agreed to provide air strikes in response to attacks against the civilian population of Sarajevo. See Caplan, *Post-Mortem on UNPROFOR*, p. 9. The UN Secretary-General subsequently instructed his Special Representative to arrange with Admiral Boorda the final plans for the use of air power. Boutros-Ghali also delegated the authority to call for strikes anywhere in Bosnia to his Special Representative, Yasushi Akashi. See also *The Blue Helmets*, p. 529.

[75] "Bosnian Serbs to Use All Available Means Of Defense if NATO Strikes," *BBC Summary of World Broadcasts*, Part 2, EE/1925, p. C/5, 18 February, 1994.

[76] "Threat to 'Slavic Allies' United Parties in Russia", *The Independent*, 10 February, 1994.

[77] *UN Document*, S/1994/152, annex, 10 February, 1994. Statement by the Ministry of Foreign Affairs of the Russian Federation. The Russian Federation also objected to the

164 *Understanding the UN Security Council*

Britain was also uncertain about the prospect of a more generalized use of air strikes. A number of senior Cabinet members were concerned about the possible consequences for British UN troops on the ground. They were also concerned that using air strikes would draw the West into a greater military involvement in Bosnia. However, the Major government overcame these objections for fear of being isolated from its two keys allies and after being warned by the US that failure to support the NATO ultimatum would threaten the Atlantic Alliance.[78]

Both the US and France supported the use of air strikes in order to deter further Bosnian Serb attacks on Sarajevo. For the Clinton administration this represented a continuation of its reliance on air power since June 1993. However, this reliance on a more militaristic approach was still isolated and not combined with any political direction.[79] The French, by contrast, had become increasingly pro-active on the issue, outraged by the callousness of the Bosnian Serb mortar attacks. They had threatened to take unilateral action against the Serbs if NATO did nothing, and were supported in this more assertive stance by the majority of the French public.[80]

With the NAC-issued 20 February deadline for air strikes less than one week away, Russia requested an urgent meeting of the Security Council in order to discuss the possibilities for demilitarising Sarajevo and placing the city under UN administration.[81] The Russian Federation, hoping to steer the UN away from adopting a coercive approach in Bosnia, used the opportunity to express its preference for diplomatic as opposed to forceful methods. Its representative stated, "we believe that it is extremely important to concentrate our efforts on preventing further bloodshed, to refrain from any action that might fan the flames of war..."[82] While advocating the demilitarisation of Sarajevo, the Russians also took issue with the procedure by which air strikes were authorized, suggesting that a further meeting of the Council on the matter was necessary in order to clarify the position of the Council.

---

apparent authority with which the NATO alliance exerted on the situation in Bosnia and Herzegovina outside the framework of the United Nations. While Russia supported the NAC statement demanding the creation of a weapons exclusion zone around Sarajevo, it objected to the interpretation of the statement as a "one sided ultimatum to the Bosnian Serbs." The Russian position stemmed in part from its traditional support for the Bosnian Serbs, but also because it resented the process on the decision and execution of air strikes being conducted outside of the control of the Security Council, and beyond the reach of the Russian veto. See also "Rift Grows Over UN action," *The Financial Times*, 12 April, 1994.
[78] "Britain 'Bowed to US pressure' Over Bosnian Ultimatum," *The Financial Times*, 11 February, 1994. The disagreement over the use of air power between the UK and the US was to significantly strain the Atlantic Alliance. Lord Douglas Hurd, interview with author, 9 December, 1999.
[79] Maynard Glitman, "US Policy in Bosnia: Rethinking a Flawed Approach," *Survival*, vol. 38, no. 4, Winter 1994, p. 71.
[80] "Air Attack Threat Against Serbs Grows," *The Financial Times*, 8 February, 1994 and "French Public Pressing for Action," *The Financial Times*, 12-13 February, 1994.
[81] *UN Document*, S/1994/152, annex, 10 February, 1994.
[82] *UN Document*, S/PV. 3336, 14 and 15 February, 1994.

Bosnia   165

This suggestion was not adopted. The French representative argued that "there is no need for these decisions [on the use of air power] of the North Atlantic Council to be submitted to the Security Council for any further decision." The representative of China stated that while his country was "opposed to the threat or use of force," with regard to the use of air power "our understanding is that it should be limited to self-defence by UNPROFOR." The Chinese concern was that the use of force by NATO and the UN would only endanger UN personnel and compromise the UN's humanitarian efforts.[83]

In general, the sentiment which emerged from the participants in the debate was that many states believed it was time for the Security Council to present a clear signal to the Bosnian Serbs that their continued attacks on Sarajevo and the other safe areas were unacceptable. Accordingly, there was widespread support for the use of punitive air strikes against Bosnian Serb positions in order to deter further attacks.[84] Indeed, there was strong criticism from some UN member states who admonished the members of the Security Council for their lack of action to protect the safe areas. The representative of Jordan worried that the Bosnian Serbs were "fully convinced that the Security Council adopted its resolutions on Bosnia and Herzegovina and on the safe areas not with a view to implementing them, but with a view only to marketing them."[85]

On 17 February, the Bosnian Serb authorities agreed to withdraw their heavy weapons from the NAC-declared exclusion zone, following the intervention of Russian envoy Vitaly Churkin.[86] Three days later, in view of the Bosnian Serb withdrawal, the members of the Council decided that air strikes were no longer appropriate.[87] An important constraint on negotiations surrounding the proposed demilitarisation of Sarajevo was the refusal of the Bosnian government to consider the prospect of completely demilitarising the Bosnian capital, as this would have required the complete withdrawal of all government military units. They considered such a move a tantamount to relinquishing their sovereign authority over their own capital city, and were thus willing to comply by only withdrawing government heavy weapons from the 20 km demilitarised zone.[88]

In practice the implementation of air strikes as policy remained hampered by the persistent vulnerability of UNPROFOR troops on the ground. General Sir Michael Rose, for example, was concerned that the use of air power would take UNPROFOR from peacekeeping to peace enforcement.[89] The threat of air strikes

---

[83] Ibid.

[84] "UN Backs NATO Over Bosnian Air Strikes," *The Financial Times*, 15 February, 1994.

[85] *UN Document*, S/PV .3336, 14, 15 February, 1994.

[86] "Churkin and Karadzic Talks End in Serb Acceptance of Russian Proposal," *BBC Summary of World Broadcasts*, Part 2, EE/1926, p. C/5, 19 February, 1994. The Russian proposal contained the NATO conditions, but when presented as a co-operative Russian initiative rather than a NATO ultimatum, it provided a "save-face" alternative for the Bosnian Serbs which was duly taken.

[87] *The Blue Helmets*, p. 530.

[88] Rose, *Fighting for Peace*, p. 65.

[89] Ibid., p. 75.

was largely promoted by the Clinton administration as a means of easing the siege of Sarajevo. There was still no long term political strategy to replace the VOPP, and Britain had only reluctantly agreed to the NAC threat of air strikes in order to protect the interests of the Atlantic Alliance.[90] Even Russia's reluctant change of position on the use of air strikes, due to the results of the open Security Council debate, was fragile.[91]

The Bosnian Serb's compliance with the NATO ultimatum had removed the need to actually use air power, and thus prevented a rift developing among the Security Council members. However, the apparent support among the western members of the P-5 for the threat of air strikes was designed as much for domestic audiences, and to mend the Atlantic Alliance, as it was for the Bosnian Serbs.[92] In the absence of any more robust demonstration of political unity from the UNSC, the principle of consent remained the most effective and practicable basis for UNPROFOR. The members of the UNSC had yet to devise an effective means of overcoming the inherent problems with UNPROFOR's reliance on the consent of the host parties or indeed a coherent political strategy with which to resolve the conflict.

Gorazde Air Attacks

The hazard of overcoming the deficiencies of consent-based peacekeeping though the use of coercive methods was sharply exposed at the end of March 1994, when Bosnian Serbs forces launched an attack on the UN designated safe area of Gorazde. In response to the danger faced by UN personnel and growing numbers of civilian casualties, UNPROFOR commanders requested the use of close air support from NATO. On 10 and 11 April NATO planes bombed Bosnian Serb positions. The attacks, slow in coming due to the complex UN/NATO authorization process, nevertheless managed to hit a Bosnian Serb artillery bunker and had some success in preventing Bosnian Serb tanks from deploying around the city. However, Bosnian Serb forces detained 15 Canadian UN troops on 14 April and imposed significant restrictions on the freedom of movement of other UN personnel.[93] Karadzic declared that the Bosnian Serbs would treat UNPROFOR as a potentially hostile force.[94] By 19 April over 130 UN personnel were being detained. Boutros-Ghali asked the NAC to authorize air strikes around Gorazde and a number of other safe areas in order to deter further attacks by Bosnian Serb

---

[90] Jane Sharp, *Honest Broker or Perfidious Albion?* Institute for Public Policy Research, London, 1997, p. 32.

[91] "Moscow Softens Stance on Bosnia Air Strikes," *The Financial Times*, 14 February, 1994.

[92] "What it Took to Bring US and Allies Together," *International Herald Tribune*, 11 February, 1994.

[93] Rose, *Fighting For Peace*, p. 163.

[94] Boutros-Ghali, *Unvanquished*, p. 147.

Bosnia 167

forces.[95] Four days later, the NAC issued an ultimatum threatening air strikes against Bosnian Serb forces if they were not withdrawn from the centre of Gorazde by 24 April, and ceased obstruction of UN personnel and humanitarian convoys. In addition, the NAC demanded the creation of a heavy weapons exclusion zone around the city.[96]

The members of the Security Council added to the political pressure being brought to bear on the Bosnian Serbs by issuing resolution 913 which condemned the attacks on Gorazde, demanded the release of all detained UN personnel, and called for closer consultation between US, Russian, and European diplomatic initiatives.[97] Yet the permanent members of the Council were not prepared to go beyond condemnation of the Bosnian Serb action and thus further endanger the UN hostages. Its members remained divided on the benefits of using air strikes to force the Bosnian Serbs to negotiate a political settlement, particularly following the taking of UN hostages. Britain questioned the effectiveness of the air strikes and was also concerned for the welfare of its troops on the ground.[98] China again voiced its reservations about the use of force by UNPROFOR in circumstances other than self-defence.[99] Even the Clinton administration appeared more reluctant to use air power to defend the city of Gorazde, in part due to pressure from Pentagon officials who questioned the effectiveness of air power in shaping the behaviour of the Bosnian Serbs.[100]

Russian opposition on air strikes however, was beginning to ease. Though a traditional ally of the Serbs in the Security Council, Russian diplomatic efforts to secure an end to the Bosnian Serb offensive against Gorazde were ignored. Though Russia remained officially opposed to the use of air strikes, there were contradictory signals coming from Moscow. Foreign Minister Andrei Kozyrev warned that if NATO air strikes continued, Russia would pull out of the Partnership for Peace initiative. At the same time however, the Russian envoy Vitaly Churkin was becoming increasingly incensed at the failure of the Pale Serbs to live up to their agreements and accused them of "using Russian politics as a shield" to hide behind.[101] His frustration with Pale's intransigence led him to appear open to a more forceful approach to defending Gorazde as he stated:

> I have never heard as many lies as I have heard from the Serbians in the last 48 hours. We should stop any type of conversation with them. The time for conversation has ended. I do not feel any desire on the Serbian side to agree on the subject [of stopping the offensive].[102]

---

[95] *UN Document*, S/1994/466, annex, 19 April, 1994.

[96] *UN Document*, S/1994/495, annex, 22 April, 1994.

[97] UNSC Resolution 913, 22 April, 1994.

[98] Sharp, *Honest Broker or Prefidious Albion?*, p. 34.

[99] *UN Document*, S/PV .3367, 22 April, 1994.

[100] Sharp, *Honest Broker or Perfidious Albion?*, p. 34.

[101] "Russian Attacks Serbs' 'Madness,'" *International Herald Tribune*, 19 April, 1994.

[102] Comments of the Russian Deputy Foreign Minister Vitaly Churkin as quoted by Bosnian Ambassador Sacirbey, *UN Document*, S/PV. 3367, 21 April, 1994.

168 *Understanding the UN Security Council*

The actual use of air strikes, despite the threat of the NAC, continued to be dictated on the ground as General Rose decided that the use of air strikes would only serve to endanger UNPROFOR personnel and take UNPROFOR into a war fighting situation.[103] Akashi took a similar position and both men used their authority to prevent the further use of air strikes. First, they declined to request air strikes against Bosnian Serb positions, claiming that the Bosnian Serbs were pulling back in order to comply with the NATO ultimatum, when if fact no such withdrawal was occurring. Rose also opted to deploy Ukrainian and British UN troops into the city, in order to reduce the potential for further air strikes.[104]

As a result of intensive negotiations by UN commanders on the ground, an agreement was reached between UNPROFOR and Bosnian Serb military and civilian officials on 23 April, 1994. Three days later Boutros-Ghali announced that the Bosnian-Serbs had largely complied with the terms of the ultimatum, and the danger facing both civilian and UN personnel in Gorazde was significantly reduced.[105]

The Gorazde episode served to emphasise the continuing importance of the consent and co-operation of the parties to the operation of UNPROFOR. Even the limited, tactical use of air strikes in self-defence had led to the taking of UN hostages. UN officials within the Secretariat and in Bosnia, eager to preserve the UN's humanitarian initiatives, recognised the limitations of using air power and thus sought to prevent its further use. In an attempt to consolidate the disparate views of the political and practical role of air power, the Secretary-General highlighted the limitations of UNPROFOR, even when augmented by the use of air power. He wrote:

> UNPROFOR's protection role is derived from its mere presence: UNPROFOR is neither structured nor equipped for combat and has never had sufficient resources, even with air support, to defend the safe areas against a deliberate attack or to hold ground...The failure of the warring parties to understand or fully respect the safe-areas concept is a particularly serious problem that has become starkly evident in Gorazde. The Bosnian government expected UNPROFOR to intervene to protect as much of the territory under its control as possible, and called for the early employment of large-scale air strikes in order to break the offensive capability of Serb forces...The Bosnian Serbs on the other hand regarded UNPROFOR's very limited use of close air support as an intervention on behalf of their opponents, and did not hesitate to attack a populated area. UNPROFOR's neutrality and credibility were strongly challenged by the different attitudes and expectations of each party...[106]

He described, in effect, a situation where the reliance of UNPROFOR on host party consent was, despite its limitations, the most effective basis for the continued operation of the force. The Secretary-General's report also alluded to the problems of trying to act both impartially and on the basis of consent in Bosnia. Remaining

---

[103] Rose, *Fighting For Peace*, pp. 173-174.
[104] Sharp, *Honest Broker or Perfidious Albion?*, p. 34.
[105] *The Blue Helmets*, p. 532.
[106] *UN Document*, S/1994/555, 9 May, 1994.

Bosnia 169

impartial between the two main parties was essential for UNPROFOR in order to promote local co-operation with UN initiatives. However, in such a highly politicised conflict, many UN initiatives proved to be contrary to the interests of either the Bosnian Serbs or the Bosnian government. This was the case even when such activities were consistent with the force's mandate. For example, air strikes against Bosnian Serb positions were seen by that party as aggressive action by the international community. Similarly, UNPROFOR efforts to enforce the demilitarized zone around Sarajevo, culminating in the forced removal of Bosnian army units from their positions on Mt. Igman, led to indignant claims from the Bosnian Parliament that UNPROFOR was failing to act impartially.[107] However, given the lacklustre UNSC commitment to resolving the conflict, remaining impartial and operating according to the principle of consent remained UNPROFOR's most effective strategy for mitigating the humanitarian impact of the conflict. Nevertheless, the issue of air strikes persisted as it was one of the few tools that the members of the Security Council were prepared to use in order to protect the Bosnian civilian population in the absence of a coherent strategy to end the conflict.

Sarajevo

During the month of August, 1994 the security situation in Sarajevo deteriorated further, with renewed Bosnian Serb attacks on the city. In response to repeated violations of the heavy weapons ban established around the city, the UN requested that air strikes be carried out by NATO warplanes. Consequently, in two separate instances, air strikes were conducted against Bosnian-Serb weapons sites. This was the result of a deliberate decision on the part of UNPROFOR's commanders not to attack a wide range of Bosnian Serb targets and risk taking the UN from peacekeeping to war-fighting. Instead, the intention was to attack individual tactical targets and pressure the Serbs to respect the Sarajevo exclusion ban. In addition, UN commanders did not want to endanger the delivery of humanitarian aid through Bosnian Serb controlled territory. This approach contrasted with that demanded by NATO commander Leighton Smith who wanted to respond with massive force against Bosnian Serb targets.[108]

The UN Secretary-General had helped to reduce the likelihood of strategic, widespread air strikes with his report to the Security Council of 17 September, 1994.[109] In it he stressed that although there was a great deal of pressure from within the international community to move the UN's involvement beyond consent, such a change would place the UN clearly on one side of the conflict. This would change the nature of the UNPROFOR presence and imply

---

[107] Rose, *Fighting For Peace*, pp. 282-283.

[108] Ibid., pp. 236-238. The approach of the UNPROFOR commanders was consistent with that espoused by the UK's "Wider Peacekeeping" doctrine.

[109] *UN Document*, S/1994/1067, 17 September, 1994.

170 *Understanding the UN Security Council*

unacceptable risks to UN personnel. Such steps, he argued, would fan the flames of war and require the withdrawal of UNPROFOR from Bosnia.[110]

Despite the demonstrated shortcomings of the air strikes and the warnings of the Secretary-General, they were again relied upon to respond to attacks on the Bihac safe area by Serb forces in the Krajina. Resolution 958 extended the authorization for air strikes into Croatia, demonstrating continued support in the Council for air strikes in the absence of a more effective policy.[111] Yet again the actions of the Security Council contrasted with the position of UNPROFOR commanders on the ground. Both General Bertrand de Lapresle, the overall Force Commander of UNPROFOR in the former Yugoslavia, and General Rose attempted to limit the use of air strikes in and around Bihac, defying intense pressure from the US Ambassador in Zagreb for a more robust response.[112]

As the fourth year of conflict in the former Yugoslavia approached, the members of the Security Council remained divided on the use of air power to augment UNPROFOR. Air power remained a substitute for a concerted, unified political approach to ending the conflict and even its limited use had created immense difficulties for UNPROFOR on the ground. This had led UNPROFOR commanders, as well as Akashi and Boutros-Ghali, to advocate adherence to a consent-based operation in the absence of a unified political direction. However, political initiatives had become increasingly focused on the five member Contact Group rather than the EU or UN. This proved to be a key factor in the eventual proactive use of force by the international community in Bosnia in 1995.[113]

The Rapid Reaction Force

During the spring of 1995, one of the most significant indications that France and Britain had become more committed to finding a solution to the conflict in Bosnia was their decision to deploy a Rapid Reaction Force to augment the self-defence capability of UNPROFOR. Together with the Netherlands, the two European Powers offered to form the RRF in order to provide UNPROFOR with well-armed, mobile personnel with which to respond to threats against UN forces.[114] The intention of the three contributing states was that the new force, operating under UN rules of engagement but without blue helmets or white vehicles, would provide

---

[110] Ibid.

[111] UNSC Resolution 958, 19 November, 1994.

[112] Sharp, *Honest Broker or Perfidious Albion?*, p. 43. Sharp notes that at one stage communications between Rose and his spotters in the field were intercepted by the US Central Intelligence Agency and revealed that Rose had instructed his men not to identify any targets, thus precluding further air strikes.

[113] The Contact Group presented their peace plan in July, 1994. See Economides and Taylor, "Former Yugoslavia," p. 85.

[114] *UN Document*, S/1995/444, 30 May, 1995.

the UNPROFOR commander with a military capacity between "strong protest" and air strikes.[115]

It was a policy shift that was instigated by the British who had become frustrated by the continued inability of UNPROFOR to protect Bosnian civilians and the vulnerability of UN troops on the ground.[116] In addition, the French and British governments had come to recognise that they would suffer politically if UNPROFOR was to fail.[117] The RRF also had a second potential role to assist in the withdrawal of UNPROFOR in the event the UNSC chose to recall the peacekeeping force.[118] The Secretary-General was careful to point out that the addition of the RRF to UNPROFOR would not change its status as a peacekeeping mission. He highlighted three factors that formed the basis for his recommendation: the humanitarian imperative, the security of UN personnel, and the need to protect the credibility of the organisation.[119]

The inclusion of the RRF in UNPROFOR seemed to reflect a growing awareness that peacekeeping doctrine required further evolution given the problems encountered in Bosnia. The RRF, while not only offering a greater ability to defend UN personnel also provided UNPROFOR with a limited offensive capability to by used, if necessary, to enforce compliance with UNSC mandates. Initial comments by the contributing nations and the Secretary-General rejected the use of the RRF in such a way. However, as events were later to demonstrate, the RRF did provide UNPROFOR with part of the capacity to adopt the guise of a peace enforcement operation.[120]

The proposed Rapid Reaction Force was accepted by the Security Council in resolution 998 which accordingly authorized an increase in the troop strength of UNPROFOR.[121] The US recognised the importance of providing UNPROFOR with an improved capability to both protect itself and fulfil its humanitarian mandate. Consequently, US officials saw the deployment of the RRF as a turning

---

[115] *UN Document*, S/1995/470, annex, 9 June, 1995.

[116] Sir Malcolm Rifkind, interview with author, 23 November, 1999; Dame Pauline Neville-Jones interview, 26 November, 1999.

[117] Sir Marrack Goulding, interview with author, 6 July, 1999.

[118] Sir Malcom Rifkind, interview with author, 23 November, 1999.

[119] *UN Document*, S/1995/470, 9 June, 1995. In effect, the addition of the RRF to UNPROFOR fell under "Option C" which the Secretary-General had identified in his 30 May report to the Security Council. The addition of the RRF would not change the mandate and methods employed by UNPROFOR, but would imply serve to bolster its ability to carry out the mandates which the operation was already assigned.

[120] This development was consistent with the increasing awareness among analysts that the combination of peacekeeping and enforcement methods, like the use of air strikes in the context of UNPROFOR, was fraught with difficulties. The development of "Wider Peacekeeping Doctrine" recognised the need to clearly distinguish between peacekeeping based on consent and peace enforcement operations. As such, the deployment of the RRF provided part of the means necessary to make a qualitative shift from peacekeeping to peace enforcement in the fall of 1995 with Operation Deliberate Force. See the discussion of the alternative peacekeeping doctrines in Chapter One.

[121] UNSC Resolution 998, 16 June, 1995.

172 *Understanding the UN Security Council*

point which not only gave UNPROFOR substantially improved ground forces, but also made the potential use of air power more effective due to the deployment of forward air control units with the RRF.[122]

There was nevertheless concern among other Council members as to how the deployment of the RRF would affect the nature of UNPROFOR. China suggested that since it was likely that the RRF would become engaged in the fighting, its authorization constituted a *de facto* change in the nature of the operation from peacekeeping to peace enforcement. Russia stressed its preference that UNPROFOR remain a peacekeeping force. Neither state however was willing to use its veto to prevent the authorization of the RRF, though it was Chinese objections that prevented the RRF being given Chapter VII authority.[123]

The Rapid Reaction Force was intended to operate within the borders of Bosnia-Herzegovnia and accordingly required the legal consent of the Bosnian government. Initially at least consent was forthcoming from both the Bosnian government and the Bosnian Serbs. On 13 June, 1995, four days after the Secretary-General announced to the Security Council the possibility of the new force, the Bosnian Minister for Foreign Affairs, Muhamed Sacirbey, wrote to the President of the Security Council indicating his country's support for the RRF. The Bosnian government, he wrote, was prepared to accept the Rapid Reaction Force "as part of the United Nations Protection Force."[124] Again in the debate among the members of the Security Council preceding the adoption of resolution 998, Sacirbey reaffirmed the consent of the Bosnian government to the deployment of the Rapid Reaction Force.[125] However, he also stressed that Bosnia was a sovereign state and as such the Bosnian government retained the power to ask the UN to withdraw if and when UNPROFOR's presence became counter-productive.[126] The Bosnian Serbs stated that they were prepared to accept the reinforcement of UNPROFOR provided its mandate was not changed without their agreement.[127]

On 28 June, the attitude of the Bosnian government towards the deployment of the Rapid Reaction Force began to change. This was brought on by two factors. First was the government's continued annoyance at criticism from New York about the lack of co-operation and outright obstruction of UNPROFOR by Bosnian government forces. Second, the Bosnians also became impatient with UNPROFOR's lack of progress at implementing its mandate. Citing this latter

---

[122] "Perry Discusses Rapid Reaction Force and Bosnia Situation," *United States Information Service*, 8 June 1995.

[123] Wolfgang Weisbrod-Weber, interview with author, 31 July, 1998. See also the comments of the Chinese and Russian representatives, *UN Document* S/PV. 3543, 16 June, 1995.

[124] *UN Document*, S/1995/483, 13 June, 1995.

[125] *UN Document*, S/PV. 3543, 16 June, 1995.

[126] "Bosnian Foreign Minister on UN Mission and General Situation," *BBC Summary of World Broadcasts*, EE/2338, p. C/6, 24 June, 1995.

[127] "Karadzic On War Situation," *BBC Summary of World Broadcasts*, Part 2, EE/2320, p. C/5, 3 June, 1995.

Bosnia 173

concern in a letter to the President of the Security Council, Sacirbey announced that his government would formally begin to review its sovereign consent to the continued operation of UNPROFOR in light of its failure to implement the relevant Security Council resolutions.[128] Though the Bosnian government was, in fact supportive of the RRF, their concern was that the new augmented UNPROFOR came in lieu of a wider, more robust intervention by the international community in order to reverse Serb territorial gains.[129] In order to delay the deployment of the RRF, and hope that a more robust intervention option was taken by the international community, the Bosnian government argued that the status of the RRF was not encompassed by the Status of Forces Agreement (SOFA) which governed the operation of the rest of UNPROFOR in Bosnia. In response, Boutros-Ghali stressed that UNPROFOR was a peacekeeping operation and that the position taken by the Bosnian government had significantly delayed the deployment of much of the force. The force deployment had originally been planned for completion by 18 July, 1995.[130]

The Security Council similarly argued that the existing SOFA constituted "an appropriate and sufficient basis" for the presence of UNPROFOR with the RRF included in it and accordingly it called upon the Bosnian government to resolve, within the framework of the existing SOFA, any outstanding issues concerning the operation of the force with the UN authorities.[131] The firm position taken by the Security Council members pressured the Bosnian government to resolve the issue through negotiation.[132]

---

[128] *UN Document*, S/1995/515, 28 June, 1995.

[129] Muhamed Sacirbey, interview with author, 14 December, 1999.

[130] According the Boutros-Ghali, the Bosnian government believed that the deployment of the RRF was not covered by the existing SOFA since resolution 998 was adopted after the original SOFA concerning UNPROFOR was signed on 15 May 1993. It also did not accept that the RRF was in fact a part of UNPROFOR or the broader UN Peace Forces (UNPF) in the former Yugoslavia. Accordingly, the UN Special Representative to Bosnia suggested that a supplementary arrangement be devised wherein the arrangements concerning the deployment of the RRF be agreed upon by the Bosnian government and then this supplementary agreement be included within the general scope of the original SOFA. This position went some way to meeting the demands of the Bosnian government which had stated that while it fully supported the arrival and activities of the RRF, it was necessary to conclude a separate agreement concerning the status of the new force. To this end the Bosnian government submitted a draft agreement to UNPROFOR representatives. See *UN Documents*, S/1995/707, 18 August, 1995 and S/1995/691, 14 August, 1995.

[131] *UN Document*, S/PV.3568, August 19, 1995.

[132] The Bosnian government signed an annex to the original 15 May, 1993 SOFA covering UNPROFOR, allowing the deployment of the RRF. The decision of the Bosnian government to argue against the deployment of the RRF was taken in the hope that a more robust intervention would be carried out by the international community, and was a means to this end. It was unlikely that the Bosnians would have pressed the issue to the extent that UNPROFOR was actually requested to leave. Muhammed Sacirbey, interview with author, 14 December, 1999.

From Peacekeeping to Peace Enforcement

On 30 May, 1995 Boutros Boutros-Ghali submitted a report to the Security Council in which he presented a bleak picture of the situation in Bosnia and the continuing problems faced by UNPROFOR. Early spring 1995 witnessed the collapse of the short-lived 31 December, 1994 cessation of hostilities agreement. The renewed fighting between Bosnian Serb and government forces also endangered the heavy weapons exclusion zone that formed the basis of the February 1994 Sarajevo agreement. While both parties violated the agreement, the violations became more flagrant as Bosnian Serb forces removed some heavy weapons from the collection sites and, in some cases, fired the weapons from inside the sites themselves.[133]

To deter further violations of the exclusion zone the new UNPROFOR-Bosnia commander, General Rupert Smith issued an ultimatum demanding the end of the fighting and the return of the heavy weapons to the collection sites. When the Bosnian Serbs failed to respect the deadline, NATO air strikes were conducted against two Bosnian Serb bunkers near Pale. Further attacks by Bosnian Serbs forces on other UN designated safe areas led to additional NATO air strikes. In response, Bosnian Serb forces surrounded some of the weapons collections points and took 300 UN personnel hostages as a deterrent against further air strikes.[134] While the UN hostages were released following a series of secret negotiations between UNPF Commander Bernard Janvier and Mladic, the Bosnian Serbs intensified their military offensive, but there were no further air strikes from the UN.[135] Their initial use in Pale had backfired despite the fact the strikes themselves were limited in number and did not constitute a serious or sustained military response by the UN.[136] The lack of such a response suggests that the UN could not afford to abandon the consensual basis of the operation, due to the continued vulnerability of UNPROFOR to Bosnian Serb reprisals.

Following this latest hostage crisis, UN officials took steps to distance themselves from air strikes as a policy option. Special Representative Akashi told his staff that the Sarajevo hostage taking incident had proven the deterrent tactic of air strikes to be ineffective. Boutros-Ghali withdrew the authority to ask NATO for air strikes from General Rupert Smith and stated that, in future, UN requests for air strikes would be made by him on an individual basis from New York.[137] This reduced the potential likelihood of further air strikes, and also reduced the coercive

---

[133] *UN Document*, S/1995/444, 30 May, 1995.

[134] Ibid.

[135] Apparently, there was substantial, if circumstantial, evidence that a deal was struck between General Janvier and Mladic wherein the UN hostages would be released in return for a guarantee that the UN would not use air power against the Bosnian Serbs again. While this was denied by UN officials, after the negotiations the Bosnian offensive continued with renewed vigour and did not bring on further air strikes. See Richard Holbrooke, *To End a War*, Random House, New York, 1998, pp. 63-64.

[136] Holbrooke, *To End A War*, p. 63.

[137] Ibid., p. 65.

means available to UNPROFOR, consequently reinforcing its identity as a consent-based peacekeeping operation. The Secretary-General stressed to the Security Council that despite the references made to Chapter VII in some of the UNSC resolutions that governed the operation of UNPROFOR, there was no Chapter VII enforcement element included in the mandate of the peacekeeping force. The authorization to use air power was intended to serve as a deterrent against attacks on the safe areas but not to enforce respect of those areas. He made a distinction between Chapter VII resolutions which are intended for the defence of a peacekeeping force, and those resolutions in which the use of force is an integral part of the mandate.[138]

As a result of this characterization, the Secretary-General recommended that the Security Council adopt one of four options in the face of continued Bosnian Serb opposition: withdraw the force; retain the existing mandate and methods of the force; change the mandate to allow a greater use of force by UNPROFOR; revise the mandate to include only those tasks which the operations could realistically be expected to perform given the prevailing circumstances in Bosnia. He recommended that the Council adopt the last option and scale back UNPROFOR so as to reconcile expectations of the force with its actual capabilities, and also reduce the risks posed to peacekeeping troops.[139]

However, this apparent retrenchment to a firm consensual basis for the operation was not to last. There had been a significant change in US policy brought on by the emergence of OpPlan 40-104, a binding NATO plan for the possible withdrawal of UNPROFOR. Consequently, the US could either deploy troops in the event of a UN withdrawal and be subject to criticism for allowing UNPROFOR to fail, or it could revise its options towards Bosnia and plan for a larger US role in resolving the conflict. In the summer of 1995, the Clinton administration chose the latter path.[140] It was also motivated by growing Congressional pressure to lift the arms embargo, a move that would have enraged its Europeans allies. In order to avoid a rift in the Atlantic Alliance and pre-empt Congressional action, Clinton decided to become more politically engaged in Bosnia.[141]

On 6 July 1995 Bosnian Serb forces attacked the UN designated safe area of Srebrenica. As reports of mass murder, ethnic cleansing, and other human rights violations emerged from Srebrenica, the pressure on the Contact Group states to take effective measures to cope with the Serb offensive reached its highest point.[142] Other safe areas such as Zepa and Gorazde were threatened and general conditions throughout the country were rapidly deteriorating.

On 21 July the Contact Group and troop contributors to UNPROFOR met in London to discuss the situation in Bosnia and decide how to respond to the latest

---

[138] *UN Document*, S/1995/444, 30 May, 1995.

[139] Ibid.

[140] Holbrooke, *To End A War*, p. 66.

[141] Caplan, *Post Mortem on UNPROFOR*, p. 29.

[142] Neville-Jones identified the fall of Srebrenica as the key turning point in British policy on Bosnia, interview with author, 26 November, 1999. Sir David Hannay made a similar characterisation, interview with author, 29 November, 1999.

176   *Understanding the UN Security Council*

Bosnian Serb aggression. In effect, the western states had come to recognise the declining utility of the threat of air strikes as a deterrent since the adoption of resolution 836. The fall of Srebrenica led to a massive qualitative change in the response of the western community to the Bosnian conflict and their response to Bosnian Serb aggression.[143]

Two important revisions to the rules of engagement which affected the use of air strikes in Bosnia emerged from the London conference. First, the NAC decided to draw "a line in the sand" around Gorazde, the safe area which lay directly in the line of the Bosnian Serb offensive, and provide it with adequate protection.[144] Secondly, the UN part of the "dual-key" system was also delegated by Boutros-Ghali to General Janvier meaning that a combined request by the UN and NATO commanders on the ground (Janvier and Admiral Leighton Smith) would lead to air strikes.[145] The renewed co-operation between the UN and NATO removed one of the main obstacles to the use of air power to respond to Bosnian Serb aggression.[146] From that point the nature of the relationship between the two organisations changed and the latter half of the 1995 summer saw NATO take a lead role in responding to instances of Bosnian Serb aggression.[147]

Despite the warning that emerged from the London Conference, the Bosnian Serbs launched a mortar attack on a Sarajevo marketplace on 28 August, 1995. The attack killed 37 people and wounded more than 80 others. The Contact Group was prompted to take action. The cities of Zepa and Srebrenica had fallen to Bosnian Serb forces, consequently reducing the deployment of UN troops in remote areas, leaving the UN force as a whole less vulnerable to further hostage taking incidents. In addition, UNPROFOR had deliberately reduced its exposure by withdrawing outlying military observer positions.[148] In addition, the increasing isolation of Pale from the Belgrade regime due to Milosevic's preference for less intransigent Bosnian Serb leaders, the reduced support of the Russians for the Serbs, and the success of a Croatian military offensive meant that conditions were ripe for a genuine cease-fire and comprehensive political settlement to be achieved.[149]

Armed with the new rules of engagement that emerged from the London conference, NATO began to attack Bosnian Serbs targets on August 30 in

---

[143] Sir David Hannay, interview with author, 29 November, 1999.

[144] Holbrooke, *To End A War*, p. 72.

[145] Boutros-Ghali, *Unvanquished*, p. 240. The dual key arrangement had been removed entirely in relation to Gorazde where NATO alone could decide if and when to launch air strikes. See Holbrooke, *To End A War*, p. 72.

[146] Dick A. Leurdijk, Before and After Dayton: The UN and NATO in the Former Yugoslavia," *Third World Quarterly*, vol. 18, no. 3, 1997, p. 461.

[147] Dame Pauline Neville-Jones, interview with author, 26 November, 1999.

[148] Wolfgang Weisbrod-Weber, interview with author, 31 July, 1998.

[149] Sir Malcolm Rifkind, interview with author, 23 November, 1999; Dame Pauline Neville-Jones, interview with author, 26 November, 1999. On Milosevic's growing dislike for the Pale Serbs see Holbrooke, *To End a War*, pp. 292-293.

Bosnia 177

Operation Deliberate Force.[150] NATO bombers, along with artillery units from the Rapid Reaction Force targeted Bosnian Serb artillery positions, ammunition dumps and anti-aircraft systems. The stated aim of the operation was to restore the heavy weapons exclusion zone around Sararjevo and also deter any further artillery attacks on the city.[151] The Bosnian government welcomed the operation and considered it to conform with all relevant UNSC resolutions. The bombing campaign was the kind of action that the Bosnian government had been seeking from the international community since the start of the conflict.[152] The Bosnian Serbs, unsurprisingly, called the NATO strikes "a huge crime" and Karadzic argued that the bombing represented "a moral catastrophe for the West."[153]

The sustained NATO air strikes and UN artillery bombardment against the Bosnian Serbs marked the start of the process which would see a cease-fire established between the Bosnian parties, and the eventual signing of the Comprehensive Peace Agreement at Dayton Ohio on 21 November, 1995.

Conclusion

The UN's experience in Bosnia demonstrated a number of problems of consent-based peacekeeping in an intra-state conflict. There were numerous belligerent parties, pursuing different political and economic agendas, some only nominally under the control of either the government or the Pale Serbs. This meant that UNPROFOR had to often cope with a sporadic and unstable consensual basis for

---

[150] There is a discrepancy between Boutros-Ghali's and Holbrooke's account of the final UN authorisation to go ahead with Operation Deliberate Force. Holbrooke claims Boutros-Ghali could not be contacted in order to authorise the air strikes but Kofi Annan, his deputy, temporarily relinquished UN control, allowing NATO to use air power when it thought necessary. Boutros-Ghali, by contrast, suggests that Rupert Smith and Leighton Smith mutually agreed that the terms of a secret MOU signed between the UN and NATO concerning the use of air strikes had been met and thus led to the air strikes. See Holbrooke *To End A War*, p. 99 and Boutros-Ghali, *Unvanquished*, p. 243.

[151] *NATO Press Release*, August 29, 1995. Procedurally, the use of air strikes had been aided by the decision of Kofi Annan, UN Under Secretary-General for peacekeeping operations, to instruct his subordinates to temporarily relinquish their authority over air strikes so as to allow NATO to more easily act against the Serbs. Annan, under pressure from Albright, agreed to order his civilian officials and military commanders to relinquish their veto over air strikes. Consequently, NATO was able to attack Bosnian Serb targets throughout the country without having to continually check back with UN officials. Similarly, the new NATO Secretary-General Willy Claes decided not to convene a meeting of the NATO Council to decide on air strikes, but chose instead to allow General Joulwan and Admiral Leighton Smith to use air strikes where they deemed it appropriate, also facilitating the use of air power. See Holbrooke, pp. 99-100.

[152] "Bosnian Government: Nato Raid Justified But Delayed," *BBC Summary of World Broadcasts*, EE/2396, p. C/5, 31 August, 1995. Muhammed Sacirbey, interview with author, 14 December, 1999.

[153] "Karadzic Calls Air Strikes a Moral Catastrophe for the West," *BBC Summary of World Broadcasts*, EE2397, p. C/11, 1 September, 1995.

its day-to-day operations. Similarly, both main belligerents actively obstructed UN initiatives when it suited their interests, as demonstrated in the case of Tuzla airport, complicating UNPROFOR's ability to implement its mandate. The UN's best efforts to remain impartial similarly created friction with the parties, given the highly political nature of UNPROFOR's activities.

Confronted with these problems of consent-based peacekeeping, the members of the UNSC attempted to bolster UNPROFOR through the threat and use of air power. At first glance, such actions suggest that the Security Council was willing to move beyond the consensual basis of the operation when the UNHCR humanitarian operation and Bosnian civilians in the safe areas were threatened by Bosnian Serb offensives. The Council's decision to authorize the use of force under Chapter VII of the Charter legally precluded the need to adhere to consent and suggests that the members of the Council demonstrated an increased willingness to ignore the usual reliance of peacekeeping operations on the consent and co-operation of the host parties. Such an analysis is misleading in its simplicity. As this chapter demonstrates, the members of the Council were, in fact, reluctant to authorize the use of air power, and even more hesitant to use it in practice.

The decision to authorize the use of air power for the self-defence of UNPROFOR represented a fragile agreement among the western powers to augment their lacklustre policy on Bosnia with the appearance of commitment and resolve. At best, resolution 836 represented "a least common denominator consensus that compromises or undercuts effective action."[154] This proved to be the case as the Council members considered the possible use of air strikes against Bosnian Serb positions to resolve the issues of Tuzla airport, the Srebrenica troop rotation, or in Sarajevo and Gorazde. China repeatedly stressed its reservations about the use of enforcement measures in Bosnia, but was willing to overcome these reservations in order to permit UNOPROFOR the means to mitigate the humanitarian impact of the conflict. The continual Russian preference for diplomacy rather than force also complicated any attempt to actually implement the provisions of resolution 836. However, it was political differences between the western members of the P-5 that precluded the expansive use of air power prior to *Operation Deliberate Force*. American concerns about limiting its involvement in Bosnia, British concerns about not endangering its troops on the ground and French vacillation between supporting strikes yet protecting its troops meant that there was rarely agreement to use air power. On the few occasions when policies converged, prior to September 1995, air strikes were used against tactical targets so as not to threaten the strategic consensual basis of UNPROFOR.

UN commanders were careful to use force only at the tactical level so as not to move UNPROFOR from a peacekeeping to a war-fighting stance. Even in the few incidents when it was used tactically, there were serious consequences such as the taking of UN hostages. This direct threat to UN personnel and the

---

[154] Ernest W. Lefever, "Reigning in the UN," *Foreign Policy*, vol. 72, no. 3, 1993, p. 19.

Bosnia 179

endangerment of the UN's humanitarian role in Bosnia further soured the appetite of the UNSC members for using air strikes.

This vulnerability of UNPROFOR in the face of continued humanitarian crises led to a change in the UNSC's strategic approach to the Bosnian conflict. The deployment of the RRF had not only improved the self-defence capability of the peacekeeping operation, but also provided an appropriate platform for a shift from peacekeeping to peace enforcement. This shift was implemented after the fall of Srebrenica. When the eventual decision was made to use punitive air strikes against Bosnian Serb positions in order to force them to the negotiating table, the use of force occurred in a limited, premeditated manner as a result of a convergence of factors such as outrage at the marketplace attack on Sarajevo, the US decision to become engaged in Bosnia, the reduction of UNPROFOR's vulnerability, the Muslim-Croat offensive and the isolation of the Bosnian Serbs from Belgrade. All these factors made the use of force at the strategic level more likely to succeed.[155] Nevertheless, it was a temporary and fragile consensus within the UNSC and NATO which permitted the shift beyond consent.

Bosnian Sovereignty

Although the members of the Council did decide to authorize the use of force in the context of UNPROFOR under Chapter VII, the manner in which they did so did not go against the wishes of the Bosnian government. Indeed, the Bosnians urged the Security Council to create the safe areas and authorize the use of force to defend them. The Bosnian government also supported the adoption of resolution 770, which urged UN member states to take "all measures necessary" to facilitate the delivery of humanitarian assistance, despite the invocation of Chapter VII.

Even on the two main issues of contention between the UN and the host government, Bosnian objections stemmed not from its concerns about the UNSC infringing on its sovereignty, but rather the failure of the Council to adequately protect the republic. For example, though the government objected to the arms embargo imposed by resolution 713 on the territory of the former Yugoslavia, it preferred the maintenance of UNPROFOR in Bosnia rather than its withdrawal. Contesting the issue of the arms embargo was a means of pressuring the west into large-scale intervention in Bosnia and ultimately defend the republic's political independence and territorial integrity. Similarly the issue of the RRF stemmed not from the Bosnian government's belief that the new force infringed on its sovereignty, but rather their concern that it came in lieu of a wider western intervention into Bosnia. Thus by contesting the RRF and delaying its deployment, the Bosnians sought to engage the west on a more substantial scale in order to protect their state from further Bosnian Serb aggression.

Given the government's weak position throughout the conflict, the greater the involvement of the international community, the more secure the position of the Bosnian republic. As a result, the occasional differences between the UNSC and

---

[155] Rose, *Fighting For Peace*, p. 350.

180   *Understanding the UN Security Council*

the Bosnian government arose primarily due to the Bosnian's objective of getting the international community more deeply engaged in the conflict and never seriously threatened to end the deployment of UNPROFOR.[156] As such, the actions of the Council in Bosnia can be viewed as reinforcing Bosnian sovereignty, and its preservation as a multi-ethnic state, rather than undermining it.

---

[156] Lord Douglas Hurd, interview with author, 9 December, 1999. This view of UNSC-Bosnian government relations never being fatally endangered by disagreements over UNPROFOR's mandate or actions was repeated to me by Sacirbey. Muhamed Sacirbey, interview with author, 14 December, 1999.

Chapter 7

Back to Iraq

Iraq remained one of the most intransigent issues faced by the Security Council in the post-Cold War period. In spite of UNSC imposed sanctions, weapons inspections and military no fly zones, the regime of Saddam Hussein nevertheless remained a thorn in the side of the international community. Its continued belligerence ensured that the Council's members had to keep continually apprised of the Iraqi situation and, between the end of the Gulf War in 1991 and December 2002, were forced to adopt 17 resolutions in regard to the situation in Iraq. Despite this intense focus of attention, the issue of Iraqi disarmament remained unresolved until it again became a global flashpoint in March 2003.

Setting the Scene

Since the 1991 Gulf War ceasefire, relations between the UNSC and Iraq had slowly simmered as the terms of the ceasefire resolution 687 were implemented. As we have seen in Chapter 2, as a result of its defeat in the first Gulf War, Iraq was kept firmly on an international leash by way of three major elements of the post-war settlement. The first of these required the complete disclosure and disarmament of Iraqi nuclear, chemical, and biological weapons - commonly referred to as weapons of mass destruction (WMD). Overseen by a team of weapons inspectors from the United Nations Special Commission (UNSCOM), and the International Atomic Energy Agency (IAEA), the weapons inspections were intended to ensure the destruction of any WMD possessed by Iraq, limit ballistic missiles to a range of not more than 150km and also ensure that Iraq did not have the ability to manufacture any prohibited weapons in future.[1] Economic sanctions provided the second term of the post war settlement and were designed to remain in place until such time as the weapons inspectors verified that Iraq had fully disarmed. A southern no-fly zone was also established as the third part of the settlement, ostensibly to provide air cover for the southern Iraqi Shias that had traditionally been persecuted by the regime of Saddam Hussein. This no-fly zone was not authorized by the United Nations, but was simply imposed by the United States and Britain.[2]

---

[1] See the terms of *UNSC Resolution 687*, 3 April, 1991.
[2] Michael Dunne, "The United States, the United Nations and Iraq," *International Affairs*, March, 2003, p. 267.

182 *Understanding the UN Security Council*

The weapons inspections were carried out from 1991 until December 1998 at which time UNSCOM was withdrawn as a result of Iraqi obstruction. Its withdrawal was followed by seventy hours of US and British air strikes against Baghdad as punishment for Iraq's failure to cooperate with the inspectors. The air strikes were not specifically authorized by the UN Security Council, except as claimed by the US and Britain under the terms of the ceasefire resolution 687.[3] In spite of the air strikes, the inspectors did not return to Iraq and the disarmament issue remained unresolved through 2002.

As the Security Council remained apprised of the Iraqi situation throughout the 1990s, the positions of the permanent members consistently reflected a joint Anglo-American willingness to use force through air strikes and maintain sanctions in order to influence Iraqi compliance with the Council's resolutions. Indeed it was the US government that adopted the most hostile posture towards the regime of Saddam Hussein and in 1998 the removal of the dictator from power became an explicit joint US-British objective.[4] To this end, both the US and Britain attempted to weaken the Iraqi regime through the selective use of air strikes and broad-brushed sanctions, with both policies pursued and justified under the authority of the UN Security Council and the perpetual authority of resolution 687 adopted in 1991. France and Russia, on the other hand, had significant economic interests in Iraq and were more inclined to use the carrot of eased economic sanctions in order to persuade the Iraqi regime to cooperate with UNSCOM and disarm in accordance with UN resolutions.[5]

Changing Attitudes

Once the Bush administration became unwilling to tolerate perceived threats to US national security following the 11 September, 2001 terrorist attacks on the US mainland, Iraq moved higher on the White House agenda and more emphasis was placed on neutralizing the threat it posed to US interests. This pressure was, in the main, politically manifest in the UN Security Council where the US sought to bring increasing pressure to bear on the Iraqi regime to complete the disarmament process that had begun following the end of the Gulf War in 1991. In order to do so, the US sought to exploit the collegiality within the Council that had allowed the rapid confrontation of the Taleban regime in Afghanistan.

The first explicit indication of the degree to which American attention had become resolutely focused on Iraq in the post 11 September world came when President George Bush made his annual State of the Union address on 29 January, 2002. In this speech he characterized North Korea, Iran and Iraq as an 'axis of evil' which demanded the attention of the United States:

---

[3] Ibid., p. 268.
[4] Adam Roberts, "Law and the Use of Force After Iraq," *Survival*, vol. 45, no. 2, 2003, p. 39.
[5] Ibid., p. 267.

States like these, and their terrorist allies, constitute an axis of evil, arming to threaten the peace of the world. By seeking weapons of mass destruction these regimes pose a grave and growing danger. They could provide these arms to terrorists, giving them the means to match their hatred. They could attack our allies or attempt to blackmail the United States. In any of these cases, the price of indifference would be catastrophic.[6]

Publicly, the Bush administration was not shy about articulating its expansive plans for Iraq. Throughout the spring and summer of 2002, options for an invasion and a public discussion of its potential military and economic impacts were openly debated, helping the Bush administration to gauge domestic and international responses to its sabre rattling. Although nothing was "official," it was nevertheless clear where American intentions lay.[7] These initiatives demonstrated that Iraq was firmly in the sights of the Bush administration.

America's public debate on war was countered by international attempts to have weapons inspectors re-admitted to Iraq. Theses initiatives, despite being led by Kofi Annan, were unproductive and began to justify American claims that the Iraqi regime had no intention of cooperating with the UN or of disarming itself.[8] Following a summer of gradually increasing focus and pressure to resolve the Iraq issue, international tension was ratcheted up by increasingly bellicose comments from within the Bush administration. At the end of August, 2002 Vice-President Dick Cheney declared that the "risks of inaction are greater than the risks of action" and that further UN inspections of the Iraqi arms programs would provide "false comfort" as to Iraqi WMD capabilities.[9] Cheney was joined in his scepticism of the United Nations by other neo-conservatives such as Donald Rumsfeld, US Secretary of Defense, who saw no need for US actions to be authorized by the UNSC.[10] Such comments and attitudes seemed to suggest that the United States had no intention of consulting the UNSC in regard to Iraq.

International fears that the US might act independently against Iraq stemmed from the dominance of neo-conservative opinion within the Bush administration. However, a second less aggressive stance was advocated by doves such as Colin Powell who preferred a multi-lateral approach and believed that weapons inspectors should be returned to Iraq as a first step in uncovering Iraq's WMD capabilities.[11] As the debate progressed, the preferred strategy that did appear to gain the upper hand within the Bush administration was one of seeking the re-

---

[6] "The President's State of the Union Address," *Office of the Press Secretary*, Washington, 29 January, 2002.

[7] "For Each Audience, Another Secret Plan to Attack Iraq," *The New York Times*, 11 August, 2002.

[8] "U.N. Talks on Iraq Inspections Resume With Sides Far Apart," *The New York Times*, 2 May, 2002.

[9] As quoted in "The World: First Among Evils? The Debate Over Attacking Iraq Heats Up," *The New York Times*, 1 September, 2002.

[10] Mats Berdal, The UN Security Council: Ineffective but Indispensable," *Survival*, vol. 45, no. 22, 2003. p. 22.

[11] "Powell Charts Low-Key Path in Iraq Debate," *The New York Times*, 2 September, 2002.

184 *Understanding the UN Security Council*

admission of inspectors to Iraq in order to provide evidence of WMD which would then justify an UN-authorized intervention, led by the United States, in order to disarm Iraq.[12] Indeed the hawks within the administration were forced to tone down their aggressive stance towards Iraq with Secretary of Defense Donald Rumsfeld withdrawing an article, due to be published in the Washington Post that defended the concept of a unilateral, pre-emptive strike against aggressive states armed with WMD.[13] It seemed that the more multilateral strategy had temporarily won the day. International pressure had in part been responsible as it had helped to give the doves in the Bush administration the upper hand when arguing that the United States should stick to the multilateral route. Opposition to independent action by the United States had been voiced by China, Saudi Arabia and even the UK supported placing pressure on Iraq to re-admit weapons inspectors rather than using force.[14] German Chancellor Gerhard Schröder stated that he would not support a war against Iraq, even if sanctioned by the UNSC, such were the risks of being distracted from the international war on terrorism.[15]

The first part of this multilateral strategy came with President Bush's address to members of the UN General Assembly on 12 September, 2002.[16] In his speech, Bush stressed the American belief that Saddam Hussein had been afforded more that enough time to comply with the demands of the UNSC and that the dictator had no serious intent to comply with UN resolutions. Similarly, he argued, the UN had to show firm resolve in the face of a regime that posed an aggressive threat to international peace and security. In the face of further obstruction, he argued, "the world must move deliberately, decisively to hold Iraq to account." But while encouraging the members of the UN to harden their combined resolve in confronting the Iraqi regime, Bush was also quick to make it clear that the United States, while working with the UN, would not allow Iraq to remain a threat to its security:

> We will work with the UN Security Council for the necessary resolutions. But the purposes of the United States should not be doubted. The Security Council resolutions will be enforced – the just demands of peace and security will be met – or action will be unavoidable. And a regime that has lost its legitimacy will also lose its power.[17]

This thinly veiled threat was directed to the Iraqi regime, but it also contained a warning to the members of the UN – Saddam Hussein would be dealt with and it

---

[12] Apparently, this strategy was advocated behind the scenes by senior Republican figures including James Baker, Lawrence Eagleburger and Brent Scowcroft. *Ibid.*

[13] "Blair, Meeting with Bush, Fully Endorses U.S. Plans for Ending Iraqi Threat," *The New York Times*, 8 September, 2002.

[14] "Pressure on Bush to Back Off," *The Guardian*, 29 August, 2002.

[15] "German Leader's Warning: War Plan is Huge Mistake," *The New York Times*, 5 September, 2002.

[16] "President's Remarks at the United Nations General Assembly," *Office of the Press Secretary*, Washington, 12 September, 2002.

[17] Ibid.

was simply the means by which this occurred that remained to be determined, either with or without the UN.

With the Iraqi issue firmly back in the UN spotlight, the other members of the Security Council were also keen to see the situation in Iraq resolved and the regime disarmed. The United States had demonstrated the seriousness with which it regarded the situation, but the preference for many states was to ensure that the situation was resolved peacefully and in the UN framework.

Such was the international concern about the prospect of the United States pursuing the war path immediately that many states sought to make their concerns public in the hope of slowing any headlong rush to war. Indeed, following President's Bush to the UN General Assembly, there was a fear that the United States was intent on removing Saddam Hussein by force without first seeking appropriate authorization from the UN. This fear was not irrational as it was fuelled by comments from within the Bush administration, the continued positioning of American military equipment in the Middle East and, most importantly, the release of the new national security strategy of the Bush administration which justified the use of preemptive attacks as an instrument of national policy. Commonly referred to as the "Bush Doctrine," it argued that in combating the threat of terror:

> While the United States will constantly strive to enlist the support of the international community, we will not hesitate to act alone, if necessary, to exercise or right of self defense by acting preemptively against such terrorists, to prevent them from doing harm against our people and our country...[18]

In response to the increasingly bellicose statements coming from the United States, UN Secretary General Kofi Annan stressed the advantages of a multilateral approach in a speech before the UN General Assembly. It was clear that his words were directed towards the Bush administration:

> I believe that every government that is committed to the rule of law at home, must be committed also to the rule of law abroad. And all states have a clear interest, as well as clear responsibility, to uphold international law and maintain international order...Any state, if attacked, retains the inherent right of self-defense under Article 51 of the charter. But beyond that, when states decide to use force to deal with broader threats to international peace and security, there is no substitute for the unique legitimacy provided by the United Nations.[19]

In spite of the continued sabre-rattling of the United States, Bush's challenge to the UN did indicate a willingness to engage with the international body as an alternative to independent action. This was, however, contingent on the US being able to obtain a resolution from the UNSC that was firm enough to severely

---

[18]"The National Security Strategy of the United States of America," *Office of the Press Secretary*, Washington, 20 September, 2002. See also "US Military Builds Up Huge Attack Force," *The Guardian*, September 13, 2002.

[19] Statement of Kofi Annan before the General Assembly, 12 September, 2002.

186   *Understanding the UN Security Council*

constrain the Iraqi regime and ensure the complete removal of any WMD it might have had.[20]   The doves in the Bush administration began to increase the diplomatic pressure within UN circles to both entrench the UN route within the administration and also complete the disarmament of Iraq.   Led by Secretary of State Colin Powell, American diplomat efforts became focused on building a coalition of partners behind a new UNSC resolution aimed at resolving the situation by pressuring Iraq to allow the return of weapons inspectors.

Once it became clear that the United States had opted to go down the multilateral route offered by the United Nations, there were two pivotal points that shaped the debate. First, it was unclear what the true objective of the United States was.   The issue under discussion, and the publicly expressed objective, was the removal of all WMD that the US and UK claimed that Iraq possessed.   The debate within the international community was primarily focused on the need to prove that such weapons existed in Iraq.   What went unarticulated was whether or not the US would try to use the United Nations mechanism to seek regime change in Iraq, consistent with its national policy objectives.   Potentially allies were keen to confine the debate to the issue of WMD and ensure that any talk of regime change was not on the table.   Dominique de Villepin, Foreign Minister of France, was quick to point out France's opposition to the idea of removing the Hussein regime:

> ...recognizing the legitimacy of a change of regime would be creating instability on the international scene that would be endless.   Where would we put the border between acceptable regimes for some and unacceptable ones for others?[21]

The United States, no doubt recognizing the extent of the opposition it would face if regime change was an explicit objective it was pursuing via the UN, instead ensured that the debate hinged around the issue of WMD.   This emphasis then brought on the second key pivot point of the debate which was how to achieve the disarmament of Iraq; through the use of inspectors and diplomacy or through the use of force?

Finding that its international partners were more amenable to action justified by the potential threat of WMD, the United States began to emphasize the Iraqi weapons arsenal.   Precisely what form any UN action would take in regard to WMD thus became the new focus of debate.   The United States proved malleable and, despite its previously aggressive stance, the Bush administration seemed willing to settle for a new UN resolution which gave Iraq one final opportunity to comply with the UNSC's demands.   Discussions centered on the terms of a new resolution which would potentially force Iraq to re-admit weapons inspections into the country.[22]   However, Iraq quickly pre-empted such discussions by unconditionally agreeing to the renewal of arms inspections on 17 September,

---

[20] "US Split On Need For Last Chance For Saddam," *The Guardian*, 6 September, 2002.

[21] Dominique de Villepin as quoted in "Bush's Step Toward U.N. is Met by Warm Welcome; Council Seems Ready to Act," *The New York Times*, 13 September, 2002.

[22] "Rift Seen at UN Over Next Steps to Deal With Iraq," *The New York Times*, 18 September, 2002.

2002. Though viewed skeptically by some as a calculated delaying action on the part of the Iraqi dictator, the admittance of inspectors back to Iraq for the first time since 1998 helped to push the crisis more firmly into the jurisdiction of the United Nations and add credence to the argument that Iraq could be disarmed using diplomatic methods.[23]

Iraq's action served to expose political differences between the P-5 member of the UNSC. From the outset, France, Russia and China had openly expressed their firm reluctance to using force as a means of resolving the situation. Russia and China both welcomed the Iraq willingness to accept renewed inspections, whereas the US administration was wary of further Iraqi deception.[24] A number of countries, including France and Russia questioned the need for a new resolution from the UNSC in light of the Iraqi offer to admit the weapons inspectors.[25]

The US and UK, keen to ensure that the Iraqi offer did not serve to further delay the resolution of the issue, continued to insist that a new resolution was imperative in order to keep up the pressure on Saddam Hussein. However, differences of opinion with the P-5 membership of the Council blunted the ability of the UNSC to sustain such pressure. The United States still retained the very real threat of war as an incentive to its international allies to support its calls for a new resolution. On 19 September, Bush submitted a draft resolution to the US Congress requesting authority to "use all means he determines to be appropriate, including force" to ensure the disarmament of Iraq and the removal of Saddam Hussein from power.[26] This clear signal of Bush's intent, combined with a letter from Saddam Hussein to the UN General Assembly on the same day in which he declared that Iraqi cooperation with the UN inspectors could not be guaranteed, serving to shift the political tide away from Iraq and back in America's favour.[27]

In addition to applying political pressure to both Iraq and its own allies with the threatened use of force, the US sought a new resolution by political bargaining. As usual, the informal Security Council meetings became a political horse-trading forum. While most states came to accept that UN involvement would center around a further resolution on the Iraqi issue, Russia made the most of its veto power to extract unrelated concessions from the US for Russian support. This is demonstrated by the abrupt change in the Russian position just days after its Foreign Minister, Igor Ivanov, had questioned the very need for a new resolution. After receiving assurances from the US that it would support Russian initiatives against Chechen "terrorists" on the Russian-Georgian border, the Russian defense

---

[23] "What Baghdad Said in Letter to Kofi Annan," *The Guardian*, 17 September, 2002.

[24] "UN Split Over Iraqi Arms Offer," *The Guardian*, 17 September, 2002.

[25] "Rift Seen at U.N. Over Next Steps to Deal with Iraq," *The New York Times*, 18 September, 2002.

[26] "Bush Seeks Power to Use 'All Means' to Oust Hussein," *The New York Times*, 20 September, 2002.

[27] As quoted in "Bush's Push on Iraq at U.N.: Headway, Then New Barriers," *The New York Times*, 22 September, 2002.

188 *Understanding the UN Security Council*

minister Sergei Ivanov clarified the position of his government and stated that it was not opposed to a further resolution of the UNSC in relation to Iraq.[28]

The Devil's in the Detail

With its fellow Security Council members finally united in their acceptance of the need for a new UN resolution regarding Iraq, US initiatives became focused on agreeing its specific terms. The Americans and British were set on obtaining a single resolution prior to the re-deployment of inspectors to Iraq demanding Iraqi cooperation with the United Nations Monitoring, Verification and Inspection Commission (UNMOVIC) and also spelling out the consequences if they did not. For the Americans the main issue under discussion was "how to keep the threat of consequences ties as closely as one can to the new requirements that will be placed on Iraq."[29] Of the other Security Council members, the Russians were initially open to the American proposal provided they received adequate assurances from the Bush administration that their vast economic interests in Iraq would be protected following any war in Iraq.[30] Germany maintained its opposition to any military action in Iraq, while the French demanded a two-resolution process; the first covering Iraqi cooperation with UNMOVIC and the second which would lay out the consequences in the event that Iraq obstructed the efforts of the weapons inspectors.[31]

During the first two weeks of October 2002, negotiations as to the shape of any new resolution on Iraq became bogged down as the French two-resolution position remained at loggerheads with that of the United States and Britain seeking a single resolution. France remained firmly opposed to offering a single resolution for fear of the United States using its terms as cover for the automatic use of force. French fears were compounded by the fact that, on 11 October, the US Congress had formally given Bush the authority to use force against Iraq.[32] This nationally sanctioned authority served to increase the pressure on the other UNSC members to ensure that the US remained engaged with the UN on the issue of Iraq, whilst still trying to limit the likelihood of the use of force. As Jean-David Levitte, the French representative to the UN, summarized:

> During the first stage, the Security Council should adopt a resolution clearly specifying the "rules of the game". It would define the inspection regime and ensure that the inspectors could fully accomplish their mission without any hindrance. This resolution should also send a clear warning to Iraq that the Council will not tolerate

---

[28] "Russia Lifts Objections After Chechen 'Deal,'" *The Guardian*, 24 September, 2002.

[29] Colin Powell, as quoted in "Council Toils Over Wording of Resolution Aimed At Iraq," *The New York Times*, 9 October, 2002.

[30] "Russia, With Much at Stake, Takes Its Time Deciding." *The New York Times*, 3 October , 2002.

[31] "France and Germany Agree on Iraq," *The New York Times*, 3 October, 2002.

[32] "Congress Authorises Bush to Use Force Against Iraq, Creating Broad Mandate," *The New York Times*, 11 October, 2002.

new violations. During the second stage, if UNMOVIC or the IAEA observe that Iraq is refusing to cooperate fully with inspectors, the Security Council will meet immediately to decide on the appropriate measures to take, without ruling anything out of hand.[33]

Russian and China, the other two veto wielding members of the UNSC, were more sympathetic to the French position. Moscow was concerned that the US and Britain were more intent about creating a legal basis for the use of force to remove Saddam Hussein from power rather than improving the inspections regime of UNMOVIC, a result with serious implications for Russian oil interests in Iraq and a position which allowed the Russian to continue bargaining for economic concessions from both the US and Iraqi governments. For its part China took a more neutral position, amenable to the idea of a new resolution but concerned that its only objective be to support the work of the inspectors.[34]

The impasse that had plagued the members of the P-5 was finally broken during the last week of October. Concerned that their stalemate had implications not only for Iraq, but also for the future of the international order both the United States and France were forced to compromise. The United States dropped its insistence that the phrase authorizing the use of "all necessary means" in the event of Iraqi non-compliance with the inspectors, normal Security Council lexicon for war, be included in the resolution. In its place, US officials suggested determining whether Iraq was in "material breech" of the Council resolution before any further action would be taken.[35] France's concern then became ensuring that the term "material breech" did not provide the United States with an automatic trigger for the US and Britain to go to war against Iraq without first consulting the Council. After repeated assurances from the United States that, in the event that Iraq was found to be in material breech of the UNSC resolution, they would consult the members of the Council before taking any action, French concerns were mollified.[36]

Resolution 1441

On 5 November, the United States submitted its draft resolution to the members of the Council, after weeks of fierce debate. With negotiations having been concluded before the formal meeting of the Council, the draft was adopted unanimously as resolution 1441. Though the resolution reaffirmed the commitment of UN member states to the territorial integrity of Iraq, the Council's

---

[33] As quoted in "On the Iraq Issue: Comments by the Council Members Holding a Veto," *The New York Times*, 18 October, 2002.

[34] Ibid.

[35] "Negotiators Seeking a Deal Retreat Behind Closed Doors," *The New York Times*, 20 October, 2002.

[36] "No Veto Threat From Security Council Negotiations on Iraq, But No Resolution Either," *The New York Times*, 31 October, 2002 and "U.S. Counting on France Will Submit Iraq Plan to U.N.," *The New York Times*, 6 November, 2002.

190 *Understanding the UN Security Council*

decision was taken under Chapter VII of the Charter. Its main provisions found Iraq to be in material breech of the obligations set out by previous UNSC resolutions, but nevertheless afforded it a "final opportunity" to comply with its disarmament obligations. Iraq was called upon to provide to UNMOVIC, the IAEA and the UNSC a complete declaration of its WMD stockpiles and programs within 30 days. Failure to do so would constitute a further material breech of its obligations and Iraq would "face serious consequences as a result of its continued violations of its obligations." Significantly, paragraph 12 of the resolution explicitly set out that in the event of Iraqi non-compliance with the terms of the resolution, the members of the UNSC would again convene in order to discuss further action. This paragraph was an important concession by the Americans to their Security Council partners, allaying concerns that the Bush administration would not consult the Council before going to war against Iraq.[37]

After the Council's vote, Kofi Annan was quick to commend the Council's action and draw attention to both the practical and symbolic natures of its terms:

> This resolution is based on law, collective effort and the unique legitimacy of the United Nations. It represents an example of multilateral diplomacy serving the cause of peace and security. It reflects a renewed commitment to preventing the development and spread of weapons of mass destruction and the universal wish to see this goal obtained by peaceful means.[38]

The American ambassador, John Negroponte, sought to further re-assure the UN members of American intentions:

> ...this resolution contains no 'hidden triggers' and no 'automaticity' with respect to the use of force. If there is a further Iraqi breach, reported to the Council by UNMOVIC, the IAEA or a Member State, the matter will return to the Council for discussions as required in paragraph 12. The resolution makes clear that any Iraqi failure to comply is unacceptable and that Iraq must be disarmed. And, one way or another, Iraq will be disarmed. If the Security Council fails to act decisively in the event of further Iraqi violations, this resolution does not constrain any Member State from acting to defend itself against the threat posed by Iraq...[39]

The French and Russians were quick to point out they had reigned in the unilateral impulses of the United States and ensured the issue remained within the forum provided by the Security Council. France's Ambassador Levitte stated:

> The resolution strengthens the role and authority of the Security Council. That was the main and constant objective of France throughout the negotiations which have just concluded. That objective was reflected in our request that a two-stage approach be established and complied with, ensuring that the Security Council would maintain control of the process at each stage. That objective has been attained...

---

[37] UNSC Resolution 1441, 8 November, 2002.

[38] *UN Document*, S/PV. 4644, 8 November, 2002.

[39] Ibid.

Sergei Lavrov, the Russian representative commented:

> At all stages of this work, we were guided by the need to direct the process of a settlement onto a diplomatic and political path and not to allow a military scenario. As a result of intensive negotiations, the resolution just adopted contains no provisions for the automatic use of force.

The Chinese representative, Mr. Wang Yingfan, expressed his country's pleasure in the fact that the resolution not only reaffirmed the territorial integrity of Iraq, but also that resolution 1441 was part of a two stage process. As a result of the reports of UNMOVIC and the IAEA the Council would be able to:

> ...draw objective, fair and realistic conclusions and decide on the next steps in the light of the situation and the views of the various parties concerned...The Security Council bears the primary responsibility for the maintenance of international peace and security – a responsibility that is entrusted to it by the Charter. Now that the Security Council has adopted this important resolution at this crucial moment, we hope that it will contribute to preserving the authority of the Council...[40]

Resolution 1441 allowed the doves in the Bush administration to pursue a multilateral approach to Iraq despite the continued build up of American military hardware in the Middle East and Congressional authorization for Bush to go to war with Iraq. Similarly, it met the French, Russian and Chinese concerns that the UNSC continue to be consulted during the disarmament process and that the territorial integrity of Iraq was reaffirmed by the Council, with no explicit mention of regime change. However, in the debates on the resolution the focus remained on the disarmament of Iraq and the best means to achieve it. No mention was made of removing the regime of Saddam Hussein. Resolution 1441 thus set the stage for a dramatic few month of international relations as the UNMOVIC and IAEA reported back to the Council on their findings and the members of the Security Council once again became embroiled in heated debates concerning the degree to which Iraq posed a threat to international peace and security.

The Inspectors Report Back

On 7 December, Iraq submitted a 12,000 page document covering its chemical, biological and nuclear weapons programs in accordance with the demands made by the Security Council in resolution 1441. After intense scrutiny of the documents, the United States and Britain declared that Saddam Hussein was again deceiving the international community and that the Iraqi declaration contained significant omissions. Jack Straw, the UK Foreign Secretary, warned "if Saddam persists in this obvious falsehood, it will become clear that he has rejected the pathway to

---

[40] Ibid.

Understanding the UN Security Council

peace laid down in resolution 1441..."[41] Similarly, Colin Powell argued that American "experts have found it to be anything but currently accurate, full or complete. The Iraqi declaration may use the language of resolution 1441, but it totally fails to meet the resolution's requirements."[42]

In contrast with these more skeptical assessments of the declaration, in a report to the Security Council, Hans Blix, Executive Chairman of UNMOVIC, wasn't so keen on finding fault with the Iraqis, "We have now been there for some two months and been covering the country in ever wider sweeps and we haven't found any smoking guns." But he was quick to add that more information was required from Iraq and that "the declaration failed to answer a great many questions."[43] Blix also criticized Iraq on not complying with certain requests such as providing UNMOVIC with a list of Iraqi weapons experts or arranging interviews with them, a lack of cooperation that had hindered the inspector's progress in Iraq.[44]

Opinion on Iraq among the P-5 remained divided as its members waited for a more comprehensive report from the weapons inspectors that was due on 27 January, 2003. The Bush administration expressed frustration with the slow progress of the inspections and again warned that it was prepared to go to war alone against Iraq, even if no new evidence of WMD was uncovered by the inspections. France and Russia remained opposed to such action. The Russian Foreign Minister, Igor Ivanov warned that any war without the sanction of the UNSC would "lead to unpredictable consequences for international peace and stability, including damage to the interests of the global struggle against terrorism."[45] France called for the inspections to be given significantly more time to produce results and non-permanent UNSC member Germany, in a position similar to that of the Russians, argued that any war against Iraq would be counter productive to the ongoing war against terrorism.[46]

In their reports to the Council on 27 January, Hans Blix and Muhamed ElBaradei, Director General of the IAEA, were not able to give definitive proof of the presence of WMD or reveal evidence of Iraq's development programs for such weapons. Blix stated that in certain areas the cooperation of Iraq authorities with the UNMOVIC inspectors could have been better and that attempts by the inspections commission to interview leading Iraqi weapons scientists had not been possible. However, he stated that "Iraq has, on the whole, cooperated rather well so far with UNMOVIC..." Blix also criticized the arms declaration provided by Iraq to the UN as incomplete in that it contained little updated information which

---

[41] As quoted in "Iraq is Lying, Say US and Britain," *The Guardian*, 19 December, 2002.

[42] "US Secretary of State Colin Powell's statement on Iraq's weapons declaration," *The Guardian*, 20 December, 2002.

[43] "Blix: No 'Smoking Guns' in Iraq," *The Guardian*, 9 January, 2002.

[44] "U.N. Inspectors Criticize Iraq Over Arms List," *The New York Times*, 10 January, 2003.

[45] "U.S. Resisting Calls For a 2nd U.N. Vote on a War With Iraq," *The New York Times*, 16 January, 2003.

[46] "Refusal by French and Germans to Back U.S. In Iraq Has Undercut Powell's Position," *The New York Times*, 24 January, 2003.

did not provide answers to questions the inspectors had concerning certain weapons programs such as research into VX nerve agent, and missile programs. Concerning the search for evidence of nuclear weapon programs in Iraq, ElBaradei reported "we have to date found no evidence that Iraq has revived its nuclear weapons program since the elimination of the program in the 1990s."[47] Both Blix and ElBaradei stated that their respective inspections regimes would need further time to complete the investigations.

In spite of the inconclusive reports of the weapons inspectors, the United States maintained its belligerent posture towards the Iraqi regime. In his 2003 State of the Union Address to the American people, Bush claimed:

> The dictator of Iraq is not disarming. To the contrary; he is deceiving. From intelligence sources we know, for instance, that thousands of Iraq security personnel are at work hiding documents and materials from the UN inspectors, sanitizing inspection site and monitoring the inspectors themselves.

Bush then went on to directly link the threat of terrorism with the Iraqi regime:

> Before September 11th, many in the world believed that Saddam Hussein could be contained. But chemical agents, lethal viruses and shadowy terrorist networks are note easily contained...It would take one vial, one canister, one crate slipped into this country to bring a day of horror like none we have ever known. We will do everything in our power to make sure that that day never comes...if Saddam does not fully disarm, for the safety of our people and for the peace of the world, we will lead a coalition to disarm him.[48]

In spite of the intense drive by the United States and Britain to seek a second UN resolution authorizing the use of force to oversee the complete disarmament of Iraq, the other members of the P-5 remained reluctant to give their support. France in particular called for the inspectors to be given more time to carry out their investigation, consistent with the requests of Blix and ElBaradei.[49]

Frustrated with the lack of support from their fellow UNSC members, Colin Powell made a special presentation to the Council on 5 February in which he laid out key evidence which the United States had gleaned form its intelligence sources in Iraq. The Bush administration hoped that the sharing of its information on Iraq would persuade other members of the Council of the threat posed to international peace and security by the Iraqi weapons programs. Powell's presentation included recordings of conversation between Iraqi military officers supposedly dealing with the hiding of prohibited weapons, images of suspect weapons sites that had been "cleansed" by the Iraqi authorities, and images of suspected mobile weapons systems. Based on this intelligence Powell argued:

---

[47] *UN Document*, S/PV .4692, 27 January, 2003.

[48] "The 2003 State of the Union Address," *Office of the Press Secretary*, 28 January, 2003.

[49] 'U.S. and Britain Press for Resolution on Iraq, but Make Minimal Headway," *The New York Times*, 4 February, 2003.

194 *Understanding the UN Security Council*

> I believe that Iraq is now in further material breech of its obligations. I believe that this conclusion is irrefutable and undeniable. Iraq has now placed itself in danger of the serious consequences called for in resolution 1441. This body places itself in danger of irrelevance if it allows Iraq to continue to defy its will without responding effectively and immediately.[50]

However passionate Powell's presentation, the other members of the Security Council took issue with his claim that Iraq was in material breech of its obligations to which the use of force was the only response. China argued "as long as there is still the slightest hope for a political settlement, we should exert our utmost efforts in achieving it." Russia similarly stressed the need to address the problem via the Security Council and using political rather than coercive means:

> We are convinced that maintaining the unity of the world community, primarily within the context of the Security Council, and our concerted action, in strict compliance with the Charter of the United Nations and the resolutions of the Security Council, are the most reliable means of resolving the problems of weapons of mass destruction in Iraq through political means.

The French representative on the Council, Mr. De Villepin, stressed:

> For now, the inspections regime favored by resolution 1441 must be strengthened, since it has not been explored to the end. Use of force can only be a final recourse. Why go to war if there still exists an unused space in resolution 1441?

Among the members of the P-5, it was only Britain that offered support for the United States, agreeing:

> There is only one possible conclusion from all of this, which is that Iraq is in further material breech, as set out in United Nations Security Council resolution 1441. I believe that all colleagues here, all members, will share our deep sense of frustration that Iraq is choosing to spurn this final opportunity to achieve a peaceful outcome...

Despite the photographs, recordings and pleading delivery of Powell's presentation to the Security Council, he failed to convince Russia, China or France to support a second resolution under Chapter VII to authorize the forcible disarmament of the Iraqi regime of its WMD. Despite lobbying phone calls from Bush to his foreign counterparts, the other members of the P-5 continued to insist that the UN inspectors be given time to complete their investigation. Stubbornly, the US and Britain continued to insist that Iraq would be disarmed with or without the support of the UNSC.[51] Again, the debate remained focused on ensuring that the Iraqi regime was disarmed of any WMD. No member of the Security Council, including

---

[50] *UN Document*, S/PV . 4701, 5 February, 2003.
[51] "France and China Rebuff Bush on Support for Early Iraq War," *The New York Times*, 8 February, 2003.

Back to Iraq   195

Iraq, whose representative attended the debates, made any mention of possible regime change.

The Debate on War

The intense debate continued during the month of February as the international community attempted to determine the extent of threat posed by Iraq to international peace and security. The US and British case in advocating the use of force against Iraq was not helped when it was revealed that a key dossier produced by the British government in support of its argument was found to be plagiarized from out of date research on Iraq.[52] Further reports from Blix and ElBaradei also did not provide sufficient evidence of Iraq's WMD capabilities for many of the UNSC members, further hindering efforts to obtain a second resolution.[53]

As the threat of war increased with continued belligerent statements from both the Bush administration and Downing St., so too did opposition to it. During 18 and 19 February, a total of fifty-five member states of the UN sought admittance to the Security Council discussions on Iraq, the majority of which sought to register their opposition to the use of force to bring about Iraqi disarmament. Their statements generally sought to emphasize the need to maintain the primacy of the UN Security Council as the central forum used to address issues of international peace and security and warned against destabilizing, unilateral initiatives of members states acting outside of the UN framework. The comments of the representative of South Africa, speaking on behalf of the membership of the Non-Aligned Movement (NAM) were typical in this respect:

> We believe that the Security Council must redouble its efforts to bring about a peaceful resolution to the situation in Iraq, in line with international law and the provisions of the UN Charter. The United Nations is the most authoritative voice in a world of complex multilateralism and interdependence. It is an Organization founded on the need to preserve international peace and security. We should not allow its legitimacy and credibility to be undermined by this issue.[54]

An emergency meeting of the heads of state of the European Union members held to debate the Iraq crisis also issued a statement that resonated with the position of the NAM and further frustrated Anglo-American initiatives to disarm Iraq using force. The EU declaration stated that its members "are committed to the United Nations remaining at the center of the international order. We recognize that the primary responsibility for dealing with Iraqi disarmament lies with the Security Council."[55] In part, the European leaders were also united in the perceived need to

---

[52] "Number 10 Admits It Used Thesis By Student," *The Independent*, 7 February, 2003.

[53] See UNMOVIC and IAEA reports made to the Security Council, *UN Document*, S/PV .4707, 14 February 2003.

[54] *UN Document*, S/PV .4709, 18 February, 2003.

[55] As quoted in "Nations See World Order Centered on U.N., Not U.S.," *The New York Times*, 19 February, 2003.

Understanding the UN Security Council

ensure that the United States, as the global superpower, operated within the framework of the United Nations rather than unilaterally.[56]

On 5 March, two days before UNMOVIC and the IAEA were due to report back to the members of the UNSC on any progress they had made with regard to overseeing the disarmament of Iraq, key members of the Security Council issued a joint declaration which directly opposed American and British initiatives. France, Russia and Germany, which held the presidency of the Security Council, stated that the objective of the full and effective disarmament of Iraq, as called for in resolution 1441, could be achieved by way of inspections. They believed that inspections were producing "increasingly encouraging results." Most importantly the declaration spelled out that they would "not let a proposed resolution pass that would authorize the use force. Russia and France, as permanent members of the Security Council, will assume all their responsibilities on this point."[57] In this context the phrase "will assume all their responsibilities" implied that, if put to the vote, both France and Russia would likely veto any proposal to authorize the use of force against Iraq. The US and Britain were dealt a further blow when China announced that it too believed a second resolution to be unnecessary and that the crisis should be resolved through peaceful means.[58]

The apprehensively awaited reports from UNMOVIC and the IAEA on 7 March again failed to produce a "smoking gun" that pointed to evidence of prohibited weapons programs. Hans Blix reported that cooperation by Iraq authorities with the inspectors had marginally improved and some significant progress had been made with the destruction of 34 declared but prohibited Al Samound II missiles. In terms of biological weapons programs, Blix reported that no evidence of any prohibited activity had been found. Similarly, ElBaradei reported that "after three months of intrusive inspections, we have to date found no evidence or plausible indication of the revival of a nuclear-weapons program in Iraq."[59]

Stalemate

Despite being presented with the latest updates from the inspections in Iraq the P-5 members of the Security Council remained firmly wedded to their respective positions as declared prior to the 7 March meeting of the Council. In what would prove to be the last formal Security Council debate on the issue, the positions of the Security Council members had a particular significance as they debated a draft resolution authorizing the use of force to disarm Iraq put forward by the US, UK

---

[56] France was particularly concerned with using the UN to balance against the power of the United States. See "L'Europe, C'est Moi – Chirac's Tactics Over Iraq," *The Economist*, 22 February, 2003.

[57] "Full Text of Joint Declaration," *The Guardian*, 6 March, 2003.

[58] "China Opposes Second UN Resolution," *The Guardian*, 6 March, 2003.

[59] *UN Document*, S/PV .4714, 7 March, 2003.

Back to Iraq

and Spain.[60] On the eve of war, both sides ironically believed that the future relevance of the Security Council and United Nations organization would be dramatically influenced by how it dealt with the Iraqi situation. The Russian representative repeated his country's position that the way in which the Iraqi crisis was handled had longer-term repercussions:

> If, through our joint efforts, we succeed in resolving the Iraqi crisis in accordance with the Charter of the United Nations, it will certainly have a positive effect on our efforts to settle other conflicts. Most significantly, it will be an important step towards a new, just and secure world order. That is why Russia has consistently and resolutely sought to solve the Iraq problem on the basis of international law and of Security Council resolutions. Today, more that ever before, we have reason to state that this is not only the proper, but also the most reliable way.

The French representative echoed similar sentiments:

> The military agenda must not dictate the calendar of inspections. We agree to accelerated timetables, but we can not accept an ultimatum as long as the inspectors are reporting progress in terms of cooperation. That would means war. That would lead to the Security Council being stripped of its responsibilities. By imposing a deadline of a few days, would we merely be seeking a pretext for war? I will say it again: as a permanent member of the Security Council, France will not allow a resolution to be adopted that authorizes the automatic use of force...Let us be clear sighted. We are defining a method for resolving crises. We are choosing how to define the world we want our children to live in.

China added its weight as a permanent member of the Security Council to those opposed to the use of force:

> Resolution 1441 did not come easily. Given the current situation, we need resolve and determination and, more importantly, patience and wisdom. The Council therefore needs to maintain its unity and cooperation more than ever so as to preserve its authority. We believe that the Council should provide strong support and guidance to the two inspection bodies in their work, let them continue inspections and seek the truth until they have fulfilled the mandate of resolution 1441...Under the current circumstances there is no reason to shut the door to peace. Therefore, we are not in favour of a new resolution, particularly one authorizing the use of force.

In the face of such hardened opposition Britain stubbornly maintained its position that the only way in which Saddam Hussein would disarm would be by the credible threat of force, authorized by the UN Security Council. The British Foreign Secretary, Jack Straw, argued:

> The paradox we face is that the only way we are going to achieve disarmament by peace of a rogue regime that, all of us know, has been in defiance of the Council for the past 12 years – the only way that we can achieve its disarmament of weapons of mass

---

[60] Ibid.

198 *Understanding the UN Security Council*

destruction, which the Council has said, pose a threat to international peace and security – is by backing our diplomacy with the credible use of force.

Colin Powell similarly argued that the United Nations must be able to meet its responsibilities with the credible threat of force when necessary:

> Last November, the Council stepped up to its responsibilities. We must not walk away; we must not find ourselves here this coming November with the pressure removed and with Iraq once again marching down the merry path to weapons of mass destruction, threatening the region, threatening the world. If we fail to meet our responsibilities, the credibility of the Council and its ability to deal with all the critical challenges we face will suffer.

Just as in past UNSC debates, the focus centered on the effectiveness of the inspections regime, the role the UNSC would play in the crisis and the wider consequences the UNSC's response to the Iraqi crisis would have for the role of the Security Council in broader issues of international peace and security. None of the members of the Council raised the issue of US and British intentions towards the regime of Saddam Hussein. It was left to the Iraqi representative in the Council chamber to suggest that the Anglo-American agenda involved more than just disarming Iraq:

> It is a very simple agenda. The objective is the complete takeover of Iraq's oil and the political and economic domination of the entire Arab region.[61]

Regardless of whether or not one accepts whether this characterization of the Anglo-American agenda is accurate, the comments of the Iraqi representative were the first and only time in the extensive UNSC debates on Iraq since November 2003 that any suggestion of an agenda beyond the disarmament of Iraq even existed. This is remarkable given US intentions of overthrowing the Saddam Hussein regime. No member of the P-5 sought to publicly raise this prospect with the US or Britain during what would prove to be the final debate on Iraq before the outbreak of hostilities.

The Security Council discussions, both formal and informal, had centered around a joint American, British and Spanish draft resolution that set a deadline of 17 March for Iraqi compliance with resolution 1441. Despite a week of intensive diplomatic activity the western allies were unable to gather the necessary nine votes that would be required for the resolution to pass in the Security Council. Based on the statements of both France and Russia, it was also a very real possibility that either P-5 member would cast a veto in order to scupper any Security Council authorization for the use of force.[62] As the possibility of failing to obtain the necessary support for the draft resolution became clear, debate in the Bush administration focused on whether or not the draft should even be put

---

[61] *UN Document*, S/PV .4714, 7 March, 2003.

[62] "Urgent Diplomacy Fails to Gain U.S. 9 Votes in the U.N.," *The New York Times*, 10 March, 2003.

forward to the vote. On this issue, Powell, Cheney and Rumsfeld were of the same position, through for different reasons. Powell believed that if the draft was put forward to a vote only to fail, and the United States took military action against Iraq regardless, it would open itself up to charges that it had violated the UN charter. Rumsfeld and Cheney preferred not to put the draft forward if it was expected to fail as that process would simply slow the onset of military operations and would expose the inability of Security Council forum to effectively cope with the crisis.[63]

To War

As a result of the perceived risks in failing to obtain support for the joint draft resolution, its sponsors chose not to formally put it to a vote. On the morning of 17 March, the decision to withdraw the draft was taken at a National Security Council meeting in the White House after American officials had consulted with their British and Spanish counterparts.[64] On the same day, the British Attorney General, Lord Goldsmith, stated that the existing authority provided by resolutions 678, 687 and 1441 gave sufficient legal grounds for military action to be taken against Iraq.[65] With the diplomatic process dead, Bush publicly gave the Iraqi regime an ultimatum:

> Saddam Hussein and his sons must leave Iraq within 48 hours. Their refusal to do so will result in military conflict, commenced at a time of our choosing...We are acting now because the risks of inaction would be far greater. In one year, or five years, the power of Iraq to inflict harm on all free nations would be multiplied many times over. With these capabilities, Saddam Hussein and his terrorist allies could choose the moment of deadly conflict when they are the strongest. We choose to meet that threat now, where it arises, before it can appear suddenly in our skies and cities.[66]

In response, Saddam Hussein rejected the American ultimatum through state controlled Iraq television and the stage for war was set.[67] As the world waited for hostilities to begin, the now sidelined members of the Security Council could only fruitlessly re-state their opposition to the settlement of the Iraqi crisis through the use of force from the floor of the Security Council chamber.[68] On the morning of 20 March, 2003 the first American and British air strikes were launched against

---

[63] "U.S. May Abandon U.N. Vote on Iraq, Powell Testifies," *The New York Times*, 14 March, 2003.

[64] "Just Another Monday, Except for Its Conclusion," *The New York Times*, 18 March, 2003.

[65] "Attorney General: War is Legal," *The Guardian*, 17 March, 2003.

[66] "President Says Saddam Hussein Must Leave Iraq Within 48 Hours," *Office of the Press Secretary*, 17 March, 2003.

[67] "Iraq Rebuffs Bush Ultimatum as War Preparations Accelerate," *The Washington Post*, 18 March, 2003.

[68] See *UN Document*, S/PV. 4721, 19 March, 2003.

200 *Understanding the UN Security Council*

Baghdad without any explicit authorization from the UN Security Council. The war had begun and diplomacy had failed to prevent the use of force.

Conclusion

What is most striking about the UNSC member's behaviour during the build up to the second Gulf War is the consistent degree of respect accorded to Iraq despite its previous twelve-year status as an international pariah state. This is similar to the degree of respect accorded Iraq following its defeat in the Gulf War in regard to the UN Guards. However ugly the regime, no matter what its history in the persecution of its own people, the community of international states still accorded it a certain degree of respect. This was manifest by France, Russia, China and numerous other UN member states arguing that the Iraqi regime should be given the time to comply with inspections. At the heart of this position were a variety of contributing factors; Iraq's sovereign status, a preference for diplomacy, economic imperatives, the role of the UNSC and the unchecked power of the United States.

A Sovereign Black Sheep

During the many Security Council debates on Iraq, the regime was consistently treated as a sovereign member of the international community and the Iraqi representative was admitted to the Security Council chamber when the situation in Iraq was being considered. Although it would be easy to disregard the seemingly formulaic phrasing used in Security Council resolution such as "reaffirming the sovereignty and territorial integrity of Iraq" they are in fact extremely important inclusions in the wording that go a long way to appeasing states, such as China, that are staunch defenders of the scope of Article 2(7).[69] Explicitly declaring UNSC recognition of and respect for a state's sovereignty consistently serves to allay any Chinese and international concerns that any UNSC action is in any way detracting from or ignoring the sanctity of state sovereignty.[70] Particularly in a time of a resurgent US super-power adopting a more aggressive role in international politics, many states would have fiercely fought to ensure that any decision on the part of the Security Council to override Article 2(7) was not taken lightly, for fear of that same power being turned on them at a later date. In spite of its status as an international pariah, Iraq was nevertheless treated with a substantial degree of respect in diplomatic negotiations.

---

[69] China's position in UNSC is consistently wary of any encroachment on Article 2(7) for its own domestic issues, particularly the issue of Taiwan. See Mats Berdal, "The UN Security Council: Ineffective but Indispensable," *Survival*, vol. 45, no. 2, 2003, p. 13.
[70] Resolution 1441 incorporates this phrase.

Back to Iraq

Diplomacy Not Force, Consent Not Coercion

Iraq was instructive in revealing the consistent preference of UNSC members for diplomatic efforts to resolve the Iraqi crisis. Diplomacy, which engenders the consent of both parties to negotiations, was in this case the method of resolving the crisis preferred by most states. Although it was diplomacy backed by the threat of force, it was nevertheless a non-coercive means of resolution. Council debates were consistently riddled with statements arguing for all diplomatic avenues to be exhausted, and for inspectors to be given more time to complete their inspections before force was used to disarm Iraq. While it was recognized that the effectiveness of diplomacy required the credible threat of force, given the willingness of the United States to go to war, it proved too difficult for members of the Security Council to effectively balance between the threat and use of force in a multilateral context.

Economic Agendas

In regions of such strategic importance like the Middle East, it was not surprising see that the political bargaining of the Security Council members, particularly the P-5, was in large part dictated by their economic interests. France and Russia were keen to protect their extensive economic interests in Iraq and used their negotiations with the United States to seek assurances that these interests would not be jeopardized in the event of any military activity in Iraq. This was more evident in the case of Russia as both the United States and Iraq sought to gain Russian support using future oil contracts as incentives.

It is these same economic factors that lie behind the treatment of the issue of regime change in an international context. Although the idea of regime change in Iraqi was an explicit goal of the Bush administration, it never entered formally into the UNSC debate on the disarmament of Iraq. Such an explicit objective would have met widespread resistance from the both the general UN membership as well as members of the P-5 simply because such a goal would require an unprecedented obfuscation of Article 2(7). Nevertheless, it appears that there was tacit acceptance within the Security Council that any US military action in Iraq would focus on the overthrow of the Saddam Hussein regime. This was what brought about a frantic Russia seeking assurances from the United States that its oil interests in Iraq would be protected after any military intervention.

Publicly however, the US sought UNSC authorization to bring about the disarmament of Iraq because that objective had a greater likelihood of success as a pretext for multi-lateral action than one of explicit regime change, which would have been a non-starter politically.[71] A regime of inspections that was left over from a previous war was manipulated by a US administration that had entirely

---

[71] There were a number of various justifications for action against Iraq cited by the United States in the lead up to the conflict including pre-emptive attack in defence of US interests, regime change, disarmament, and the war on terrorism. See Adam Roberts "Law and the Use of Force After Iraq," p. 39.

different goals in regard to Iraq. This in part explains why the US persisted with trying to justify UN action on the basis of the threat posed by Iraqi WMD. The general weakness of the case against Iraq on WMD, the failure of UN inspectors to produce evidence indicating the existence of any significant weapons or weapons programs and the at times farcical quality of the US and UK "evidence" purporting to prove the existence of such weapons, suggests that they needed to garner authorization on the basis of WMD because it was the only possible grounds for action that might be accepted by the UNSC.

The failure of any member of the Security Council to take the debate beyond the immediate issue of disarmament and hold the US to account concerning its intentions towards the Iraqi regime in power is remarkable. The Security Council had previously authorized regime change in the cases of Haiti and Sierra Leone, but given the strategic interests of other states in Iraq, the same could not be done in this case.[72] It is unlikely that had the United States received authorization from the UNSC for the use of force to disarm Iraq, Saddam Hussein would have been left in power. Given the explicit goal of regime change repeatedly stressed by the Bush administration, it is difficult to see that any UN-authorized coalition invasion would have left Saddam Hussein in power. However, this outcome was never publicly debated in a comprehensive manner as a possible eventuality of UN authorized Anglo-American action.

Protecting the Primacy of the Security Council

Perhaps one of clearest goals of members of many Security Council members and the UN membership in general that guided the debate on Iraq was the desire to ensure that the Iraqi crisis was dealt with through the mechanism of the United Nations and that any decisions in regard to Iraq, whether authorizing force or not, were taken by the Security Council. A danger, recognized and commented on many times during the debate, was that if the UN were sidelined, its credibility would be undermined. Many of the Security Council members therefore sought to ensure the UNSC's role in the crisis not only in specific reference to Iraq, but also in order to re-affirm the primary role of the Security Council in matters concerning international peace and security for any future crises as well.

It was an issue that was raised soon after Bush's September 2002 challenge to the UN to deal with Iraq and continued to permeate the debate with the UNSC until March 2003. Indeed, the UNSC members repeatedly stressed the need for the Iraqi crisis to be resolved in the forum of the Security Council in order to maintain its international authority. Ironically, it was this same threat to the credibility and relevance of the UN Security Council that was raised by the United States and Britain as a rationale why the Council members should have supported the use of

---

[72] See Adam Roberts' discussion of the UNSC adapting to new circumstances, including the authorisation of regime change in Adam Roberts "Intervention Without End?" *The World Today*, 22 December, 2002.

Back to Iraq 203

force against Iraq.[73] At the heart of this debate lay a fundamental disagreement as to the consequences of any UN-authorized use of force against the Iraqi regime.

Reigning in the United States

The Iraqi case was the first evidence that the United States was willing to act more aggressively in response to the terror threat that it faced following 11 September, 2001. Evidenced by Bush's 2002 State of the Union Address, identifying Iraq, Iran and North Korea as a new "axis of evil" and the release of the Bush doctrine in September 2002, many states became wary that a super-power with the ability and freedom to act unhindered in its fight against terrorism would create a much more unstable and unpredictable world and undermine the existing international order. By ensuring that the debate on Iraq occurred with the forum of the Security Council, other states attempted to contain and restrict the options available to the United States using a framework of international law centered on the UN Charter. In this way Iraq reflects a peculiar situation in which it, as a UN member state, was being protected by the provisions of the UN Charter, based on international law while simultaneously this same legal framework was being used by other UN member states in order to constrain the actions of the world's most powerful state.[74] The United States was simply unwilling to take unilateral action without first attempting to gain support from the UNSC. Contrast the comments of Marlin Fitzwater in 1991 in the administration of George Bush senior stating America's golden rule of US-UN politics "If you don't need it, don't ask."[75] While Fitzwater was referring to the decision of the US and Britain not to seek explicit Security Council authorization for the humanitarian intervention into northern Iraq beyond a malleable interpretation of resolution 688, this behavior contrasts markedly with US behavior in 2002. In the latter case, the Americans preferred to put the issue before the United Nations, suggesting that even as the lone super power the United States would prefer to work in conjunction with its fellow UNSC members, just as they would similarly prefer.

The manner in which the members of the Security Council dealt with the Iraqi crisis served to emphasize the degree to which the same motivations, concerns and interests governed the attitudes and positions of the Council members as they sought to disarm the Iraqi state as had concerned them in the immediate aftermath of the Cold War. In spite of a more bellicose United States, the debate centered around concerns of respecting state sovereignty, protecting the international legitimacy of the United Nations and its Security Council and behind the scenes the P-5 members of the Council were engaged in bi-lateral negotiations designed to mitigate the affects of any conflict on their economic and political

---

[73] This fear of irrelevance has been used before to pressure UNSC members to authorise the use of force. See Roberts, "Intervention Without End," p. 12.

[74] For a discussion of the UNSC being used as a mechanism to balance against US power see Michael J. Glennon, "Why the Security Council Failed," *Foreign Affairs*, May/June 2003.

[75] See Chapter 2.

interests. There was an overwhelming preference for consensual diplomatic methods to be used to resolve the dispute, rather than relying on the use force. In this way, the Iraqi case of 2002-2003 was no different from the cases examined from the early 1990s. The same motivations and factors were behind the decisions and actions of the Security Council members, with most members seeking to reaffirm the existing international order by continuing to emphasize its key constituent elements and norms such as state sovereignty and non-intervention. The major new development demonstrated by the Iraqi crisis was the use of the United Nations forum and the Security Council in particular by the members of the P-5 to reign in the United States and attempt to keep the US operating in a multilateral context. While these efforts eventually failed, they did serve to demonstrate the continuing utility of the UNSC in this regard as it allowed the other Great Powers to work cooperatively in order to circumscribe the actions of the United States.

Chapter 8

Beyond Consent and Sovereignty?

The post-Cold War period was met with a dramatic increase in the number of UN peacekeeping operations deployed around the world.[1] The apparent willingness of the UNSC to authorize the use of force in these operations led some analysts to suggest that the Council was increasingly willing to override the restrictions imposed by Article 2(7) in order to resolve the conflicts and mitigate their humanitarian consequences. Such suggestions, if accurate, would have reflected an increased humanitarian motivation in international politics with potentially significant, long-term implications for the sovereign rights of states. Other commentators, however, took a more conservative view of the UNSC's actions.[2] What was commonly accepted amongst analysts of peacekeeping operations was that the challenges of post-Cold War conflicts had tested peacekeeping techniques and principles as never before. The wisdom of the increasing reliance by the UNSC on enforcement measures, at the expense of alternative methods based on consent, came to be a dominant feature in the debate on peacekeeping doctrine.

By examining the degree to which peacekeeping operations mandated by the Security Council adhered to the principle of consent or instead resorted to the use of coercion, this book had three main objectives. First, it was intended to examine the problems faced by consent-based peacekeeping techniques in the early 1990s and investigate the degree to which members of the Security Council relied on the use of force to overcome them. Second, it aimed to understand the implications of these Security Council decisions for the principle of non-intervention, the importance of state sovereignty in international politics, and the strength of the humanitarian imperative within international politics. Third, it sought to determine whether or not an understanding of the motivations of the UNSC members in the early 1990s assists in understanding the more recent decisions of the Security Council leading up to the second Gulf War. Were the same motivations evident in Iraq in 2002-2003 in regard to the use for force, non-intervention and sovereignty?

---

[1] From May 1988 until October 1993, twenty new peacekeeping operations were set up as compared with a total of seventeen from 1946 until 1988. See Roberts, "The Crisis in UN peacekeeping," p. 299.
[2] As noted in Chapter 1.

Consent or Coercion?

In order to address the myriad challenges posed by the numerous intra-state conflicts that sprang up in the wake of the super power rivalry, the international community chose to use the UN as the preferred tool of conflict resolution. Yet traditional UN peacekeeping methods were found wanting. Instead, the members of the Security Council occasionally agreed to arrogate to themselves the authority to use any means necessary to find solutions to these challenges. However, the scope and scale of these challenges were so vast that UNSC scrambled to cope. The channels of safe navigation through the waters of intra-state conflict, ethnic cleansing, displaced persons and regional war, were uncharted. In giving themselves Chapter VII authority, the Council members were in effect doing two things; demonstrating to the conflicting parties involved and the broader international community that the Council was "serious" in addressing the conflicts, and also giving themselves the broadest possible arsenal of tools, including the use of force, with which to address the conflicts as necessary.

The record of the immediate post-Cold War demonstrates that there was a substantial reluctance on the part of the Security Council members to move beyond the consensual basis of traditional peacekeeping methods towards using more coercive methods. The ultimate choice of consensual or coercive methods stemmed from both the attitude of the international community attitude towards the use of force by UN-mandated forces as well as the vagaries of each conflict. Both factors led to an emphasis on consent that was clearly reflected in the strategic considerations governing the deployment of UN mandated peacekeeping operations. Even in cases where the Council members chose to invoke their Chapter VII authority, the main emphasis that emerges from a detailed examination of recent UNSC actions is that they did so reluctantly, preferring the continued centrality of consent to peacekeeping initiatives. In practice, although there were instances of force being used in the context of peacekeeping operations such incidents proved to be rare.[3]

Problems with Consent

The challenges of post-Cold War conflicts exposed a number of problems with consent-based peacekeeping. In many conflicts, the plethora of belligerent parties meant that it was extremely difficult for a peacekeeping operation to acquire a consistent and dependable consensual basis on which to fulfil its mandate. In Bosnia, for example, UNPROFOR often encountered situations in which consent given at the operational level did not materialise at the tactical level. In other instances, operational or tactical level consent given on one day could be revoked without warning on the next. Such uncertainties made it extremely difficult for consent-based peacekeeping operations to implement their mandates effectively.

---

[3] Examples include the clash between UNOSOM II troops and Somali clansmen or NATO air strikes against Bosnian Serb positions.

Beyond Consent and Sovereignty?

The application of a traditional peacekeeping approach to the conflict was precluded by the internal nature of the conflict and the expansive mandate, which was given to UNPROFOR by the Security Council. The protection of humanitarian convoys and "safe areas" in particular were tasks that left UNPROFOR widely dispersed throughout the country and reliant on the consent and co-operation of the numerous belligerent local parties in spite of official Chapter VII authority to fulfill elements of the mandate.

Adhering to consent also significantly affected the type of role the UN was able to play in a particular situation. In northern Iraq, for example, the Council members initially appeared willing to act to protect the rights of the Kurdish people at the expense of the sovereign rights of Iraq by linking the refugee flows emanating from Iraq with a threat to international peace and security in resolution 688. However, a closer examination of this resolution, and the UNSC's subsequent decisions, demonstrate that the sovereign rights of Iraq remained a significant restraint on UN action. The Council members could not agree to authorize *Operation Provide Comfort* under Chapter VII. Despite efforts of members of the western coalition to justify their multi-lateral intervention under the terms of resolution 688, there is significant evidence to suggest the resolution did not give sufficient legal authority to undertake such action. Consequently, because of the unwillingness of the Security Council members to clearly characterize the situation as a threat to international peace and security under Article 42, they were forced to cope with the humanitarian crisis through co-operative measures undertaken with the agreement of the government of Iraq. Saddrudin's attempts to obtain Iraqi agreement to the deployment of a UN peacekeeping mission to protect Kurdish refugees and provide them with relief aid were rejected. In its place the UN was only able to deploy a significantly less robust UN Guards contingent. When the Iraqi government refused to permit the deployment of a UN force, it forced a dramatic revision of a proposed peacekeeping operation in the face of severe humanitarian need. However, the UNSC members did not resort to Chapter VII to address the situation, but instead sought to work with the Iraqi authorities.

In other cases too, proposed peacekeeping deployments were significantly shaped by the absence of local consent. In Somalia the proposed deployment of UNOSOM I was significantly delayed and circumscribed by the demands of Aidid. Regardless of whether or not the local power brokers represented a national governing body or not, there was a reluctance on the part of the Security Council members to act without their cooperation despite the obvious shortcomings of UNOSOM I. Likewise in Haiti the vulnerability of consent-based peacekeeping operations was again demonstrated with the failed deployment of UNMIH in the face of orchestrated domestic opposition. Sensitivity within the United States to the prospect of further casualties in the wake of Somalia meant that the main troop contributor to UNMIH was unwilling to deploy in conditions other than those of near unanimous local consent and co-operation. In Haiti, the Council members were initially more patient and willing to bear with low intensity efforts based on consent and cooperation, rather than force, to bring about the restoration of Aristide. From October, 1993 until July, 1994 the UNSC members attempted to

208   *Understanding the UN Security Council*

pressure the *de facto* government to agree to a peaceful transfer of power. Eventually, this political pressure was augmented by sanctions and the imposition of a naval blockade around the country. The invocation of Chapter VII to authorize these measures troubled members of the Council however, and Aristide's consent was necessary before the proposed resolutions could be passed. This same hesitation also meant that, during this time, there was little consideration given within the UNSC to the use of force to restore Aristide. The absence of sufficient political will combined with the haunting spectre of Somalia ensured that consent was a primary requirement of the UN's initial involvement in Haiti.

From Challenge to Change

In the face of the shortcomings of a consent-based approach to peacekeeping in the post-Cold War world, the UNSC adopted a variety of measures according to the nature of each situation. In some cases, like Iraq in 1991, there were limits to the Council invoking the Chapter VII provisions. The UN had demonstrated during the Gulf War that its collective enforcement mechanisms could effectively respond to a threat to international peace and security posed by a classic case of inter-state aggression. However, the Kurdish crisis presented the members of the UN Security Council with a more complex issue to resolve since it lay at the boundary between international jurisdiction and the rights of the Iraqi sovereign state. In this situation, the international community was prepared to work with the Iraqi government, bolstered by the provisions of the Gulf War ceasefire, which included air protection in the northern no-fly zone.

By contrast, the outbreak of famine in Somalia presented an early post-Cold War test of the degree to which the ineffectiveness of traditional peacekeeping methods would be tolerated by the UNSC in the face of a clear humanitarian imperative. Indeed, it caused a robust response by the international community. When faced with a lack of consent from the SNA in Mogadishu which paralysed UNOSOM I, the members of the UNSC were willing to overcome the operation's reliance on local consent by using Chapter VII to authorize the deployment of UNITAF. This authorization to use "all necessary means" to overcome the problems of consent and implement the UNITAF mandate had been a precondition of US participation in the coalition. Four months later, buoyed by post-Cold War optimism about the potential role of the UN in international security and the need to assist the collapsed Somalia state, the members of the Council were willing to extend this Chapter VII authorization to UNOSOM II due to the complexity of the mandate and the perceived risk to UN personnel.[4]

The predominant nature of the UNSC's response to the Rwandan genocide was significantly moulded by the UN experience in Somalia. Although the foundation of the Arusha Peace Agreement appeared fragile, the UNSC nevertheless decided to deploy a consent-based peacekeeping operation to oversee

---

[4] See the UNSC debate prior to the adoption of resolution 814 as noted in Chapter 3.

its implementation. In spite of its shortcomings, only lacklustre attempts were made to bolster the operations strength or increase political pressure on the parties involved. The short sightedness of these decisions turned fatal following the assassination of Habyarimana and the collapse of the Rwandan government. Extreme elements of the armed forces revoked their consent to the presence of UN peacekeepers and directly attacked UN personnel. Faced with this hostility and still reeling from the UN deaths in Somalia, the members of the Council decided to reduce UNAMIR down to a skeletal force, appearing to hide from the crisis rather than confront it. This was in spite of the fact that Rwanda was experiencing a severe humanitarian crisis, and instead required the rapid reinforcement of UNAMIR.

Even as the nature of the conflict and the scale of the killings became clear, the Council members still remained reluctant to get involved. The absence of political will among any of the Security Council members to counter the genocide became evident as the UN Secretariat had difficulty in finding adequate resources for a reinforced UNAMIR II operation. France alone had sufficient means and interest to make UNAMIR II a viable mission, but its participation was prevented by RPF objections. Indeed, French motives behind this offer were questionable given its support for the Habyarimana regime.

In Bosnia, the Security neither confronted the situation nor shied from it, but rather seemed to muddle through. The failure of a more consent-based approach to limit the territorial expansion of Bosnian-Serb forces and prevent ethnic cleansing led the Council to authorize the use of air power, under Article 42 of the Charter, to defend the "safe areas" and protect UNPROFOR troops. Yet while the Security Council had gone beyond consent with resolution 836, it was largely political posturing at the behest of the United States. The authority given to UNPROFOR and NATO to use force was rarely implemented on the ground. Nevertheless, this combined reliance of UNPROFOR on consent and coercion effectively made it a "middle ground" peacekeeping operation.

This variable basis of operation resulted in a strategic approach that often appeared muddled. For example, when NATO air strikes were launched, the UN Secretariat went to great lengths to stress that they did not change the consensual nature of UNPROFOR since air power was only used to defend peacekeeping personnel. Although a consent-based approach had proved vulnerable to obstruction by the host parties, the consequences of using air power also proved significant. The taking of UN hostages, for example, prompted UNPROFOR to re-emphasise the consensual basis of the operation.

The Problems With Force

Limited moves beyond consent towards the threat and use of force as a conflict resolution mechanism seemed to create more problems that they solved. In Somalia, just as UNOSOM I's adherence to consent had left it paralysed, the move beyond consent in UNOSOM II was to demonstrate significant shortcomings when combined with an expansive mandate for which there was inadequate support among the host parties. Despite its Chapter VII authorization, UNOSOM II experienced significant losses of personnel following the outbreak of hostilities between UN forces and the SNA. In response, the UNSC members decided to return UNOSOM II to a firmly consensual basis, despite the fact this left it largely ineffective. Many UNSC members subsequently questioned the use of coercive methods in the face of local resistance to UN initiatives. Ultimately, Somalia proved to be the nadir of post-Cold War peacekeeping operations. Consent based peacekeeping in an intra-state conflict had failed as had the attempt to allow UNOSOM II to use coercion to implement its mandate. In turn, the UN's failure in Somalia was to have severe repercussions on subsequent peacekeeping initiatives.

In northern Iraq, the UNSC had chosen to work with the Iraqi government, with reasonable success. In Somalia, the choice to use force lead to severe problems after which there was a re-emphasis on conducting peacekeeping operations on the basis of consent. Subsequently, the use of force became authorized only in circumstances where there was sufficient pressure from key members of the P-5 to resolve a situation. Such pressure in turn emanated from situations where calculations of national interest dictated something be done to address the situation by way of the United Nations.

In the case of Haiti, it was only after the issue of Haitian refugees became of pressing domestic political concern to the Clinton administration, and Aristide's restoration to power became a political objective of the US, that more emphasis was placed on securing his return to Port-au-Prince through any means necessary. This renewed US pressure led to the adoption of resolution 940 but there had been significant opposition, particularly among Latin American states, to the invocation of Article 42 in it. Their concerns about a US-led intervention in the Caribbean basin were only overcome by an express request from Aristide for action by the international community. This request had been solicited by supporters of the resolution and had only been reluctantly given by the exiled leader. Political machinations among three of the UNSC's permanent members - the US, France and Russia - also facilitated the resolution's adoption. These three states had reached an informal agreement on the use of Chapter VII in their respective areas of interest.

This fragile combination of support and reluctant acquiescence to the terms of resolution 940 ultimately made its adoption possible, but this also demonstrates the political fragility which lay behind the decision to use coercion to restore Aristide to power. Concerned by the possible consequences of actually using force, the US unsurprisingly placed severe pressure on the *de factos* in order to get them to consent to the MNF deployment, culminating in the dramatic despatch of the last minute Carter/Powell/Nunn mission to negotiate the peaceful transition of power. This threat of force, like that used in UNITAF, demonstrates that the members of the Council, particularly the United States were treating host consent as a malleable factor that could be achieved through the threat of force once the UN Security Council had authorized its use.

In a similar manner, the genocide in Rwanda was belatedly addressed once a member of the P-5 was willing to take the lead, followed meekly by its discredited fellow Security Council members. Following the abject failure of the UN to deploy UNAMIR II with sufficient rapidity to protect Rwandan civilians, pressure within the Security Council, primarily from non-permanent members such as New Zealand, pushed the UNSC to take action. Consequently, the UNSC members reluctantly decided to provide the French with Chapter VII authorization for *Opération Turquoise*, despite reservations as to French motives. Though this action was taken under Article 42, and thus can be said to have shifted beyond consent, it was a shift that occurred reluctantly, after much prevarication on the part of Council members concerned that France might abuse the power vested in it by the UNSC. This reluctance was expressed in the debate on resolution 929 and the narrowness with which it was eventually passed. There is also evidence to suggest that the use of Chapter VII in Rwanda to authorize *Opération Turquoise* was part of the reciprocal agreement on the use of Chapter VII reached in the Haitian case between the US, France and Russia. This suggests that the Council's use of Chapter VII in Rwanda was primarily a function of French military requirements to ensure the security of its force, and belated action by the rest of the UNSC to protect Rwandan civilians. Overall, the case of Rwanda serves to indicate that the UNSC will go beyond consent only in specific, extenuating circumstances. It also suggests that such action is more likely to occur in response to conflicts in which permanent members of the UNSC have an interest rather than situations of exceptional humanitarian need.

In Bosnia, eventual determination to resolve the conflict, including the more robust use of coercion by UN forces, only came about as a result of predominantly political considerations. It was only after two years of vulnerability and limited effectiveness that the situation in Bosnia deteriorated to such an extent that the members of the UNSC were prompted to take the necessary steps to reinforce UNPROFOR. In the summer of 1995, the "middle ground" approach was clearly rejected in preference for a more coercive international response to Bosnian Serb intransigence.[5] It was a change in policy brought on by the continuing humanitarian impact of the conflict and well as the deteriorating credibility of the international community. Thus the deployment of the RRF and the withdrawal of vulnerable outlying UNPROFOR units, combined with the change in the balance of power between Bosnian Serb, government and Croatian forces, created conditions in which air power could be applied effectively. This helped to force the Bosnian Serbs to the negotiating table and end the conflict. Like the cases of Haiti and Rwanda, the move towards coercion and away from consent was taken reluctantly, despite the humanitarian consequences of the conflict, and only once the political interests of key members of the Security Council were placed in jeopardy.

---

[5] Every British official involved in Bosnia interviewed by the author agreed that a qualitative shift occurred over the summer of 1995 in terms of the international community's policy towards Bosnia from consent towards enforcement.

212 *Understanding the UN Security Council*

The Continuing Advantages of Consent

In combination, the underlying preference for peacekeeping operations to be deployed on a consensual and cooperative basis and the tragic lessons learned from the use of force in the UNOSOM II operations left members of the Security Council in a situation where subsequent operations after Somalia went beyond consent only in very specific and limited circumstances. The main alternative to consent-based peacekeeping became a Chapter VII authorized, member state led coalition intervention. This was demonstrated in both Haiti and Rwanda. The Article 42 authorization for both *Operation Uphold Democracy* and *Opération Turquoise* came only after intense debate in the Council, and the perceived lack of alternative options to resolve the situations. In each case, the decision to use Article 42 was a function of the requirements of the states leading the interventions and not general support for such measures within the Council.[6] This preferred emphasis for consent was also highlighted in UNPROFOR where, despite the broad authorization for the use of coercion in resolution 836, in practice the sharp differences on policy among the members of the Security Council prevented this authorization from being robustly implemented in practice until the summer of 1995.

It is important to recognise why consent remained a central principle of post-Cold War peacekeeping despite its demonstrated limitations in intra-state conflicts. Following the peacekeeping casualties suffered by UNOSOM II, this issue of risk limitation became of even greater importance for troop contributors, dramatically affecting subsequent UN operations. In effect, host party consent to a peacekeeping operation remains a risk-minimising factor which states consider carefully before deciding whether or not to contribute personnel to a particular peacekeeping mission.[7] When such consent is withdrawn or the UNSC acts to move an operation beyond the basis of consent, troop contributors can decide to reconsider the presence of their contingent in that operation. As demonstrated by the cases of UNOSOM II, UNAMIR I and UNMIH such concerns frequently mean the complete withdrawal of individual national contingents from a UN operation, or cause the operation to dramatically circumscribe its activities.[8]

When deployment risks are not offset by host consent, the primary alternatives are either no deployment or the authority to use force under Article 42 in order to implement a UNSC mandate. This is evidenced by the Chapter VII authorizations of *Opération Turquoise*, *Operation Uphold Democracy*, UNITAF and UNOSOM II. In each of these cases the stability of host party consent was

---

[6] Another consideration that may have led to a preference for Chapter VII authorised operation within the UNSC and particularly on the part of the US, is the fact that UN-authorised, member state led MNF's are assessed out of voluntary contributions and not the regular UN budget. Michel Duval, interview with author, 17 December, 1999.

[7] The problems of the early 1990s peacekeeping operations have served to diminish troop contributors' confidence in consent as the main guarantee of the security of their troops. Ian Johnstone, interview with author, 17 June, 1999.

[8] Dmitry Titov, interview with author, 22 July, 1998.

Beyond Consent and Sovereignty? 213

poor. UN member states were more willing to contribute troops to the operations because they had to authority to use force to both implement the mission mandate and, more importantly, protect their personnel, consequently offsetting some of the risk created by the lack of reliable host party consent. In theory, this appeared to provide the United Nations with the possibility of a dynamic response option, when a consent-based peacekeeping option is unsuited to a particular conflict.[9] However, even when provided with robust terms of self-defence or Chapter VII authorization to use force, issues of troop security mean that troop contributors remain reluctant to use force. In Bosnia, the general vulnerability of UNPROFOR troops limited the degree to which an expanded concept of self-defence could be implemented beyond the tactical level. In Haiti the US went to great lengths to secure the agreement of the *de factos* to the deployment of US forces and in Rwanda France was careful to remain within its circumscribed area of operation in order to avoid clashes with the RPF.[10]

What is most evident from the cases examined in this study is the continuing advantage provided by the principle of consent to peacekeeping initiatives in the face of a lack of commitment on the part of the P-5 towards conflict resolution. First, the principle of consent can served to facilitate UN involvement in a conflict and allow the organisation to work towards its resolution. For example, the principle of consent allowed the deployment of UN Guards into northern Iraq to replace the coalition troops. This minimised the possibility of further hostilities between coalition forces and the government of Iraq, and simultaneously allowed the UN to provide assistance to the Kurdish refugees. Similarly in Bosnia, consent-based peacekeeping facilitated the delivery of humanitarian supplies throughout the country, albeit on a limited scale. A more belligerent posture by UNPROFOR without additional resources would have likely been counter productive and brought the operation's humanitarian activities to a halt, most likely leading to many more civilian casualties. Based on this evidence, adherence to consent still offers UN peacekeeping operations significant advantages and, in the absence of P-5 commitment to deploying a peace enforcement operation, still represents an effective collective response to conflict situations. The likelihood of a consent-based operation's success is enhanced if the limitations of such an approach are recognised and applied only to appropriate situations in which the consensual basis is judged to be stable in the long term.

---

[9] The development of such a peace enforcement option with Chapter VII authorisation goes some way to resolving the criticism placed on early 1990s UN peacekeeping initiatives by analysts such as Betts, Asada and Stedman who argued that the UN should either do traditional peacekeeping operations or collective enforcement operations under Chapter VII of the UN Charter. See Chapter 1.

[10] This wariness about using force in the context of a peacekeeping operation , so as to not take it beyond consent at the strategic level is a constant theme throughout Michael Rose's account of his command in Bosnia. See Rose, *Fighting For Peace.*

Humanitarianism versus Sovereign Rights

Ironically, in a post-Cold War era characterized by international political rhetoric about the need to protect human rights and a plethora of Chapter VII resolutions adopted by the Security Council, it is clear that concerns among UNSC members about non-intervention and risk outweighed those about humanitarian need. These concerns, when combined with the fact that many of the conflicts involved sovereign states in turmoil, suggest that rather than detracting from the relevance of sovereign status in the international system, the actions of the UNSC were instead often directed towards its reinforcement.

This conclusion is demonstrated by two factors. First, in many of the cases considered in this study, it is evident that members of the Security Council were willing to consider issues such as refugee flows, or gross abuses of human rights as threats to international peace and security, thus enabling the use of Chapter VII enforcement measures to address them. This link between violations of human rights and credible threats to international peace and security is vital in order for the UNSC members to arrogate to themselves the authority to deal with each individual case.[11] Such decisions have consequently served to broaden the overall scope of Chapter VII. However, the rationale behind such decisions was often case specific, suggesting that similar decisions taken in future will also be dictated by the specific characteristics of each conflict. This is particularly the case since such actions only establish non-binding political as opposed to legal precedents.[12] Somalia represents the only case in which the move from consent to coercion was fully supported for its humanitarian objectives by the members of the Security Council at the time.

Second, it is important to recognize that in each case, the UNSC became involved in situations concerning states in turmoil, in which the exercise of internal sovereign authority was inadequate. This created problems of refugee flows impacting adjacent states, internal conflict, ethnic cleansing and famine. In seeking to resolve these issues the actions of the Security Council, although often adopted under Chapter VII of the Charter and obviating the terms of Article 2(7), can be viewed as taken in order to reaffirming and re-establish the sovereign status and stability of the state in question. Indeed, the very fragility of a sovereign state often creates the need for international involvement and simultaneously limits the negative implications such involvement ultimately has for the sovereign status of the state concerned, even if such action is taken under Chapter VII of the UN Charter.[13]

The decision of the Security Council to adopt resolution 688 and the explicit connection made between the Kurdish refugee flows and the threat to international peace and security was the first indication that members of the UNSC were willing to use Chapter VII expansively in the post-Cold War period. Indeed, a state's

---

[11] Derek Boothby, interview with author, 18 June, 1999.

[12] Louis Fréchette, interview with author, 17 December, 1999.

[13] However, Rwanda demonstrates that humanitarian crisis alone is sometimes not enough to spur the UNSC into effective action.

persecution of its citizens was an issue that had, theretofore, normally been considered within the domestic jurisdiction of that state. Yet the resolution was only narrowly adopted, its main opponents arguing that the treatment of Kurdish refugees in Iraq was solely the concern of the Iraqi government. As a result of this division within the UNSC, resolution 688 was not a clear and unambiguous statement of intent, but was instead a political compromise. While drawing attention to the threat to international peace and security, it specifically did not invoke the enforcement measures available to the Council under Article 42 due to Chinese objections. Consequently, the UNSC was not acting under the exception to Article 2(7), and therefore did not prejudice the sovereign rights of Iraq.[14] The members of the UNSC were primarily motivated by concerns about international peace and security and the threat posed to state such as Turkey and Iran as a result of the refugee flows. As such, it was not a response based solely on humanitarian concerns, but was instead directed toward stabilizing the surrounding region by halting the flow of refugees.

The members of the UNSC were similarly willing to determine that the dire humanitarian situation in Somalia constituted a threat to international peace and security, again utilising an expansive interpretation of what constituted such a threat. This determination was primarily one of necessity in order to provide the UNSC with the legal jurisdiction to act in response to the crisis and allow UNITAF recourse to the use of coercion to fulfil its mandate. The Somali crisis was in fact confined within the country's borders and had limited external consequences, highlighting the convenient use of Article 39 in order to facilitate international action. The initiative to circumvent the restrictions of Article 2(7) with regard to Somalia was not opposed in the Security Council because of the humanitarian situation and also because of the virtual collapse of the Somali government. Because there was no functioning government that could act as interlocutor between the Somali people and the UN there was no sense within the Council that its actions and use of Chapter VII were a deliberate means of overriding the sovereign wishes of the Somali state. In fact, many of the Council's members justified the use of Chapter VII as restoring the sovereign identity of Somalia by coping with the severe humanitarian situation and re-establishing viable political institutions and therefore the UNSC's initiatives in Somalia are best viewed as ultimately intended to restore Somalia as a stable and effective member of the community of sovereign states.

An expansive interpretation of Chapter VII again led the UNSC members to characterize the Haitian refugees flows to other states in the Caribbean basin as a threat to international peace and security. They accordingly acted under Chapter VII to implement the economic embargo and eventually authorized the deployment of *Operation Uphold Democracy*. However, the members of the UNSC proved reluctant to agree to the use of Chapter VII provisions in order to respond to the crisis. This reluctance stemmed from two main considerations. First, not all UNSC members agreed that the situation was a threat to international peace and

---

[14] Chapter VII, Article 40, UN Charter.

security. Second, some were worried by the prospect of a US-led intervention in the Caribbean basin, concerns that were only overcome once Aristide had agreed to the proposed UNSC initiatives. This serves to demonstrate that even in the wake of northern Iraq and Somalia, members of the Security Council were uncomfortable with a continued broad interpretation of the Council's jurisdiction and the consequent narrowing of Article 2(7).

The underlying motives behind the UNSC engagement in Haiti are more difficult to interpret. Countries such as Brazil, Canada and Venezuela wanted to restore a democratically elected government. This would suggest that the UNSC's characterization of the situation as a threat to international peace and security was one of necessity in order to permit its reestablishment. However, such a conclusion is tempered by the fact that the actual restoration of Aristide only came about following the US decision to become more fully engaged on the Haitian issue. This renewed US proactivity had been sparked by the fact that the issue of Haitian refugees had become a political liability for the Clinton administration. Additionally, there is substantial evidence to indicate that US motivations were not a function of Aristide's democratic credentials. Instead, American efforts appeared to be directed towards the establishment of a Haitian government that would be able to stop to outflow of Haitian refugees to US shores. Consequently, UNSC agreement to adopt resolution 940 was only possible because of the linkage between the two issues.

In terms of sovereignty, it is clear is that the *de facto* government was not considered a legitimate member of international society. The willingness of the international community to continue to tolerate the *de factos* hold on power declined significantly following their failure to implement the GIA and halt the outflow of refugees. In its place, the members of the Council restored the elected Haitian government under Aristide, expecting that it would be more able to halt the flow of refugees from Haitian shores. As such, the UNSC's actions and particularly those of the United States, can be viewed promoting a very traditional conception of a "sovereign" power - one that is able to effectively exercise both internal and external sovereignty.

In Rwanda, the genocide and consequent refugee flows had clear implications for regional stability and therefore the conflict constituted a clear threat to international peace and security. When Chapter VII was initially invoked by the Security Council in resolution 918 in order to establish the arms embargo, the members of the UNSC agreed to characterize the situation as such. Like the cases of northern Iraq and Haiti before it, the destabilizing threat of refugees flows from Rwanda was accepted as falling under the jurisdiction of the UNSC.

The motive behind the use of Chapter VII was initially to allow the imposition of the arms embargo in resolution 918 in order to prevent the spread of the conflict, but this motive had changed by the time *Opération Turquoise* was authorized with resolution 925. By then, the failure to deploy UNAMIR II had become evident and the Security Council was pressured to belatedly take action to protect Rwandan civilians. In response, they chose to authorize a French intervention motivated primarily by French political considerations rather than any humanitarian imperative.

Beyond Consent and Sovereignty?

What the Rwanda case demonstrates most clearly is that the existence of a severe humanitarian crisis alone does not automatically lead to effective Chapter VII action from the UNSC to mitigate its impact or confront its causes. The Security Council's behaviour was shaped more by concerns about the potential risks of UN engagement in the wake of Somalia and a lack of political will among most of the Council members. Clearly, in Rwanda, the potential risks of the operation outweighed the humanitarian imperative.

The UNSC's use of an expansive interpretation of its Chapter VII authority to respond to the Rwandan refugee flows potentially infringed on the sovereign status of the host state by skirting Article 2(7). However, the chaos of the crisis meant that there was, temporarily, no acting government and instead the Council's actions can be more accurately viewed as attempts to contain the situation until such time as a stable sovereign government emerged. This hypothesis is supported by the UNSC's decision to respect the RPF's request that UNAMIR II be withdrawn after the former Rwandan exiles had secured their hold on power.

The Rwandan case also demonstrates that the members of the Security Council are willing to revoke the rights and privileges normally accorded to a state government if that government is seen as responsible for outrageous human rights violations against its own people. For this reason, the objections of the interim Rwandan government to the imposition of the arms embargo were dismissed by other members of the Council who questioned its legitimacy. This effective withdrawal of representative status from the interim government also helped to ensure that there were no objections within the UNSC to the invocation of Chapter VII despite the fact that its members were deliberately becoming involved in the internal affairs of the Rwandan state.[15]

A more nuanced picture is presented by the Bosnian case where there were two primary motivations behind the UNSC's invocations of Chapter VII. First, the conflict was characterized in the Security Council as a threat to international peace and security due to the possibility of the conflict spreading to neighbouring European states. Second, the members of the Security Council did appear concerned by the humanitarian consequences of the conflict. In particular, they sought to end the practice of ethnic cleansing and preclude the flow of refugees to neighbouring states. This resulted in the adoption of resolution 770 which authorized the use of all necessary means to ensure the delivery of relief supplies as well as the creation of the safe areas under Chapter VII in resolutions 819 and 824. While the measures implemented in practice to fulfill the UN's mandate were lacklustre, like the cases of Iraq, Rwanda and Haiti, the invocation of Chapter VII in response to humanitarian issues demonstrates that the members of the Security Council were prepared to become involved in issues that are normally considered within the domestic jurisdiction of a state.

Despite the UNSC's frequent reliance on Chapter VII measures to contend with the Bosnian conflict, such actions did not occur at the expense of Bosnian

---

[15] Concerns about the use of Chapter VII were instead brought on by concerns about the motives of the French intervention, the combination of peacekeeping with enforcement methods, and the lack of RPF consent for the intervention. See Chapter 5.

218 *Understanding the UN Security Council*

sovereignty. On certain issues such as the arms embargo, initial agreement from the host state (the FRY) was withdrawn once the federal government had been dissolved and the Bosnian government assumed sovereign status. Yet, the Bosnian government's opposition to the imposition of the arms embargo later disappeared after it became apparent that UNPROFOR would be withdrawn if the embargo was lifted. Indeed, it appears that Bosnian objections to both the arms embargo and the RRF deployment were sophisticated negotiating strategies designed to increase the involvement of the UNSC in the conflict. Other actions of the Security Council were more clearly directed towards the protection of Bosnian sovereignty in the face of aggression from Bosnian-Serb forces. Particularly in the case of resolution 836, it is evident that the members of the Council were acting to protect the rights, including those of territorial integrity and political independence, due to the Republic as a member of the United Nations. Indeed it is doubtful that Bosnia-Herzegovina as a sovereign state would have survived without the involvement of the United Nations.

Understanding Iraq

Although separated by a decade, the lessons learned from the analysis of Security Council decision making in regard to consent and coercion in the early 1990s find resonance in the politics of the Council prior to the outbreak of the second Gulf War in 2003. The same political interests, concerns and objectives can be seen to underwrite the positions taken by the UNSC members during the Council's debate on the disarmament of Iraq. The manner in which the issue of Iraq became a focus of such dramatic debates within the Security Council arose simply because the issue became of such importance to the United States, one of the P-5, that it forced consideration of the item on the UNSC's agenda. As US and British pressure on Iraq was slowly ratcheted up in the post 11 September world during the spring and summer of 2002 and the members of the Council began to consider the possible use of force against Iraq in order to disarm it, it was a pattern similar to that of the early 1990s. Where the national interests of one of the P-5 members are at stake, it greatly facilitates the UNSC's consideration of the issue and the potential use of Chapter VII authority in order to resolve it.[16] In this case the threat of Iraqi WMD programs to international peace and security had been previously established and accepted by the members of the Security Council in the wake of the first Gulf War in 1991. The provisions of those resolutions were thus resurrected by the United States in 2002 once it, for reasons of its own national interest, sought to do so. Indeed, UN efforts to disarm Iraq had persisted since 1991 but primarily through

---

[16] In the case of Iraq in 2002, the US initiated such action proactively, in pursuit of its interests. In the early 1990s similar actions on the part of the P-5 members occurred *in response to* threats to their national interests.

Beyond Consent and Sovereignty?   219

diplomatic means. After September 2001, the United States was no longer willing to tolerate their continued ineffectiveness.[17]

While US interests were sufficient to galvanize the Security Council to consider the purported threat of Iraq's WMD program, they could not produce unanimity within the Council. The other P-5 members, particularly France and Russia, did not agree with American and British assessment of the threat posed by Iraq to international peace and security in absence of concrete evidence that WMD existed. Consequently they were content to continue with a strengthened United Nations weapons inspections regime, UNMOVIC, in order to bring about the complete disarmament of Iraq. They did not agree with the United States and Britain that the Council should authorize the use of force under Chapter VII of the Charter to forcibly disarm the regime of Saddam Hussein.

Their refusal to support the US and Britain was the result of their failure to agree on the degree of threat posed by Iraqi WMD, their desire to ensure that the United States, with its explicit national policy of pre-emptive intervention and "axis of evil" target list, could not proceed to use the United Nations in order to neutralize those threats, and lastly to prevent the removal of an Iraqi regime that was of benefit to both French and Russian economic interests.[18] Like many of the cases in the early 1990s like Haiti, Rwanda and Bosnia where P-5 interests led to the use of Chapter VII to authorize the use of force, in the case of Iraq in 2003, P-5 interests prevented it.

Pre-emptive Intervention

The circumstances in which the Council's members considered the issue of Iraq had significantly changed from a decade earlier. The short-term legacy of the terrorist attacks on the United States had left that country with a unwillingness to tolerate threats to its security, whether at home or abroad. The invasion and route of the Taleban was followed by the orchestrated campaign against Iraq as the first of three states forming the "axis of evil." To meet this threat of terrorism the United States released its new national security policy, the Bush doctrine, which articulated the concept of "preemptive" strikes as a legitimate policy against perceived threats to American security and interests. In effect, preemptive intervention represented an attempt to develop a new doctrine of intervention, in

---

[17] Whether or not the threat posed by WMD programmes in Iraq was the true motivation behind US efforts to remove Saddam Hussein from power or not is not the concern of this study. What is important is that the United States, for whatever reason, sought to confront the Iraqi regime and sought to do so by way of the UNSC and it was the US's interest that caused the matter to be considered with such gravity in the Security Council.

[18] See Michael J. Glennon's discussion of Russian, France and China seeking to counter a resurgent US power in the Security Council, "Why the Security Council Failed," *Foreign Affairs*, May/June, 2003.

Understanding the UN Security Council

addition to the early 1990s attempted development of a doctrine of humanitarian intervention.[19]

It was with this preemptive doctrine that American and British policy makers sought to secure UN backing for their conflict against Iraq. While formally, they sought to find Iraq in breech of previous UN resolutions governing its disarmament, the new attitude of the United States towards risk and the means by which it sought to neutralize those risks - preemptive strikes - in effect meant that they sought to have the members of the Security Council back their new policy of pre-emptive intervention using the Council's provisions under Chapter VII.[20]

Back to the Future

Although the United States and Britain invaded Iraq without the backing of the United Nations, the same factors that led to the stalemate of the Security Council in 2003 had governed Security Council politics in the early 1990s and permitted cases of international intervention under UN auspices. Gone were the considerations of humanitarianism, issues of multi-lateral pre-emptive intervention were left unspoken, but what were at stake were national interests. And it was because the interests of the P-5 members were so diametrically opposed in Iraq that the Security Council was deadlocked.

At the broadest level, the United States and Britain were asking the other members of the Security Council to authorize direct action against Iraq under Chapter VII in an audacious circumvention of Article 2(7) of the Charter. While legal, such action would nevertheless have indicated a UNSC that was much more aggressive and willing to back the United State's doctrine of pre-emptive intervention. Ultimately, the resistance among the other members of the Security Council to such action proved too great, not only because of the paucity of evidence against Iraq but also because of the implications such a decision would have had for international peace and security. In future, as other issues are considered by the UNSC, they will arise do so as a result of the interests of one of the P-5 members of the Security Council. This may be Iran or North Korea, the two other states in the US "axis of evil," but the only way in which the use of force will be authorized by the UNSC will be if sufficient common ground is found between its members in terms of threats to their individual national interests.

When the threat to their interests or to the stability of the international order is created by a P-5 member with a specific international agenda, the most likely common ground that will emerge among the UNSC members will be promoting the primacy of the UNSC forum and limiting the use of its Chapter VII authority. A UN Security Council that can be seen to serve as an effective curb of unilateral action will be an important factor in reducing any perceived threat of America to

---

[19] See Adam Roberts, "Law and the Use of Force After Iraq," *Survival*, vol. 45, no. 2, 2003.

[20] Without the legacy resolutions concerning the disarmament of Iraq, the Anglo-American lobbying of their fellow Security Council members would have been more visible as an attempt to gain UNSC backing for the doctrine of pre-emptive intervention.

Beyond Consent and Sovereignty?   221

North Korea or Iran and consequently serve to ameliorate that threat. If either of those states come to view the UNSC as offering no protection from the United States, it is likely that they will simply increase their efforts to develop or acquire WMD in order to defend themselves against attack. The remaining UNSC members will likely therefore seek to ameliorate any perceived threat created by American actions.[21]

At its heart, the United Nations Security Council is a political body and the political interests of its constituent members are what drive it. It is a seemingly obvious conclusion but one that is all too frequently forgotten by those who have greats aspirations for the United Nations organization. In the early 1990s it was the interests of its member-states that enabled the Council to authorize the use of force and international intervention in Haiti, Bosnia, Rwanda, and Somalia. It was these same interests that could not find common ground on the issue of Iraq's WMD in 2003 and resulted in a stalemated Security Council. As we have seen, intervention by one state or group of states, into the affairs of another has been a feature of international politics since the rise of the modern nation state four centuries ago. What changes is simply its form and the reasons that are used to justify it.[22] In the early 1990s interventions were justified under the humanitarian banner and more recently under the banners of terrorism and preemption, but they were interventions nevertheless.

As new justifications for intervention emerge they will remain restricted by the more stable norms of international politics. As intra-state conflicts sprang up around the globe in the early 1990s, humanitarian crises seemed to converge with threats to international peace and security. In response, the members of the UNSC arrogated to themselves the authority to become involved in issues normally considered within the domestic jurisdiction of states. Yet there were limits to the humanitarian impulses of the international community. They were contained by the continuing hesitation among UN states to infringe on the sovereign rights of states. Additionally the difficulties of second generation peacekeeping operations made troop contributing nations wary of exposing their personnel to danger regardless of how great the humanitarian need. The consistent preference for consent-based peacekeeping operations and the reluctance to authorize the use of force demonstrates the continuing need to both minimize the risk to UN personnel and respect the sovereign rights of the host state.

A doctrine of humanitarian intervention has failed to be generally accepted or codified by the international community.[23] In the early twenty-first century, the

---

[21] As this book goes to print, it appears that the relative power of the UNSC *vis à vis* the US will increase as the post war crisis in Iraq grows in severity. See "Bush Asks For UN Help in Iraq," *The Guardian*, 4 September, 2003.

[22] See S. Neil MacFarlane, "Intervention in Contemporary World Politics," *Adelphi Paper 350*, The International Institute for Strategic Studies, August, 2002.

[23] 14 Heads of State met in the UK in July, 2003 to ratify the recommendations of the International Commission on Intervention and State Sovereignty, backing the principle of humanitarian intervention. However, they failed to do so. See "Blair's New World Order Blocked," *The Daily Telegraph*, 15 July, 2003.

United States chose to pursue a doctrine of pre-emptive intervention, but in Iraq this failed to be supported by the Security Council, again due to calculations of national interest and an unwillingness to relax international restrictions on intervention and the use of force. These same attitudes will continue to restrict the scope for international interventions authorized under Chapter VII of the Charter, irrespective of any emergent intervention rubric. During the challenging times of the post-Cold War period the members of the Security Council have repeatedly and consistently acted towards preserving a state system based on the sovereign equality of each member state and similar considerations will continue to permeate the decision making of the UN Security Council as it confronts new threats to international peace and security.

List of Interviews

Aust, Anthony. Legal Counsellor, British Foreign and Commonwealth Office; former Legal Advisor to the UK Permanent Mission to the United Nations. Interviewed 8 December, 1999 at the Foreign & Commonwealth Office, London.

Bergstrom, Runo. Lessons Learned Unit, Department of Peacekeeping Operations,UN. Interviewed 23 July, 1998, UN Headquarters, New York.

Boothby, Derek. Formerly Director, Europe Division, Department of Political Affairs, UN. Interviewed 18 June, 1999 at UN Headquarters, New York.

Coleman, Chris. Political Affairs Officer, Policy and Analysis Unit, Department of Peacekeeping Operations, UN. Interviewed 21 June, 1999 at UN Headquarters, New York.

Duval, Michel. Deputy Permanent Representative of Canada to the United Nations. Interviewed 16 December, 1999 at the Permanent Mission of Canada to the United Nations, New York.

Fréchette, Louise. Deputy Secretary-General of the United Nations; formerly Permanent Representative of Canada to the United Nations. Interviewed 17 December, 1999 at UN Headquarters, New York.

Goulding, Sir Marrack. Warden, St. Anthony's College, Oxford; formerly UN Under-Secretary-General, Department of Political Affairs. Interviewed 7 and 21 July, 1999, at St. Anthony's College, Oxford.

Hannay, Sir David. Former Permanent Representative of the United Kingdom to the United Nations. Interviewed 29 November, 1999, London.

Hirsch, John. Vice-President, International Peace Academy. Interviewed 4 August, 1998, at the International Peace Academy, New York.

Hurd, Lord Douglas. Former British Foreign Secretary. Interviewed 9 December, 1999 at offices of Hawkpoint Partners, London.

Johnstone, Ian. First Officer, Executive of the Secretary-General, UN. Interviewed 17 June, 1999 at UN Headquarters, New York.

Keating, Maria. Humanitarian Affairs Advisor, Office of the Iraq Programme, UN. Interviewed 21 June, 1999 at UN Headquarters, New York.

Lindenmayer, Elizabeth. Special Assistant to the Secretary-General, UN. Interviewed 17 June, 1999 at UN Headquarters, New York.

Liu, F.T. Formerly Special Assistant to Ralf Bunche, Special Representative of the Secretary-General in the Congo. Interviewed 16 June, 1999, New York.

Malone, David. President of the International Peace Academy; formerly Deputy Permanent Representative of Canada to the United Nations. Interviewed 17 December, 1999 at the International Peace Academy, New York.

Mengesha, Yohannes. Principal Officer, Executive Office of the Secretary-General, UN. Interviewed 18 June, 1999, UN Headquarters, New York.

Mochida, Shigeru. Senior Political Affairs Officer, Africa I Division, Department of Political Affairs, UN. Interviewed 5 August, 1998 at UN Headquarters, New York.

Neville-Jones, Dame Pauline. Former Political Director, British Foreign and Commonwealth Office. Interviewed 1 December, 1999 at offices of Hawkpoint Partners, London.

Renninger, John. Deputy Director, Europe Division, Department of Political Affairs, UN. Interviewed 29 July, 1998 at UN Headquarters, New York.

Rifikind, Sir Malcolm. British Foreign Secretary, 1996-1997. Interviewed by telephone, 23 November, 1999.

Riza, S. Iqbal. Chef de Cabinet, Executive Office of the Secretary-General, UN. Interviewed 15 December, 1999 at UN Headquarters, New York.

Rudasingwa, Major Thougene. Chief of Staff, Office of the Rwandan President. Interviewed 23 March, 2000 in Kigali, Rwanda.

Rugangazi, Ben. Former Spokesman for the Rwandan Patriotic Front. Interviewed 21 March, 2000 in Kigali, Rwanda.

Sacirbey, Muhammed. Permanent Representative of the Republic of Bosnia-Hercegovina to the United Nations. Interviewed 14 December, 1999 at the Permanent Mission of Bosnia-Hercegovina to the United Nations, New York.

Sherry, George. UN Senior Political Advisor in Leopoldville, Congo, 1964. Interviewed 18 June, 1999 at the International Peace Academy, New York.

Titov, Dmitry. Officer-in-Charge, Africa Division, Department of Peacekeeping Operations, UN. Interviewed 22 July, 1998 at UN Headquarters, New York.

Verheul, Adriann. Political Affairs Officer, Department of Peacekeeping Operations, UN. Interviewed 22 July, 1998 at UN Headquarters, New York.

Vogt, Margaret. Director, Africa Programme, International Peace Academy. Interviewed 13 July, 1998 at the International Peace Academy, New York.

Weisbrod-Weber, Wolfgang. Senior Political Affairs Officer, Europe and Latin America Division, Department of Peacekeeping Operations, UN. Interviewed 31 July, 1998 at UN Headquarters, New York.

Zhou, Fei. First Secretary, Permanent Mission of the People's Republic of China to the United Nations. Interviewed 15 December, 1999 at the Permanent Mission of the PRC to the UN, New York.

Selected Bibliography

The following selected bibliography contains bibliographic information for all citations made in this study as well as additional sources consulted during the course of research.

Books

Abdullahi, Mohammed Dirye. *Fiasco in Somalia: US-UN Intervention*. African Institute of South Africa. 1995.

Abi-Saab, Georges. *The United Nations Operation in the Congo, 1960-1964*. Oxford University Press. London. 1978.

Adelman, Howard and Astri Suhrke. *The International Response to Conflict and Genocide: Lessons From the Rwanda Experience*. Steering Committee of the Joint Evaluation of Emergency Assistance to Rwanda. 1996.

Albrecht-Carrie, René. *The Concert of Europe*. Macmillan Press. London. 1968.

Arend, Anthony C. and Robert J. Beck. *International Law and the Use of Force: Beyond the UN Charter Paradigm*. Routledge. London. 1993.

Bailey, Sidney D. and Sam Daws. *The Procedure of the UN Security Council*. 3rd edition. Clarendon Press. Oxford. 1998.

Beitz, Charles. *Political Theory and International Relations*. Princeton University Press. Princeton. 1979.

_____. ed. *International Ethics*. Princeton University Press. Princeton. 1985.

Benton, Barbara, ed. *Soliders For Peace*. American Historical Publications. New York. 1996.

Berdal, Mats. *Whither UN Peacekeeping?* Adelphi Paper 281. International Institute for Strategic Studies. London. 1993.

Best, Geoffrey. *Humanity in Warfare*. Weidenfield and Nicolson. London. 1980.

Bodin, Jean. *On Sovereignty*. Edited by J.H. Franklin. Cambridge University Press. Cambridge. 1992.

Boutros-Ghali, Boutros. *Unvanquished*. I.B. Tauris Publishers. London. 1999.

Bowden, Mark. *Black Hawk Down*. Bantam Press. New York. 1999.

Bull, Hedley. *The Anarchical Society*. Macmillan Press Ltd. London. 1977.

_____. Intervention in World Politics. Clarendon Press. Oxford. 1984.

Burns, E.L.M. *Between Arab and Israeli*. Harrap. London. 1962.

Bush, George and Brent Scowcroft. *A World Transformed*. Vintage Books. New York. 1998.

Calvocoressi, Peter. *World Politics Since 1945*. 6th edition. Longman Group Ltd. London. 1991.

Camilleri, Joseph A. and Jim Falk. *The End of Sovereignty?* Edward Elgar Publishing Ltd. Aldershot. 1992.

226 *Understanding the UN Security Council*

Cassese, A., ed. *The Current Legal Regulation of the Use of Force.* Martinus Nijhoff Publishers. Lancaster. 1986.

————. *International Law in a Divided World.* Clarendon Press. Oxford. 1986.

Clarke, Walter and Jeffrey Herbst, eds. *Learning From Somalia: the Lessons of Armed Humanitarian Intervention.* Westview Press. Oxford. 1997.

Coulon, Jocelyn. *Soldiers of Diplomacy: The United Nations, Peacekeeping, and the New World Order.* University of Toronto Press. Toronto. 1998.

Cox, David and Albert Legault, eds. *UN Rapid Reaction Capabilities: Requirements and Prospects.* The Canadian Peacekeeping Press. Clementsport. 1995.

Crocker, Chester A. and Fen Osler Hampson, eds. *Managing Global Chaos.* United States Institute of Peace Press. Washington D.C. 1996.

Daniel, Donald C.F., Bradd C. Hayes with Chantal de Jonge Oudraat. *Coercive Inducement and the Containment of International Crises.* United States Institute of Peace Press. Washington D.C. 1999.

Dannreuther, Roland. *The Gulf Conflict: A Political and Strategic Analysis.* Adelphi Paper 264. International Institute of Strategic Studies. London. 1992.

Dayal, Rajeshwar. *Mission For Hammarskjold: The Congo Crisis.* Oxford University Press. London. 1976.

de Waal, Alex and Rakiya Omaar. *Rwanda: Death, Despair and Defiance.* African Rights. London. 1994.

Dobbie, Charles. *Wider Peacekeeping.* British Army Field Manual, 4th draft. Wiltshire.1995.

Drew, Elizabeth. *On the Edge: The Clinton Presidency.* Simon & Schuster. New York. 1994.

Drysdale, John. *Whatever Happened to Somalia?* Haan Associates, London, 1994.

Dupuy, Alex. *Haiti in the New World Order.* Westview Press. Oxford. 1997.

Durch, William J. *The Evolution of UN Peacekeeping.* St. Martin's Press. New York. 1993.

————. ed. *UN Peacekeeping, American Policy and the Uncivil Wars of the 1990s.* Macmillan Press Ltd. London. 1997.

Farer, Tom J. ed. *Beyond Sovereignty: Collectively Defending Democracy in the Americas.* The Johns Hopkins University Press. Baltimore. 1996.

Fauriol, Georges A. ed. *Haitian Frustrations.* The Centre for Strategic and International Studies. Washington D.C. 1995.

Fincham, Charles B.H. *Domestic Jurisdiction.* A.W. Sijthofff Uitgeversmaatschappig. Leiden. 1948.

Fisler Damrosch, Lori, ed. *Enforcing Restraint: Collective Intervention in Internal Conflicts.* Council on Foreign Relations Press. New York. 1993.

Gong, Gerrit W. *The Standard of 'Civilization' in International Society.* Clarendon Press. Oxford. 1984.

Goodrich, Leland, Edvard Hambro, and Anne Patricia Simons. *Charter of the United Nations: Commentary and Documents.* 3rd revised ed. Columbia University Press. New York. 1969.

Gourevitch, Philip. *We Wish To Inform You That Tomorrow We Will Be Killed With Our Families.* Picador. Oxford. 1998.

Selected Bibliography 227

Grenville, J.A.S. *Europe Reshaped 1848-1878*. The Harvester Press. Sussex. 1976.

Harrison, Selig S. and Masashi Mishihara, eds. *UN Peacekeeping: Japanese and American Perspectives*. Carnegie Endowment for International Peace. Washington D.C. 1995.

Heiberg, Marianne, ed. *Subduing Sovereignty: Sovereignty and the Right to Intervene*. Pinter Press Ltd. London. 1994.

Higgins, Rosalyn. *United Nations Peacekeeping 1946-1967*. Oxford University Press. London. 1969.

————. *UN Peacekeeping*, vol. 3. Oxford University Press. Oxford 1980.

Hinsley, F.H. *Sovereignty*. C.A. Watts & Co. Ltd. London. 1966.

Hirsch, John and Robert Oakley. *Somalia and Operation Restore Hope*. United States Institute of Peace Press. Washington D.C. 1995.

Holbrooke, Richard. *To End a War*. Random House. New York. 1998.

Jackson, Robert H. *Quasi-States: Sovereignty, International Relations, and the Third World*. Cambridge University Press. Cambridge. 1990.

————. ed. *Sovereignty at the Millennium*. Blackwell Publishers Ltd. Oxford. 1999.

James, Alan. *Sovereign Statehood*. Allen & Unwin Ltd. London. 1986.

Klinghoffer, Arthur Jay. *The International Dimension of Genocide in Rwanda*. Macmillan Press Ltd. London. 1998.

Kluyver, Mrs. C.A. *Documents on the League of Nations*. A.W. Sijthoff Uitgeversmaatschappig. Leiden. 1920.

Liu, F.T. *United Nations Peacekeeping and the Non-Use of Force*. Lynne Rienner Publishers. London. 1992.

Lyons, Gene M. and Michael Mastanduno, eds. *Beyond Westphalia? State Sovereignty and International Intervention*. The Johns Hopkins University Press. Baltimore. 1995.

Lyons, Terrence and Ahmed I. Samatar. *Somalia: State Collapse, Military Intervention and Strategies for Political Reconstruction*. The Brookings Institution. Washington D.C. 1995.

MacFarlane, S. Neil. *Intervention and Regional Security*. Adelphi Paper No. 196. International Institute of Strategic Studies. London. 1985.

————. *Intervention in Contemporary World Politics*. Adelphi Paper No. 350. The International Institute for Strategic Studies. London. 2002.

Macartney, C.A. *National States and National Minorities*. Oxford University Press. London. 1934.

Mair, L.P. *The Protection of Minorities*. Christophers. London. 1928.

Major, John. *John Major: The Autobiography*. HarperCollins Publishers. London. 1999.

Makinda, Samuel. *Seeking Peace From Chaos: Humanitarian Intervention in Somalia*. IPA Occasional Paper Series. Lynne Rienner Publishers. London. 1993.

Malone, David. *Decision-Making in the UN Security Council: The Case of Haiti, 1990-1997*. Clarendon Press. Oxford. 1998.

Maren, Michael. *The Road to Hell: The Ravaging Effects of Foreign Aid and International Charity*. The Free Press. New York. 1997.

Mayall, James, ed. *The New Interventionism, 1991-1994.* Cambridge University Press. Cambridge. 1996.

Melvern, L. R. A People Betrayed: *The Role of the West in Rwanda's Genocide.* Zed Books. London. 2000.

Moore, Keith B. *Illustrated Catalogue of UNITAF Aerial Leaflets Used in Support of Operation Restore Hope, Somalia.* Blatter Catalogue. April 1995.

Murphy, Sean D. *Humanitarian Intervention: The United Nations in an Evolving World Order.* University of Pennsylvania Press. Philadelphia. 1996.

Otunnu, Olara A. and Michael W. Doyle, eds. *Peacemaking and Peacekeeping for the New Century.* Rowman and Litttlefield Publishers, Inc. New York. 1998.

Owen, David. *Balkan Odyssey.* Victor Gollancz Publishers. London. 1995.

Pearson, Lester B. *The International Years.* Victor Gollancz Ltd. London. 1974.

Pérez De Cuellar, Javier. *Pilgrimage For Peace: A Secretary-General's Memoir.* St. Martin's Press. New York. 1997.

Prunier, Gérard. *The Rwanda Crisis: History of a Genocide.* Hurst & Company. London. 1995.

Rajan, M.S. *United Nations and Domestic Jurisdiction.* Asia Publishing House. New York. 1961.

Ramsbotham, Oliver and Tom Woodhouse. *Humanitarian Intervention in Contemporary Conflict.* Polity Press. Oxford. 1996.

Ratner, Stephen R. *The New UN Peacekeeping.* Macmillan Press Ltd. London. 1995.

Ridgeway, James, ed. *The Haiti Files: Decoding the Crisis.* Essential Books/Azul Editions. Washington. 1994.

Rikhye, Indar Jit. *The United Nations of the 1990s and International Peacekeeping Operations.* Southampton Papers in International Policy. Number 3. Southampton. 1992

Rikhye, Indar Jit, Michael Harbottle, and Bjorn Egge. *The Thin Blue Line.* Yale University Press, New Haven, 1974.

Rodley, Nigel S. ed. *To Loose the Bands of Wickedness.* Brassey's (UK) Ltd. London. 1992.

Roper, John and Masashi Nishihara. *Keeping the Peace in the Post-Cold War Era.* The Trilateral Commission. New York. 1993.

Rose, General Sir Michael. *Fighting For Peace.* Warner Books. London. 1998.

Rosner, Gabriella. *The United Nations Emergency Force.* Columbia University Press. London. 1963.

Ruhela, Satys Paul, ed. *Mohammed Farah Aidid and His Vision of Somalia.* Vikas Publishing House PVT Ltd. New Delhi. 1994.

Sahnoun, Mohammed. *Somalia: The Missed Opportunities.* United States Institute of Peace Press. Washington D.C. 1994.

Schenk, H.G. *The Aftermath of the Napoleonic Wars.* Kegan, Paul, Trench, Trubner & Co. Ltd. London. 1947.

Sharp, Jane. *Honest Broker or Prefidious Albion?* Institute for Public Policy Research. London. 1997.

Simm, Bruno, ed. *The Charter of the United Nations.* Oxford University Press. Oxford. 1994.

Selected Bibliography 229

Smith, Edwin M. and Michael G. Schechter, eds. *The United Nations in a New World Order*. The Keck Center for International and Strategic Studies. 1994.

Smith, James D. D. *Canada in Croatia: Peacekeeping and UN Reform*. Strategic and Combat Studies Institute, No. 15, 1995.

Stotzky, Irwin P. *Silencing the Guns in Haiti*. University of Chicago Press. London. 1997.

Stowell, Ellery C. *International Law: A Restatement of Principles in Conformity with Actual Practice*. Sir Issac Pitman & Sons Ltd. London. 1931.

The Blue Helmets: A Review of United Nations Peacekeeping. 2nd ed. UN Department of Public Information. New York. 1990.

_____. 3rd ed. UN Department of Pubic Information. New York. 1996.

Vincent, R.J. *Nonintervention and International Order*. Princeton University Press. Princeton. 1974.

Weiss, Thomas G., David P. Forsythe and Roger A. Coate. *The United Nations and Changing World Politics*. 2nd Edition. Westview Press. Oxford. 1997.

Weller, Marc, ed. *Iraq and Kuwait, The Hostilities and Their Aftermath*. Cambridge International Documents Series. vol. 3. Grotius Press. Cambridge. 1993.

White, N.D. *The United Nations and the Maintenance of International Peace and Security*. Manchester University Press. Manchester, 1990.

Wilkinson, Philip. *Sharpening the Weapons of Peace: The Development of a Common Military Doctrine for Peace Support Operations*. International Security Information Service. Briefing No. 68. London. 1998.

Woodhouse, Tom and Oliver Ramsbotham. *Peacekeeping: Terra Incognita: Here Be Dragons*. INCORE. Londonderry. 1996.

Woodward, Susan L. *Balkan Tragedy*. The Brookings Institution. Washington D.C. 1995.

Zartmann, I. William, ed. *Collapsed States*. Lynne Reiner Publishers. London. 1995.

Chapters in Books

Adam, Hussein M. "Somalia: A Terrible Beauty Being Born," in I. William Zartmann, ed. *Collapsed States*. Lynne Rienner Publishers. London. 1995.

Akehurst, Michael. "Humanitarian Intervention," in Hedley Bull, ed. *Intervention in World Politics*. Clarendon Press. Oxford. 1984. pp. 95-118.

Annan, Kofi. "Challenges of the New Peacekeeping," in Olara A. Otunnu and Michael W. Doyle, eds. *Peacemaking and Peacekeeping for the New Century*. Rowman and Littlefield Publishers, Inc. New York. 1998. pp. 169-187.

Asada, Masahiko. "Peacemaking, Peacekeeping, and Peace Enforcement: Conceptual and Legal Underpinnings of the U.N. Role," in Selig S. Harrison and Masashi Nishihara, eds. *UN Peacekeeping: Japanese and American Perspectives*. Carnegie Endowment for International Peace. Washington D.C. 1995. pp. 31-70.

230 *Understanding the UN Security Council*

Canham-Clyne, John. "Selling out Democracy," in James Ridgeway, ed. *The Haiti Files: Decoding the Crisis.* Essential Books/Azul Editions. Washington. 1994. pp. 108-117.

Chopra, Jarat. "The Obsolescence of Intervention under International Law," in Marianne Heiberg, ed. *Subduing Sovereignty: Sovereignty and the Right to Intervene.* Pinter Press Ltd. London. 1994. pp. 33-61.

Clark, Jeffrey. "Debacle in Somalia: Failure of the Collective Response," in Lori Fisler Damrosch, *Enforcing Restraint: Collective Intervention in Internal Conflicts.* Council on Foreign Relations Press. New York. 1993. pp. 205-239.

Clarke, Walter. "Failed Visions and Uncertain Mandates," in Walter Clarke and Jeffrey Herbst, eds. *Learning From Somalia.* Westview Press. Oxford. 1997. pp. 3-19.

————. "Somalia and the Future of Humanitarian Intervention," in Walter Clarke and Jeffrey Herbst, eds. *Learning From Somalia.* Westview Press, Oxford, 1997. pp. 239-253.

Dallmeyer, Dorinda G. "National Perspectives on International Interventions: From the Outside Looking In," in Donald C.F. Daniel and Bradd C. Hayes, eds. *Beyond Traditional Peacekeeping.* Macmillan Press Ltd. London. 1995. pp. 20-39.

Diego Arria. "Diplomacy and the Four Friends of Haiti," in Georges A. Fauriol, ed. *Haitian Frustrations.* The Centre for Strategic and International Studies. Washington D.C., 1995. pp. 90-97.

Drysdale, John. "Foreign Military Intervention in Somalia: The Root Cause of the Shift from UN Peacekeeping to Peacemaking and its Consequences," in Walter Clarke and Jeffrey Herbst, eds. *Learning From Somalia.* Westview Press. Oxford. 1997. pp. 19-134.

Economides, Spiros and Paul Taylor. "Former Yugoslavia," in James Mayall, ed. *The New Interventionism, 1991-1994.* Cambridge University Press. Cambridge. 1996.

Eknes, Age. "The United Nations and Intra-State Conflicts," in Marianne Heiberg, ed. *Subduing Sovereignty: Sovereignty and the Right to Intervene.* Pinter Press Ltd. London. 1994. pp. 96-115.

Freedman, Lawrence and David Boren. "Safe Havens for Kurds in Post-War Iraq," Nigel S. Rodley, ed. *To Loose the Bands of Wickedness.* Brassey's (UK) Ltd. London. 1992. pp. 43-91.

Howe, Jonathan T. "Relations between the United States and the UN in Somalia," in Walter Clarke and Jeffrey Herbst, eds. *Learning From Somalia.* Westview Press. Oxford, 1997. pp. 173-190.

Ives, Kim. "The Coup and US Foreign Policy," in James Ridgeway, ed. *The Haiti Files: Decoding the Crisis.* Essential Books/Azul Editions. Washington. 1994. pp. 87-103.

Johnston, Harry and Ted Dagne. "Congress and the Somali Crisis," in Walter Clarke and Jeffrey Herbst, eds. *Learning From Somalia.* Westview Press. Oxford. 1997. pp. 148-172.

Lewis, Ioan and James Mayall. "Somalia," in James Mayall, ed. *The New Interventionism, 1991-1994.* Cambridge University Press. Cambridge. 1996.

Selected Bibliography

Lowis, W. Roger. "The Era of the Mandates System and the Non-European World," in Hedley Bull and Adam Watson, eds. *The Expansion of International Society*. Clarendon Press. Oxford. 1984.

Luban, David. "Just War and Human Rights," in Charels R. Beitz, ed. *International Ethics*. Princeton University Press. Princeton. 1985.

Maingot, Athony P. "Sovereign Consent versus State-Centric Sovereignty," in Tom Farer, ed. *Beyond Sovereignty: Collectively Defending Democracy in the Americas*. Johns Hopkins University Press. Baltimore. 1996. pp. 189-379.

Osterud, Oyvind. "Sovereign Statehood and National Self-Determination," in Marianne Heiberg, ed. *Subduing Sovereignty: Sovereignty and the Right to Intervene*. Pinter Press Ltd. London. 1994. pp. 18-31.

Prunier, Gérard. "The Experience of European Armies in Operation Restore Hope." in Walter Clarke and Jeffrey Herbst, eds. *Learning From Somalia*. Westview Press. Oxford. 1997. pp. 135-147.

Roberts, Adam. "The Crisis in UN Peacekeeping," in Chester A. Crocker and Fen Osler Hampson, eds. *Managing Global Chaos*. United States Institute of Peace Press. Washington D.C. 1996. pp. 297-319.

Rodley, Nigel S. "Collective Intervention to Protect Human Rights and Civilian Populations: The Legal Framework," in Nigel S. Rodley, ed. *To Loose the Bands of Wickedness*. Brassey's (UK) Ltd. London. 1992.

Schechter, Michael G. "The United Nations in the Aftermath of Somalia: The Effects of the UN's Handling of Article 2(7) on the United Nations," in Edwin M. Smith and Michael G. Schechter, eds. *The United Nations in a New World Order*. The Keck Center for International and Strategic Studies, 1994.

Stedman, Stephen John. "UN Intervention in Civil Wars: Imperatives of Choice and Strategy," in Donald C.F. Daniel and Bradd C. Hayes, eds. *Beyond Traditional Peacekeeping*. Macmillan Press Ltd. London. 1995. pp. 40-63.

Stoessinger, John G. "The World Court Advisory Opinion," in John G. Stoessinger, ed. *Financing the United Nations System*. The Brookings Institution. Washington. D.C. 1964. pp. 140-156.

Stromseth, Jane E. "Iraq's Repression of its Civilian Population: Collective Responses and Continuing Challenges," in Lori Fisler Damrosch, *Enforcing Restraint: Collective Intervention in Internal Conflicts*. Council on Foreign Relations Press. New York. 1993. pp. 77-117.

Tharoor, Sashi. "The Changing Face of Peacekeeping," in Barbara Benton, ed. *Soldiers For Peace*. American Historical Publications. New York. 1996. pp. 209-223.

Vaccaro, J. Mathew. "The Politics of Genocide: Peacekeeping and Rwanda," in *UN Peacekeeping, American Policy and the Uncivil Wars of the 1990s*, William J. Durch, ed. Macmillan Press Ltd. London. 1997. pp. 367-408.

Verwey, Wil D. "Humanitarian Intervention," in A. Cassese, ed. *The Current Legal Regulation of the Use of Force*. Martinus Nijhoff Publishers. Lancaster. 1986.

Walzer, Michael. "The Rights of Political Communities," in Charles Beitz, ed. *International Ethics*. Princeton University Press. Princeton. 1985.

232 *Understanding the UN Security Council*

Weiss, Thomas G. "Rekindling Hope in UN Humanitarian Intervention," in Walter Clarke and Jeffrey Herbst, eds. *Learning From Somalia: the Lessons of Armed Humanitarian Intervention.* Westview Press. Oxford. 1997. pp. 207-228.

Journal Articles

Adelman, Howard. "Humanitarian Intervention: The Case of the Kurds." *International Journal of Refugee Law.* vol. 4. no. 1. 1992. pp. 4-38.

Adelman, Howard and Astri Suhrke. "Early Warning and Response: Why the International Community Failed to Prevent the Genocide." *Disasters.* vol. 20. no. 4 1995. pp. 295-304.

Ashton, Barry. "Making Peace Agreements Work: United Nations Experience in the Former Yugoslavia." *Cornell International Law Journal.* vol. 30. no. 3. 1997. pp. 769-788.

Aykan, Mahmut Bali. "Turkey's Policy in Northern Iraq, 1991-95." *Middle Eastern Studies.* vol. 32. no. 4. October, 1996. pp. 343-366.

Barkey, Henri J. "Kurdish Geopolitics." *Current History.* vol. 96, no. 606. 1997. pp. 1-5.

Barkin, J. Samuel and Bruce Cronin. "The State and the Nation: Changing Norms and the Rules of Sovereignty in International Relations." *International Organisation.* vol. 48. no. 1. 1994. pp. 107-130.

Berdal, Mats. "Fateful Encounter: The United States and UN Peacekeeping." *Survival.* vol. 36. no. 1. 1994. pp. 30-50.

————. "Lessons Not Learned: The Use of Force in 'Peace Operations' in the 1990s." *International Peacekeeping.* vol. 7. no. 4. 2000. pp. 55-74.

————. "The UN Security Council: Ineffective But Indispensable." *Survival.* vol. 45. no. 22. 2003. pp. 7-30.

Betts, Richard K. "The Delusion of Impartial Intervention." *Foreign Affairs.* vol. 73. no. 6. 1994. pp. 20-33.

Bolton, John R. "Wrong Turn in Somalia." *Foreign Affairs.* vol. 73. no. 1. 1994. pp. 56-66.

Boutros, Boutros-Ghali. "An Agenda For Peace - One Year Later." *Orbis.* vol. 37. no. 3. 1993. pp. 323-332.

Bratt, Duane. "Explaining Peacekeeping Performance: The UN in Internal Conflicts." *International Peacekeeping.* vol. 4. no. 3. 1997. pp. 45-70.

Bryden, Matthew. "Somalia: The Wages of Failure." *Current History.* April 1995. pp. 145-151.

Bunce, Valerie. "The Elusive Peace in the Former Yugoslavia." *Cornell International Law Journal.* vol. 28, no. 3. 1995. pp. 709-718.

Burkhalter, Holly J. "The Question of Genocide: The Clinton Administration and Rwanda." *World Policy Journal.* vol. 11. no. 4. 1994. pp. 44-54.

Burton, Michael L. "Legalising the Sublegal: A Proposal for Codifying a Doctrine of Unilateral Humanitarian Intervention." *The Georgetown Law Journal.* vol. 85. 1996. pp. 417-454.

Selected Bibliography

Campbell, Kenneth J. "Once Burned, Twice Cautious: Explaining the Weinberger-Powell Doctrine." *Armed Forces and Society.* vol. 24. no. 3. 1998. pp. 357-374.

Carr, Caleb. "The Consequences of Somalia." *World Policy Journal.* vol. 10. 1993. pp. 1-4.

Chopra, Jarat and Thomas G. Weiss. "Sovereignty is no Longer Sacrosanct: Codifying Humanitarian Intervention." *Ethics and International Affairs.* vol. 6. 1992.

Ciechanski, Jerzy. "Enforcement Measures Under Chapter VII of the UN Charter: UN Practice after the Cold War." *International Peacekeeping.* vol. 3. no. 4. 1996. pp. 82-104.

Clapham, Christopher. "Rwanda: The Perils of Peacemaking." *Journal of Peace Research.* vol. 35. no. 2. 1998. pp. 193-210.

Clark, Jeffrey. "Debacle in Somalia." *Foreign Affairs.* vol. 72. no. 1. 1993. pp. 109-123.

Clarke, Walter and Jeffrey Herbst. "Somalia and the Future of Humanitarian Intervention," *Foreign Affairs.* vol. 75, no. 2, 1996. pp. 70-85.

Cohen, Lenard J. "Bosnia and Herzegovina: Fragile Peace in a Segmented State." *Current History.* vol. 1995. no. 599. 1996. pp. 103-112.

Constable, Pamela. "Haiti: A Nation in Despair, A Policy Adrift." *Current History.* March 1994. pp. 108-114.

———. "A Fresh Start for Haiti?" *Current History.* February 1996. pp. 65-69.

Damrosch, Lori Fisler. "The Constitutional Responsibility of Congress For Military Engagements." *The American Journal of International Law.* vol. 89, 1995. pp. 58-70.

Dandeker, Christopher and James Gow. "The Future of Peace Support Operations: Strategic Peacekeeping and Success." *Armed Forces & Society.* vol. 23. no. 3. 1997. pp. 327-348.

Daniel, Donald C.F. and Bradd C. Hayes. "Securing Observance of UN Mandates Through the Employment of Military Force." *International Peacekeeping.* vol. 3. no. 4. 1996. pp. 105-125.

Delbruck, Jost. "A Fresh Look at Humanitarian Intervention Under the Authority of the United Nations." *Indiana Law Journal.* vol. 67. 1992. pp. 887-901.

De Wall, Alex and Rakiya Omaar. "The Genocide in Rwanda and the International Response." *Current History.* April 1995. pp. 156-161.

Dobbie, Charles. "A Concept for Post-Cold War Peacekeeping." *Survival.* vol. 36. no. 3. 1994. pp. 121-48.

Doyle, Kati. "Hollow Diplomacy in Haiti." *World Policy Journal.* vol. 11. no. 1. 1994. pp. 50-58.

Dunne, Michael. "The United States, the United Nations and Iraq." *International Affairs.* March 2003. pp. 257-77.

Ellerman, Christine. "Command of Sovereignty Gives Way to Concern For Humanity." *Vanderbilt Journal of Transnational Law.* vol. 26. 1993. pp. 341-371.

Ero, Comfort and Suzanne Long. "Humanitarian Intervention: A New Role for the United Nations?" *International Peacekeeping.* vol. 2. no. 2 1995. pp. 140-56.

Falk, Richard. "The Haiti Intervention: A Dangerous World Order Precedent for the United Nations." *Harvard International Law Journal*. vol. 38. no. 2. 1995. pp. 341-358.

Farrell, Theo. "Sliding into War: The Somalia Imbroglio and US Army Peace Operations Doctrine." *International Peacekeeping*. vol. 2. no. 2. 1995. pp. 194-214.

Fetherston, A.B., O. Ramsbotham and T. Woodhouse. "UNPROFOR: Some Observations From a Conflict Resolution Perspective." *International Peacekeeping*. vol. 1. no. 2. 1994. pp. 179-203.

Franck, Thomas M. and Nigel S. Rodley. "After Bangladesh: The Law of Humanitarian Intervention by Military Force." *The American Journal of International Law*. vol. 67. 1973. pp. 275-305.

Fuller, Graham E. "Kurdistan: Raised Hopes, Empty Promises." *Foreign Affairs*. vol. 72. no. 3. 1993. pp. 108-121.

Gagnon, Mona Harrington. "Peace Forces and the Veto: The Relevance of Consent." *International Organisation*. vol. 21. no. 4. 1967. pp. 812-836.

Galbraith, Peter W. "Washington, Erdut and Dayton: Negotiating and Implementing Peace in Croatia and Bosnia-Herzegovina." *Cornell International Law Journal*. vol. 30. 1997. pp. 643-649.

Garvey, Jack Israel. "United Nations Peacekeeping and Host State Consent." *The American Journal of International Law*. vol. 64. 1967. pp. 241-269.

Glennon, Michael J. "Sovereignty and Community After Haiti: Rethinking the Collective Use of Force." *The American Journal of International Law*. vol. 89. 1995. pp. 70-74.

_____. "Why the Security Council Failed." *Foreign Affairs*. May/June. 2003.

Glitman, Maynard. "US Policy in Bosnia: Rethinking a Flawed Approach." *Survival*. vol. 38. no. 4. 1994. pp. 66-83.

Goose, Stephen D. and Frank Smyth. "Arming Genocide in Rwanda." *Foreign Affairs*. vol. 73. no. 5. 1994. pp. 86-96.

Goulding, Marrack. "The Evolution of United Nations Peacekeeping." *International Affairs*. vol. 69. no. 3. 1993. pp. 451-464.

_____. "The Use of Force by the United Nations." *International Peacekeeping*. vol. 3. no. 1. 1996. pp. 1-18.

Gow, James. "Deconstructing Yugoslavia." *Survival*. vol. 33. no. 4. 1991. pp. 291-311.

_____. "The Use of Coercion in the Yugoslav Crisis." *The World Today*. vol. 48. no. 1. 1992. pp. 198-202.

_____. "Bosnia I: Stepping Up the Pace?" *The World Today*. vol. 51. no. 7. 1995. pp. 126-128.

_____. "For The Long Haul." *The World Today*. vol. 54. no. 5. 1998. pp.121-122.

Gow, James and Christopher Dandeker. "Peace-support Operations: The Problem of Legitimation." *The World Today*. vol. 51. no. 8. pp. 171-174.

Gros, Jean-Germain. "Towards a Taxonomy of Failed States in the New World Order: Decaying Somalia, Liberia, Rwanda and Haiti." *Third World Quarterly*. vol. 17. no. 3. 1996. pp. 455-471.

Selected Bibliography 235

_____. "Haiti's Flagging Transition." *Journal of Democracy*. vol. 8. no. 4. 1997. pp. 94-111.

Hagglund, Gustav. "Peacekeeping in a Modern War Zone." *Survival*. vol. 32. no. 3. 1990. pp. 233-240.

Hayden, William. "The Kosovo Conflict and Forced Migration: The Strategic Use of Displacement and the Obstacles to International Protection." *Journal of Humanitarian Assistance*. Http://www.jha.sps.cam.ac.uk/b/b597.htm posted on 14 February 1999. pp. 1-25.

Higgins, Rosalyn. "The New United Nations and Former Yugoslavia." *International Affairs*, vol. 69. no. 3. 1993. pp. 465-483.

Hintjens, Helen M. "Explaining the 1994 Genocide in Rwanda." *The Journal of Modern African Studies*. vol. 37. no. 2. 1999. pp. 241-286.

Hoffmann, Stanley. "In Search of a Thread: The UN in the Congo Labyrinth." *International Organisation*. vol. 16. 1962. pp. 331-363.

_____. "The Crisis of Liberal Internationalism." *Foreign Policy*. vol. 98. 1995. pp 159-177.

Holst, Johan Jorgen. "Enhancing Peacekeeping Operations." *Survival*. vol. 32. no. 3. 1990. pp. 264-275.

Hutchinson, Mark R. "Restoring Hope: UN Security Council Resolutions For Somalia and an Expanded Doctrine of Humanitarian Intervention" *Harvard International Law Journal*. vol. 34. 1993. pp. 624-640.

Jakobsen, Peter Viggo. "The Emerging Consensus on Grey Area Peace Operations Doctrine: Will It Last and Enhance Operational Effectiveness?" *International Peacekeeping*. vol. 7. no. 3. 2000. pp. 36-56.

_____. "National Interest, Humanitarianism or CNN: What Triggers UN Peace Enforcement After the Cold War?" *Journal of Peace Research*. vol. 33. no. 2. 1996. pp. 205-215.

Jones, Bruce D. "Intervention Without Borders: Humanitarian Intervention in Rwanda, 1990-1994." *Millennium*. vol. 24. no. 2. 1995. pp. 225-249.

Koh, Harold Hongju. "The Haiti Paradigm in United States Human Rights Policy." *The Yale Law Journal*. vol. 103. 1994. pp. 2391-2435.

Koshy, Ninan. "The United Nations, the US and Northern Iraq." *Economic and Political Weekly*. vol. 31. no. 4. 1996. pp. 2760-2765.

Krasner, Stephen D. "Pervasive Not Perverse: Semi-Sovereigns as the Global Norm." *Cornell International Law Journal*. vol. 30. no. 3. 1997. pp. 651-680.

Kresock, David M. "Ethnic Cleansing in the Balkans: The Legal Foundations of Foreign Intervention." *Cornell Journal of International Law*. vol. 27. 1994. pp. 203-239.

Lauterpacht, Eli. "Sovereignty-Myth or Reality?" *International Affairs*. vol. 73. no. 1. 1997. pp. 137-150.

Lefever, Ernest W. "Reigning in the UN." *Foreign Policy*. vol. 72. no. 3. 1993. pp. 17-20.

Leurdijk, Dick A. "Before and After Dayton: The UN and NATO in the Former Yugoslavia." *Third World Quarterly*. vol. 18. no. 3. 1997. pp. 457-470.

McCormick, Shawn H. "The Lessons of Intervention in Africa." *Current History*. April 1995. pp. 162-166.

McCoubrey, Hilaire. "Kosovo, NATO and International Law." *International Relations*. vol. 14. no. 5. 1999. pp. 29-46.

McHugh, Lois B. and Susan Epstein. "Kurdish Refugee Relief and Other Humanitarian Aid Issues in Iraq." *Congressional Research Service Issue Brief.* The Library of Congress. 31 May, 1991.

McMullen, Ronald K. and Augustus Richard Norton. "Somalia and Other Adventures For the 1990's." *Current History*. April 1993. pp. 169-174.

McNulty, Mel. "France's Role in Rwanda and External Military Intervention: A Double Discrediting." *International Peacekeeping*. vol. 4. no. 3. 1997. pp. 24-44.

MacInnis, John A. " Peacekeeping and International Humanitarian Law." *International Peacekeeping*. vol. 3. no. 3. 1996. pp. 92-97.

Mackinlay, John. "Powerful Peacekeepers." *Survival*. vol. 32. no. 3. 1990. pp. 241-250.

Mackinlay, John and Jarat Chopra. "Second Generation Multinational Operations." *The Washington Quarterly*. vol. 15. no. 3. 1992. pp. 113-130.

Mackinlay, John. "Improving Multifunctional Forces." *Survival*. vol. 36. no. 3. 1994. pp. 149-173.

Macleod, Alex. "French Policy Toward the War in the Former Yugoslavia: A Bid For International Leadership." *International Journal*. vol. LII. no. 2. 1997. pp. 243-264.

Maingot, Anthony P. "Haiti and Aristide: The Legacy of History." *Current History*. February, 1992. pp. 65-69.

_____. "Haiti: The Political Rot Within." *Current History*. Febuary, 1995. pp. 59-64.

Makinda, Samuel M. "Somalia: From Humanitarian Intervention to Military Offensive?" *The World Today*. October 1993. pp. 184-186.

Malesic, Marjan. "International Peacekeeping: An Object of Propaganda in Former Yugoslavia." *International Peacekeeping*. vol. 5. no. 2. 1998. pp. 82-102.

Malone, David. "Haiti and the International Community: A Case Study." *Survival*. vol. 39. no.2. 1997. pp. 126-46.

Mandelbaum, Michael. "The Reluctance to Intervene." *Foreign Policy*. no. 95. Summer, 1994. pp. 3-18.

_____. "Foreign Policy As Social Work." *Foreign Affairs*. vol. 75. no. 1. 1996. pp. 16-32.

Maren, Michael. "Somalia: Whose Failure?" *Current History*. May, 1996. pp. 201-205.

Martin, Ian. "Haiti: Mangled Multilateralism." *Foreign Policy*. no. 95. 1994. pp. 72-89.

Mayall, James. "Non-intervention, Self-determination and the 'New World Order'. *International Affairs*. vol. 67. no. 3. 1991. pp. 421-429.

Melvern, Linda. "Genocide Behind the Thin Blue Line." *Security Dialogue*, vol. 28. no. 3. 1997. pp. 333-346.

Selected Bibliography

Mermin, Jonathan. "Television News and American Intervention in Somalia: The Myth of a Media-Driven Foreign Policy." *Political Science Quarterly.* vol. 112. no. 3. 1997. pp. 385-403.

Morley, Morris and Chris McGillion. "Disobedient Generals and the Politics of Redemocratization: The Clinton Administration and Haiti." *Political Science Quarterly.* vol. 112. no. 3. 1997. pp. 363-384.

Morris, Justin. "Force and Democracy: UN/US Intervention in Haiti." *International Peacekeeping.* vol. 2. no. 3. 1995. pp. 319-412.

Murphy, Sean D. "The Security Council, Legitimacy, and the Concept of Collective Security After the Cold War." *Columbia Journal of Transnational Law.* vol. 32. no. 2. 1994. pp. 199-275.

Neville-Jones, Pauline. "Dayton, IFOR and Alliance Relations in Bosnia." *Survival.* vol. 38. no. 4. 1996. pp. 45-65.

Norton, Augustus R. and Thomas G. Weiss. "Superpowers and Peace-keepers." *Survival.* vol. 32. no. 3. 1990. pp. 212-220.

O'Connell, Mary Ellen. "Continuing Limits on UN Intervention in Civil War." *Indiana Law Journal.* vol. 67. 1992. pp. 903-913.

Osterud, Oyvind. "The Narrow Gate: Entry to the Club of Sovereign States." *Review of International Studies.* no. 23. 1997. pp. 167-184.

Patman, Robert G. "Disarming Somalia: The Contrasting Fortunes of United States and Australian Peacekeepers during United Nations Intervention, 1992-1993." *African Affairs.* vol. 96. 1997. pp. 509-533.

Peace, Kelly Kate and David P. Forsythe. "Human Rights, Humanitarian Intervention, and World Politics." *Human Rights Quarterly.* vol. 15. 1993. pp. 290-314.

Picco, Giandomenico. "The UN and the Use of Force." *Foreign Affairs.* vol. 73. no. 5. 1994. pp. 14-18.

Pugh, Michael. "Military Intervention and Humanitarian Action: Trends and Issues." *Disasters.* vol. 22. no. 4. 1998. pp. 339-351.

Ramet, Sabrina Petra. "War in the Balkans." *Foreign Affairs.* vol. 71. 1991-92. pp. 78-98.

Ramsbottham, Oliver. "Humanitarian Intervention 1990-5: A Need To Reconceptualize?" *Review of International Studies.* vol. 23. 1997. pp 445-468.

Reed, William Cyrus. "Exile, Reform, and the Rise of the Rwandan Patriotic Front." *The Journal of Modern African Studies.* vol. 34. no. 3. 1996. pp. 121-138.

Reisman, Michael W. "Sovereignty and Human Rights in Contemporary International Law." *The American Journal of International Law.* vol. 84. 1990. pp. 866-876.

Rieff, David. "The Illusions of Peacekeeping." *World Policy Journal.* vol. 11. no. 2. 1994. pp. 1-18.

Roberts, Adam. "Humanitarian War: Military Intervention and Human Rights." *International Affairs.* vol. 69. no. 3. 1993. pp. 429-449.

———. "From San Francisco to Sarajevo: The UN and the Use of Force." *Survival.* vol. 37. no. 4. 1995. pp. 7-28.

238   *Understanding the UN Security Council*

————. "Communal Conflict as a Challenge to International Organisation: The Case of Former Yugoslavia." *Review of International Studies*. vol. 21. 1995. pp. 389-410.

————. "Intervention Without End?" *The World Today*. 22 December. 2002. pp. 10-12.

————. "Law and the Use of Force After Iraq." *Survival*. vol. 45. no. 2. 2003. pp. 30-56.

Rodley, Nigel S. "Human Rights and Humanitarian Intervention: The Case Law of the World Court." *International and Comparative Law Quarterly*. vol. 38. 1989. pp.321-333.

Ruddick, Elizabeth E. "The Continuing Constraint of Sovereignty: International Law, International Protection, and the Internally Displaced." *Boston University Law Review*. vol. 77. pp. 429-482.

Ruggie, John Gerard. "Wandering in the Void." *Foreign Affairs*. vol. 72. no. 5. 1993. pp. 26-31.

————. "The UN and the Collective Use of Force: Whither or Whether?" *International Peacekeeping*. vol. 3. no. 4. 1996. pp. 1-20.

Ryan, Christopher M. "Sovereignty, Intervention, and the Law: A Tenuous Relationship of Competing Principles." *Millennium*. vol. 26. no. 1. 1997. pp. 77-100.

Salmon, Trevor C. "Testing Times for European Political Co-operation: The Gulf and Yugoslavia, 1990-1992." *International Affairs*. vol. 68. no. 2. 1992. pp. 233- 253.

Sikkink, Kathryn. "Human Rights, Principled Issue-Networks, and Sovereignty in Latin America." *International Organisation*. vol. 43. no. 3. 1993. pp. 411-441.

Slim, Hugo. "Military Humanitarianism and the New Peacekeeping: An Agenda For Peace?" *Journal of Humanitarian Assistance*. http://www-jha.sps.cam.ac.uk/a/a015.htm posted no 22 September, 1995. pp. 1-11.

Smith, Gaddis. "Haiti: From Intervention to Intervasion." *Current History*. vol. 94. no. 589. 1994. pp. 54-58.

Smith, Tony. "In Defense of Intervention." *Foreign Affairs*. vol. 73. no. 6. 1994. pp. 34-46.

Sorenson, Georg. "An Analysis of Contemporary Statehood: Consequences for Conflict and Co-operation." *Review of International Studies*. no. 23. 1997. pp. 253-269.

Stedman, Stephen John. "The New Interventionists." *Foreign Affairs*. vol. 72. no. 1. 1993. pp. 1-16.

Stevenson, Jonathan. "Hope Restored in Somalia?" *Foreign Policy*. no. 91, 1993. pp. 138-154.

Stoltenberg, Thorvald. "Introducing Peacekeeping to Europe." *International Peacekeeping*. vol. 2. no. 2. 1995. pp. 215-223.

Surke, Astri. "Facing Genocide: the Record of the Belgian Battalion in Rwanda." *Security Dialogue*. vol. 29. no. 1. 1998. pp. 37-48.

————. "Dilemmas of Protection: The Log of the Kigali Battalion." *International Peacekeeping*. vol. 5. no. 2. 1998. pp. 1-18.

Selected Bibliography

Szasz, Paul C. "Peacekeeping in Operation: A Conflict Study of Bosnia." *Cornell International Law Journal*, vol. 28. no. 3. 1995. pp. 685-699.

Talbott, Strobe. "Democracy and the National Interest." *Foreign Affairs*. vol. 75. no.6. 1996. pp. 47-62.

Thakur, Ramesh. "From Peacekeeping to Peace Enforcement: the UN Operation in Somalia." *The Journal of Modern African Studies*. vol. 32. no. 3. 1994. pp. 387-410.

Thornberry, Cedric. "Peacekeepers, Humanitarian Aid, and Civil Conflicts." *Journal of Humanitarian Assistance*. http://www-jha.sps.cam.ac.uk/a/a017.htm, posted 15 September, 1995. pp. 1-13.

Thornton, Rod. "The Role of Peace Support Operations Doctrine in the British Army." *International Peacekeeping*. vol. 7. no. 2. 2000. pp. 41-62.

Tharoor, Shashi. "United Nations Peacekeeping in Europe." *Survival*. vol. 37. no. 2. 1995. pp. 121-134.

_____. "Should UN Peacekeeping Go 'Back to Basics?'" *Survival*. vol. 37. no. 4. 1995. pp. 52-64.

Tulchin, Joseph S. "The Formulation of US Foreign Policy in the Caribbean." *The Annals of the American Academy of Political and Social Science*. no. 533. 1994. pp. 177-187.

Urquart, Brian. "Beyond the 'Sheriff's Posse." *Survival*. vol. 32. no. 3. 1990. pp. 196-205.

Varady, Tibor. "The Predicament of Peacekeeping in Bosnia." *Cornell International Law Journal*. vol. 28. no. 3. 1995. pp. 701-707.

Vulliamy, Ed. "Bosnia: The Crime of Appeasement." *International Affairs*. vol. 74. no. 1, 1998. pp. 73-92.

von Hippel, Karin. "Democratisation as Foreign Policy: The Case of Haiti." *The World Today*. January 1995. pp.11-14.

Weiss, Thomas G. "Triage: Humanitarian Interventions in a New Era." *World Policy Journal*. vol. 11. no. 1. 1994. pp. 59-68.

_____. "Military-Civilian Humanitarianism: The 'Age of Innocence' Is Over." *International Peacekeeping*. vol. 2. no. 2. 1995. pp. 157-74.

Weiss, Thomas G. and Kurt M. Campell. "Military Humanitarianism." *Survival*. vol. 33. no. 5. 1991. pp. 451-465.

Welhengama, G. "New Developments of International Law Through the Second Phase of the Gulf Crisis - An Analysis." *The Liverpool Law Review*. vol. 13. no. 1. 1991. pp. 115-137.

Wheeler, Nicholas J. "Pluralist or Solidarist Conceptions of International Society: Bull and Vincent on Humanitarian Intervention." *Millennium*. vol. 21, no. 3, 1992. pp. 461-487.

White, Nigel D. "The UN Charter and Peacekeeping Forces: Constitutional Issues." *International Peacekeeping*. vol. 3. no. 4. 1996. pp. 43-63.

Wilentz, Amy. "Love and Haiti," *New Republic*. 5 July. 1993. pp. 18-19.

Wilkinson, Philip. "Sharpening the Weapons of Peace: The Development of a Common Military Doctrine for Peace Support Operations." *International Security Information Service Briefing Paper*, No. 18. April 1998. pp. 1-10.

240 *Understanding the UN Security Council*

Zhang, Yonhjin. "China and UN Peacekeeping: From Condemnation to Participation." *International Peacekeeping.* vol. 3 no. 3. 1996. pp. 1-15.

Magazines and Newspapers

The Economist (London)
Economic and Political Weekly
The Financial Times (London)
The Guardian (London)
The Independent (London)
The International Herald Tribune (London)
Jane's Defence Weekly
Le Monde (Paris)
New Statesman & Society
The New Yorker
The New York Review of Books
The Times (London)

Unpublished Papers, Theses and Government Publications

Berdal, Mats R. *Beyond Peacekeeping: Reflections on the Evolution of International Peacekeeping After the Cold War.* Paper presented at the Japan Institute for International Affairs. Tokyo. June 1994.

Boutros Boutros-Ghali. "An Agenda for Peace: Preventative Diplomacy, Peacemaking and Peace-keeping," *UN Document,* S/24111, 17 June, 1992.

"Bush, Clinton Say US Support for UN Will Continue," Statements of President Bush and Presidential Candidate Bill Clinton to the UN Association of the USA. *United States Information Agency.* 9 October, 1992.

Clinton Administration Policy on Reforming Multilateral Peace Operations (PDD-25). Bureau of International Organisation Affairs. US Department of State. 22 February, 1996.

Comprehensive Report on Lessons-Learned From United Nations Operation in Somalia. Friedrich Ebert Stiftung. Life and Peace Institute, Norwegian Institute of International Affairs in co-operation with the Lessons Learned Unit, DPKO. December 1995.

Cook, Helena. *The Safe Havens in Northern Iraq.* Human Rights Centre. University of Sussex. 1995.

DHA Review of the United Nations Guard Contingent in Iraq (UNGCI). Iraq Programme. Department of Humanitarian Affairs. United Nations. New York. 15 August, 1997.

Dictionary of Military Terms. The United States Department of Defence. 1999.

FM 100-23: Peace Operations. Department of the Army (US). Washington D.C. 1994.

Jan, Ameen. *Peacebuilding in Somalia.* International Peace Academy Policy Briefing Series. July 1996.

Selected Bibliography 241

Liu, F.T. *Evolution of United Nations Peacekeeping Operations Over the Past Fifty Years.* Unpublished Paper. International Peace Academy. New York. 1 July 1998.

McHugh, Lois B. and Susan Epstein. "Kurdish Refugee Relief and Other Humanitarian Aid Issues in Iraq." *Congressional Research Service Issue Brief.* The Library of Congress. 31 May, 1991.

O'Connell, Christine. *France and the United Nations in Somalia.* M.Phil Thesis. University of Oxford. 1996.

Peacemaking and Peacekeeping for the Next Century. Report of the 25th Vienna Seminar. An International Peace Academy Report. New York. 1995.

Report of the Independent Inquiry into the Actions of the United Nations During the 1994 Genocide in Rwanda. United Nations. New York. 15 December, 1999.

Sens, Allen G. *Somalia and the Changing Nature of Peacekeeping.* Commission of Inquiry into the Deployment of Canadian Forces to Somalia. Ottawa. 1997.

Stapleton, Barbara. *The Shias of Iraq.* Report to the Parliamentary Human Rights Group. March, 1993.

The Responsibility to Protect. Report of the International Commission on Intervention and State Sovereignty. International Development Research Centre. Ottawa. 2001.

"The United Nations Dumbarton Oaks Proposals for a General International Organisation", *The United Nations Conference on International Organisation,* United Nations Information Organisation, London, 1945. Document No. 1 G/1.

Index

Aga Khan, Prince Sadruddin, 54
Aidid, Mohammed Farah, 65, 66, 68, 69, 70, 71, 72, 74, 82, 89, 91
air strikes, 148, 151, 154, 159
  and safe havens, 151, 152
  "dual-key" system, 176
  UNSC views on, 163, 164
Akashi,Yasushi, 160, 161
Akehurst, Michael, 15, 16
Albright, Madeleine,
  and Bosnia, 155
  and Rwanda, 130, 132, 135, 137
  and Somalia, 86, 90
Alexander I, 8
Ali Mahdi, Mohamed, 65, 66, 67, 69, 71, 74, 82
Amin, Idi, 15
An Agenda for Peace
  and Somalia, 74, 85
  Supplement to, 26
Annan, Kofi, 1, 19, 31
  and Bosnia, 177
  and Iraq, 183, 185, 186, 190
  and Rwandan genocide, 130
Aristide, Jean Bertrand, 98, 100, 101, 103, 105
  election of, 99
  position on international intervention in Haiti, 116
  return to Haiti, 120
Arteh Qhalib, Omer, 66, 69
Article 2(7), 4, 11, 12, 21, 32, 34, 35
  circumvention of, 3
Arusha Accords, 126, 127, 128, 131, 139, 145
Asada, Masahiko, 23, 24
Aust, Anthony, 51

Baker, James, 52
Barre, Siad, 65
Beitz, Charles, 18, 19
Belgian peacekeepers
  killings of, 128
Berdal, Mats, 25, 26, 30

Betts, Richard K., 23
Blix, Hans
  reports to UNSC, 192, 196
Bodin, Jean, 5
Booh-Booh, Jacques-Roger, 133
Bosnia-Herzegovina
  attitude to RRF, 172
  membership of United Nations, 150
  no-fly zones, 151
  safe areas, 156
Boutros Boutros-Ghali, 1, 20, 22, 26
  and Haiti, 104
  and redefinition of peacekeeping, 27
  and Somalia, 66, 93
  expansion of UNPROFOR, 149
  response to genocide, 130, 133
  view on air strikes in Bosnia,160
Brahimi Report, 31
Britain
  frustration with UNPROFOR, 170
  and Kurdish crisis, 40
  and Rwanda, 132
British Army
  concept of wider peacekeeping, 27
Brochard, E.M., 7
Brownlie, Ian, 7
Bush administration
  and plans for Iraq, 182, 201
Bush Doctrine, 185
Bush, George W., 2, 202
  and Iraq, 193
  challenge to UN, 185
Bush, George, 1, 57
  and Kurdish crisis, 40, 51
  and Somalia, 80

Carter, Jimmy, 119
Cédras, Raoul, 99
Chapter VII
  UNSC interpretation of, 215
China
  and Haiti, 100
  and Kurdish crisis, 43
  concerns over Somalia, 69, 78, 87, 95

Index

position on Iraq, 194
Chopra, Jarat, 31
Christian Wolff, 7
Churkin, Vitaly, 52, 165, 167
Clinton administration
and Somalia, 88
attitude towards Haiti, 103
coercive inducement, 29, 30
Concert of Europe, 7
Conference on Security and Cooperation
in Europe, 45
Connaughton, Richard, 27
Consent
advantages of, 211
blurring of, 34
definition of, 22
levels of, 31
problems with, 206

Dallaire, Roméo, 127, 128, 130
Dandeker, Christopher, 30
Dayton Agreement, 177
Dobbie, Charles, 26, 26, 27
Dulles, John Foster, 12
Dumbarton Oaks, 12, 14

Eagleburger, Lawrence, 76
ElBaradei, Muhamed
reports to UNSC, 192
ethnic cleansing
in Bosnia, 153
European Convention on Human Rights,
15
European Union (EU)
position on Iraq, 196

Farrell, Theo, 25
Fitzwater, Marlin, 47, 51, 52
Forces Armées Rwandaises (FAR), 126
France
and Haiti, 104, 105
and Iraq, 182, 186, 187, 188, 189,
190, 193, 194, 197, 198, 200, 201
and northern Iraq, 40, 41, 42
and Rwanda, 132
and Somalia, 78, 80, 81, 91
attitude to Kurdish crisis, 40
Front Révolutionnaire pour
l'Avancement et le Progrès Haitien
(FRAPH), 109

Gallagher, Robert, 70
General Assembly, 2, 13, 15, 16, 17, 24
Germany
and Somalia, 80
Gharekhan, Chinmaya, 138
Gorazde Air Attacks, 166
Goulding, Sir Marrack, 27, 29
Government of National Unity in
Rwanda (GNU), 142
Governors Island Agreement, 106
Gow, James, 27, 29
Great Powers, 7, 10

Habyarimana, Juvenal
appointment of, 125
assassination of, 127
Haiti
Group of Friends, 103, 105
Hinsley, F.H., 5, 16
Holy Alliance, 8
Howe, Jonathan, 88
human rights
and UN Charter, 13, 14
protection of, 11
humanitarian intervention, 4, 7, 8, 10,
11, 12, 17, 18, 38, 39
advocates of, 16
doctrine of, 4, 9, 12, 37
failure of states to support doctrine of,
221
impetus towards, 16
humanitarian need versus sovereignty,
213
Hurd, Douglas, 48
Hussein, Saddam, 181, 187, 199
and Shiite uprising, 39
attitude of US towards, 181
repression of Kurds, 39
response to American ultimatum in
2003, 201

India
intervention in East Pakistan, 15
position on northern Iraq, 43
interahamwe, 128, 129
International Atomic Energy Agency
(IAEA), 181, 190, 191, 192, 196
International Civilian Mission in Haiti
(MINCIVIH), 104

International Commission on
   Intervention and State Sovereignty,
   19
international peace and security, 1, 2, 3,
   13, 14, 18, 20, 35, 39
Intervention, 3, 6, 7, 8, 9, 10, 11, 12, 13,
   14, 16, 18, 19, 34
   definition of, 6
Iran
   and Iraqi refugees, 39, 40, 44, 46, 62
Iraq
   Kurds, 4, 37
   no-fly zone in southern, 180
   refugee crisis, 37
Ivanov, Igor, 187
Ivanov, Sergei, 188

Jackson, Robert, 19
James, Alan, 17
Janvier, Bernard, 174
Jonah, James, 64, 66
Jonassaint, Emile, 112, 118

Kagame, Paul, 133
Karadzic, Radovan, 150, 151, 159, 160,
   162, 165, 166, 172, 177
   attitude to UNPROFOR expansion,
   150
Kirkuk, 49
Korean War
   and UN General Assembly, 22
Kouyate, Lansana, 89
Kurds
   repression of, 38, 39

League of Nations, 9, 10, 11, 12
   and Minorities Treaties, 11
Liu, F.T, 21, 27, 28, 30, 31
Luban, David, 21
Luxembourg summit, 47

Mackinlay, John, 30, 31
Major, John, 52
   and creation of safe havens in Iraq, 47
Mayall, James, 4
Montevideo Convention, 10
Multi-National Force (MNF)
   in Haiti, 116, 118

New Zealand
   position on Rwanda, 135
new world order, 1
norm of non-intervention, 6, 9, 10, 11,
   13
North Atlantic Treaty Organisation
   (NATO), 46
   and Bosnia, 162

Oakley, Robert, 82, 83
Operation Amaryllis, 129
Operation Deliberate Force, 177
Operation Poised Hammer, 60
Operation Provide Comfort, 44, 206
Operation Restore Hope, 80, 82, 83, 84,
   88, 89, 90
Operation Safe Haven, 48
Opération Turquoise, 140, 141
   deployment of, 142
Operation Uphold Democracy, 119
OpPlan 40-104, 175
Organisation of African Unity (OAU),
   67, 74, 125
Organisation of American States (OAS)
   and Haiti, 99
Owen, David, 160

Peace enforcement operations
   definition of, 21
Peace Support Operations
   doctrine of, 34
peacekeeping
   debate on doctrine, 22, 23, 24, 25, 26
   deficiencies of, 24, 37
   'grey area' of operations, 26
   increased demand for, 37
   second generation, definition of, 22
   traditional peacekeeping definition of,
   21
Pentagon
   and Rwanda, 132
   and Somalia, 79
Pérez de Cuéllar, Javier, 20
   and Somalia, 63
Pezullo, Lawrence, 103
Powell, Colin, 183, 192, 193, 194, 195,
   198, 199

Quick Reaction Force (QRF)
   in Somalia, 87, 92

Index

Rapid Reaction Force (RRF)
    deployment in Bosnia, 170
    in Iraq, 61
Ratner, Stephen, 27
Rieff, David, 23
Riza, Iqbal, 30
Roberts, Adam, 4, 25, 26
Rocard, Michel, 55
Rose, Michael, 160
Rwandan Patriotic Front (RPF) 125, 128,
    132, 134, 141
    attitude to French intervention, 129
    attitude to transitional government,
    126
    attitude to UNAMIR, 126
    attitude to UNAMIR II, 135
    importance of consent, 144
    UN monitors report on, 144
Ruggie, John Gerard, 23, 27, 28
Rumsfeld, Donald, 183, 199
Russia
    and Haiti, 113
    and Iraq, 187, 189, 194 197, 198, 200,
    201
    concerns about air strikes in Bosnia,
    163, 164
    position on Somlia, 77
Rwanda
    Belgium withdrawal from 130

Sacirbey, Muhamed, 172
Sahnoun, Mohammed, 70, 71, 72, 73, 95
Sanctions
    and Haiti, 105, 110
    and Iraq, 181
Sarajevo
    Airport Agreement, 149
    deteriorating security situation, 169
    exclusion zone, 162
Schröder, Gerhad, 184
Second Gulf War, 199
Security Council
    characterisation of Somali crisis, 66
    deadlocked on Iraq (2002), 198
    debate before second Gulf War, 188-
    96
    humanitarian concerns in Bosnia, 154
    response to Rwandan genocide, 130
Shias, 180
Sikkink, Kathryn, 17
Smith, General Rupert, 174

Somalia
    Addis Ababa conference on 89
    and Australia 83
    and Pakistan, 72
Somali National Alliance (SNA), 66
Sorenson, Georg, 17
sovereign equality, 5,
sovereignty, 5, 13, 16, 17
    centrality of, 4
    definition of,
    relevance of, 14, 16, 35
    theory of, 5, 7, 17
Srebrenica
    air strikes, 159
State of the Union address
    in 2002, 182
    in 2003, 193
state system
    moral basis of, 18
Stedman, Stephen John, 23
Stowell, Ellery, 7
Straw, Jack, 191, 197, 200

Tanzania
    intervention in Uganda, 15
Tharoor, Shashi, 25, 30
Tontons Macoutes, 99
Turkey
    and Kurdish crisis, 44, 45

UN Charter, 3, 11, 12, 13, 14, 20, 21
UN Guards, 38, 39, 56, 57, 58, 59, 60,
    61, 63
UN Military Observers in Somalia, 67,
    68
United Nations Assistance Mission
    in Rwanda (UNAMIR) 127, 128,
    129, 130, 137, 138, 143, 145, 146
    bolstering of, 143
    deployment of, 126
    GNU's attitude towards, 144
    mandate renewal, 131
    reduction of, 144
    understanding of genocide, 128
    withdrawal of, 145
UNHCR, 150
    concerns about Tuzla airport, 160
Unified Task Force (UNITAF) 81
Union of Soviet Socialist Republics
    (USSR), 14, 101
United Nations Mission in Haiti

(UNMIH) 107
United Nations Monitoring, Verification
  and Inspection Commission
  (UNMOVIC), 188, 189, 190, 191
United Nations Protection Force
  (UNPROFOR), 147
  air strikes, 153
  and delivery of relief supplies, 150
  creation of Bosnian command, 149
  deployment of, 148
  expansion of mandate, 150
  marketplace attack, 162
  problems fulfilling mandate, 159
United Somalia Congress (USC), 64
United States
  loss of Rangers in Somalia, 91
  policy on Haiti, 101, 102
  policy on northern Iraq, 40
  terrorist attacks on, 182
UNOMUR, 125
UNOSOM I, 70, 72
UNOSOM II, 89
  and Pakistani deaths, 90
and US deaths, 91
  withdrawal of, 95
United Nations Security Council
  (UNSC)
  agreement on Iraq, 189
  attempts to improve peacekeeping
  operations, 208

attitude to consent, 206
opinions on Iraq, 187-91
pre-emptive intervention, 218
relations with Iraq, 181
response to challenges of post Cold
  War, 208
UNSCOM, 181, 182
  withdrawal of, 182
US Agency for International
  Development (USAID)
  in Somalia, 79
US Army
  approach to peacekeeping doctrine,
  31
USS Harlan County incident, 109
Uwilingiyimana, Agathe, 127

Vance-Owen Peace Plan, 157
Vattel, 7
Vietnam
  intervention in Cambodia, 18
Vincent, Father Jean-Marie, 119
Vincent, R.J., 17, 24

Walzer, Michael, 18
Weapons of Mass Destruction (WMD),
  33, 186, 190
Wilsonian ideals, 10
World Court, 15
Wörner, Manfred, 162

Printed in the USA
CPSIA information can be obtained
at www.ICGtesting.com
LVHW011205150324
774517LV00047B/2151